# Counseling Psychology:
An Integrated Positive Psychological Approach

# Counseling Psychology

## *An Integrated Positive Psychological Approach*

Ruth Chu-Lien Chao

WILEY Blackwell

This edition first published 2015


*Registered Office*
John Wiley & Sons, Ltd, The Atrium, Southern Gate, Chichester, West Sussex, PO19 8SQ, UK

*Editorial Offices*
350 Main Street, Malden, MA 02148-5020, USA
9600 Garsington Road, Oxford, OX4 2DQ, UK
The Atrium, Southern Gate, Chichester, West Sussex, PO19 8SQ, UK

For details of our global editorial offices, for customer services, and for information about how to apply for permission to reuse the copyright material in this book please see our website at www.wiley.com/wiley-blackwell.



*Library of Congress Cataloging-in-Publication Data applied for*

HB ISBN: 9781118468128
PB ISBN: 9781118468111

A catalogue record for this book is available from the British Library.

Cover image: Pine cone in grass © Catherine Lane / Getty Images

Set in 10/13pt Minion by SPi Publisher Services, Pondicherry, India

Printed in Singapore by C.O.S. Printers Pte Ltd

1 2015

*To KM*

*The One and Only*

*Sine qua non*

# Contents

# Acknowledgments

Twelve years ago, when I was an international student in the University of Missouri, I was struggling with a group of severely distressed clients in my practicum. One day, my supervisor came to give a warning, "Ruth, you need to do something definitive today to help these clients. Or else, you might fail in this practicum. You are too quiet, and you haven't given any intervention to treat any symptom." I was shocked. "Are you saying that I just need to do something to pass this practicum?" My supervisor bluntly confirmed, "Yes, just do something positive."

Well, needing to "do something" to pass told me that all I was here for was for therapy alone, i.e., reducing symptoms. Were the clients *happy* after such therapy, however? Honestly, I could not tell. So, I assigned homework, that these clients simply identify one thing they want to do over the weekend, to make them happy. All of them looked at me in disbelief. Some said they never heard of such odd homework. Others said this is too easy to be homework. Then, thorough discussions on each client's homework followed. In the next session when clients returned, every client's face was *shining*. We reviewed the homework, and I was much impressed to learn that it is clients' mutual laughter that makes the real difference in life.

Today, now serving as an Associate Professor, as I look back to my work with that group, I am so much more appreciative of my *clients* who taught me that reducing symptoms is not identical to being happy, as a lack of problems does not always imply being proud of oneself. In that group therapy, my co-therapists and I were able to combine treatment to reduce symptoms while promoting positive affect, to make counseling a holistic process toward clients' happy and confident living.

All this amounts to my journey in integrating traditional counseling therapies with positive psychology of joy. In this journey, I was inspired by my personal awareness of myself as a Taiwanese whose positive personality features differ considerably from positive features in Western culture, such as forbearance, which could be seen as pessimism in the West is, in contrast, thoughtfulness admired in Asia and Taiwan. Thus, positive personality characters are intensely culture-related. The present book attempts to integrate these cultural differences in positive characters to assist multicultural clients.

My writing of this book was supported by countless people in countless ways. My precious clients taught me how to manage distress while enhancing their well-being. My professors in the University of Missouri, Drs. Puncky Heppner and Glenn Good, gave their endless assistances during my struggling years as an international student. My friend and colleague, Dr. Wendy Jordanov at Tennessee State University, shared much laughter and tears to invigorate my teaching.

Here at the University of Denver, I am lucky to have mentors Drs. Cyndy McRae, Kathy Green, and Maria Riva, who provide tireless and immediate support at various junctures! Finally, but not the least, I much appreciate my family who always stand by me, and my KM who unfailingly stands solidly behind me in my lonely struggles. These are just a handful of precious people, among many others, without whom this book would never have seen the light of day.

# PART I

# Conceptual Framework

# 1

# Introduction: Toward an Integrative Approach in Counseling

**Learning Objectives**

- Discover the importance of theory.
- Review the development of deficit model of the traditional counseling theories.
- Consider the necessity of positive psychology in counseling.
- Understand the importance of culturally appropriate counseling.

In the world of various theories in counseling, counselors and scholars face a challenge regarding how to apply theories to explain clients' symptoms. Before selecting the "best theory," this book explores a fundamental question behind it, "why do we need a theory?". Prochaska and Norcross (2010) say,

> Without a guiding theory …, clinicians would be vulnerable, directionless creatures bombarded with literally hundreds of impressions and pieces of information in a single session. Is it more important to ask about color preferences, early memories, parent relationships, life's meaning, disturbing emotions, environmental reinforcers, thought processes, sexual conflicts, or something else in the first interview? (p. 4)

Thus a solid theory is basic and essential to practice. Theory is key to integrating practical applications which can otherwise become directionless. Theories also enable counselors to become competent to identify and use the most appropriate assistance to resolve their clients' bewilderingly varied problems. Meanwhile, conversely, with practical experiences in

*Counseling Psychology: An Integrated Positive Psychological Approach*, First Edition. Ruth Chu-Lien Chao.

mental health services, counselors become able to evaluate critically the theoretical knowledge. It is the purpose of this book that readers will understand how to integrate theory and counseling, thereby enriching both, and thus become skilled in providing coherent and effective services to clients.

Successful integration of theory and practice requires careful consideration of the relationship between the two. Handling theory independently of practice prevents their integration and hinders the application of theory to practice. Actually, the integration of theory and practice advances the current trend of training of mental health professionals. When education and training focus only on either research or practice, this education fails to meet the fundamental requirements of the current training trend (Belar & Perry, 1992).

Thus integration of theory and practice in this volume elucidates three assumptions: (a) integration of traditional counseling theory with positive psychology, (b) multicultural contextualization of such integration, and (c) indispensability of integrating theory and practice. Let us expand on each of these assumptions.

The *first* assumption in this book is that traditional counseling theory can at most describe the mechanisms of people's psychological distress. Unfortunately, such explanation still fails to promote people's well-being and strengths, and their symptom-free status does not equate to positive affects (Seligman & Csikszentmihalyi, 2000). Therefore, this book introduces and incorporates positive psychology to complement traditional counseling theory, and to fill the gaps it leaves. Positive psychology is the scientific study of the strengths and virtues that enable individuals and communities to thrive. In counseling, the principles of positive psychology assist clients to manage their problems and even thrive against their distress (Seligman, Steen, Park, & Peterson, 2005). Positive psychology is founded on the premise that people want to lead meaningful and fulfilling lives, to cultivate what is best within themselves, and to enhance their experiences of love, work, and play. This integration highlights the main purpose of this book: while traditional counseling theory demystifies clients' psychological issues, positive psychology provides the indispensable conceptualization to promote positive emotions of clients. With the two approaches together, people are able to move to a happier and fuller life.

The *second* assumption in this book is contextualization of this integrative approach into the clients' multicultural backgrounds. To counsel multicultural clients effectively, counselors should possess multicultural counseling awareness, knowledge, and skills (Sue & Sue, 2012). Multicultural competence in part entails approaching the counseling process from the context of the personal culture of the client (Sue, Arrendondo, & McDavis, 1992; Sue & Sue, 2012). Professional ethics compel counselors to ensure that their cultural values and biases do not override those of the client (American Counseling Association, 2005). To date, many books on traditional counseling theories and techniques are still based on Western culture (Arredondo, Toporek, Brown, Jones, Locke, Sanchez, & Stadler, 1996). It is apparent that the major reason for therapeutic ineffectiveness for multicultural clients lies in the monoculturalism of Western counseling to them (Sue, 2004). Unfortunately, most books on counseling theories treat multicultural counseling in a single chapter and it is often still treated as ancillary and not an integral part of counseling theories. That is, if anything at all is included about multicultural and cross-cultural issues, they tend to be treated as a chapter in the later part of the book, or a few brief paragraphs at the end of each chapter. These arrangements demonstrate a sad reality: multicultural cultural competence or counseling multicultural clients is still seen in isolation (and as unnecessary) from the overall presentations of most books on counseling theories.

This book plans to set up a new direction to contextualize the integration of counseling theories and positive psychology and to make such integration sensitive to multicultural clients' needs. Thus, it is believed that to multiculturalize counseling theories, counselors need to be aware of their racial biases, have multicultural knowledge, and possess culturally sensitive skills (Arredondo, Toporek, Brown, & Jones, 1996).

Importantly, it is hoped that this book will serve as an agency for social justice in counseling (Landrine & Klonoff, 1996; Pettigrew, Tropp, Wagner, & Christ, 2011). Social justice mission in counseling endorses an application of theory–practice integration to the clients' contexts. The American Psychological Association indicated that sensitivity to clients' contexts is an ethical consideration (American Psychological Association, 2010). Such application requires being sensitive to clients' cultural contexts, and this sensitivity is an index to practitioners' multicultural counseling competence. Counselors who want to have more multicultural counseling competence need to work on two tasks. First, they deepen their multicultural training. Second, they contextualize their integration of theory and practice. Having knowledge about clients' backgrounds and providing services with culturally sensitive skills are important aspects for multicultural counseling. These culturally sensitive skills are consistent with the American Counseling Association's (2005) *Code of Ethics*. Thus, being multiculturally competent is an integral part of professionals' ethical conduct.

Furthermore, contextualizing mental health services has an important self-reflective ramification. Contextualizing counseling inevitably obliges counselors to reflect on their own worldviews and cultural values, as they provide services which are theory–practice integrated. Imbalanced focus between clients' cultural backgrounds and practitioners' own cultural values may hinder their therapeutic relations and therapeutic effectiveness (Kearney, Draper, & Barón, 2005). To apply in practice the integration of theory and practice to culturally diverse clients, it might be helpful for both white and racial/ethnic minority counselors to reflect on how relevant their own cultural values are to their services to multicultural clients. For white counselors, it would be important for both themselves and their clients to reflect on their respective privileges and how likely they are to inherit the racial biases of their forebears (White & Parham, 1990). That is, it would be a critical awareness for whites to understand how they have directly or indirectly benefited from individual, institutional, and cultural biases on being members in majority (Helms, 1990). For racial/ethnic minority counselors, it might be useful to examine how they themselves are struggling to work through marginalization or discrimination in their *own* life (Sue & Sue, 2008; Vinson & Neimeyer, 2003).

The *third* assumption of integration in this book highlights the role of practitioners as consumers of research, according to the principle that science without practice would be abstract, and practice without science could be blind. Stoner and Green (1992) posed the question: "What scientific knowledge bases form the foundations of the professional practice of psychology, and how should a knowledge base influence practice?" (p. 158). Thus, counselors incorporate relevant knowledge into professional practice. And yet, it requires sensitive skills to judge what specific components of theoretical variables are to be integrated, and how they are to integrate. These crucial themes will be discussed in each chapter throughout this book.

Moreover, to provide effective counseling, counselors should be equipped with both theoretical knowledge and practical skills. For this reason, in this book there will be a case study and application for major theories. This assumption indicates that counselors well versed in knowledge and practice will be knowledgeable of theory and skilled in counseling. Such theoretical knowledge facilitates an evaluation of psychotherapy outcomes. Thus, the delivery of effective services in clinical practice may depend on counselors' knowledge of empirical studies and specific theoretical approaches. This highlights the importance and necessity of considering case studies after each theoretical exploration; the case study represents the integration between science and practice. Furthermore, it is hoped that counselors are able to appreciate scientific research in order to evaluate the effectiveness of a chosen service, and vice versa to meet the clients' needs effectively.

## Historical Background

The journey of treatment or psychotherapy can be traced back thousands of years. In ancient Greece, mental illness was regarded as a medical disease, more than a visitation of malevolent deities. While ancient Greeks' understanding of the nature of the mental illness was not always correct in the present perspective, they did recognize the value and importance of treatment or psychotherapy. In the Middle Ages, supernatural causes were believed to be the reason for mental illness, and thus the use of torture was popular to gain confessions of demonic possession. However, some physicians also began to support the use of psychotherapy to treat patients. For example, Paracelsus (1493–1541) was credited with providing the first clinical/scientific mention of the unconscious, and advocated psychotherapy for the treatment of mental illness (Webster, 2008). Despite scattered information about "talking" in the treatment of emotional problems, the English psychiatrist Walter Cooper Dendy was an important figure in treating mental illness from a psychological perspective. Dendy (1853) first introduced the term *psychotherapeia* to refer to the "helpful influence of a healer's mind upon that of a sufferer." Within this term *psychotherapeia* he described the growing belief in the benefits of talking with the patient suffering from emotional problems.

Although the history of psychotherapy or counseling is quite ancient, counseling as a profession is a relatively new occupation, traceable back to some events in the twentieth century. Counseling as a profession arose in response to societal problems that plagued the United States at the turn of the nineteenth century, such as industrial revolution and urbanization. The advent of World War I and World War II further stimulated the development of psychology as a science and an occupation. Additionally, the US government furthered progress in professional counseling by formally sponsoring counseling services. After World War II, a deficit model of treating people led to remarkable progress in treating a variety of mental illnesses.

In recent decades, mental health services have been controlled and developed not by new ideas, but by economic issues. Traditionally, psychotherapy was a long process, often involving years of treatment. As mental health services became more widely available, emphasis was placed on briefer forms of treatment. This trend was further driven by the arrival of managed care insurance plans and limitations to coverage for mental health issues in Western countries. Today, virtually all therapeutic modalities offer some sort of brief therapy designed to help the persons themselves deal with their own distinct problems. Another influence came from government-sponsored grants such as the National Institute of Health which tended to fund research on treating existing illness more than preventive intervention or enhancement of well-being (Seligman, 2001). At present, the new integration approach presented in this book has two scenarios, enumerated as follows.

## Integration I: Counseling in Positive Psychology

This Introduction elucidates the reasons for the development of integrative counseling, which attends to clients with an understanding of their *strengths* as well as their symptoms. Thus "positive psychology" is an indispensable component in this book, in addition to traditional mainstream theories. Both traditional counseling theories and positive psychology together make this book a comprehensive and interesting sourcebook for graduate students. An understanding of clients' symptoms within the traditional approach, integrated with a new appreciation of their *strengths*, captures the burgeoning trend in counseling, and moves beyond the traditional deficit model of traditional counseling focusing solely on clients' negative aspects.

In the human quest for knowledge, each phenomenon presents us with the desire to probe its purpose, though the phenomenon itself is not its purpose. This is the same for counselors when presented with clients' symptoms. The appearance of psychological issues that counselors and practitioners treat appeals for discovery of its purpose and meaning. For example, Corsini (1995) indicated that,

> Psychotherapy is a formal process of interaction between two parties, each party usually consisting of one person but with the possibility that there may be two or more people in each party, for the purpose of amelioration of distress in one of the two parties relative to any or all of the following disability or malfunction: cognitive functioning (disorders of thinking), affective functions (suffering or emotional discomforts), or behavioral functions (inadequacy of behavior), with the therapist having some theory of personality's origins, development, maintenance and change along with some method of treatment logically related to the theory and professional and legal approval to act as a therapist. (p. 1)

Because psychotherapy and counseling seem interchangeable to some people, Sommers-Flanagan and Sommers-Flanagan (2004) defined counseling as a process in which,

> … a trained person who practices the artful application of scientifically derived principles for establishing professional helping relationships with a person who seek assistance in resolving large or small psychological or relational problems. This is accomplished through ethically defined means and involves, in the broadest sense, some form of learning or human development. (p. 9)

From the above two definitions of psychotherapy and counseling, three points are derivable. First, to date, the service that counselors and practitioners provide appears to be mostly repairing and solving psychological, affective, and cognitive problems. Do treatment and reducing symptoms alone compose the identity of counselors? Second, and perhaps most importantly, therapists should ask themselves why they avoid defining the purpose of treatment as they provide it. In other words, should counselors pursue only treating and repairing symptoms? Or else, should they define themselves as "cheerleaders" to clients and only attend to rosy aspects of clients by avoiding immediate and urgent distress? Or, as a third alternative, should counselors balance their help between these two approaches by providing treatment of symptoms together with enhancement of strengths?

Across time and space, traditional counseling and psychotherapeutic modalities have typically included the following:

1. A suffering, confused, or distressed person or group of persons seeks relief from mental, spiritual, and physical distress. They seek mental services mostly because their daily life is disturbed by their mental distress. Or else, their symptoms may make them unable to function well enough to meet daily life adequately.
2. A mental health professional is expected to treat his or her clients. This professional acts as a mental health expert and guide.
3. This system of treatment is based on a few assumptions such as "the client is sick" and "the practitioner acts like a doctor who prescribes a mental guide to reduce negative symptoms." When the symptoms are treated, it is time to end this therapeutic relationship.
4. Because the traditional therapy model is based on a deficit perspective on the client, and the professional attempts to explain the origins of the client's distress, there appears no need to address clients' strengths, well-being, and resources.
5. There are a series of contacts (e.g., 6–10 sessions) over time, and these contacts are defined as therapeutic in nature. Although symptom-free does not equate to feeling happy, the traditional approach in counseling still focuses on the former more than the latter.

In sum, within the general framework espoused here, it is recognized that many forms of traditional treatment or therapy are deeply embedded in the system of disease. But it may be misleading and restrictive to focus only on treating symptoms, instead of perceiving clients as human beings with various dimensions. Essential as it is, fixing symptoms alone cannot compose a whole therapy. It is *both* the treatment of symptoms and attending to clients' well-being that compose the total therapy, for both components are interdependent. Without treatment of symptoms, clients' strengths may be overshadowed by weaknesses. Without enhancement of strengths, clients may have no energy to fight against their symptoms. So, a beneficial therapy depends on (a) a well-defined plan of treatment of symptoms, and (b) that focus to be collaborated with clients' strengths. Otherwise, the self vanishes into some scattered haphazard collection of mental diseases, and well-being is neglected.

To be ready for therapy in the twenty-first century, many scholars proposed to redefine the focus of the mental health profession. This newly defined focus in the counseling profession should reflect what human beings are. Human beings, while experiencing loss, have hope. While knowing the cruelty of sorrows, they also taste the sweetness of joy. In other words, when treatment of symptoms is *integrated* with enhancement of positive strengths, human beings turn out holistically wholesome. In this way, an integrated treatment (i.e., treatment of symptoms together with enhancement of strengths) issues a clarion call to a new approach in counseling. This new call is a much better place to adequately tackle common, basic, and actual psychological phenomena, positive and negative combined.

To integrate treatment of symptoms into enhancement of strengths is not to put "vintage old wine in a new and better bottle" as Sternberg and Grigorenko said (2001, p. 1078). Instead, the integration is to keep the vintage wine out of the bottle, and then neither symptoms nor strengths will overshadow the other. Thus, to better serve clients in need, integration has been seen as inevitable and could become a new trend in counseling (Seligman, 2002). Scheidlinger (1999) mentioned a *mother group therapy* where the mother role represents nurturing and healing. The mother group is the mother milieu that consolidates diverse positive and negative experiences. Integration of treatment of symptoms and enhancement of strengths invigorates holistic recovery (Seligman, 2002). In Scheidlinger's (1999) example, integration is possible only in the motherly milieu of concerted focuses (i.e., traditional psychology and positive psychology). Here the integration of these two approaches facilitates enrichment of one another and moves toward an unbiased and holistic approach to better understand human beings (see Table 1.1).

Now, in addition to integrating traditional treatment of symptoms and positive psychology into a holistic approach, it is critical to know that the integration has four features.

*First*, neither the integrated approach nor a particular theory can be the orthodox principle for the human mind. Yet, they must complement one another to exist respectively as themselves. That is to say, after finding the integrated approach between traditional counseling and positive psychology, it is important to explore how to connect the integrated approach to clients. The principles of the integrated approach are based on the traditional theories in counseling and positive psychology, thus, without an understanding of the traditional theories, the integrated approach could be empty, abstractly without focus or base.

*Second*, counseling theories are irreplaceable for the integrated approach, just as arms cannot do what eyes do. So this book does not attempt to discard the traditional theories. Instead, what this book does is to synthesize individual theories with positive psychology to become an integrated approach which can accurately describe clients. The synthesis could be a unique process making use of traditional counseling theories alongside positive psychology to conceptualize clients' issues.

**Table 1.1** Traditional counseling vs. positive psychology

| | *Traditional counseling* | *Positive psychology* |
|---|---|---|
| Conceptualization | Disease model | Strengths-based model |
| Focuses | Dysfunction<br>Mental illness or other psychological problems | Well-being; strengths |
| Purposes of counseling | Reduce symptoms | Promote people's positive affects, strengths, and positive characters |

*Third*, each theory (e.g., psychoanalysis) thus collaborates with positive psychology to carry out a task. Such collaboration happens when a traditional approach opens itself from a symptomatic mode to a balanced approach to appreciate the human mind. Thus, the integration of traditional counseling theories and positive psychology shifts our perspectives from only fulfilling the mission of reducing negative symptoms to comprehensively embracing human beings, including their weaknesses and strengths. What is crucial here is how counselors best apply the integrated approach in order to energize the client's fullest potentials. Such careful studies of human nature are important. A lack of theories disables the integrated approach, turning it quite haphazard and ineffective. Therefore the integrated approach relies on counselors' thorough understanding of theories and effective application to clients.

*Finally,* this book weaves new perspectives on psychology into a healthy wholesome system which supports improving the client's health. This is created through the above considerations on the indispensability of traditional counseling theories and positive psychology into an integrated approach. Counselors' urgent task is not to debate whether traditional theories should be kept or replaced with other approaches. Counselors do not debate which counseling theory should receive more attention than others. In this book, it is believed that all components of counseling theories and positive psychology have their unique contribution to counseling. That is, different theories (e.g., cognitive therapy, psychoanalysis) are indispensable and play significant roles in counseling.

## Integration II: Counseling in Multicultural Populations

This approach highlights how integrative counseling can benefit multicultural clients. Integration in a multicultural context can effectively benefit culturally diversified clients, according to Sue et al.'s (1982) key article. This multicultural context reveals three interpretations of psychological distress and its treatments:

### The psychosocial interpretation

For centuries, healing has been a focus in many cultures. For example, Albert Ellis, the founder of relational emotive behavior therapy, credited Epictetus (c. AD 50–138) with providing a foundation for his system of psychotherapy (Ellis & Dryden, 2007). This Greek philosopher proposed that individuals are responsible for their own actions, which they can examine and control through rigorous self-discipline, and individuals have a duty to care for all fellow humans. These principles of self-examination, together with caring for fellow humans, will help people achieve happiness (Seligman, 2002; Stephens, 2007).

While the Stoic Epictetus explored happiness and peace of mind, Buddha, Siddhartha Gautama (563–483), encouraged people to follow a path of balance rather than extremism, and to keep a peaceful mind, saying, "The secret of health for both mind and body is not to mourn for the past, nor to worry about the future, but to live the present moment wisely and earnestly" (Wilkson, 2008, p. 64). Thus, despite coming from different cultures, languages, regions, and period of time, both Epictetus and Buddha can be considered forebears of contemporary cognitive theory and therapy. Similar to therapists in our modern days, they proposed theories and principles to help people reduce their struggles and suffering. Additionally, for many Native American tribes, tribe authority and spiritual leaders still hold as much or more salience for healing than do most forms of counseling or psychotherapy (Sue & Sue, 2008). The same holds true for many other native indigenous peoples. Many Asian and African cultures also have their respective cultural interpretations about psychological matters. Thus, to reduce symptoms and promote well-being seem to have a long history in various cultures.

Even though psychological treatment has received scholarly attention from philosophers and healers of different cultures over the centuries, after Freud, psychotherapy has been dominantly claimed by Western culture as "Western." Psychotherapy approaches from cultures outside the West are taken as "other" and considered unorthodox. This West ethnocentrism on psychotherapy is being challenged by numerous scholars and practitioners in multicultural counseling. To counter the Western-centered psychotherapy or counseling, this book will incorporate theories that respect diverse cultures.

## The religious/spiritual interpretation

Psychological suffering is a topic which has been discussed over millennia by clergymen, shamans, mystics, monks, elders, and other religious and spiritual leaders. Religion refers to individual and corporate beliefs and practices dealing with our relationship with some ultimate being or reality, and is distinguished from spirituality. Spirituality typically refers to the more experiential component of that relationship, or more broadly to one's core values or search for meaning. Such religion also specifies a code of behavior by which individuals may judge the personal and social consequences of their actions.

As one of the eternal themes of all cultures, religion has been of interest to psychologists and practitioners for centuries. For example, William James's (1902) *The Varieties of Religious Experience* initiated a tradition of phenomenological work in the psychology of religion. Later, Jung (1939) and Allport (1953) provided a basis for personality and social psychologists to examine religion, following which a rich empirical and theoretical literature has developed.

Two factors have, however, limited our understanding of the issue of religion in psychotherapy or counseling. First, the discipline of psychology has had an ambivalent relationship with religion. Most twentieth-century philosophies of science in psychology followed the trend of European positivism, which saw religion as an impediment to be eliminated. Freud largely adopted this positivistic stance toward religion as a primitive defense mechanism that had no place in a modern scientific world. Second, practitioners and researchers have neglected the relation between culture, religion, and psychotherapy. Even if religion is incorporated, most practitioners and scholars focused on Western versions of Christianity in populations of European and North American Caucasians. Despite these two factors limiting the relationship between counseling and religion, people of diverse backgrounds may believe that religion is the only way to promote their well-being. Thus, it is important to understand the relationship between these two entities.

Recently, some scholars and practitioners have recognized the significance of religions of non-Western culture (e.g., Taoism, Zen, Buddhism) for psychotherapy, and some practitioners also acknowledge healing potentials in non-Western spiritual practices and beliefs (Olson, 2002). Religious and spiritual leaders often have great wisdom, compassion, and insight into the human condition. Some theories we'll cover in this text are more open than others to these spiritual dimensions of humanity, though this book will not directly address spiritual practices as such in psychotherapeutic theories.

Since the clients' religious and spiritual backgrounds are an integral part of multicultural counseling, an effective therapist would do well to take into account the totality of the client's conditions, biological and spiritual, in treatment. Of course, counselors will vary in the relative weights they give to these dimensions. But our task at hand is to recognize that the totality of the client's cultural conditions must *all* be understood, in the context of traditional theories of psychotherapy and counseling, and integrated with the vigorous approach of positive psychology.

## The current status of multiculturalism in psychotherapy

Since the 1800s, psychology originating in Euro-American regions has been written about by white men. As with many psychology and mental health specialties, counseling resulted from World War II. Despite some differences of historical interpretation, scholarly consensus is that counseling was developed at a time when women and under-representative populations (e.g., racial/ethnic minorities, homosexuals, immigrants) deserved no higher education. Consequently, much of the history of modern psychology is written from the perspective of the privileged class of white males. Unfortunately, this perspective also came to pervade the specialty of counseling.

Now, however, as racial/ethnic minority populations increase in Western countries, how to work effectively with culturally diverse clients has become a predominant quest for almost all Western practitioners. It has been over three decades since Sue et al. (1982) published the landmark article on multicultural counseling, thanks to which the American Psychological Association (1993) changed its accreditation standards, even mandating multicultural training, for trainees to acquire knowledge and skills relevant to clients of diverse cultural backgrounds.

In this multicultural context, *theories* on counseling are essential to explaining psychological changes of depression or well-being that differ among different cultural backgrounds. Therefore, those who use Eurocentric theories to conceptualize treatment planning and prognosis of non-Western people will encounter potential problems (Kearney, Draper, & Barón, 2005; Lucas & Berkel, 2005).

Ignorant of the cultural worldviews of non-Western groups, counselors may unintentionally misconceptualize or psychopathologize multicultural clients (Anderson, 2003), as Western-centered theories may misinterpret their situation of mental health. Using culturally insensitive theories would legitimately raise the question as to whether current counseling theories in general are meeting the needs of this population. This suspicion was confirmed when the US Surgeon General's (2001) Supplement, *Mental Health: Culture, Race, and Ethnicity*, concluded that the mental healthcare and services provided to racial/ethnic minorities are inadequate. The absence of adequate counseling theories for racial/ethnic minorities' mental health contribute to a misunderstanding of them (Clark, Anderson, Clark, & Williams, 1999; Landrine & Klonoff, 1996). Theorists urged development of a conceptual model that organizes, explains, and leads to understanding the psychological behavior of racial/ethnic minorities based on their own worldview, not on the Western worldview (Williams, Neighbors, & Jackson, 2003). For example, constructs and theories which have been developed without considering the cultures of racial/ethnic minorities have often been inappropriate for these minority populations (Cokley, Caldwell, Miller, & Muhammad, 2001), because marginalized people have lived in a framework distinct from the whites'. Such differences could contribute to the different etymology of psychological distresses (Constantine & Sue, 2006; Ridley, 2005; Sue & Sue, 2008). Thus, the *Diagnostic and Statistical Manual of Mental Disorders* (*DSM-IV-TR*) says that racial/ethnic minorities may have their own unique and different definitions or expressions of specific distress (American Psychiatric Association, 2000).

Despite a long list of adverse conditions and centuries of exclusion from the socioeconomic mainstream, racial/ethnic minorities have surprisingly managed to forge notable contributions to American society, with vibrant cultural independence and a legacy of social activism. Understandably, some scholars and practitioners are interested in exploring what protective factors supported and enabled many racial/ethnic minorities successfully to manage their deleterious circumstances and even soar high in achievements. To date, empirical evidence points to cultural resources as supportive of positive coping behaviors. Culture has been shown to shape how racial/ethnic minorities define stressors, evaluate their coping resources, and thereby provide a supportive context for positive coping (Daly, Jennings, Beckette, & Leashore, 1995).

Although these cultural resources cannot remove racial/ethnic minorities from harm or psychological distress, they do appear to buffer the negative effects of psychosocial barriers (Chao & Green, 2011). Researchers reported that individuals with greater resources, such as social networks, tend to be more mentally healthy than do individuals with fewer resources (Simoni, Martone, & Kerwin, 2002; Wilson & Miles, 2001). Since many racial/ethnic minorities do succeed despite adversity, current counseling theories extrapolated from traditional psychology and a disease-focused model may fail to explain adequately the reasons for racial/ethnic minorities' psychological health vigor (Caldwell-Colbert, Parks, & Eshun, 2009; Davidson, Wingate, Slish, & Rasmussen, 2010).

Additionally, because the development of most counseling theories has been taken primarily from research involving, and conducted by, Caucasian whites without racial/ethnic minority groups, counseling theories today represent no *total* spectrum of human diversity (Okazaki & Sue, 2000). How to use traditional counseling theories when working with racial/ethnic minorities is a problem here. This book will integrate traditional theories and positive psychology, and contextualize them into multicultural clients' environments.

## Suggestions for the Use of this Book

Here are some recommendations on how to get the full value from this book. There are five steps to mastering this book:

- Step 1: Be familiar with traditional counseling theories, including the historical context, perspective on human nature, and theoretical principles.

- Step 2: Understand positive psychology (see Chapter 4).
- Step 3: Integrate traditional theories and positive psychology.
- Step 4: Contextualize Step 3 to multicultural clients' backgrounds.
- Step 5: Apply Steps 3 and 4 to case studies.

Thus, the book tells you to be sensitive to five points. First, as you read through Chapters 2–4, you will accumulate knowledge of positive psychology and how important it is for human cognition, affection, and behavior. You will also recognize that without addressing people's strengths and positive aspects, counseling or psychology manifests itself as unfinished. You may also notice that some components (e.g., resilience, hope) in positive psychology could be what you appreciate most in your counseling.

Second, this book does not tell you to discard traditional counseling theories. Instead, the author believes that traditional counseling theories, limited as they are, are a first starting point for interpreting the behavior, emotion, and cognition of human beings. Without mastering the traditional counseling theories, practitioners would have no first base to integrate these theories with positive psychology, to develop a solid new approach to understanding human beings. Moreover, without knowing traditional counseling theories, we would be unable to contextualize theories into the cultural environment of racial/ethnic minorities. Thus, we must not discard traditional theories but must master all traditional theories in counseling, and then go beyond them into positive cultural contextualization.

Third, after providing discussion of positive psychology and traditional counseling theories in the chapters that follow, this book will move on to integrating these two seemingly opposite groups of theories. To begin, traditional psychotherapy and counseling focus on repairing the client's distress and negative symptoms more than enhancing their strengths and well-being, which ignores the fact that distress and well-being are often two sides of a human coin.

Thus, this book will not argue which side of the coin (distress vs. well-being) should dominate. On the contrary, this book will integrate the two sides. Traditional repairing is integrated with appreciation of strengths in positive psychology, to compose a comprehensive framework of theory in counseling.

This integration of repairing and enhancing is closer to the actual situation of an approach to counseling which is most likely to benefit clients. When readers read through each chapter, some will reflect on their own counseling experience to find that they have actually been addressing clients' strengths, although these integrative aspects were neglected for decades (Seligman, 2002); and others may notice that such awakening of their clients to appreciating their own strengths, while their negative troubles are treated, is a therapeutic approach which is comprehensively effective.

Fourth, after integration, readers will learn how to *apply* the integrated theoretical framework to culturally different clients. Although this is not a manual on multicultural counseling, the book will effectively respond to practitioners' needs to serve emerging racial/ethnic minority clients. As racial/ethnic minority populations in the United States increase, US-based practitioners should particularly note the importance of providing a culturally sensitive service to those clients with distinctive cultural lifestyles. This book thus contextualizes our new approach that integrates traditional theories into positive psychology to multicultural clients.

Fifth, to strengthen the application of theory to concrete situation, Chapters 5 to 14 will be supplemented with a case study. These case studies provide readers with opportunities to sharpen their skills in applying theories to practice. The case studies will facilitate readers' transition of learning, from theory to practice, as both are interdependent resources for effective counseling.

Finally, in this book, there are several terms used interchangeably: counseling and psychotherapy; counselors, therapists, psychotherapists, and mental health professionals. In terms of counseling and psychotherapy, at times, they are differentiated by length of treatment (counseling may have fewer sessions than psychotherapy); clientele (counseling may be more often used with "healthy" people than psychotherapy); types of problems (counseling may be used to deal with interpersonal problems, but psychotherapy sometimes tends to be used to manage severe psychological problems). However, this book is written from the perspective that counseling and psychotherapy are similar and may be exchanged throughout this book. Both counseling and psychotherapy are based on helping foundations, so the two terms are used interchangeably to enhance readability.

The terms counselors, therapists, psychotherapists, and mental health professionals are also used interchangeably. Sometimes there are differences in the qualifications of these professionals; counselors may have Master's or doctoral degrees, but most psychotherapists are professionals with doctorates. However, the focus of this book is about counseling theories and positive psychology, so there is interchangeable use of these professionals' titles throughout.

## Concluding Remarks

Theories in counseling provide scholars and practitioners with guidelines to conceptualize psychological problems and understand the human mind. Without theories, counselors would get lost in hundreds of impressions and pieces of information. Clients would be helped with directionless counseling. Thus, theories help counselors transform daunting presenting problems into sound rationales to look into clients' distresses and symptoms. However, what types of theories do practitioners adopt to fit best with clients? Should we continue using the traditional theories? Most traditional theories were based on Western culture many decades ago, so it is questionable how and whether they can provide culturally sensitive interpretation for people of different cultures in the modern world (Van der Zee & Van Oudenhoven, 2013). To respond to the challenges of how theories can explain the problems and minds of people in the twenty-first century with accuracy and cultural sensitivity, this book attempts (a) to integrate positive psychology into current counseling theories, and (b) to multiculturalize this integration to meet multicultural people's backgrounds.

It is believed that the integration of traditional counseling theories and positive psychology could help counselors respond to the challenges they encounter in practice. Counselors could apply the integrative approach to assist clients reduce their symptoms, promote their strengths, and enhance their well-being. With multicultural clients, counselors could tailor this integrative approach of counseling to their cultures.

This book does not suggest that we discard the traditional counseling theories, instead, it is recommended that readers familiarize themselves with these theories. Thus, the first step of using this book is to capture the essential concepts of each counseling theory. The other important theory in this book is positive psychology and readers will learn to integrate each theory with positive psychology (from Chapters 5 to 14). The third component of this book is to multiculturalize the integrative approach to culturally different clients. The process of multiculturalization fulfills the ethical guidelines in the American Psychological Association's (2005) and American Counseling Association's (2005) ethic codes by being sensitive to clients' cultures, values, and beliefs. Moreover, the multiculturalization begins with counselors' self-awareness, and follows up with multicultural knowledge and skills (Sue & Sue, 2012).

## Review Questions: What Do You Think?

1. Describe counseling in your own words.
2. Imagine yourself as a counselor. What top five issues would you like to accomplish in your counseling?
3. Is "symptom-free" the same as or different from "feeling good?" Why, or why not?
4. Do you think that you are a product of your culture? Why, or why not?
5. What is likely to happen if counselors do not multiculturalize their counseling?

# 2

# Therapeutic Relationship: Exploring Clients' Symptoms and Strengths

**Learning Objectives**

- Learn about the positive empathetic rapport.
- Reflect on the appropriateness of the traditional intake checklist which is limited to symptoms and problems.
- Explore a balanced intake checklist which includes symptoms and positive character strengths, talents and abilities, and positive aspects of the client.
- Discover the character strengths in positive psychology.
- Consider the positive empathetic rapport in a multicultural context.

This chapter describes how counselors develop positive empathetic rapport with clients and use basic interpersonal skills to strengthen working relationships. This chapter also highlights that counselors discover and appreciate clients' strengths and various positive aspects, as they understand clients' symptoms and assess their readiness to change.

## What is Positive Empathetic Rapport?

With traditional counseling, counselors usually follow the "disease-focused model" by focusing on clients' problems, symptoms, difficulties, and concerns (Corsini & Wedding, 2013). During a typical first session, clients are asked to complete an intake checklist. Several common questions in this checklist are closely related to the *Diagnostic and*

*Counseling Psychology: An Integrated Positive Psychological Approach*, First Edition. Ruth Chu-Lien Chao.

*Statistical Manual of Mental Disorders* (DSM), and the question list overall asks clients to focus on the message: "What's wrong? What concerns bring you in?". Many intake checklists in counseling and mental health centers ask clients to check specific items as their concerns or presenting problems. Some example items are: academic concerns; episodes of manic behavior; obsessive thoughts; addictions; faculty/advisor concerns; panic attacks; ADHD/learning problems; family problems; paranoia; feeling doomed or helpless; phobias; adjustment to new situations; financial concerns; physical abuse or assault; alcohol or drug concerns; graduation preoccupations; procrastination; anger management; harassment; anxiety, fear, nervousness; identity/sense of self; relationship concerns; career/job concerns; impulse control; sexual abuse or sexual assault; compulsive behavior; internet/videogame concerns; sexuality concerns; concentration difficulties; intimate relationship concerns; sleep difficulties; concern with other's well-being; interpersonal concerns; spiritual or religious concerns; cultural/multicultural concerns; legal concerns; stress or tension; cutting or self-injury; loneliness; thinking about suicide; depression, sadness; loss, grief, death; thoughts racing through your mind; self-esteem; trouble making decisions or getting things done; eating concerns/body image; medical or health concerns; emotional or psychological abuse; mood swings.

If a therapeutic relationship is built upon a disease model or repair of clients' deficits, this relationship may only conceptualize clients as people with problems and miss other important characteristics and even good qualities. As Peterson and Seligman (2004) indicated,

> We can now measure and describe much of what is wrong with people, but what about those things are right? When psychiatrists and psychologists talk about mental health, wellness, or well-being, they mean little more than the absence of disease, distress, and disorder … [T]he perspective of positive psychology … means that we are as focused on strength as on weakness, as interested in building the best things in life as in repairing the worst (p. 4).

Accordingly, the positive empathetic rapport focuses on clients' two sides of mental status: their psychological difficulties and their strengths and positive affects. When the therapeutic relationship between counselor and client incorporates the strength and difficulty of a client, counselors may redirect their therapy from an almost totally disease-based model to a strength-building approach (Aspinwall & Staudinger, 2003). Yet, the positive empathetic rapport does not mean that counselors should completely disregard the DSM, ICD, or intake checklists. Instead, the positive empathetic rapport emphasizes the balanced relationship between disorders and strengths. For example, while there is an intake checklist to measure the problems of clients, should counselors also have a comparable list of strengths for clients to select? To enhance the appreciation of clients' strengths, mental health professionals should have an in-depth understanding of clients' positive characteristics. To increase the understanding of positive aspects of clients, Peterson and Seligman (2004) developed a classification of positive characters or the so-called "manual of the sanities" (p. 4). In their classification of positive aspects of human beings, they connect characteristics to positive individual traits. Further, they encourage counselors eventually to include the identification or creation of environments that enable good character. Moreover, the positive empathetic rapport focuses not only on clients' positive strengths, but also on their talents and abilities, on conditions that enable or disable strengths, on scenarios that are related to the strengths, and on the consequences that may ensue from these strengths.

Various scholars have argued that counseling has traditionally protected the status quo in society (Prilleltensky, 1989; Sue & Sue, 1977). The professional identity of counseling historically has had a remedial focus, with a one-to-one approach, and a general tendency to deal with crises and past or ongoing problems. Professional counseling training programs have long had a tendency to focus on remediation of problems and not on preventive counseling techniques and approaches (Cartwright, Daniels, & Zhang, 2008). Thus, the positive empathetic rapport promises to renew traditional counseling by inspiring counselors to balance their appreciation of clients regarding their problems and character strengths. As such, the positive empathetic rapport adopts a holistic and comprehensive approach to understanding clients. Counselors will interview clients regarding their presenting problems, but also, equally importantly, counselors will ask clients about their character strengths. Some typical questions for counselors to consider are as follows:

- What makes clients seek counseling despite their severe mental illness? Does seeking counseling imply that they still have some hope of having a good life? Does coming to see a counselor suggest that clients do not want to give up on themselves? Does talking to someone indicate that they still believe that they can recover from symptoms?
- Despite the symptoms and distresses, what character strengths help clients maintain their daily work, relationship with family members, and even care for those in need? What does it look like to them to live with struggles with psychological disorders and simultaneously fulfill their responsibilities in life and work? What resources do they use to manage their symptoms and life?
- As we know, John Nash is a winner of the Nobel Laureate in Economics, yet, he has been diagnosed with developing paranoid schizophrenia and has endured delusional episodes since his early adulthood. What makes him thrive against his paranoid schizophrenia and endure these delusional episodes? Are his character strengths of perseverance and resilience contributing to his success? Or does his success come from his love of learning and self-acceptance of his schizophrenia symptoms?
- There are so many successful and even influential people who have struggled with psychological disorders. For example, Abraham Lincoln suffered from what we now call depression, if we use the standard diagnostic criteria from the DSM. But this diagnosis is only one side of a story about how Lincoln wrestled with mental illness. Diagnosis, after all, seeks to assess a patient at just one moment in time, with the aim of treatment. But Lincoln's depression is part of a whole life story; exploring it can help us see that life more clearly, and discern its lessons. Thus, a question for us to consider is what made Lincoln a great president despite his struggles with depression (Shenk, 2006).

## Understand Clients' Strengths and Characters

To know the importance of clients' strengths is one thing, but to understand deeply what strengths *are* is quite another. Strength can be defined as the quality or state of being strong, capacity for exertion or endurance, power to resist force, power to resist attack, or degree of potency of effect or of concentration (Compton, 2004). Although the word "strength" may appear easy to understand, in fact its meaning has been the subject of much reflection by numerous poets, scholars, writers, philosophers, and educators. For example, "That which does not kill us makes us stronger" (Nietzsche, 1990, p. 34). This saying is used to give people encouragement after they have gone through trying times and have survived such. The saying can also be used to show others how strong they are after suffering and pain. Gandhi also had his thoughts on strengths and said, "The weak can never forgive. Forgiveness is the attribute of the strong" (Gandhi, 1993). How powerful can strengths be? Strengths can inspire us to pursue love and beauty, as said by one of our greatest artists, Vincent van Gogh: "It is good to love many things, for therein lies the true strength, and whosoever loves much performs much, and can accomplish much, and what is done in love is well done" (Van Gogh, 1963, p.110).

In counseling, this appreciation of the importance of character strengths assists counselors in understanding a client as a whole person, rather than simply focusing on the client's problems. To further appreciate clients' strengths and how their strengths contribute to counseling, Peterson and Seligman (2004) developed 10 criteria regarding how strengths contribute to clients' mental status. These 10 criteria of strengths highlight people's persistence, their ability to conquer obstacles, perseverance, and endurance. Strengths also involve self-belief, through which a person encourages herself or himself despite all kinds of barriers. Strengths also include multiple aspects of human beings, from thoughts to actions. Additionally, strengths do not happen in a vacuum or overnight, they require that "the larger society provides institutions and associated rituals for cultivating strengths and virtues and then for sustaining their practice" (Peterson & Seligman, 2004, p. 27).

Moreover, Peterson and Seligman (2004) identify 24 strengths in six categories (see Appendix A for this list in more detail):

*Category One* Wisdom and Knowledge – Wisdom and knowledge refers to the cognitive strengths that entail the acquisition and use of knowledge. Based on Peterson and Seligman's (2004) classification, the category of wisdom and knowledge includes five strengths: creativity, curiosity, judgment, love of learning, and perspective.

In counseling, what is important is to link these character strengths to understand clients. While traditional counseling theories provide some explanation to conceptualize clients' symptoms, personality, and presenting problems, the understanding of the above character strengths will facilitate counselors' holistic understanding of clients. The process of identifying clients' strengths helps counselors highlight clients' positive aspects which may be used to help reduce their symptoms. For example, the recognition of a client's strengths in wisdom and knowledge can help the client appreciate his or her own wisdom. When a client is recognized to have strengths (e.g., wisdom), he or she would be more willing to learn to use the strengths to reduce their symptoms.

The other function of character strengths in counseling is that counselors can help clients cultivate their strengths. For example, when noticing a client's love of reading, counselors can suggest various resources such as a book club. From elaborating upon this interest in reading, this client may develop strengths such as joy of learning and may find that such joy relieves them from daily life stress (Snyder, Irving, & Anderson, 1991).

*Category Two* Courage – According to Peterson and Seligman (2004), the category of courage stresses that people use emotional strengths to accomplish goals in the face of opposition or difficulty. There are four strengths under this category: bravery, perseverance, honesty, and zest.

People may question the necessity of courage in counseling, although courage is the ability and willingness to confront uncertainty, fear, pain, stress, and various difficulties (Osho, 1999). Unfortunately, such important characteristics appear to be neglected in counseling which assumes clients to be in a weak or sick position. In traditional counseling theories, clients are usually perceived as people with presenting issues. They are also believed to seek help, advice, guidance, and treatment. Thus, the concept of courage is contradictory to the traditional theories which psychopathologize or conceptualize clients from the deficit perspective. While positive psychology brings the concept of courage to psychology, what is critical in counseling is how to help clients develop and appreciate their courage. To make courage an essential part in counseling, counselors also need to move away from traditional counseling theories to recognize and incorporate clients' courage into counseling.

Courage covers a wide range of definitions and presentations. When clients seek help to manage their experiences in cancer, they may actually demonstrate physical courage which suggests that in the face of physical pain, hardship, death, or threat of death, they still strive to live. Moral or psychological courage is the ability to act correctly in the face of popular opposition or discouragement. Before clients come to counseling, they might have worked hard to manage their problems. Such efforts to handle their problems in fact could be a demonstration of psychological courage. Their seeking counseling help should be conceptualized as a part of their efforts to improve their difficulties, instead of reinforcing their failure roles.

*Category Three* Humanity – This category indicates that individuals have interpersonal strengths that involve tending and befriending others. Three strengths are listed here: love, kindness, and social intelligence.

In traditional counseling, clients tend to be seen as people with low social intelligence and lacking the ability to love. Such perceptions may reinforce clients' weaknesses and problems. When someone is not believed to succeed, he or she might fail. Likewise, when clients are not believed that they have ability to love, they may have lower confidence in themselves that they can love. Thus, in counseling, counselors are the crucial people who not only observe clients' symptoms, but also their character strengths such as humanity or the ability to love (Gilbert, 2009). In positive psychology, humanity includes love, kindness, and social intelligence.integrating these strengths into counseling can shift clients' thoughts from negative aspects such as self-dislike to being able or willing to love people. Additionally, clients may be also very hard or critical on themselves; yet, being compassionate and kind to oneself could be a beginning toward a healthy life (Neff & Costigan, 2014). Counselors can observe how clients treat themselves and then install several critical steps to help them cultivate their self-compassion. For example, counselors can help clients stop being so hard on themselves, manage difficult emotions with greater ease, motivate themselves to practice self-compassion in everyday life, and learn to be their own best teachers. Importantly, clients may have already demonstrated some self-compassion. Counselors should recognize the level of self-compassion clients have, and help them build upon it. As Thomas Carlyle (1929) said, "The wealth of a man is the number of things which he loves and blesses, which he is loved and blessed by."

Moreover, in traditional counseling theories, clients are assumed to have difficulties with their social intelligence and thus it is usually neglected. Yet, social intelligence can affect clients' emotions, which may contribute to their presenting problems. Therefore, counselors can examine the levels of clients' social intelligence. In addition to understanding its impact, counselors should help clients cultivate social intelligence. When clients develop better social intelligence, they have the capacity to effectively negotiate complex social relationships and environments because it demonstrates clients' self- and social awareness – an ability and appetite to manage complex social change (Sheldon, 2004).

*Category Four* Justice – The category of justice refers to individuals' civic strengths that underlie healthy community life. This category includes three strengths: teamwork, fairness, and leadership.

In traditional counseling theories, the concept of justice has been neglected and psychologists rarely conceptualize human problems based on justice. According to the "father of experimental psychology," the German physician Wihelm Wundt, psychology focused on breaking down mental processes into the most basic components. Such an approach only addressed individual problems, not relationships with others and environments. Thus, it is not surprising that justice, a concept of fairness to others and environments, is not within the realm of traditional counseling theories.

However, in current days, people are increasing their interactions with others, and the missing of context amounts to isolating clients' issues in the therapy room. Justice refers to a concept of moral rightness based on ethics, rationality, law, fairness, and equity. When clients keep others' feelings and perspectives in mind and consider a fair solution to manage the conflicts, they should experience calmness and peacefulness. That is, as clients strive to maintain justice, they are creating positive emotions toward themselves. As Gandhi (1965, p. 270) said, "Let the first act of every morning be to make the following resolve for the day … I shall not submit to injustice from anyone. I shall conquer untruth by truth. And in resisting untruth, I shall put up with all suffering."

*Category Five* Temperance – The category of temperance focuses on self-control which includes strengths that protect against excess such as forgiveness, humility, prudence, and self-regulation.

Western culture encourages people to be active, direct, and action-oriented, thus temperance may be perceived as a passive or negative personality. Temperance refers to moderation marked by personal restraint. Temperance is generally defined by control over excess, so that it relates to several self-restraint concepts such as abstinence, chastity, and modesty. Unfortunately, temperance has been largely ignored in personality trait psychology, where references to character and morally tinged terms were completely avoided (Allport, 1955). Worse, some traditional counseling theories, such as psychoanalysis, conceptualize positive traits (e.g., temperance) as unconscious impulses.

Theoretically, temperance is more of an overarching concept that houses a number of more specific traits and patterns that can be specifically operationalized. That is, temperance may include forgiveness, humility, prudence, and self-regulation. When counselors help clients forgive their transgressors, clients may experience several benefits, for example, they may: (a) have less negative affects such as anger, anxiety, depression, and hostility; (b) act in a more socially desirable manner; (c) be empathetic to someone who had been previously been rude to them; (d) have higher levels of agreeableness. Thus, forgiveness is not to suggest that clients compromise or give in; instead, it helps clients helps clients to stop dwelling on the offense. When clients are able to forgive, they may also increase their positive states while decreasing negative ones.

Humility is another key features of temperance. Humility is characterized by "letting one's accomplishments speak for themselves and not regarding oneself as more special than one is." Humility also includes important character strengths: (a) an accurate (not underestimated) sense of one's abilities and achievements; (b) the ability to acknowledge one's mistakes, imperfections, gaps in knowledge, and limitations, especially those in a power position; (c) openness to new ideas, contradictory information, and advice; (d) appreciation of the value of all things, as well as the many different ways that people and things can contribute to our world. In counseling, humility may help cultivate clients' self-esteem which fosters their management on stress. However, when clients' humility is low, there are several behavioral or emotional problems such as being hostile, angry, competitive, aggressive, conflicting with others, and less grateful. Thus, learning to develop humility could be an important approach to deal with clients' presenting problems (McCrae & Costa, 1999).

Temperance also includes prudence which is characterized by "being careful about one's choices, not taking undue risks, and not saying or doing things that might later be regretted." Although prudence is usually used in reference to financial situations, it could also be a strength that clients can develop. According to Peterson and Seligman (2004), prudence has the following attributes: (a) a foresighted stance toward people's future, thinking and caring about it, planning for it, and holding long-term aspirations; (b) an attitude that resists self-defeating impulses. Putting prudence into counseling, counselors can help clients develop a style of thinking about everyday life choices that is reflective and deliberate. Clients can also learn to harmonize their various goals and interests to create a stable and coherent life.

*Category Six* Transcendence – The category of transcendence concentrates on the strengths that forge connections to the larger universe and provide meaning. This category includes five strengths: appreciation of beauty and excellence; gratitude; hope; humor; and spirituality. Transcendence is also associated with experiencing spiritual or religious ideas such as considering oneself an integral part of the universe. In counseling, counselors can help clients increase their transcendence. As clients feel gratitude toward others and environments, they begin to treasure their family, friends, and themselves. They start to feel hopeful about their future. Thus, transcendence could be clients' internal resources, which in turn serve as their resources against stress and presenting problems.

## Positive Empathetic Rapport in a Multicultural Context

In addition to understanding the principles of positive psychology, it is important to address positive traits that exist within a client's context. Indeed, the isolation of the DSM from the positive traits of the respective context has been criticized in past years. In addition to narrowly focusing on disease, other problems related to the DSM and traditional counseling are that the DSM lacks an overall scheme, fails to be exhaustive, and given its medical root, fails to attend clients' culture and backgrounds. Thus the DSM is often applied in a uniform way to all clients, whether men or women, clients from culturally diverse backgrounds, or clients with disability issues (Van der Zee & Van Oudenhoven, 2014).

Park and Peterson (2003) proposed that scholars, educators, and mental help professionals should characterize the properties of settings that enable strengths and virtues. They suggested that such characterization would point to the features of the physical environment (e.g., beauty, naturalness), the social environment (e.g., empowerment as studied by social workers and community psychologists); and both (e.g., predictability and controllability as studied by the learning psychologists). While it is important to examine the relationship between the environment and positive traits, for counselors and mental health professionals what is indispensable is to understand how a client's culture defines positive traits. For example, although independence is a positive trait in Western culture, it may not be seen so positively in Asian culture. Being independent in Western culture refers to not being influenced or controlled by others in matters of opinion or conduct, and thinking or acting for oneself not for others. Other meanings of independence include: not being subject to another's authority or jurisdiction; not being influenced by the thoughts or actions of others; not depending or being contingent upon something else for existence or operation; and not relying on others for aid or support. In Western culture, these characters may be judged as merits or quality toward maturity or other positive traits. However, in Asian culture, individuals should treat others' needs as being as important as one's own needs. Asians also pursue the other-centered perspective in interpersonal relationships, as Mencius (2005) said, "As people starve, I starve. As they drown, I drown." In Asian culture, if individuals only consider their own needs and goals, they would be judged as "self-centered" or "selfish." Thus, positive traits should be placed in a client's specific cultural context.

Putting Peterson and Seligman's (2004) classification of strengths into a multicultural framework, counselors and mental health professionals need to be aware that these 24 strengths originated in Western culture. It remains questionable whether different cultures would have a similar interpretation of these 24 strengths, or include the same strengths in their own list. Importantly, many cultures may identify other strengths which are not listed in the strengths identified by Peterson and Seligman (2004). Working with multicultural clients, critical questions for the counselor to explore include: What are your culture-specific strengths? How does your culture define strength? How do people in your culture use strengths to promote their well-being?

In sum, applying the concept of "strengths" to multicultural clients does not mean that counselors "sell" the 24 strengths to them. In contrast, the process of identifying strengths in a multicultural context includes a few steps: (a) counselors recognize the 24 strengths by

Peterson and Seligman (2004) are based on Western culture; (b) counselors are knowledgeable that these 24 strengths may overlap with some cultures and beliefs; and (c) counselors respect that there are culture-specific strengths neglected or missed by Peterson and Seligman (2004).

## Concluding Remarks

Because traditional counseling is built upon a "disease model" which focuses on the repair of clients' deficits, the typical traditional intake session stresses clients' problems and symptoms, and aims to identify concerns such as feeling depressed, family problems, addictions, obsessive thoughts, panic attacks, and so on. Such a disease model may directly or indirectly push the therapeutic relationship toward the repair and fixing of problems, while neglecting the important character strengths of clients. That is, the intake checklist within the disease model overlooks positive aspects of clients and may lead to misunderstanding them as human beings. In order to use an intake interview as a tool which can provide a balanced and holistic understanding of clients, it is critical to add clients' positive aspects such as character strengths, virtues, and positive affects, thereby supporting the development of a positive empathetic rapport. This is why a positive empathetic rapport includes clients' two sides of mental status: their psychological difficulties as well as their strengths (Peterson & Seligman, 2004).

According to Peterson and Seligman (2004), there are 24 strengths in six categories: Wisdom and Knowledge; Courage; Humanity; Justice; Temperance; Transcendence. If positive characteristics and strengths are included in an intake checklist, counselors could more easily build an appreciation of the client as a person, rather than just someone with problems.

Finally, to provide a balanced and comprehensive intake checklist with multicultural clients, counselors need to be aware of how to interpret and adapt these 24 strengths in six categories, in order to develop an understanding of multicultural clients in a culturally sensitive way. Counselors should also possess multicultural knowledge, and understand how a positive empathetic rapport would be useful for multicultural clients. Additionally, it is important to appreciate that some culture-specific strengths are not identified by Peterson and Seligman (2004). However, whether identified in the list or not, counselors must respect these culturally specific strengths and be willing to incorporate them into counseling.

## Review Questions: What Do You Think?

1. What do you think should be included in an intake checklist? Please provide your rationale.
2. Imagining yourself as a client, how would you feel if someone only asked you questions regarding your problems, and no questions about your strengths?
3. Do you believe that character strengths are universally recognized and understood?
4. What is the role of culture in shaping and interpreting character strengths?

# 3

# Powered by Struggles and Strengths

**Learning Objectives**

- Overview current counseling theories, including background, philosophy, and counselor's roles.
- Critically review current counseling theories, and reflect on their shortcomings.
- Evaluate why, whether, and how positive psychology can complement current counseling theories.

Applying theory to the counseling of clients can be challenging and daunting. There are various approaches to understanding clients (e.g., psychoanalysis, client-centered therapy) and each approach has its limitations. What is important for the counseling of clients is to develop an integrative approach, combining the traditional counseling theories with positive psychology, which can enhance clients' growth and development. This chapter covers current theories as it introduces positive psychology. This chapter also provides a comprehensive interpretation of problems and symptoms using current theories, and the application of positive psychology to attempt to enhance clients' strengths. Finally, this chapter explains the necessity of doing the above, by elucidating how focusing on clients' positive aspects (e.g., strengths) can support the management of their symptoms.

*Counseling Psychology: An Integrated Positive Psychological Approach*, First Edition. Ruth Chu-Lien Chao.

## Current Counseling Theories: Are They Enough?

Overall, the current or traditional counseling theories focus on the interpretation of problems and seek solutions to treat or fix the issues brought by clients. Below is an overview of the current counseling theories which demonstrates that the focus of these theories is on weaknesses, problems, or concerns.

### Psychoanalytic therapy

Psychoanalytic therapy, founded by Freud (1856–1939), is considered to be dynamic, meaning that there is an exchange of energy and transformation. Freud used the term "catharsis" to describe this release of energy, and saw the personality as composed of a conscious mind, a preconscious mind, and an unconscious mind. The conscious mind has knowledge of what is happening in the present. The preconscious mind contains information from both the unconscious and the conscious mind. The unconscious mind contains hidden or forgotten memories or experiences. In psychoanalytic therapy, the personality has three parts: the id, the ego, and the superego.

1. The id is present at birth and is part of the unconscious. The id is the site of the pleasure principle, the tendency of an individual to move toward pleasure and away from pain. Because it is present at birth, the id does not have a sense of right or wrong, is impulsive, and is not rational. It contains the most basic of human instincts, drives, and genetic endowments.
2. The ego is the second system to develop, and it functions primarily in the conscious mind and in the preconscious mind. It serves as a mediator between the id and the superego, controlling wishes and desires. The ego is the site of the reality principle, the ability to interact with the external world with appropriate goals and activities.
3. The superego sets the ideal standards and morals for the individual. The superego operates on the moral principle which rewards the individual for following parental and societal dictates (Moore & Fine, 1995).

Using the perspective of developmental stages, psychoanalytic therapy conceptualizes the human mind. First, the oral stage is centered on the mouth as a source of pleasure. Second, the anal stage is centered on the anus and elimination as a source of pleasure. Third, the phallic stage is centered on the genitals and sexual identification as a source of pleasure. The Oedipus complex is described as the process whereby a boy desires his mother and fears castration from the father. In order to create an ally of the father, the boy learns traditional male roles. In contrast, the Electra complex is similarly described but is less clearly resolved in the female child with her desire for the father. A girl competes with the mother, and thus learns the traditional female roles. Fourth, the latency stage is characterized with peer activities, academic and social learning, and development of physical skills. Fifth, the genital stage begins with the onset of puberty. If the other stages have been successfully negotiated, the young person will take an interest in and establish sexual relationships. Freud's psychoanalysis emphasizes the defense mechanisms of ego which protects the individual from being overwhelmed by anxiety. He considered ego defense mechanisms normal and operating on the unconscious level.

The role of the counselor in psychoanalytic therapy is to encourage the client freely to explore difficult material and experiences from their past, gaining insight and working through unresolved issues (Moore & Fine, 1995). In psychoanalytic therapy, the counselor is an expert and interprets for the client. There are three main goals of psychoanalytic therapy: (a) to help the client bring the unconscious into the conscious; (b) to help the client work through a developmental stage that was not resolved or where the client became fixated; and (c) to help the client adjust to the demands of work, intimacy, and society. In psychoanalytic therapy, counselors use techniques such as free association, dream analysis, analysis of transference, analysis of resistance, and interpretation. *Free association* is a process whereby the client verbalizes any thoughts without censorship, no matter how trivial the thoughts or feelings may be. *Dream analysis* is a process whereby the client relates their dreams to the counselor. The counselor interprets the obvious or manifest content and the hidden meanings or latent content. *Analysis of transference* is a process whereby the client is encouraged to describe to the counselor those issues that have caused difficulties with significant authority figures in their lives. The counselor helps the client gain insights into the conflicts and feelings expressed. *Analysis of resistance* is a process where the counselor helps the client to understand what factors can cause a halting in therapy. *Interpretation* is a process where the counselor helps the client gain insight into past and present events.

### Adlerian therapy

Alfred Adler (1870–1937) believed that an individual's feelings should be understood in a holistic approach, spanning from the past, present, and to the future. Adler believed that people are mainly motivated toward a feeling of belonging. Thus, social interest is innate could be enhanced by social training. Adler expressed that people strive to become successful and to overcome the areas that they perceive as inferior. He referred to this process of personal growth as striving for perfection. Those who do not overcome feelings of inferiority develop an inferiority complex, but those who overcompensate for feelings of inferiority develop a superiority complex. Adler also believed that an individual's conscious behavior, not the unconscious, is the mainstay of personality development. Because of this concept, Adlerian theory emphasizes personal responsibility for how an individual chooses to interpret and adjust to life's events. For Adler, maladjustment is defined as choosing behavior resulting in a lack of social interest or personal growth. Adler believed that misbehavior will take place when a person has become discouraged or when positive attempts have failed to get the needed results (Carlson, Watts, & Maniacci, 2006).

According to Adler, the family is changed by the birth of each child. He also thought that the birth order of the children in the family influences many aspects of their personality development. For example, the oldest children are usually high achievers, parent pleasers, conforming, and well behaved, while the youngest child is the most capable of pleasing or entertaining the family. While they run the risk of being spoiled, they are also the most able to get what they want through their social skills and ability to please. They are often high achievers, because of the role models of their older siblings.

In general, Adler saw the family as the foundation of socialization for the child. He believed that a child's interpretation of the events in their life is determined by the interaction with family members before the age of five. The family interactions teach the child to perceive events and situations through evaluations of themselves and the environment. These perceptions that guide the child's behavior are called fictions. Basic mistakes could be made based on these fictions. Adlerians believe that some of those mistakes are as follows (Muzak, 2009). *Over-generalizing* refers to the individual's belief that everything is the same or alike. *False or impossible goals of security* means that the false feeling of security leads the individual to try to please everyone, in order to seek security. *Misperceptions of life and life's demands* indicate that these misperceptions lead the individual to expect more accommodation than is reasonable. *Minimization or denial of one's worth* suggests that the minimization leads individuals to believe that they never succeed in life.

Yet, Adler believed that life requires the courage to take risks without knowing the outcome. He believed that a person with a healthy life style contributes to society, has meaningful work, and has intimate relationships. He proposed cooperation between the genders as opposed to competition. He believed that well-adjusted people live in an interdependent relationship with others in a cooperative spirit.

For Adler, counselors play various roles in counseling. The counselor is as a diagnostician, teacher, and model. The counselor helps the client to explore conscious thoughts, beliefs, and logic for behaviors that are not in their best benefits. The therapeutic relationship is an equal one with the counselor sharing insights, impressions, opinions, and feelings with the client, in order to promote the therapeutic relationship. Therapy is a very cognitive process, with an emphasis on the examination of faulty logic. Therapy also empowers the client to take responsibility to change through a re-educational process. The counselor encourages the client to behave "as if" they were who they wished to be and often provides the client with "homework" assignments outside the sessions. Adlerian therapists are eclectic in technique with an emphasis on encouragement and responsibility (Carlson et al., 2006).

In Adlerian therapy, the goals of counseling are to help the client develop a healthy life style and social interest. The counselor assists the client through the four goals of the therapeutic process: (a) establishing a therapeutic relationship; (b) examining the style of life; (c) developing client insight; and (d) changing behavior. The behavior change goal is only achieved as the result of the individual taking personal responsibility for behavior. The most commonly used techniques are establishing rapport, defining style of life, and helping the client to gain insight (Carlson & Slavik, 1997).

## Person-centered counseling

Carl Rogers (1902–1987) viewed human nature as basically good, and believed that if given the appropriate environment of acceptance, warmth, and empathy, the individual will gain self-actualization. For Rogers, self-actualization is the motivation that makes the individual move toward growth, meaning, and purpose. Person-centered counseling also proposes that most people are provided conditional acceptance as children, which leads them to behave in ways that will assure their acceptance. However, in their need for acceptance, the individual often behaves in ways that are incongruent with the real self. Thus, the greater this incongruence between the real self and the ideal self, the more maladjusted the person becomes. The role of the counselor is to facilitate the client's awareness, self-actualization, and growth. The counselor sets up an environment where the client feels safe and comfortable to explore their own issues. In counseling, counselors demonstrate a special I–Thou relationship of unconditional positive regard, empathy, and warmth (Rogers, 1939).

The person-centered counselor uses psychological testing on a limited basis. The Q-sort is sometimes used in assessment. This is a series of 100 statements written on cards. The statements are self-descriptions such as "I am capable," "I am dependent," or "I am worthless." The client is asked to read and sort each of these statements into nine piles, from "most like me" to "least like me." Then the stacks are recorded. The client re-sorts the cards into an order expressing what they want to be like. The Q-sort gives an indication of the incongruence between the perceived real self and the ideal self. However, the use of diagnostic categories is discouraged as incompatible with the philosophical view of the individual as unique. Diagnosis places the counselor in a position of authority and imposes a treatment plan.

In person-centered counseling, the client or individual is the main focus. Thus, the goal for the counselor is to facilitate the client to move toward realistic self-perception, greater confidence and self-direction, a sense of positive worth, profound maturity, social skill, and also to be more fully functioning in all aspects of their lives.

The history of person-centered counseling shows that different periods of this theory had specific focuses. For example, during the nondirective period (1940–1950), Rogers believed that the counselor should focus on listening and creating a permissive atmosphere. The counselor did not provide interventions, but communicated acceptance and clarification. During the reflective period (1950–1957), counselors emphasized being nonjudgmental of the client, stressing that the counselor's job is to reflect client's affect accurately. Finally, during the experiential period (1957–1980), counselors focused on empathy, warmth, and genuineness. *Empathy* is the ability of the counselor to understand the emotions of the client and correctly communicate this understanding. *Warmth* (also referred to as acceptance and positive regard in person-centered literature) is the ability of the counselor to convey unconditional acceptance. *Genuineness* is the ability of the counselor to be themselves without assuming roles or facades. The counselor helps the client through accurate reflections of feelings, keeping the client focused on the concern, and clarification of feelings and information. The counselor uses open-ended questions or phrases to help the client gain insight into experiences and necessary changes in their lives (Rogers, 1951).

### Existential therapy

Existential therapists (e.g., Rollo May, Viktor Frankl) believe that individuals write their own life story through the choices that they make. Therefore, psychopathology is defined by existentialists as neglecting to make choices.

Lack of freedom to choose may cause anxiety for clients. Anxiety is seen as the motivational force that propels clients toward reaching their potential. Conversely, anxiety is also seen as the paralyzing force that prevents clients from reaching their full potential. Therefore, through awareness, this anxiety can be helpful in living more fully. Frankl

(1905–1997) believed that each person searches for meaning in life, and that while this meaning may change, the meaning never ceases to be. According to Frankl, life's meanings can be discovered in three ways: (a) doing a deed (accomplishments or achievements); (b) experiencing a value (beauty, love, nature, and arts); and (c) suffering (reconciling ourselves to fate).

In existential therapy, counselors do not play the role of an "expert." In fact, each client is considered unique, with the counselor focusing on being authentic with the client and entering into a deep personal sharing relationship. The counselor models how to be authentic, how to realize personal potential, and how to make decisions with an emphasis on mutuality, wholeness, and growth (May, Angel, & Ellenberger, 1958). Existential counselors do not diagnose, nor do they use assessment models like the DSM. Existential counseling aims to have the clients take responsibility for their life and life decisions. Another goal is to help clients to develop self-awareness in order to promote potential, freedom, and commitment to better life choices. Existential therapists also help clients develop an internal frame of reference, as opposed to the outward one. Existential therapists occasionally use techniques, with the most common technique focusing on the relationship with the client. Confrontation is also used by existential counselors, when they challenge clients to take responsibility for their own lives (Van Deurzen, 2012).

### Gestalt therapy

A gestalt means a whole, and gestalt therapy is based on the person feeling whole or complete in their life. Gestalt therapy is considered to be a "here-and-now" therapy. When a person focuses on what they actually are, rather than what they wish to become, they become self-actualized. The idea is that through self-acceptance one becomes self-actualized. Gestalt therapists believe that the individual naturally seeks to become an integrated whole, living productively. Gestalt therapists are antideterministic because they believe that people have the ability to change and become responsible. Moreover, gestalt therapy borrows various viewpoints from existentialism, experientialism, and phenomenology, with the emphasis on the present and awareness. Gestalt therapy focuses on the individual's own inner world of interpretation and assessment of their present life situation. When individuals emphasize intellectual experience and diminish the importance of emotions and senses, they lose the ability to respond emotionally to situations or events in their life. Additionally, gestalt therapy believes that thoughts, feelings, and reactions to past events or situations can impede personal functioning and prevent here-and-now awareness. The most common "unfinished business" is that individuals cannot forgive their parents for perceived mistakes in parenting. Awareness is considered on a continuum, with the healthiest person being most aware. These people are aware of their needs, and they deal with them one at a time. The emphasis of gestalt therapy is on reality and not on embellished or imagined needs. The individual recognizes their internal need, and meets the need through manipulation of the need and the environment (Breshgold, 1989).

In gestalt therapy, psychological difficulties are considered to arise in several ways: through loss of contact with the environment and its resources; through loss of contact with the self through over-involvement with the environment; through failure to put aside unfinished business; through experiencing conflict between what one should do and what one wants to do; and through experiencing the difficulties with individuals' dichotomies such as love/hate, pleasure/pain, masculinity/femininity.

In gestalt therapy, the role of the counselor includes creating an environment for the client to explore their needs in order to grow. The counselor is fully present with the client in the here-and-now, with intense personal involvement and honesty. The counselor also helps the client to focus on blocking energy and to use that energy positively and adaptively. Finally, the counselor helps the client to discern life patterns (Perls, Hefferline, & Goodman, 1994).

Additionally, counselors follow some rules in counseling clients. For example, the principle of the "now" requires the counselor to use the present tense; and "I and Thou" means that the client must address to the person causing their distress directly rather than talk about them or to the counselor about them. The counselor also helps the client to use "I" instead of referring to their own experiences in the second (you) or third (he/she) person. The counselor pays attention to the use of an awareness continuum that focuses on *how* and *what* rather than on *why*. The counselor has the client convert questions into statements.

In regard to diagnosis, gestalt therapists believe that diagnoses and standardized assessments are not necessary within this theory (Gladding, 1996). In counseling, gestalt therapists have a few goals: (a) the emphasis is on the here-and-now; (b) the client is encouraged to make choices based on the present ("now") as opposed to the past; (c) the counselor helps the client resolve the past and assist the client to become congruent; and (d) the counselor helps the client to reach maturity intellectually, and helps the client shed neuroses.

Gestalt therapy appreciates and incorporates techniques in counseling. Techniques in gestalt therapy have one of two forms, either an exercise or an experiment. The exercises include activities such as fantasy role playing and psychodrama. The experiments are unplanned creative interventions that grow out of the here-and-now interaction between the client and the counselor. The dream work in gestalt therapy consists of the client telling the dream and then focusing their awareness on the dream from the perspective of each character or element in the dream. The technique of empty chair is a process where the client addresses parts of the personality, as if it were an entity sitting on an empty chair. The client may switch perspectives by switching chairs or may simply address the chair. In gestalt therapy, confrontation is another exercise that is very powerful, in which the counselor calls attention to the incongruence between the client's verbal comments and observed emotions or behaviors.

Gestalt therapy also uses group exercises, such as "making the rounds" in which the client is instructed to say the same sentence to each member of the group and then add something personal for each person. Each client then repeats the phrase "I take responsibility" in response and finish it with their personal statement. For example, one client may say "I take the responsibility of having a fight with my husband;" the other client may finish the sentence as "I take the responsibility of having a bad grade." The process is to help the client to integrate their internal perceptions and behaviors. Other techniques include exaggeration, which is used to overdramatize the client's gestures and movements to help the client gain more insight into their meaning. And in another technique, "May I feed you a sentence?" is the question that the counselor asks before giving the client a more specific expression of what the counselor believes is the underlying message of the client (Perls et al., 1997).

## Rational emotive therapy

Albert Ellis (1913–2007) assumed that the individual has the capacity to be completely rational, irrational, sensible or crazy, which he believed is biologically inherent. He was most concerned with irrational thinking especially that which creates upsetting or irrational thoughts (Ellis, 1984, p. 266). These irrational beliefs are as follows:

1. It is absolutely essential to be loved or approved of by every significant person in one's life.
2. To be worthwhile, a person must be competent, adequate, and achieving in everything attempted.
3. Some people are wicked, bad, and villainous and therefore should be blamed or punished.
4. It is terrible and a catastrophe whenever events do not occur as one hopes.
5. Unhappiness is the result of outside events, and therefore a person has no control over such despair.
6. Something potentially dangerous or harmful should be cause to great concern and should always be kept in mind.
7. Running away from difficulties and responsibilities is easier than facing them.
8. A person must depend on others and must have someone stronger on whom to rely.
9. The past determines one's present behavior and thus cannot be changed.
10. A person should be upset by the problems and difficulties of others.
11. There is always a right answer to every problem, and a failure to find this answer is a catastrophe.

Ellis considered that people feel distressed mostly due to their irrational beliefs, and people are easily disturbed because of their gullibility and suggestibility. He was also a proponent of the idea that the individual can think of their behavior as separate from their personhood, i.e., "I did a bad thing" rather than "I am a bad person." He believed that each individual has the ability to control their thoughts, feelings, and actions. In order to gain this control, a person must first understand what they are telling themselves (self-talk) about the event or situation. Finally, he believed that cognitions about events or situations can be of four types: positive, negative, neutral, or mixed. These cognitions result in the same type of thoughts – in other words, positive cognitions lead to positive thoughts, negative cognitions lead to negative thoughts, etc.

In rational emotive behavior therapy (REBT), counselors are direct and active in their teaching and also in their correcting of the client's cognitions. Ellis believed that a good REBT counselor must be bright, knowledgeable, empathetic, persistent, scientific, and interested in helping others; and that they should use REBT in their personal lives (Ellis, 1980). Despite focusing on the scientific approach, the REBT counselor does not rely heavily on the DSM categories. The primary goal in counseling is to help people live rational and productive lives. REBT helps people see that it is their thoughts and beliefs about events that create difficulties, not the events or situations themselves. REBT helps the client to understand that wishes and wants are not entitlements to be demanded. Thinking that involves the words "must," "should," "ought," "have to," and "need" are demands, not an expression of wants or desires. Ellis believed that REBT also helps clients to stop perceiving a catastrophe when their needs and desires are not met. Additionally, REBT also stresses the appropriateness of the emotional response to the situation or event. A situation or event need not elicit more of a response than is appropriate. Thus, REBT assists people in changing self-defeating behaviors or cognitions, and espouses acceptance and tolerance of self and of others in order to achieve life goals.

REBT frequently incorporates techniques in counseling. The first few sessions are devoted to learning the ABC principle: "A" refers to the activating event, "B" means belief or thought process, and "C" indicates the emotional consequences. Throughout the counseling, the technique of cognitive disputation is aimed at asking the client questions which challenge the rationale, logic, or philosophy of the client's thinking. The technique of imaginary disputation asks the client to use imagery to examine a situation where they become upset. This technique is used in one of two ways: first, the client imagines the situation, examines the self-talk, and then changes the self-talk leading to a more moderate response. Secondly, the client imagines a situation in which they respond differently than is habitual, and are asked to examine the self-talk in this imagery. The technique of "Emotional Control Card" is an actual card intended for the client to carry in their wallet which has a list of inappropriate or self-destructive feelings countered with appropriate nondefeating feelings. In a difficult situation, the client has this reference card on their person to help them intervene in their own self-talk.

The technique of behavioral disputation involves having the client behave in a way that is opposite to the way they would like to respond to the event or situation. The technique of confrontation occurs when the counselor challenges an illogical or irrational belief that the client is expressing. Counselors may also use encouragement, explicitly urging the client to use REBT rather than to continue self-defeating responses.

## Behavioral therapy

Behavioral therapists, with the exception of cognitive behaviorists, concentrate on observed behaviors. A basic tenet of behaviorism is that all behavior is learned, whether the behavior is maladaptive or adaptive. Behaviorists believe that adaptive behavior can be learned to replace maladaptive behavior. This theory also endorses well-defined, measurable, and observable goals in therapy. Because of the focus on learning, behaviorists reject the idea that human personality is composed of traits. Instead, behaviorists strive for empirical evidence to support their use of specific techniques and to support the usage of behavioral therapy techniques.

Based on learning theories in behavioral therapy, *respondent learning* (also often referred to as *stimulus–response learning*), is learning in which the learner does not need to be an active participant. The outcome is the conditioning of involuntary responses. The unlearning of these conditioned responses is called counterconditioning. Conversely, *operant conditioning* requires that the participant be actively involved. This type of learning involves rewarding the desired behavior or punishing the undesired behavior until the person learns to discriminate the desired behavior that elicits the reward. Operant conditioning differs from respondent conditioning in that operant conditioning is the conditioning of voluntary responses through rewards or reinforces. *Social modeling* is a process in which new behavior is learned from watching other people and events without experiencing the consequences from the behavior or engaging in the behavior.

In behavioral therapy, the counselor's roles are varied and include being a consultant, a reinforcer, and a facilitator. Behavioral therapists are active in counseling and apply behavioral principles to achieve the goals of therapy. Behavioral therapists use social learning to model the desired behavior, while respondent and operant conditioning counselors are more directive and prescriptive in their approach to the therapy goals. When counseling clients, behavioral therapists frequently use tests, though the role of diagnosis varies greatly among behavioral counselors (Kazdin, 1979; 1984).

Behavioral therapists mainly attempt to achieve two goals. The first goal is to improve the life of the client through better adjustments to life and to achieve personal goals professionally and personally. The second goal is to help the client achieve behavioral changes through the development of therapeutic goals. There are four steps involved in the development of these therapeutic goals, as follows:

1. Define the problem concretely specifying when, where, how, and with whom the problem exists;
2. Take a developmental history of the problem, eliciting conditions surrounding the beginning of the problem, and what solutions the client has tried in the past;
3. Establish specific sub-goals in small incremental steps toward the final goal; and
4. Determine the best behavioral method to be used help the client change.

In counseling, behavioral therapists use a range of techniques. Reinforcers increase the desired behaviors, when they follow the behavior, and reinforcers can be negative or positive. Positive reinforcers are those that are desired by the client, while negative reinforcers are contingencies to be avoided. Behavioral therapy also focuses on *schedules of reinforcement*. For example:

- A *fixed-ratio schedule* means that the reinforcer is delivered after a set number of responses.
- A *fixed-interval schedule* means that the reinforcer is delivered after a set time lapses.
- A *variable-ration schedule* means that the reinforcer is delivered after varying numbers of responses.
- A *variable-interval schedule* means that the reinforcer is delivered at varying time intervals.

Another important technique in behavioral therapy is *shaping*, which is learning behavior broken down into small steps that are considered as *successive approximations* toward the final desired behavior. The order of the desired sequence of skills leading to the desired behavior is referred to as *chaining*. Other important concepts include *generalization*, which is the transfer of the learning from the behavioral therapy room to the outside world, and *maintenance* which is the consistent continuation of learned behaviors without support of external sources to the client's self-control and self-management. Furthermore, *extinction* is the elimination of a behavior through withholding a reinforcer, while *punishment* is the delivery of aversive stimuli resulting in suppressing or eliminating a behavior. Behavioral therapists also use the technique of *systematic desensitization*, which is a process accomplished through successive approximations to reduce anxiety toward an anxiety-provoking event or situation (Kazdin & Hersen, 1980). The steps needed to accomplish the behavior are listed and prioritized, from "no anxiety" through to "most anxiety." The hierarchy is reviewed, with the counselor helping the client to learn relaxation techniques to reduce or overcome anxiety. As a client cannot feel anxious and relaxed at the same time, the phenomenon is termed *reciprocal inhibition*. Through this process, the client can ultimately perform the desired behavior. Assertiveness training is a technique frequently used in behavioral therapy. Assertiveness training is used where the client is taught to express their appropriate feelings without hostility, anxiety, or passivity. The actual training may include all of the other behavioral techniques to achieve the desired behaviors. Other techniques used by behavioral therapists include: *time out*, *covert sensitization*, and *thought stopping* (Kearney, 2006).

### Reality therapy

Reality therapy was founded in the 1960s by William Glasser, who maintained that people act on a conscious level and that they are not driven by instincts and the unconscious. Glasser believed that there is a health/growth force in every person, and that this force seeks both physical and psychological health/growth. He separated these into the "old brain," or primitive physical needs, and the "new brain," or psychological needs. While the old brain contents itself with maintaining life, the new brain seeks belonging, power, freedom, and fun. He also believed that identity or a healthy sense of self is necessary. A "success identity" comes from being loved and accepted. A "failure identity" comes from *not* having needs for acceptance, love, and worth met. A person must experience identity before they can perform a task. According to him, children ages 2 to 5 first learn socialization and learn to deal with frustrations and disappointments. Children not getting support and love from their parents during this critical time begin to establish a failure identity. Glasser also pointed out that the second critical period is between 5 and 10 years or the early school years. Children who have socialization or academic problems may establish a failure identity. Moreover, he suggested that human learning is a life-long process; therefore, one can change one's identity at any time in one's personal history by learning what needs to be learned. Moreover, Glasser believed that humans are self-determined and each person has within themselves a picture or perception of themselves. Each person then behaves in a way that is determined or controlled by this image of themselves, so that the self-image can be maintained (Glasser, 1965).

In reality therapy, the role of the counselor includes acting as a teacher/model to the client and as someone who creates an atmosphere of acceptance and warmth helping the client to focus on the control of displayed thoughts and actions. In Glasser's approach (Glasser, 1981; 1984), the counselor also uses "ing" verbs to help clients describe their thoughts and actions, i.e., angering, bullying, intimidating, excusing. The focus of reality therapy is on the behavior that the client needs or wants to change, and on how to change that behavior in a positive manner. Reality therapy does not generally use formal assessment techniques or diagnostic categories.

There are several goals of reality therapy:

1. To help the client to be autonomous and behave responsibly toward self and others.
2. To help the client determine what they want in life.
3. To help the client to develop a practical plan to accomplish their personal needs and desires.
4. To establish an involved and meaningful relationship with the client.
5. To put the past behind and focus on the present and the outcome of present behaviors.
6. To accept no excuses and to eliminate punishment from the client's life.

In terms of techniques, reality therapy incorporates three techniques: (a) through involvement with the client, the counselor helps the client to see reality, and to understand how a behavior is unrealistic; (b) the counselor separates the client from the behavior and rejects the behavior without rejecting the client; and (c) the final step is to teach the client how to fulfill their needs realistically and positively. Glasser's approach also uses humor to point out absurdity without being sarcastic, and uses confrontation to help the client accept responsibility for behavior. In summary, reality therapy uses a system of establishing what the clients want, what they have been doing, evaluate how helpful their actions have been, and to plan for how they want to behave in the future.

### Feminist therapy

Feminist therapy, rather than having been founded by a specific theorist (e.g., psychoanalysis was mainly founded by Freud), is a philosophy or approach of therapeutic intervention that recognizes the impact of varied social practices on personal problems. It has its roots in the feminist and equal rights movements of the 1960s, and it embraces the conviction that "the personal is political." In other words, feminist therapy focuses on how the macro-level issues affect an individual's psychological issues. Feminist therapists practice from a variety of theoretical perspectives and represent individuals striving for political and social changes that exemplify justice and equality for all peoples.

The principles of feminist therapy include: recognition of societal or political impacts; multiple oppressions; acknowledgment of power differentials inherent in the therapeutic relationship and in society; and responsibility for personal involvement in engendering individual and social changes that equalize power.

First, feminist therapy acknowledges and advocates the awareness of societal or political impacts on personal problems. Perhaps stemming from women's movements which pursue equality between men and women, now feminist therapy also seeks equality among people from diverse backgrounds, including but not limited to sex, heritage, race, class, age, physical ability, religion, and sexual orientation. While each of these aspects alone may create personal difficulties for an individual within society, most individuals suffer from multiple oppressions. In large part, providing didactic experiences that illuminate these inequalities provides the framework for the therapeutic process. Additionally, feminist therapists remain aware of the complexity of human diversity and of how their own personal attributes and differences from the client may be affecting the process of healing.

Because feminist therapists strive to achieve equality in their therapeutic relationships and to empower their clients, they are continuously aware of the intrinsic power differential, especially early in therapy, that exists in the therapeutic relationship. Feminist therapists use the therapeutic relationship as a model to demonstrate to clients how to build an equalitarian relationship with someone else. In counseling, throughout the therapeutic process, there is a continuous focus on equalizing the client–therapist relationship and on avoiding taking responsibility for or coercing the client. The intent of this focus is to work collaboratively with clients, who are considered to be the experts in their own experiences, to achieve goals that are meaningful to them. A strong emphasis is placed on consciousness raising, which assists clients in understanding the context of their psychological distress. Within this relationship, therapists are far more likely to be self-disclosing, especially in relation to their own experiences of oppression and empowerment, than in most formal schools of psychological thought.

Feminist therapy emphasizes being active in efforts to bring about change that equalizes social and personal power. Because feminism is multifaceted, the focus of such change efforts may vary greatly; however, personal investment in altering power differentials is considered of primary importance for the therapist and, eventually, for the client. Advocacy requires continuous awareness of both positive outcomes and unanticipated negative consequences of efforts to equalize power and promote social justice. While feminist therapy has no formal theory of development, it does view society's construction of what is right and good as having considerable impact on individual identity development. For example, it has been suggested by our society that girls develop through connection with their primary caregiver, usually a woman, while boys avoid this connection in favor of autonomy. Girls are expected to adhere to common gender role stereotypes, including nurturance (playing with dolls), sensitivity, and cooperativeness. Boys, conversely, are expected to be sturdy, power seeking, and self-determining. Society, in various forms, stresses similar messages in relation to a plethora of other personal attributes.

Feminist therapists believe that psychopathology, or problems in daily living, closely relate to society, public policies, and the macro-system where we are living in. Thus, there is consistent recognition that psychological distress is engendered by environmental conditions, especially those conditions which produce disproportionate power or limitations of choice. As Brown and Ballou (1992) note, it is difficult to label an individual with a "disorder" and to believe that this "disorder" is located exclusively within the person, while ignoring the context of distress. In counseling, feminist therapists play roles as individual counselors, social change agents, and even policy-makers in social policies. Or feminist therapists play roles as educators to cultivate clients' understanding of the relationship between multiple oppressions and personal problems. Therapists may also serve the role of a coach to demonstrate how to build an equalitarian relationship.

To meet therapeutic goals, feminist therapists incorporate several techniques in counseling. First, feminist therapists utilize *consciousness raising*, to examine the role that social power differentials and bias play in personal distress and relationships. Helping clients appreciate the systematic nature of personal constructions and relationships, following from cultural constructions and mandates, provides a holistic perspective of mental distress and well-being that diminishes self-blame. Secondly, *personal validation* is an additional technique utilized in feminist therapy. Feminist therapy may also use *assertiveness* to assist clients in finding their own voices to tell their own stories in ways that are self-validating and self-enhancing.

## Family therapy

Family therapy treats the family as a unit, thus it emphasizes the relationships and roles of family members to each other (Minuchin & Fishman, 1981). Family therapy focuses on family issues, for example, the loss of a family member, trauma, divorce conflicts, issues in blended or remarried families, family violence, substance abuse, or behavioral problems in children. Family therapists practice in community mental health agencies, managed care organizations, hospitals, private practice, employee assistance programs, and other settings. They provide individual, couples, and family counseling; prevention programs, including parent education programs; crisis management, and other intervention and educational services.

Different from individual counseling which focuses on individual clients, family therapists with an experiential focus have goals for families to develop a sense of togetherness and autonomy, build self-esteem, relieve family pain, and overcome blocks to personal growth. There are different approaches within family therapy (Goldenberg & Goldenberg, 2008).

- Transgenerational family counselors focus on reducing anxiety, increasing self-differentiation, and rebuilding trust and fairness.
- Family therapists with an emphasis in structural family theory have a goal of restructuring the family organization, reducing symptoms, and creating flexible boundaries.
- Behavioral or cognitive counselors and therapists focus on modifying behavioral sequences, eliminating maladaptive behaviors, alleviating presenting symptoms, and restructuring cognitions.
- Social constructionists emphasize learning, creating new viewpoints, and giving new meanings to problems.
- Counselors identifying with the narrative approach focus on alternative stories helpful to the family, separating the person from the problem, re-envisioning the family's past and rewriting their future.

All approaches have in common building a strong alliance with a family and its members based on trust and respect, assessment and utilization of support systems, and the negotiation of expectations, hopes, and resources to make counseling useful.

Modern families exist in a wide variety of ways, including divorced families, blended families, single-parent families, gay and lesbian families, and families with specific problems (e.g., sexual abuse, substance abuse). Because of the changes in family organization, the current system of families goes beyond one which focuses on core family, and therefore family therapists need to play different roles and incorporate different techniques to meet each system of families they work with.

## What is Missing from the Current Theories?

The above overview of current counseling theories reveals several important issues as follows.

First, the discipline of counseling psychology has been overly focusing on the negative sides of the human mind. No matter which counseling theory counselors adopt, the counseling and mental health profession overall remains focused on clinical and problematic aspects of people. In fact, the word root of "clinical" continues to influence counselors' thinking about this field, even though the etymology has perhaps been forgotten. The word "clinic" derives from the Greek *klinikos* which means "one who receives baptism on a sick bed." This could be a reason why, to date, most mental health professions focus on the "sick" side of human mind.

Over the past decades, counseling has been increasing its focus on psychopathology, with particular emphasis on issues such as historical backgrounds and resource allocations. Several factors encouraged psychology and counseling disciplines to devote their attention to psychopathology and to view people through the lens of the disease or deficit model.

1. Traditional counseling theories strive to explain psychological problems, that is, what factors contribute to mental illness. For example, Freud's psychoanalysis mainly focuses on what causes anxiety, neuroses, depression, and other psychological distresses. Indeed, psychoanalysis is rarely used to explore how to promote well-being or strengths. This deficit approach in counseling theories relates to the training students receive. Although counselors' or other mental professionals' academic training has usually taken place in graduate schools of universities, their practitioner training will probably have occurred primarily in hospitals, mental health centers, university counseling centers, and clinics (Routh, 2000). In these settings, counselors are primarily asked to focus on diagnosis, develop a treatment plan, help clients make progress in their mental diseases, and terminate the sessions whenever clients were free of symptoms. None of the focus would have been on the promotion of strengths or well-being.
2. Historical issues have also contributed to the reinforcement of the traditional and disease model in counseling psychology. After World War II, the Veterans Administration (VA) joined forces with the American Psychological Association in developing training centers and standards for psychologists and mental health professionals. Because these early treatment centers were located in VA hospitals, the training of clinical psychologists continued to occur primarily in psychiatric settings. The impacts of this historical placement within psychiatric medicine are still alive today in counseling. Additionally, because the VA hospitals provided training resources to graduate students in counseling psychology, the VA disease model still continues to influence the conceptualization of clients' issues. Moreover, the National Institute of Mental Health (NIMH) was established in 1949, and "thousands of psychologists found out that they could make a living treating mental illness" (Seligman & Csikszentmihalyi, 2000, p. 6). Many scholars in counseling noticed that they could get funded by the NIMH or other funding agencies if their

projects were focused on repairing or treating psychological problems, instead of promoting well-being.

3. The development of the DSM has further reinforced the role of psychopathology in counseling psychology. Having been overly focused on the deficit model in treating clients, the critical flow of counseling or professional mental health training has "distorted and damaged" the training of clinical or counseling psychology (Albee, 2000, p. 247). Worse, the uncritical acceptance of the deficit-based explanation of mental disorders further reinforces the approach of treating problems only and neglects the necessity of promoting strengths. The language, forms of expression, and terms used by current counseling theories remain the language of medicine and psychopathology. Some examples include symptom, disorder, illness, diagnosis, and treatment. These examples are still popular in the present day, and are all consistent with the four deficit-based assumptions about the human mind. Moreover, consistent with the emphasis on psychopathology, current counseling theories (e.g., psychoanalysis, behavior therapy, etc.) emphasize abnormality over normality, maladjustment over adjustment, and sickness over health. They promote the dichotomy between normal and abnormal behaviors and focus on treating the abnormal behaviors, while neglecting to promote clients' strengths. Counseling theories so far unfortunately conceptualize human adjustment and maladjustment as the central focus of an individual. Such conceptualization dismisses other dimensions of human beings, such as interaction with the environment or sociocultural forces such as prejudice and oppression. That means these counseling theories also dismiss how people develop their strengths despite their struggles with psychological problems.
4. Finally, the last, but not the least important, implication of the present counseling theories is the DSM. In 2013, the American Psychiatric Association published the fifth edition of the DSM (i.e., DSM-5). This publication reinforces the DSM as the "standard" for diagnosis and treatment. In being recognized as the "standard," the DSM has dominated psychology and other mental health professionals for many decades. Unfortunately, the dominance of the DSM also implies that the main approach of counseling theories is still focused on negative aspects of the human mind. Because the DSM has dominated the field of mental health professions for such a long period, it would most likely be difficult to abandon the language and ideology used by it in order to adopt the language of positive psychology. Furthermore, the DSM is enshrined as the most authoritative book in various mental health professions such as psychiatry and psychology. The DSM was first published in 1952 (American Psychiatric Association [APA], 1952), and is now in its fifth edition (APA, 2013). The DSM provides the organizational structure for virtually every textbook and course on abnormal psychology, psychopathology, and other courses. Many schools or psychology departments also assign these courses using the DSM as a required reference for undergraduate and graduate students. Meanwhile publishers strive increasingly to publish more books on the assessment, diagnosis, and treatment of psychological problems, most of which use the DSM approach and/or structure. This dominance by the DSM thus impacts on the training and education of future professionals, the ideology and conceptualization of the human mind, and the development of counseling theories.

## Positive Psychology: A New Blood to the Field?

If traditional counseling theories are inadequate in interpreting the human mind, we need to ask what theories *could* meet this challenge. If merely addressing the problems or fixing mental illnesses cannot satisfy people's need to feel happier, then the task for us is to develop a theoretical framework which can accurately and sufficiently explain the complexity of the human mind. To tackle this challenge, this book attempts to integrate current counseling theories with positive psychology in order (a) to examine ways to interpret, explain, or reduce symptoms; and (b) to explore a theoretical framework to promote positive aspects of human beings.

Thus, this book integrates positive psychology because it shows therapeutic benefits when counselors promote mental professionals' appreciation of clients' strengths and well-being. The strengths cultivated in counseling will help clients to manage their presentation problems. Cultivating clients' strengths serves numerous purposes in counseling, including: (a) facilitating clients' own management of their problems; (b) increasing clients' use of their resources; (c) assisting clients to prevent relapse; and (d) enhancing clients' positive affect.

The classification of strengths presented in this book is intended to reclaim the study of character, virtue, strengths, and well-being, as legitimate topics of psychological inquiry and informed societal discourse. By providing ways of talking about character strengths and measuring them across the life span, this classification will start to make possible a science of human strengths that goes beyond armchair philosophy and political rhetoric. We believe that good character can be cultivated, but to do so we need conceptual and empirical tools to craft and evaluate interventions.

## Concluding Remarks

This chapter provides an overview of each of the main current counseling theories. It is demonstrated that, in general, current counseling theories have two characteristics: (a) they stress the deficit model, and (b) they seek solutions to treat or fix the problems presented by clients. Through this overview, it is found that current counseling theories are almost always dominated by clients' weaknesses, problems, or concerns. Such a skewed perspective reveals the incomplete understanding of the human mind. To make our appreciation of the human mind more comprehensive, the strength-based approach of positive psychology will be indispensable for the development and improvement of current counseling theories.

## Review Questions: What Do You Think?

1. What are the strengths and limitations of current counseling theories?
2. Based on the overview of current counseling theories, which theory do you like most and which theory do you like least? Please explain.
3. How does positive psychology strengthen or complement current counseling theories? Or do you think that positive psychology cannot benefit current counseling theories? Explain your answer.

# PART II

# Integration of Counseling Theories and Positive Psychology

# 4

# Positive Psychology in Counseling: What is it?

**Learning Objectives**

- Define positive psychology.
- Explore the historical background of positive psychology.
- Examine the theoretical principles of positive psychology.
- Consider positive psychology in a multicultural context.

Positive psychology, as a subfield in psychology, is an approach that focuses on the positive aspects of human beings, such as strengths and virtues, as opposed to the deficit-repair model of psychotherapy. Positive psychology embraces the study of the processes and conditions that contribute to optimal functioning and flourishing in human beings. Topics in positive psychology include at least three areas: (a) the study of positive emotions, such as well-being, hope, curiosity, and love; (b) the study of individual strengths, such as problem-solving skills, wisdom on living in general, and courage in face of threatening adversity; and (c) the study of positive practices in institutions, such as school policies that foster students' intrinsic motivation to learn. Although interest in such topics has existed since the earliest days of psychology, the term and concept of positive psychology were coined as part of a concentrated effort by psychologists who saw a need to highlight these relatively neglected areas of research.

An important impetus for the emergence of positive psychology came from the reaction to the dramatic increase in attention devoted to the understanding and treatment of psychopathology, and to the biological and environmental factors contributing to mental

*Counseling Psychology: An Integrated Positive Psychological Approach*, First Edition. Ruth Chu-Lien Chao.

illness (Seligman & Csikszentmihalyi, 2000). Positive psychology, as a focus of study, arose as a concerted and coordinated effort to promote theoretical and research attention toward psychological functioning at its best (Keyes, 2002). Thus, positive psychology creates a better balance with the work being done on mental illness.

Positive psychology emphasizes positivistic and empirical research methods, and it is a scientific exploration of positive aspects of human beings. Such exploration deals with holistic human strengths which support vigorous living, and so naturally the investigation is interdisciplinary. Cutting across traditional boundaries of clinical, social, and developmental psychology, positive psychology examines the nature of happiness, the power of hope, and fundamental human strivings such as the search for meaning. For example, positive psychology is also appreciative of the specialty of counseling psychology that has traditionally focused on "normal" or nonclinical populations with a model to prevent mental illness. The following sections include a definition of positive psychology, a brief review of its history, its theoretical principles, and its application to multicultural populations.

## Definition of Positive Psychology

Positive psychology aims to initiate a shift of focus from a traditionally exclusive emphasis on repairing symptoms, moving instead toward discovering human potential to nurture positive qualities. Positive psychologists work on three levels: subjective level; individual level; and group level. At the subjective level, the positive psychologist focuses on positive experiences of the subject such as well-being, satisfaction, hope, and optimism. Well-being and satisfaction relate to one's hope and optimism when looking forward to the future. Moreover, well-being is also related to flow and happiness regarding present living (Seligman & Csikszentmihalyi, 2000). The individual level addresses positive personal traits: the ability to love with courage, perseverance, forgiveness, originality, spirituality, and wisdom. The group level emphasizes the indispensable significance of civic virtues, together with the institutions that help individuals aspire toward becoming better citizens with responsibility, moderation, tolerance, altruism, and ethical conscience.

## Historical Context

Although the term "positive psychology" was coined only recently by Martin Seligman and his colleagues (Seligman & Csikszentmihalyi, 2000), the fact is that the concept of positive psychology is far from novel. For decades before the term was coined, psychologists evidently showed interest in topics now classified under positive psychology. For example, psychologists have examined the nature of aspects of positive mental health such as well-being (English, 1946; Guyer, 1931), the effects of hope (Callander, 1922; Rusk & Taylor, 1949), and the correlates of happiness (Hartmann, 1934). There are three reasons why positive psychology is often characterized as a new subfield. One, since World War II, psychology, particularly clinical psychology, has aimed to understand what goes wrong with people to reduce symptoms of distress. This overall deficit model approach was designed to treat patients, not to acknowledge and enhance human strengths (Seligman & Csikszentmihalyi, 2000). These efforts made a remarkable progress in treating mental illness, but neglected the strengths that people draw on to defy negative symptoms and thereby to function vigorously in daily living.

Historically, the research in psychology was dominated by a psychopathological model that focused on human flaws, problems, and weaknesses. A study of psychological literature, published in 1995, noted a ratio of 17 studying negativities to 1 studying positive human aspects (Myers & Diener, 1995). Specifically, studies on mental disorders are recognized by clinicians, researchers, pharmaceutical regulation agencies, health insurance companies, the legal system, and policy makers together with alternatives such as the International Statistical Classification of Diseases and Related Health Problems (ICD). Unfortunately, even in the twenty-first century, studies on positive psychology are still not recognized by the above parties or organizations.

Three, before its seminal article by Seligman and Csikszentmihalyi (2000), positive psychology had been excluded from empirical studies to assess and cure suffering symptoms, studying psychological disorders and negative environmental stressors such as divorce, academic failures, or substance abuse. Thus, empirical investigation bypassed positive psychology until the late 1980s and early 1990s.

Since then, and as interest in positive psychology has grown, a gradual academic recognition of this imbalance has developed. Research in positive psychology became more common, and then blossomed in the 2000s. Notable topics and scholars in the history of positive psychology (and their respective areas of research) have studied subjective well-being, hope, problem-solving, forgiveness, flow, character strengths, self-compassion, resilience, psychological well-being, learned optimism, and meditation and spirituality. Indeed, the list still goes on. The key researchers here have become leaders in positive psychology for over a decade, providing the foundation for its movement through to today.

The brief history of positive psychology can be used to identify some common misconceptions about its nature and goals. Positive psychology does not just focus on positive sides of humanity. For example, although happiness is important, positive psychology is not a hedonistic pursuit of pleasure. Rather, positive psychology attempts to address the current imbalance of attention between mental illness and positive aspects (Seligman, 2002). Positive psychology does not discard previous psychological research. A misleading impression of the title, "positive psychology," is that all other psychologies are "negative psychology" or "problematic psychology." In fact, this is an unfair characterization and a wrong dichotomization. The goal of positive psychology is not to replace past studies but to enhance the progress psychologists have made in understanding and treating mental illness by balancing them with a comprehensive understanding of the nature of mental health that includes factors promoting well-being.

Positive psychology distinguishes itself from unconfirmed formularies of self-help by building on factual empirical confirmations. Empirical discoveries of positive psychology have a strong potential to facilitate optimal human functioning. The application of positive psychology is firmly grounded in empirical scientific researches.

## Theoretical Principles

Positive psychology is broadly conceptualized as the study of the factors contributing to the positive aspects of humanity. In this broad setting of positive psychology, most attention focuses on two particular research areas of positive psychology (Seligman & Csikszentmihalyi, 2000): positive subjective experiences of positive emotions (e.g., well-being, contentment, and joy) and positive individual differences of traits (e.g., hope and curiosity). Additionally, positive psychology is also applied to schools and workplaces. There is no hierarchical relationship or sequential order between the three areas, though most research to date has focused on the first two areas. This chapter will review the current state of research in the areas of (a) positive subjective experiences, (b) positive individual traits, and (c) positive mental health.

### A. Positive subjective experiences

There is a strong need for understanding positive subjective experiences, for purposes both of public decision making and of people's private life orientation. Yet, our empirical investigation of positive emotions is still at an early stage. Currently psychologists know more about depression than about positive emotions. The need for a better understanding of emotions has been growing. In recent decades, some positive psychology scholars have begun to explore questions about the potency and potentialities of positive subjective experiences.

Feeling good can have strong impacts on different dimensions of life. When experiencing mild positive emotions, people are more likely to have positive behaviors such as helping other people, being flexible in their thinking, and finding creative solutions to daily problems. Interestingly, Pressman and Cohen (2012) also found that positive emotions are related to longevity, as seen in deceased psychologists. They examined whether specific types of positive and negative emotional words used in the autobiographies of 88 well-known deceased psychologists were associated with longevity. Using existing emotion scales and models of emotion categorization, Pressman and Cohen calculated and categorized the percentile of emotional words used by each of these 88 psychologists. After controlling for sex, year of publication, disclosed illness, native language, and year of birth, the use of more positive emotional words (e.g., lively, humorous) was associated with increased longevity. In another study, while testing a model of positive emotions, Fredrickson and Branigan (2005) discovered that the experience of joy expands the realm of what a person feels like doing at a given time. Following an emotion-eliciting film clip (the clips induced one of five emotions: joy, contentment, anger, fear, or a neutral condition), the experimenter asked research participants to list everything they would like to do at that moment. Those participants who experienced joy or contentment listed significantly more desired possibilities than did the people in the neutral or negative conditions. Furthermore, those expanded possibilities for future activities would in turn lead the joyful individuals to initiate more subsequent expanded actions. Those participants who expressed more negative emotions, in contrast, tended to shut down their thinking about subsequent possible activities. Simply put, joy appears to open us up to many new thoughts and behaviors, whereas negative emotions dampen even our existing ideas and actions, and to shut us in the status quo.

Putting positive emotions into the context of behavior, positive emotions such as joy also increase our likelihood of behaving positively toward other people, along with developing more positive relationships. Joy also induces playfulness, which is evolutionarily adaptive behavior used to acquire necessary resources to thrive in unexpected contingencies (Frijda, 1994). By the same token, juvenile play builds (a) enduring social and intellectual resources by encouraging attachment, (b) higher levels of creativity, and (c) brain development (Fredrickson, 2001). Thus positive emotions, by broadening processes, also can help an individual to build more resources than possessed at present. In 2002, Fredrickson and Joiner demonstrated this positive building by assessing people's positive and negative emotions and broad-minded coping, as demonstrated through solving problems with creative means on two occasions.

Researchers have found that an individual's initial levels of positive emotions are good predictors of overall increases in creative problem solving. These changes in improved coping then also lead to further increases in positive emotions, which in turn result in further improved coping. These predictions were all confirmed. These results held true for positive emotions, but not for negative emotions. Thus, it is confirmed that positive emotions such as joy may help generate resources, maintain and enhance vital energy, which in turn lead to the acquisition of more positive emotions, and thereby create even more numerous and more diverse resources. Fredrickson and Joiner (2002) referred to this positive sequence as the "upward spiral" of positive emotions.

Moreover, joy and contentment might function as antidotes or buffers to negative emotions. People in a condition of joy and contentment might be able to undo the effects of the negative emotions more quickly than were the people in the other reverse conditions. Or when people feel joyful may interpret things differently from others who feel miserable. Thus, there is an incompatibility between positive and negative emotions, and the potential effects of negative experiences can be offset by positive emotions such as joy and contentment.

Given that positive emotions help people build sustaining resources to recover from negative experiences, positive emotions might be associated with optimal mental health or flourishing (Fredrickson & Losada, 2005). In other words, positive psychological emotions and social well-being could be related to each other. When individuals experience happiness and excitement, it is possible that the whole of society may have more happy people.

## B. Positive individual traits

*Character strengths* Positive psychology has made great strides in the identification, classification, and measurement of character strengths (Peterson & Seligman, 2004). Although much of this research has been conducted by researchers examining the nature and effects of a particular strength, there has also been great progress in developing a meaningful classification and omnibus measure of strengths. This work has been spearheaded by the Values in Action Institute and has culminated in the publication of *Character Strengths and Virtues* (Peterson & Seligman, 2004). This system is a comprehensive classification of character strengths that integrates the knowledge of classical traditions and modern psychological science. The system is intended to complement the DSM as a "manual of the sanities" (Easterbrook, 2001, p. 23). As such, the current Values in Action (VIA) classification system is considered the first iteration of a developing understanding of character strengths, matching the progress of how the DSM gradually evolved and improved clinicians' understanding of the various forms of mental illness.

The VIA classification system is a hierarchical system. At the highest level are the six virtues that Peterson and Seligman (2004) identified from a broad survey of the major philosophical traditions across history. The six virtues identified from this survey include wisdom, courage, humanity, justice, temperance, and transcendence. Additionally, these six virtues are characterized by 24 strengths that the researchers identified as the psychological traits and processes by which these virtues could be achieved. The 24 strengths identified by these criteria and included in the VIA classification system are creativity, curiosity, open-mindedness, love of learning, perspective, bravery, persistence, integrity, vitality, love, kindness, social intelligence, citizenship, fairness, leadership, forgiveness and mercy, humility/modesty, prudence, self-regulation, appreciation of beauty and excellence, gratitude, hope, humor, and spirituality. The VIA system conceptualizes these strengths as natural categories that encompass related traits. For example, the character strength of hope also entails concepts such as optimism and future-mindedness, and integrity also entails authenticity and honesty (see Appendix A for a more detailed description of the traits).

Character strengths also have been examined in relation to life satisfaction (Peterson, & Seligman, 2004). It is important for us to know which strengths are associated with life satisfaction and whether there are costs associated with having too much of a particular strength. Hope and optimism were the strengths most associated with life satisfaction, but strengths of modesty, creativity, and appreciation of beauty exhibited the weakest associations with life satisfaction. There were no indications that too many "strengths" were associated with lessened life satisfaction. Those individuals with the lowest levels of hope and zest exhibited particularly low levels of life satisfaction.

*Hope* Snyder (2002) conceptualized human behavior in terms of the pursuit of goals, and defined hope as the perceived ability to identify meaningful goals, to identify pathways or routes to achieve them, and to have a sense of active agency or motivation. People can hope to use the identified pathways to achieve the desired goals. Although conceptually similar to Scheier and Carver's theory of optimism (to be discussed subsequently), hope theory is distinct in that it places the individual as the central active agent in the pursuit and attainment of desired goals. High levels of hope are associated with improved functioning in a variety of domains (Snyder, 2002), and hope and optimism are related but each distinctly contributes to flourishing mental health (Gallagher & Lopez, 2007).

*Optimism* Michael Scheier and Charles Carver (1992) defined optimism as the individual difference in general expectations of achieving future positive outcomes, together with expectations of avoiding future negative outcomes. Optimism is believed to produce positive outcomes by affecting individuals' pursuit of goals and their forms of coping with challenges. Optimistic individuals, as compared to pessimistic individuals, exhibit higher levels of subjective well-being and more adaptive forms of coping, as well as faster physical recovery after surgery (Scheier & Carver, 1992).

### C. Positive mental health

In addition to positive subjective experiences, and positive individual traits, a third area in which positive psychology has made important strides is in the identification and explanation of positive mental health. Although as early as 1948 the World Health Organization proclaimed that mental health was more than mere absence of mental illness, psychology in the twentieth century was dominated by the medical model which identified health as an absence of disease. The dominance of this medical model has changed in recent years, as it has become increasingly apparent that mental health and mental illness are distinct. Moreover, an understanding of the nature and causes of mental health might facilitate both treatment and prevention of mental illness (Ryff & Singer, 1998). Three different models of positive mental health have been examined in recent years, namely: subjective well-being; psychological well-being; and social well-being. Although the early debates focused on which of these models was the "best" model (Ryff & Singer, 1998), recent discussions have focused on how these three models are complementary, and work together to serve as distinct but related indicators of positive mental health (Keyes, 2005; Keyes, Shmotkin, & Ryff, 2002).

*Subjective well-being* Subjective well-being (SWB) is the first and most well studied of the three models (Diener, Suh, Lucas, & Smith, 1999). It also has been referred to as hedonic or emotional well-being (Keyes, 2005). SWB is made of three related components of well-being: (a) presence of positive affect; (b) absence of negative affect; and (c) life satisfaction. SWB is an extension of the philosophy of hedonism, which identifies pursuit of pleasure and avoidance of pain as the ultimate goals of life (Ryan & Deci, 2001). This model also assumes that individuals are the best judges of whether they are happy (Diener, Sapyta, & Suh, 1998).

Two studies have demonstrated that SWB can be explained by genetics, and individuals may have a biologically determined "set-point" for happiness that accounts for about 50 percent of levels of happiness (Lyubomirsky, Sheldon, & Schkade, 2005). Personality research has demonstrated that SWB is relatively stable across the lifespan and has identified physical, psychological, and demographic factors associated with SWB (see Diener et al., 1999, for a review).

*Psychological well-being* Psychological well-being (PWB) is an alternative model intended as a more holistic and theoretically grounded theory of well-being. An extension of the Aristotelian philosophical tradition that identified the ultimate goal in life as the pursuit of one's "daemon," or true self, this theory is also known as eudaimonic well-being (Ryan & Deci, 2001). Ryff and her colleagues have identified six related but distinct factors that they believe encompass the ideal of well-being: autonomy, environmental mastery, personal growth, positive relations with others, purpose in life, and self-acceptance. Individuals who are high in these factors are believed to demonstrate a few characteristics: (a) being independent and driven by their own standards (autonomy); (b) managing and interacting effectively with external opportunities (environmental mastery); (c) continually seeking opportunities to grow and develop (personal growth); (d) engaging in mutually satisfying, trusting, and meaningful relationships (positive relations with others); (e) identifying and pursuing meaningful goals (purpose in life); and (f) having a positive attitude about one's past and present (self-acceptance). Many researchers support the contention that psychological well-being represents a different facet of positive mental health not captured by the emotion-oriented subjective well-being model (Keyes et al., 2002; Ryff, 1989; Ryff & Keyes, 1995).

*Social well-being* Although psychological and subjective well-being provide two compelling and empirically supported models of individual well-being, they provide a limited account of how interpersonal and social forces can promote and reflect holistic well-being. Keyes (1998) argued that this intrapersonal focus reflects a bias in psychological research, because only focusing on individual differences does not properly consider an individual's social condition and social experiences that also impact his or her personal well-being. Keyes has therefore proposed that social well-being is an additional important facet of positive mental health that should be studied in conjunction with subjective and psychological well-being for a more holistic description of positive mental health.

Social well-being consists of five factors that represent the "appraisal of one's circumstance and functioning in society" (Keyes, 1998, p. 122). These five factors are social acceptance, social actualization, social coherence, social contribution, and social integration. Individuals who are high in these factors also show five qualities: (a) favorable views of others and feeling comfortable with other people (social acceptance); (b) believing that the institutions and individuals of a society are helping to reach the individuals' and institutions' potentials (social actualization); (c) perceiving order and quality in the social world and expressing concern about their social world (social coherence); (d) believing themselves to be important and efficacious members of society (social contribution); (e) and feeling that they are a part of their society similar to other such members (social integration).

*Complete mental health* These models of subjective, psychological, and social well-being have recently been unified into a complete model of mental health that identifies the three theories of well-being, as related though distinct indicators of flourishing mental health (Keyes, 2005). This model considers mental health and mental illness to be distinct dimensions of functioning rather than ends of a single spectrum. Thus, psychologists now have both continuous and categorical measures and models of well-being that have been empirically tested and supported in a broad variety of samples.

## Limitations of Positive Psychology

Now, diverse observations on the actual situation today must be made. To begin, today's positive psychology research is plagued by the same issues that have affected much of psychological research, including overuse of conveniently cross-sectional samples of primarily white middle-class college students. These issues limit the potential significance and interpretation of findings. Another primary limitation of positive psychology is that it appears at times as if the cart is put before the horse. The state of the research is not sufficiently developed to justify some of the claims being made. Part of this problem stems from the attractive nature of the subject matter. Topics such as hope and happiness have long been the domain of pop psychology, and it will be important for researchers in positive psychology to avoid the temptation to follow popular fashion and instead to ensure that the conclusions being articulated are confirmed by scientific findings.

Regarding future direction of positive psychology, the first essential step is the continued evaluation and validation of the current models and measures we have on positive mental health, character strengths, and positive emotions. It will be critical for the development of positive psychology that these basic building blocks are developed, by using the most sophisticated and rigorous psychometric and experimental techniques. It will also be important for positive psychology in the twenty-first century to investigate more culturally diversified populations. Encouraging and interesting work has been done examining character strengths in such diverse populations as the Maasai of Kenya and the Inuit of Northern Greenland (Biswas-Diener, 2006), but additional work is needed to follow them up to providing a more complete picture of global well-being and the enormous factors that promote it. Longitudinal work is needed to examine how well-being develops, and this work needs to be promoted over time so that researchers can begin to draw up causal contexts and potential pathways to well-being. Finally, further research is needed to examine the biological markers and neural processes associated with flourishing mental health, and how these physiological processes are related to psychological factors such as hope and optimism found to contribute to flourishing mental health.

## Positive Psychology for Multicultural Populations

Understanding how to apply positive psychology to culturally diverse clients is a critical issue in counseling. It is critical to extend the relevance of multicultural development to positive psychology when counseling racial/ethnic minority clients. Integral to any successful application of positive psychology is the infusion of multiculturalism throughout every step of therapy and counseling. A counseling model that does not attend to clients' culturally diverse environments is incomplete and even harmful. Clearly, culturally sensitive counselors facilitate clients' strengths and decrease their symptoms, while contextualizing counseling according to clients' cultural backgrounds (Galassi & Akos, 2007; Ponterotto, Utsey, & Pedersen, 2006).

In the United States, as the country becomes more culturally diverse, development of diverse multicultural strengths will grow increasingly important to promote mental health, life satisfaction, and socio-emotional health (Galassi & Akos, 2007; Ponterotto et al., 2006). In Europe, the total number of national minority populations is estimated at 105 million people, or 14 percent of 770 million Europeans (Heredia Montesinos, 2015). Thus, it appears that there is a great need of cultural toleration and diversity in Europe. This section addresses multicultural sensitivity and integrated counseling between positive psychology and traditional therapy. Although integrated counseling is relatively new to the literature, it is theoretically robust and warrants the attention of counselors and psychologists.

Let us first consider the situation in the United States. To date, as counselors are generally aware that the demographic profile is changing rapidly, it is important to examine precise projections of population growth and understand the impact of an increasingly diverse population. From 2010 to 2050, the projected population growth rate for the US white population will be only 5 percent, while the comparable growth rates for racial/ethnic minority groups are as follows: blacks, 58 percent; Hispanics (of any race), 154 percent; Asian Americans, 180 percent; and American Indian, Alaskan native, other Pacific islanders, and biracial/multiracial Americans, 186 percent. As a result, by the year 2050, the white population of the United States will be a numerical minority (at 49 percent). These projections provide convincing evidence that counselors will have many clients from culturally diverse backgrounds.

In other Western societies such as some countries in Europe, there might be mixed reactions about diversity. Specifically, evidence on the effect of cultural diversity for attitudes toward immigrants in Europe is mixed (e.g., Sandhu & Moosa, 2013). Thus, when the attitudes regarding diversity impact on people's health, it is crucial for psychologists to understand when cultural diversity does, and when it does not, elicit prejudice in order to help prevent the pernicious consequences of discrimination. Moreover, research has repeatedly attempted to explain such attitudes with the presence of cultural diversity arising from an increasing number of immigrants. Thus, counselors need to (a) recognize the increasingly diverse demographics in Europe and (b) be sensitive to multicultural clients' needs in counseling. Moreover, counselors need to be aware how collectively shared norms and values permeate all spheres of social life.

Thus, applying positive psychology to diverse populations requires us to attend to two issues: First, similar to traditional psychology or counseling, positive psychology has originated in Western, individualistic culture. Positive psychology in Western culture focuses on individualistic needs, such as one's private well-being, life satisfaction, kindness, and so on. Yet, from a non-Western perspective, culture-related strengths such as harmony, forbearance, and collective coping are critical for mental health. The lack of application of positive characteristics which are relevant within an individual's' own cultural context parallels the insensitivity of applying Western psychology to non-Westerners. Thus, in order to be more multicultural in approach, positive psychology needs to find culture-related positive characteristics appropriate to the culture of each client.

Second, racial/ethnic minority clients' positive multicultural personality is enhanced by recognizing and appreciating their culture-related strengths. The concept of multicultural sensitivity can be traced in Ramirez's (1999) work on providing counseling to culturally diverse peoples. His counseling aims at helping other culturally diverse clients to develop their own positive multicultural personality. To help develop positive multicultural personality, it is critical to synthesize the resources learned from different peoples and cultures to create multicultural coping styles (Ramirez, 1999). Counselors and mental health professionals should foster creative problem-solving skills, and help multicultural clients to be proactive in social justice for themselves (Ramirez, 1999).

Subsequently, Van der Zee and Van Oudenhoven (2014) identified five factors in expatriate populations toward building a model which can make positive psychology more multicultural. The first factor is *cultural empathy*, which is the ability to empathize skillfully with the thoughts and feelings of those culturally different from oneself. The second factor is *open-mindedness*, which is an open, unprejudiced attitude toward cultural differences. The third factor is *emotional stability*, which refers to stable mental health to stay calm under stressful and/or unfamiliar situations. The fourth factor is *social initiative*, which involves embracing and initiating cultural interactions in a wide variety of contexts. The last factor is *flexibility*, which involves cognitive resiliency that promotes seeing new cultural situations as a positive challenge rather than as a stress marker.

Most recently, anchored in a counseling and positive psychology framework, Ponterotto's (2010) model on multiculturalism and positive psychology reviewed and integrated varied theories such as social psychology to arrive at a model that is broader than that proposed by Ramirez (1999) or Van der Zee and Van Oudenhoven (2013). Ponterotto's (2010) model expands the focus of multicultural personality development to American adolescents and adults adapting to school, work, and life in an increasingly culturally diverse context. This model is seen as a strength-based cluster of personality dispositions or traits that can be subsumed under broader models of personality (such as McCrae and Costa's [1999] five-factor theory of personality). Multicultural personality is hypothesized to predict cultural adjustment and to enhance quality-of-life outcomes in culturally heterogeneous societies such as the United States (Ponterotto, 2010).

As other Western countries outside of the United States have been increasingly diverse, it is an emerging issue to address how to multiculturalize positive psychology in other Western countries. Specifically, other Western countries can examine the impact of diverse demographics such as how diversity promotes people's cross-cultural interaction and inspires people with different perspectives. Yet, it is also important to explore how multicultural clients may suffer racism and discrimination. Counseling multicultural clients requires counselors' sensitivity to these clients' cultures, values, and beliefs. In addition to understanding their psychological problems, counselors also need to appreciate their positive characters such as resilience, perseverance, and spirituality. That is, counselors need to appreciate how multicultural clients adjust to culturally different environments and help them pursue a high quality of life.

## Concluding Remarks

Positive psychology focuses on positive aspects of human beings, as opposed to the deficit-repair model of psychotherapy and psychopathology. Because it is different in its philosophy about the human mind from current theories, it is important to understand its historical context and theoretical principles. Examples of themes in positive psychology include the study of positive emotions, such as well-being, hope, curiosity, and love. Incorporating these topics into counseling may increase the positive emotions of clients.

However, the inclusiveness of these positive emotions does not mean that counselors discard current counseling theories. Similarly, to include clients' strengths such as problem-solving skills, wisdom, and courage does not suggest that counselors neglect clients' symptoms. In contrast, the integration of positive emotions and strengths into current counseling theories attempts to enhance treatment effectiveness.

This chapter also provides an overview of major concepts in positive psychology such as hope, optimism, happiness, perseverance, wisdom, and courage. These concepts in positive psychology enrich current counseling theories and reflect clients' mentality as well. Positive psychology also contributes to achieving a better balance between rigorous research and innovative theoretical orientation. Positive psychology emphasizes empirical research methods, and it is a scientific exploration of positive aspects of human beings. With such rigorous evaluation, positive psychology appears to have a strong position to stress holistic human strengths and vigorous living. However, positive psychology encounters several challenges. First, it needs to move from individual level to organizational, institutional, and societal levels in order to demonstrate that well-being and strengths may go across different levels of social organization. Second, positive psychology may be new to multicultural people, and it is the task of proponents of positive psychology to articulate how it will benefit multicultural clients.

## Review Questions: What Do You Think?

1. What is your definition of positive psychology?
2. Describe the historical background of positive psychology.
3. Describe the theoretical principles of positive psychology. How do these principles make sense to you?
4. Would you use positive psychology for your counseling? Why or why not?
5. How might clients react when counselors talk about their strengths and well-being?
6. Based on your knowledge of multiculturalism and diversity, can you think of examples of positive affects, emotions, strengths, or well-being that have originated in a non-Western culture?

# 5

# Psychoanalytic Therapy

**Learning Objectives**

- Learn about psychoanalytic therapy, its historical background and theoretical principles.
- Learn about the criticisms on psychoanalytic therapy and how positive psychology complements it.
- Understand how to integrate psychoanalytic therapy into positive psychology.
- Think critically about how to set the integration between psychoanalytic therapy and positive psychology into a multicultural context.
- Apply the integration to a case study.

Psychoanalysis was founded by Sigmund Freud (1856–1939) who believed that people could be cured by making conscious their unconscious thoughts and thus to gain "insight." The aim of psychoanalysis therapy is to release repressed emotions and experiences, that is, to make the unconscious conscious. In general, psychoanalytic psychologists or counselors see psychological problems as rooted in the unconscious mind. Based on Freudian principles in psychoanalysis, manifest symptoms are caused by latent or hidden disturbances. In psychoanalysis, the typical causes include unresolved issues during development or repressed trauma, and therefore, the treatments focus on bringing the repressed conflict to consciousness, where the client can manage it.

*Counseling Psychology: An Integrated Positive Psychological Approach*, First Edition. Ruth Chu-Lien Chao.

## Historical Context

Psychoanalytic therapy is considered to be one of the earliest theories in counseling and psychology. Expanding from Europe to the United States, psychoanalytic therapy developed a complex and multifaceted conceptualization of the human mind, and created an impact on clinical practice and academic theory. Psychoanalysis came from Freud's early experiments with hypnosis and "talking cure;" thus, psychoanalysis allowed clients to reveal their inner feelings and thoughts. Historically, Freud's views regarding sexual conflict as the origin of neurosis met with professional insults and suspicion, particularly in his home town of Vienna where "sex" was considered a dirty word and a taboo subject (Molino & Benvenuto, 2009). For years, Freud courageously developed his theory with painful self-analysis and overcame his own neurosis via studying his unconscious (Freud, 1930, 1953). In his lifetime, Freud revolutionized psychology with many seminal concepts such as his theories about sex. He also recruited a number of psychologists to catalyze other psychodynamics. Some extended his model, others modified it, and still others reacted against it. All these reactions further enriched the field of psychology.

## Theoretical Principles

For Freud, the human mind has three components: the conscious; the preconscious; and the unconscious. The conscious is present awareness, thoughts, feelings, and perceptions. The preconscious is what we are currently unaware of, but can become aware of easily. The unconscious is what we are unaware of and most of the contents of the unconscious are unacceptable or unpleasant, such as feelings of pain, anxiety, or conflict. Yet, the unconscious continues to influence our behavior and experience, even though we are unaware of these underlying influences (Freud, 1926).

According to Freud (1930), these three levels of mind can be presented like an iceberg. The top of the iceberg that people can see above the water represents the conscious mind. The part of the iceberg that is submerged below the water but is still visible is the preconscious. The bulk of the iceberg lies unseen beneath the waterline and represents the unconscious. Even though the unconscious is beyond people's awareness, it can still influence people's acts, ideas, and feelings. Freud also believed that there could be conflicts between the three levels of mind, and that such conflicts may result in abnormal behavior, symptoms, or psychological distress. To further conceptualize the human mind, Freud proposed: (a) a structural model of personality; and (b) psychosexual stages (Roudinesco, 2003) to describe human personality and developmental stages.

### A. Structural model of personality

According to Freud (1930), each person possesses a certain amount of psychological energy that forms the three basic structures of personality: the *id*; the *ego*; and the *superego*. Each of these three structures has different roles and operates at different levels of the mind. In general, there are two basic forces motivating behavior: *sexual drive* (the libido) and *aggressive drive*. Energy of these drives seeks release via the psychological systems of the id, the ego, and the superego. In the unconscious, operating from the pleasure principle, the *id* is where the libido and aggressive drives emerge. Although the id is based on the pleasure principle and seeks immediate gratification, it also provides *all* of the energy necessary to drive personality. That is, the id strives to fulfill our most basic urges, many of which are tied directly to survival (Roudinesco, 2003).

Because the id seeks immediate gratification of sensual needs and drives, it acts based on the idea that needs should be met immediately. For example, when people are hungry, the pleasure principle motivates them to eat. When they are tired, it motivates them to rest. But of course in real life, people cannot always satisfy their urges or needs immediately. Waiting can therefore be a negative experience, since most people have to wait until the moment they can fulfill their needs. When immediate satisfaction is impossible or difficult for people, tension results because the id relies on the "primary process" to temporarily relieve the tension. The primary process functions to relieve people's tension by creating a mental image either through daydreaming, fantasizing, hallucinating, or some other process. When direct action is prevented, fantasies or memories meet the id's needs. For example, infants may imagine their mother's breast (Roudinesco, 2003).

Although the id is present at birth, children begin to recognize that it is impossible immediately to fulfill wishes without difficulties, and therefore they slowly develop the *ego* to fulfill wishes in a socially acceptable way. The ego is the center of consciousness, and it follows the "reality principle," not the pleasure principle, to satisfy needs within social limits. The ego also regulates conflict between the id's instinctual drives and the outside demands for maximal gratification of instincts as they relate to the world. The ego uses secondary process thinking, or rational deliberation, as its primary mode of operation. For example, a preschooler wishing to continue breastfeeding may realize that he or she is no longer allowed to do so and may be satisfied with snuggling with mother (Roudinesco, 2003).

Later in childhood, the *superego* develops out of the ego, as a set of internalized moral attitudes learned from parents and from the ethical standards of society. People internalize these moral standards because following social ethical standards makes people feel good and reduces anxiety. Because the superego is typically thought of as the heart of our conscience, it often becomes the source of feelings of guilt, or it instructs humans on all of the things they should do. No wonder id, ego, and superego often clash, with competing wishes and demands. Wishes, desires, needs, and memories sometimes work their way into the preconscious from the unconscious mind, but they rarely enter the conscious mind. The purpose of preventing these desires and wishes from appearing in the conscious is to protect the conscious, as these wishes are unacceptable to the person or society. Freud (1930) further described the relationship as follows:

> One might compare the relation of the ego to the id with that between a rider and his horse. The horse provides the locomotor energy, and the rider has the prerogative of determining the goal and of guiding the movements of his powerful mount towards it. But all too often in the relations between the ego and the id we find a picture of the less ideal situation in which the rider is obliged to guide his horse in the direction in which it itself wants to go (Lecture 31).

### B. The development of psychosexual stages

Psychoanalytic theory contends that a child's early childhood relationships, particularly those with his or her caregivers, are important influencers of personality development. Freud (1930) claimed that as children develop, they go through a universal series of psychosexual stages, and each stage has its specific conflicts of id, ego, and superego. Additionally, each stage focuses on a different sexually excitable zone of the body (Freud, 1957a, 1957b). How a child learns to fulfill the sexual desires in each stage becomes an important component of the personality, and successful negotiation depends on the caregiver's responses to the child's attempts to satisfy basic needs. If a child does not successfully adjust or solve the conflicts in each stage, then fixation occurs, wherein the child can become trapped at an earlier stage (Freud, 1959). Thus, each stage may have its respective "fixation."

The first stage is the oral stage, which lasts from infancy to about 18 months, when libidinal impulses are satisfied by stimulating the mouth in feeding or sucking. If the caregiver does not adequately satisfy the child's needs, the child may develop a deep sense of mistrust and fear of abandonment. Fixation at this stage results in excessive dependence on others and habits related to the mouth, such as smoking and excessive eating and drinking later in this person's life.

The anal stage is from 18 months to about 3 years. The focus of gratification in this stage is the anus, with children expressing great interest in passing and retaining feces. If parents are too harsh or critical with toilet training, the child may become fixated at this stage and have traits such as being stubborn, rigid, stingy, and too focused on orderliness.

Next is the phallic or Oedipal stage which is from 3 to 6 years. In this stage, the focus of pleasure is the genitals and this stage is where the most important sexual conflicts occur, as a boy's Oedipus complex and a girl's Electra complex. Boys are supposed to love their mothers, and fear that their fathers will castrate them. Resolving this fear turns into strong superego, identifying with father's values. Girls in Electra complex love their fathers and fear retaliation by their mothers. So according to Freud, girls do not develop superegos and are not as moral, but are motivated more by emotions than morals and by penis envy. Unsuccessful resolution of the phallic stage results in not adopting a proper gender, or in a heterosexual orientation into excessive seductive relationships (Jones, 1953).

From age 6 to 12 is the latency stage, which involves avoiding the opposite sex, and using energy to develop skills and interests. The last stage is the genital stage, which begins about age 12 at puberty. If children have successfully passed previous stages, their sexual interests turn to heterosexual relationships, to pursue romantic relationships and learn to negotiate romantic sexual encounters with the opposite sex (Benvenuto & Molino, 2008).

## Defense mechanisms

When unacceptable unconscious desires seep into the conscious mind, this process could create distress for people. As a way of coping, people develop defense mechanisms to help disguise or transform the unacceptable unconscious desires. All people use defense mechanisms on occasion to protect themselves from their unconscious desires or to shape personality. However, when maladaptive mechanisms are used or when people's behaviors become extremely governed by the defense mechanisms, then such inappropriate use of defense mechanisms can lead to abnormal behaviors.

Freud's 10 defense mechanisms are as follows (Jones, 1953):

1. Repression – not allowing painful or dangerous thoughts to become conscious (e.g., a witness of murder may repress his or her memory of the event, not remembering it).
2. Denial – refusing to acknowledge the existence of source of anxiety (e.g., a parent insists her fatally ill child will recover).
3. Projection – attributing one's own unacceptable desires to others (e.g., a husband who is sexually attracted to a friend accuses his wife of infidelity).
4. Rationalization – creating socially acceptable reasons to justify being denied by others (e.g., a student who did not get a job of choice rationalizes this through claiming he did not like where the job was based).
5. Reaction formation – acting in opposition to what one fears to acknowledge (e.g., a man afraid of being feminine joins a "manly" football team to prove his masculinity).
6. Displacement – displacing hostility to an object onto a safe substitute (e.g., a wife angry at boss goes home to yell at her family).
7. Regression – retreating from an upsetting conflict to an earlier developmental stage to assuage anxiety (e.g., a toilet-trained boy has accidents after his baby brother's birth).
8. Identification – adopting ideas and values of a superior (e.g., prisoners adopting attitudes of their captors).
9. Sublimation – expressing sexual or aggressive energy in socially acceptable ways (e.g., a man with strong aggressive impulses plays professional football).
10. Intellectualization – adopting a distanced attitude on quite unpleasant issues (e.g., a man distressed at going through a divorce settlement discusses his court arrangements with detachment).

Rigid repeated use of defense mechanisms is problematic, yet not all defenses are unhealthy coping strategies. For example, sublimation can involve love, work, altruism, and even humor – all rechanneling raw sexual and aggressive impulses. Love is quite powerful sublimation, allowing sexual gratification in a socially acceptable form. In fact, Freud took all forms of sublimation as constructive mature defense mechanisms (Jacobs, 2001).

In all, Freud's psychoanalysis in the late nineteenth and early twentieth centuries has been a huge influence on counseling and therapy, expanded in different directions by Freud's colleagues and students such as Carl Jung and Alfred Adler with the following five themes: One, besides a person's inherited constitution, a person's growth is determined by early childhood events. Two, human behavior, experience, and cognition are largely determined by basic drives which are largely unconscious. Three, the attempts to bring those drives into awareness meet psychological resistance in defense mechanisms. Four, conflicts between materials conscious and unconscious (repressed) can result in neurosis, anxiety, depression, and so on. Five, liberation from the effects of the unconscious material is achieved through bringing this material into the conscious mind (via skilled guidance).

As the target of attention in the last few decades, psychoanalysis has been criticized for lacking scientific evidence in techniques. The theoretical bases of psychoanalysis cannot lead to scientific investigation. While personality traits in oral, anal, Oedipal, and genital phases can be observed, they are not stages in a child's development, nor do they result in adult traits.

As we know, Freud believed that human beings are motivated by unconsciousness. Yet, the idea of unconscious is contested because human behavior can be observed while human mental activity has to be inferred. Unconsciousness and its transference have been widely researched and validated in cognitive psychology and social psychology, but Freud's interpretation cannot be validated (Westen & Gabbard, 2002).

Despite its significant position in counseling therapy, psychoanalysis is being criticized here also. According to Freud, people are passively influenced by their environment, and do not determinately decide and change their environment. However, human beings are active and able to make decisions, to control their behaviors, and to regulate their emotions (Peterson & Seligman, 2004). There are numerous examples that support people as active decision-makers, and these examples appear to go beyond what the psychoanalytic theory can explain. We see persons risking dangers to help strangers, yet psychoanalysis cannot explain such cases, for Freud picked only what he noticed (sex, negative distortions) and created his theory around them. To complete what psychoanalysis misses in conceptualizing the human mind, it is important to understand people from the other side: human beings are active. Positive psychology, a strength-based approach in counseling and psychology, complements psychoanalytic therapy to enrich our conceptualization of human minds. Positive psychology is finally here to infuse psychoanalysis with life's positive features harmonizing with negative ones.

## An Integration: Positive Psychology and Psychoanalytic Therapy

Positive psychology can integrate with psychoanalysis in three areas: (a) harmony between conscious and unconscious; (b) mutual appreciation between id, ego, and superego; and (c) changing defense mechanisms into self-enhancement mechanisms.

### A. Seeking harmony between conscious and unconscious

In psychoanalysis, people are caught in conflicts between motivations which originate in the conscious and the unconscious; to understand the unconscious we must consider the conscious. "Conscious" comes from Latin *conscientia* made of "con," "with" "together," and "sci," "knowing". So "conscious/consciousness" means shared knowledge, knowing together, inner awareness, and ability to think/perceive (Merriam-Webster, 2005). "Unconscious" is not knowing/perceiving; lacking consciousness, shared knowledge, and self-recognition of one's acts and feelings; unconscious is linked to "knowledge," as "not self-knowing" (Merriam-Webster, 2005). Freud (1957a) contributed unconscious as central to psychology. He perceived the unconscious not as a state of being but as an active mechanism. He was the first to oppose the prevalent assumption that the human mind is all-conscious. Consciousness is only one part of a combination of mental processes, in the context of the underlying unconscious in which different impulses fly around. Thus, conscious frequently conflicts with unconscious.

Developing harmony is a key theme in positive psychology: conflicts can be resolved by mutual understanding between the conscious and unconscious. Impulses, assumed to be negative, are locked in the unconscious. Using the new principle of harmony, counselors can help clients to release impulses from the unconscious – for the conscious to accept them. Also, impulses of the unconscious can be taken as critical messages to the self. People can learn to listen to their desires in order to help them find a new self. For Freud, impulses exist outside the body only by assuming the forms of such media as thought, speech, or visualization (even dreams). Thus, the counselor can help the client to release impulses from the unconscious by expressing, not repressing, impulsive contents. A counselor can also help a client to connect impulses with words or verbal images.

The integration of psychoanalysis with positive psychology lies in connecting the unconscious to the conscious. As the impulse of the unconscious is highly reliant on some types of relief to avoid developing symptoms of hysteria and neuroses, the conscious could be a forum for healthy expression of desires from the unconscious. Moreover, if possible, the conscious can help channel impulses into creativity and inspiration for the individual.

### B. Mutual appreciation between id, ego, and superego

Freud (1962) described the tripartite psychic structure of the id, the ego, and the superego, three theoretical constructs in terms of whose activity and interaction mental life is described. The id is uncoordinated instinctive responses; the ego is a realistic organizer; the superego is critical moralizer. Freud believed that there is a tight and even tense relationship between id and ego, and he said, "Where id is, there shall ego be" (Freud, 1962). He also described the relationship between id and ego with a metaphor of a horse and its rider. But id's impulses cannot be always satisfied, and individuals feel pain. The id's desires clash with the ego's reality principles and the superego's morality, to become anxiety and other problems. Furthermore, these three psychic entities compete. As the id pursues pleasure, the moralistic superego tries to control the id, while the ego tries to negotiate pleasure pursuit and outside judgment.

Thus, a counselor is challenged to help the client to manage the tripartite conflicts, by using positive psychology that focuses on strengths of id, ego, and superego. Id is assumed as childish impulsiveness, but it also honestly expresses needs for pleasure. As positive psychology advocates the identification of strengths, a counselor can help the client to listen to id's desires for pleasure. When id's strengths (e.g., alerting us to basic needs and pleasure) are recognized, such recognition may satisfy its demand when given attention. Thus, from the perspective of positive psychology, instead of repressing id's needs, what ego can manage is how to help id express its needs and facilitate people's understanding of its strengths. Id in fact functions to attend to our basic needs and maintain our survival, thus id plays an indispensable role in human beings' survival and even prosperity against various hurdles in life.

Psychoanalysis sees ego as adjusting internal desires to fit external restrictions. As Freud (1962) says, ego decides the goal for id and guides the direction for moving toward success. According to positive psychology, to achieve happiness requires goal-directed action, deliberate thinking, and purposeful planning (Locke, 2002a). Thus, to mediate between the id's needs for pleasure and the external conditions, the ego makes efforts to enhance the individual's pleasure without breaking the environment into a chaotic condition. For this, it is important to recognize that ego promotes people's well-being despite various environmental restrictions.

Superego is a moral parental controller of id's desires, and even a suppressor of them with external judgments. But id, ego, and superego have strengths and weaknesses; no component of psyche is all good or all bad. A counselor must help clients see each of these, and to learn to integrate the strengths of id, ego, and superego to enhance mental health and to reduce distress. Recognizing the strengths of id, ego, and superego does not imply justifying the competition among them. Instead, with a new perspective from positive psychology, it is possible to conceptualize these three entities of the human mind with a strength-based approach.

## C. Transform defense mechanisms into self-enhancement

According to Freud, defense mechanisms are psychological strategies to manipulate, deny, or distort reality. These strategies of manipulation or denial are completed through processes including, but not limited to, repression, identification, or rationalization to maintain a socially acceptable self-image. Sometimes healthy individuals use different defenses to protect themselves from anxiety and social sanctions. Additionally, defense mechanisms also provide people a refuge from things that the individual cannot cope with. Defense mechanisms can thus occur in the following situations: (a) when different impulses conflict with each other; and (b) when impulses conflict with superego values. Moreover, when there is no solution to meet the id's impulses, defense mechanisms may present as a concealing drive to suppress anxiety. These mechanisms turn pathological when their persistent use leads to maladaptive behavior which adversely affects health.

Freud first identified the major defense mechanisms in 1894, as follows: (a) repression, in order to exclude unacceptable desires from consciousness; (b) reaction formation representing the opposite of what one feels; (c) projection, attributing one's ideas, feelings, or attitudes (especially blame, guilt, or responsibility) to others; (d) regression, reverting to an earlier mental or behavioral level; (e) denial, refusing the existence of painful fact; (f) rationalization, substituting rational creditable motives for true threatening ones; and (g) sublimation, diverting instinctual desire from its primitive form to a socially acceptable form. Years after Freud's original definition of defense mechanisms, different theorists differently categorize defense mechanisms.

Through positive psychology, defense mechanisms may reveal another perspective, and the integration between positive psychology and defense mechanisms may alter perspectives, interpretations, and research practices (Peterson & Seligman, 2004). A positive outlook on defense mechanisms is correlated with positive outcomes such as self-esteem. High self-esteem relates to adaptive coping, optimism, self-efficacy, less negative affect, and to better well-being and more life satisfaction. Taylor and Armor (1996) say, "People who have high self-esteem and high self-confidence, who report that they have a lot of control in their lives, and who believe that the future will bring them happiness are more likely than people who lack these perceptions to indicate that they are happy at present" (p. 884).

Defense mechanisms aim to prevent conscious awareness of several factors including disturbing content that would generate anxiety or other negative emotions, threaten ego, and relate to negative affect and the self. They also act to buffer against anxiety to prevent further distress (A. Freud, 1935). Below are descriptions of how the different traditional defense mechanisms can be integrated with positive psychology.

1. Repression and positive psychology – For psychoanalysis, repression is a mechanism suppressing painful risky thoughts from consciousness. It reinforces the avoidance mechanism as a means to forget the issue temporarily, with the individual unable to self-accept those thoughts with honesty. By embracing the integrity and honesty of positive psychology, clients learn how to be authentic, to be true to themselves in pain, to accept and be responsible to feelings and behaviors, and to own those behaviors rather than striving to be popular as a priority.
2. Denial and positive psychology – In psychoanalysis, denial is the refusal to admit an external source of anxiety, and appears often when an individual is unable to face obvious reality. For example, drug addicts or alcoholics may deny their problem, and victims of a painful event may deny the event. While protecting the individual from anxiety or pain, denial requires a great deal of energy, and needs other defenses to keep unacceptable feelings from consciousness. Or at most, denial is a "band aid" which can to cover up troubles but likely makes them worse.

   Positive psychology has another way to manage denial – using open-mindedness, receptiveness to new different ideas, and a willingness to search for evidence against favored beliefs (Peterson & Seligman, 2004). It is a most efficient strategy to deal with new possibilities, not "no problem at all" but "always revise on new evidence."
3. Projection and positive psychology – In psychoanalysis, projection is attribution of one's unacceptable impulses to others. For example, a CEO considering moving to another company might accuse his employees of infidelity. Projection is unhealthy because it only hides unwanted unconscious impulses, not letting the conscious mind recognize them. Positive psychology integrates projection in order to broaden perspective, opening up one's outlook to address difficult questions freely with knowledge and insights, for example by looking at the past to gain a wider perspective on the present.
4. Rationalization and positive psychology – Rationalization creates socially acceptable reasons to hide unseemly motives. The reasons for doing this include preventing anxiety, protecting self-esteem, putting down others, and self-protection through becoming out of touch with the real world.

   Rationalization overlooks forgiveness, which can be offered by positive psychology. Forgiveness occurs when someone offers a free pardon to give up all claim on an offence or debt, regardless of the offender's response. Rationalization justifies disappointment; forgiveness accepts mistakes in order to stop anger, and moves individuals toward well-being through finding compassion for those who wronged them, as psychologists recommend.
5. Reaction and positive psychology – Reaction formation acts in opposition to the impulses one is afraid to acknowledge (e.g., a man fearing being feminine joins a "manly" football team for masculinity). Within positive psychology, being true to oneself initiates the process of self-understanding, which enables the persistence to achieve one's goals successful. Persistence determinedly supports the individual to overcome

difficult opposition (Peterson & Seligman, 2004), and never give up on dreams. As persistence empowers pursuit, people need no behavior opposite to their feelings. So, in our example, a man need not adopt masculine behaviors to avoid being criticized as feminine. Simply being true to his feelings on his gender identity makes him a true person.

6. Displacement and positive psychology – Displacement substitutes dangerous objects or situations with ones that are perceived as safe (e.g., someone is angry at their boss and then aggressively yells at family and pets). Venting anger solves no problem, but hurts innocent others. Within positive psychology, being kind to oneself effectively releases frustration. Self-kindness is acting compassionately to oneself in a difficult time, or in failure, or when disliking things. It is to admit that those difficulties exist, but in true understanding to enable the individual to focus on achieving health and happiness, as well as honoring and accepting one's humanness. It is important and efficient to stay with our own feelings and care for our needs, thereby being open to reality, and not displacing frustrations onto others.
7. Regression and positive psychology – Regression describes the retreat from upsetting conflict in the present to an earlier developmental stage, in order to prevent anxiety and satisfy current needs (e.g., a toilet-trained boy begins to have accidents after his new baby brother is born). With positive psychology, persistence could be a characteristic which helps people manage upsetting conflicts that trigger such regression. Persistence in positive psychology means "a voluntary continuation of a goal-directed action in spite of obstacles, difficulties, or discouragement" (Peterson & Seligman, 2004, p. 229). By integrating persistence into regression, people learn how to accept the difficulties they encounter in life, and maintain positive attitudes in the face of challenges. Although regression functions to prevent people from being overwhelmed by anxiety, such short-term management of anxiety leaves the issue as it is. For example, when facing an exam, a student's regression to earlier developmental stage such as poor self-care only amounts to avoiding anxiety for a short while. To manage the issue effectively, persistence would help the student accept the difficulties, persevere through barriers, and maintain their goal-directed attitudes. Thus, while regression could provide a brief relief from anxiety, persistence would provide a long-term solution to anxiety or stress.
8. Identification and positive psychology – Identification adopts the values of someone in a superior position (e.g., prisoners adopt their captors' attitudes). In psychoanalysis, identification assimilates an aspect, property, or attribute of the other and is transformed, wholly or partially, by the model of the other. The more identified people feel with superior others, the lower self-esteem or self-confidence they would have, and may feel negative about themselves. Positive psychology, an approach that highlights individuals' strengths, such as integrity, can help promote their well-being. Integrity, a concept of positive psychology, means that people are true and honest to themselves. Therefore, people with integrity would accurately represent their internal states, intentions, and commitments. While identification with superior others may make people feel good or get attention, they may miss the essential quality of being human – being true and honest to oneself. As long as one can accurately represent one's internal status and commitments, people know that they need not seek attention and recognition by

conforming with superior others. With integrity, people would be guided by their own values and standards, whereas identification only pursues superior others. Thus, people with integrity feel committed to their own beliefs, and such honesty to themselves would be likely to make them proud of themselves.

9. Sublimation and positive psychology – Sublimation expresses sexual or aggressive energy in ways that are socially acceptable (e.g., a man with strong aggressive impulses plays professional football). It is believed that sublimation is a sign of maturity (indeed, of civilization) and allows people to function normally in culturally acceptable ways. Freud defined sublimation as the process of deflecting sexual instincts into acts of higher social valuation. He also said, being "an especially conspicuous feature of cultural development; it is what makes it possible for higher psychical activities, scientific, artistic or ideological, to play such an important part in civilized life" (Freud, 1930, p, 286). In positive psychology, "citizenship" could be integrated with sublimation to promote people's well-being. Citizenship represents "a feeling of identification with and sense of obligation to a common good that includes the self but that stretches beyond one's own self-interest" (Peterson & Seligman, 2004, p. 370). Thus, when people have in mind a common good or collective well-being, they may endeavor to fulfill such a mission to actually increase people's happiness. For example, Mother Teresa dedicated her whole life to those in poverty and promoted human meanings in life. Moreover, she said "Let us more and more insist on raising funds of love, of kindness, of understanding, of peace. Money will come if we seek first the Kingdom of God – the rest will be given" (Mother Teresa, 1989).
10. Intellectualization and positive psychology – Intellectualization adopts cold distanced perspectives on issues of displeasure (e.g., a distressed man during a divorce settlement coolly discusses the logistics of court proceedings). Intellectualization would allow people temporarily to escape from unpleasant topics, but not solve the issue. Individuals intellectualize unpleasant issues because these issues trigger their anxiety. Although intellectualization temporarily protects people from difficult or hurtful feelings, it cannot promote wellness. To manage painful or unpleasant feelings effectively, the concept of empathy in positive psychology can help people deepen their emotions. Empathy is "an other-oriented emotional response elicited by and congruent with the perceived welfare of someone else" (Batson, Ahmad, Lishner, & Tsang, 2002, p. 486). Empathy gives people a perspective from others on unpleasant issues which usually involve others. This other-perspective can reduce the tendency to intellectualize.

## Multiculturalize the Integration

The American Psychological Association (APA) has published *Guidelines on Multicultural Education, Training, Research, Practice, and Organizational Change for Psychologists* (APA, 2002) within which it defines "multicultural" as being used "… to refer to interactions between individuals from minority ethnic and racial groups … in the dominant European-American culture" (p. 3). In the Western culture, what is important is to appreciate the cultural diversity of communities within a given society and the policies that promote this diversity. Thus, multiculturalism is the simple fact that people from all cultures or backgrounds celebrate differences and embrace diversity, though people do have their uniqueness. Such celebration of differences should exist at different levels, including individuals, organizations, neighborhoods, cities, and nations. Multiculturalism encourages ideologies and policies that promote this diversity or its institutionalization. In this sense, multiculturalism exists in a society which appreciates the rich tapestry of human life and the desire among people to express their own identity in the manner they see fit.

To align the principles of multiculturalism, to better serve increasingly diverse populations, integration of psychoanalysis and positive psychology cannot be done uniformly, but must be culturally sensitive and tailored to each client's background. Thus, considering how to contextualize this integration to a particular client's background depends on the counselor's multicultural competence. Integration of psychoanalysis and positive psychology should be situated in a client's context.

Counseling psychology today has taken the lead in incorporating multicultural diversity into curricula, training, and practice (Constantine & Gloria, 1999; Murphy, Wright, & Bellamy, 1995; Norcross, Sayette, Mayne, Karg, & Turkson, 1998; Ponterotto, 2010; Ponterotto, Alexander, & Grieger, 1995; Quintana & Bernal, 1995; Speight, Thomas, Kennel, & Anderson, 1995; Sue & Sue, 2012). Multicultural counseling competence has been defined as an aggregate of counselors' attitudes/beliefs, knowledge, and skills in working with individual clients from various cultural groups (racial, ethnic, gender, social class, and sexual orientation) (Sue, Arredondo, & McDavis, 1992; Sue et al., 1998).

Multiculturalizing integrated psychoanalysis and positive psychology inevitably requires counselors' competence in multicultural self-awareness and multicultural skills, in the specific *client's* context, background, values, and worldview. But both psychoanalysis and positive psychology came from Western culture. As positive psychology's stress on personal strengths and assets and environment have been neglected until recently (Seligman & Csikszentmihalyi, 2000), so positive psychology itself lacked attention to cultural diversity. This lack of information on different cultural strengths, integration with psychoanalysis, and cultural diversity, has limited counselors' understanding of how culturally diverse people thrive against various odds.

Thus, multiculturalization of the integration begins with counselors' self-awareness of their own ethnic customs, biases, values, and cultural attitudes, and should progress to consider how these aspects may influence counseling and counselor–client interactions (Sue et al., 1992). "Awareness" includes developing culturally accurate and appropriate attitudes, judgments, and assumptions (McRae & Johnson, 1991), to prevent unintentional blindness to clients' needs, values, and worldviews.

## A. Multiculturalizing integration of positive psychology with the unconscious/conscious

Counselors may integrate psychoanalysis and positive psychology, unaware of their own cultural biases, values, and assumptions. Clients from diverse cultures may find it hard to understand psychoanalysis. For Freud, consciousness is only part of the mental processes, and the unconscious is like a large hall where different impulses fly around.

Counselors, being familiar with psychoanalysis, may take it for granted that the unconscious is a milieu in which impulses are hidden, ready to integrate with the conscious and with positive psychology. All such attitude comes from counselors' own awareness developed through years of training and familiarity with psychoanalysis and positive psychology. Yet, for multicultural clients, the first conversation with a counselor could also be the first time they have heard about the concepts of psychoanalysis and positive psychology. Therefore, culturally sensitive counselors must see the integration from the clients' perspective.

Conscious–unconscious conflicts may be resolved with harmony. This resolution benefits multicultural clients only if it is adjusted to the *client's* values and worldviews. Counselors need to explore the principle of "harmony" from within clients' worldviews and cultures. Counselors must be aware that clients may see "harmony" differently from how they see it. With counselors' awareness of cultural differences, multicultural clients learn to appreciate how harmony helps them learn to listen to their desires in the unconscious, and to find their new self.

To Freud, impulses need expression in order to mediate their emergence from being trapped within the body, and counselors can help clients facilitate this expression. Here counselors must be aware of their biases on such matters, and must be sensitive to how multicultural clients interpret such connection from their culture. Putting integration in a multicultural context, counselors must be sensitive to how this connection from unconsciousness to consciousness helps clients in a way that is in keeping with their cultural background, to help clients transform their impulse into creativity and inspiration effectively.

How might a client's culture use the concept of harmony in order to harmonize the unconscious with conscious? It might be impossible for some cultures. Or some cultures may instead debate or negotiate to resolve differences. Counselors can explore culturally equivalent concepts to reconcile unconscious with conscious. In Western culture, harmony is prompted by the positive psychology approach; counselors can help multicultural clients explore strengths of unconscious and conscious and to connect both.

Similarly, culturally skilled counselors create an inclusive relationship in order to celebrate diversity. But some multicultural clients may prefer direct styles of communication, and counselors must be sensitive and creative enough to explore the different ways in which the integration can be adapted to match multicultural clients' communication styles. By developing their own multicultural skills, counselors incorporate multicultural clients' modes of thinking and interactions into integrative therapy. By integrating harmony and id/ego/superego, counselors do not force multicultural clients to answer questions. If multicultural clients endorse no "harmony" to reconcile id, ego, and superego, counselors should respect them, not requiring clients to learn harmony and reconciliation according to a Western understanding.

### B. Multiculturalize the integration of positive psychology and id/ego/superego

For Freud, id, ego, and superego are indispensable to personality, yet create conflicts. It is still doubtful if positive psychology's stress on the strengths of id, ego, and superego is compatible with multicultural clients. Culturally sensitive counseling first examines how integration between positive psychology and id/ego/superego is appreciated by other cultures, aware that different cultures differently interpret "integration."

Because the id is assumed as childish impulsiveness, recognition of the strengths of the id (honestly expressing needs for pleasure) is one way to manage the id. But counselors must be careful about whether recognizing the id's strength matches a client's cultural values. If not, counselors should explore with multicultural clients how they manage id, ego, and superego in their cultures. Although Freud stressed that superego is the agent to suppress internal needs with external judgments, positive psychology stresses how to use superego's strength to enhance well-being. However, multicultural clients may appreciate superego and depreciate id. Before highlighting superego's strengths, counselors must first explore with multicultural clients whether their culture overstresses superego's power.

Culturally skilled counselors know how oppression, racism, discrimination, and stereotyping can negatively affect multicultural clients personally. Here, the concept of appreciation may be difficult for some marginalized clients who suffer disadvantages. For example, Hope and Klonoff (1996) found that among 153 African American participants, only 3 (1.9 per cent) blacks reported experiencing absolutely no racist discrimination of any type. Counselors need a sufficient understanding of how racist discrimination impacts on clients' mental health, and how to support clients in surviving day-to-day problems when they are already exhausted.

A question in counseling is "Would racist discrimination reduce multicultural clients' belief in appreciation?" Some cultures (African American) have a history of slavery, and it is important to understand how these cultures perceive appreciation. Sue and Sue (2012) stressed that for white counselors, multicultural knowledge may mean that white counselors understand how they may have directly or indirectly benefited from individual, institutional, and cultural privileges. The knowledge of white privilege and racist discrimination can be combined to provide a more comprehensive understanding of racism and mental health, and to better help multicultural clients see the strengths of id, ego, and superego.

To enhance their multicultural skills, it is important that counselors create a culturally sensitive therapeutic relationship, by affirming each client's uniqueness and diversity. With multicultural skills, a counselor can incorporate a multicultural client's mode of thinking and interaction into integrative therapy. In the integration between appreciation and id/ego/superego, counselors must not force multicultural clients to answer questions. If multicultural clients endorse no appreciation in recognition of the strengths of id, ego, and superego, counselors should respect them, and not require them to learn what that appreciation is according to Western culture.

## C. Multiculturalize the integration of positive psychology and defense mechanisms

Multicultural awareness involves counselors' awareness of clients' perceptions of defense mechanisms in *the clients'* cultures. According to Freud, defense mechanisms are strategies to protect oneself. Integrated with positive psychology, defense mechanisms promote well-being. This integration should be contextualized within clients' cultural values and worldviews. The concept of defense mechanisms may not exist in some cultures, much less a perspective highlighting the strengths of defense mechanisms. Counselors may collaborate with multicultural clients to examine the integration from the clients' cultural perspective.

1. Repression in positive psychology – Understanding how to multiculturalize this integration has challenged counselors and scholars. Repression in psychoanalysis allows no painful or dangerous thoughts to enter the conscious mind, and for positive psychology repression must be used to strengthen and promote well-being.

Yet, some multicultural clients may feel odd about defense mechanisms and positive psychology. With multicultural knowledge about a client's values, the counselor can help the client to find the equivalent concept of repression in *their* culture. For example, Asians stress sacrificing one's benefits for others. Asians also believe that people should build their happiness on others' well-being. With multicultural skills, counselors can help clients to integrate repression with positive psychology's integrity, authenticity, and honesty. Importantly, because culturally skilled counselors constantly seek to understand themselves as racial and cultural beings, they do not assume the integration of repression and positive psychology (in integrity, authenticity, honesty, etc.) as the only way to promote clients' well-being.

Culturally skilled counselors could explore with multicultural clients the meanings and functions of integrity, authenticity, or honesty in their culture, and how such positive characteristics can help them manage repression. Specifically, in view of the fact that Western culture assumes that an individual can reap benefits from honestly facing oneself, counselors can explore if such a concept is universally shared across different cultures. Counselors can then sensitively use such a concept – facing up to oneself to promote well-being of those multicultural clients.

2. Denial and positive psychology – In psychoanalysis, denial can be perceived as a "band aid" covering an individual's source of anxiety without dealing with it. In positive psychology, the most effective way of managing the problem is to be open-minded. Open-mindedness in Western culture is defined as when an individual is receptive to new and different ideas. Open-mindedness is the willingness to search for evidence against one's favored beliefs and plans. Despite sound integrations between denial and open-mindedness, culturally sensitive counselors need to tailor such integration to multicultural clients' background. For example, the counselor can explore whether the client's culture contains the concept of open-mindedness or something similar. If yes, what does open-mindedness mean to the multicultural client? The concept of "denial" also may have different implications from those in Western culture.

In order to pursue such multicultural exploration, culturally skilled counselors must be aware of how their own cultural background and experiences, attitudes, and values and biases, influence this integration of denial and open-mindedness as they work with multicultural clients. With open-mindedness or the equivalent concept in their culture, multicultural clients can openly explore how open-mindedness might help them to manage their denial. According to Sue, Arredondo, and McDavis (1992), one standard for the culturally sensitive counselor is actively to engage verbal and nonverbal helping responses. Culturally sensitive counselors are also aware that response styles, thinking processes, and value systems may be related to cultures. In general, to apply integration to multicultural clients requires counselors to provide services based on clients' cultures.

## Application in Counseling: Case Study

Amy has come to a free "drop-in" counseling clinic to get some information and advice. When Amy was 10 years old, her father, whom she says was a very heavy drinker, left her mom and her sisters and never came back. At 14, Amy started drinking, and at 16, she started dating Jack and very soon dropped out of high school. After a few months of seeing Jack, Amy found herself pregnant. Jack felt trapped by Amy's pregnancy and left. In order to pay for the rent, Amy applied for jobs and then worked for long hours everyday, usually from 6am till 11pm and occasionally till early morning the next day. She was fatigued, sad, and miserable, and experienced symptoms related to pregnancy.

Amy says her presenting problems include financial stress and relationship troubles. Being pregnant, she feels fatigued very often. As an African American woman, she also experienced verbal and behavioral discrimination. For example, her coworkers seem to assume that her working performance is worse than others. Her supervisor tends to check her work several times a day, while he checks others' work only once a day. Amy was trying to communicate about this issue with him, but he neglected her feedback and attributed her request to her feeling of insecurity. She is thoroughly confused, and does not know what she should do with her life or with her relationship with Jack, or how to deal with discrimination in work.

### How to help Amy

By using the integration of psychoanalytic therapy and positive psychology to help Amy, her counselor can focus on three tasks: (a) promote harmony between Amy's conscious and unconscious; (b) help Amy appreciate her id, ego, and superego; and (c) encourage Amy to transform defense mechanisms into self-enhancement mechanisms.

Because Amy has problems with drinking that originated in troubled relations with her father and boyfriend, the first step is to help Amy to deal with her problematic relationships. She may be eager to have a nurturing, affectionate, and even warm relationship with her father; unfortunately, she was abandoned. She may unconsciously be looking forward to being with her father and having a positive father–daughter relationship; yet in her consciousness she believes that her traumatic childhood came from her irresponsible father. Thus, Amy lives in the conflict between unconscious needs and conscious reality. Her way of coping with such conflict was to resort to alcohol, and to find a boyfriend to replace her need of her father.

Despite the conflict between her unconsciousness and consciousness, there is still hope for her to have a peaceful and less traumatic life. Her counselor can help her see the positive aspects of unconsciousness and consciousness. Specifically, maintaining the harmony between these two aspects may help her to avoid resorting to alcohol. Her unconsciousness alerts her that she needs to rebuild a positive relationship with her father, and her consciousness reminds her to be realistic since she has never contacted her father since he left. In order to maintain the harmony between her unconsciousness and consciousness, she can use realistic strategies from consciousness to satisfy her unconscious eagerness to reunite with her father. As she becomes capable of managing her internal conflict, she actually moves toward a healthy relationship with herself. She may notice that she feels relieved and drinks less.

In the second task, her counselor can help her to appreciate her id, ego, and superego. Although most people believe that the id represents a "trouble-maker," it in fact contains a human's basic and instinctual drives. Through exploring her id, Amy may notice that she has some unsatisfied desires. Unfortunately, she might not take a deep look at her desires which could be inspiring for her, and so she might fail to manage her impulses from id. Her counselor can facilitate Amy's appreciation of the contributions from id, ego, and superego and how each makes a difference (positive and/or negative) to her life.

To facilitate her appreciation of id, ego, and superego, the counselor can explore with her some important enquiries: "What would happen if your life had no id (e.g., desire, impulse, pleasure)?" "What are the pros and cons of having ego in your life?" and "What do you like most and least about your superego?" When Amy reflects on her id, ego, and superego in a deeper way, she may notice the role that each of them plays in her presenting problems such as drinking, her life, and her worldview. Because appreciation refers to the recognition and enjoyment of the good qualities of something, such exploration of the positive qualities of id, ego, and superego may help Amy to develop new insights to advance her self-understanding and well-being.

The third task that her counselor can work on with Amy is to turn defense mechanisms into self-enhancement mechanisms. Defense mechanisms aim to prevent awareness of disturbing content that generates anxiety and/or other destructive emotions. If the counselor helped Amy by using psychoanalysis alone, Amy would only learn how her defense mechanisms function. But when integrated into positive psychology, defense mechanisms can be empowered as part of an approach toward self-enhancement.

For example, Amy uses repression to suppress painful thoughts from her consciousness that originated in abandonment by her father, by turning to alcohol to reinforce avoidance to try to forget her traumatic childhood. All this is defeatism that never actually helps her to overcome the difficulties. If the counselor introduces her to the concept of empowerment with the characteristics of integrity and honesty, she will learn how to be authentic in facing up to herself, being true to herself even when it is painful, and thereby courageously accept responsibility for her own feelings and behaviors, whatever they are.

Importantly, such transformation from repression to integrity and honesty need not mean she has to discard her self-defense mechanisms. Abandoning self-defense mechanisms may trigger her hurtful pain of being abandoned by father. After all, defense mechanisms are her unconscious reactions of self-protection. Amy needs to accept and practice functions, with awareness of their meaning, in order to let her self-defense mechanisms play their indispensable roles. It is through this approach that, while defense mechanisms are at work, she will learn to use her defense mechanisms with a new perspective.

Concretely put, repression can only temporarily allow her to avoid pain. As she adds integrity to repression, she learns to accept the needed function of repression, for the purpose of self-protection, but then look at painful experiences with a new perspective of integrity and honesty. Through this, she can recognize negative pain, which indicates issues that need addressing and help Amy understand how to look forward to a hopeful future when those needs are fulfilled. She can then strive to fulfill those needs as *positive* needs.

This situation parallels hunger as the catalyst to eating food. When hungry, people see delicious foods in front of them and strive to get them. Thus negative hunger is a conduit to positive consumption of food, in the same way as negative pain catalyzes positive characteristics still ahead to be obtained. Pain can make for a life full of hope ahead. Learning to live through this integrated approach, Amy can now broaden her methods of self-protection, from temporary forgetting to healthy management, and then into empowerment with overflowing well-being.

Such vibrant health can be experienced in the very midst of tough stresses of all types, such as Amy's abandonment by her father and boyfriend, her struggles during pregnancy and the discrimination she faces at work, among many more. Moreover, Amy is now quite capable of facing up to the uncertain days ahead. Amy may even be able to assist other people struggling under similar circumstances! Positive psychology calls this situation the *vigorous health of well-being.*

### Follow-up: You Continue as Amy's Counselor

Consider how you would help Amy if you were her counselor. Here are a series of questions to provide some structure in your thinking about her case:

- How much interest would you have in Amy's early childhood? What are some of the ways in which you would help her to see patterns between her childhood issues and her current problems?
- Consider the transference relationship that is likely to be established between you and Amy. Because positive psychology is integrated into the counseling with Amy, consider whether you would continue to include positive psychology in your therapeutic relationship with her.
- In working with Amy, what counter transference issues might arise for you?
- What role might cultural difference play between you and Amy? What does her cultural background mean to you when you work with her, with the integration between psychoanalysis and positive psychology?

## Concluding Remarks

Psychoanalysis, founded by Freud, has been an influence on psychology and counseling through to the present day. Freud's theories changed how we think about the human mind and behavior, and left a lasting mark on psychology. The psychoanalytic approach provides counselors with a conceptual framework to understand the origins and functions of symptoms. Psychoanalysis benefits counseling in several ways, by enabling an understanding of: (a) resistances from the psychoanalytic perspective; (b) the potential contribution of childhood issues to the current problem; (c) the roles of transference and countertransference in counseling; and (d) how the overuse of ego defense may keep clients from functioning effectively.

Additionally, the unconscious, conscious, and dream symbolism in psychoanalysis remain popular topics among both counselors and laypersons, despite the fact that Freud's work is viewed with skepticism by many today. A number of Freud's observations and theories were based on clinical cases and case studies, making the findings in psychoanalysis difficult to generalize to a larger population (Angers, 2011). Freud's psychoanalysis is also limited in what it can do to build clients' strengths and well-being. The deterministic emphasis of psychoanalysis puts clients into an inactive role and overlooks opportunities to help them explore different possibilities to solve their problems. The integration between psychoanalysis and positive psychology can instead help clients gain insights into their problems while building their well-being and positive affects.

Psychoanalysis has been criticized because of the difficulties involved in attempting to generalize its concepts to clients from different cultures. For example, psychoanalysis assumes that resistance can take the form of canceling counseling appointments or refusing to look at the counselor (Corey, 2012). However, this overlooks the transportation difficulties faced by some clients which can result in them having to cancel appointments (Sandell, Blomberg, Lazar, Carlsson, & Broberg, 2000). Other clients do not feel comfortable examining their problems in a psychoanalytic way due to their cultural values. Generally based on upper- and middle-class values, not all clients share the values implied within the psychoanalytic approach, and for some the cost of treatment is prohibitive. For multicultural clients, the overemphasis on internal psychological conflicts may be inconsistent with their social framework and environmental perspectives. Thus, multicultural scholars (e.g., Suzuki & Ponterroto, 2008) indicate the importance of adding external sources of clients' problem, especially those who suffer from an oppressive environment. Because psychoanalysis is limited in addressing the social, cultural, and political factors that result in a multicultural client's problem, the above section titled "Multiculturalize the Integration" attempts to balance the external factors relating to client's problems with the internal factors.

## Review Questions: What Do You Think?

1. Describe the three components (i.e., the conscious, the preconscious, and the unconscious) in psychoanalysis. How does positive psychology promote these three components to enhance people's well-being?
2. What are the primary functions of ego defense mechanisms? How does positive psychology complement ego defense mechanisms to build well-being?
3. Reflect on your personal or professional experiences of interacting with people from different cultures. What difficulties would you expect if you apply: (a) psychoanalysis; (b) positive psychology; and (c) integration between psychoanalysis and positive psychology to work with culturally different people?
4. In the case study, Amy appeared to be suffering from many problems. How would you feel if she discusses racial issues with you? How would you conceptualize her racial confrontation with the perspectives of: (a) psychoanalysis; (b) positive psychology; and (c) integration between psychoanalysis and positive psychology?

# 6

# Adlerian Therapy

**Learning Objectives**

- Learn about the historical background of Adlerian therapy.
- Distinguish between Adlerian therapy and Freud's psychoanalysis.
- Describe striving with purpose, social interest, birth order, sibling relationships, and life style.
- Learn about the impact of inferiority and compensation.
- Integrate Adlerian therapy into positive psychology.
- Multiculturalize the integration between Adlerian therapy and positive psychology.
- Apply the integration to a case study.

Adlerian therapy is based on the individual psychology of Alfred Adler (1870–1937), a Viennese contemporary of Sigmund Freud. Individual psychology emphasizes the individual's social cultural backgrounds and holistic view of personality. Adlerian therapy stresses that people need to take personal responsibility, strive to achieve life goals, and grow toward a sense of completion and belonging. Since these values are universally shared, some concepts in Adlerian therapy are still contemporary expressions in today's therapy.

*Counseling Psychology: An Integrated Positive Psychological Approach*, First Edition. Ruth Chu-Lien Chao.

## Historical Context

Adler's view on psychology and therapy can be tracked back to his childhood, family, and living environment. Alfred Adler started as a medical practitioner who had a keen interest in the social and political structure of society. He explored the effects of environmental and psychological influences on the symptomatology of physical disorders. Early in his adulthood he was influenced by political theory, especially that of Marx, though this interest changed as he developed his theory. By 1898, he wrote his first paper on education. In 1902, Freud asked Adler to join his small group and recognized his talent in psychology and neurosis. In a very short period of time, Adler was named Freud's successor, becoming President of the Vienna Psychoanalytical Society.

However, it quickly became apparent that the two men had developed different theoretical perspectives. For example, Adler argued that behavior is determined by expectations about what we hope to achieve in the future, not by what we have done in the past, or what others have done to us. He resigned from the Psychoanalytical Society in 1911, and then founded the Society for Free Psychoanalytical Research (later called Individual Psychology). Adler was a theoretician and therapist of considerable stature and a number of his theoretical concepts are still influential even in current thinking. He is best known for his emphasis on power as the individual goal (cf. Freud's focus on sex). Many components of his theory were based on the child's experience of impotence and humiliation, resulting in the creation of a self-ideal, the expression of which is linked for the individual with feelings of strength and power, and hence overcoming feelings of helplessness and inferiority. His therapeutic approach concentrated on current difficulties and is concretely based on a social and cultural context. During his later years, having established himself in America, he travelled and taught widely in Europe. He influenced analytical thought including the work of Sullivan, Horney, and Fromm, and indirectly, contemporary cognitive and existential therapies.

## View of Human Nature

Adler abandoned Freud's basic theory because he believed Freud was too narrowly focused on biological aspects and instinctual mechanisms. Although Adler claimed that people begin to form their personality and their approach to life in the first six years of living, his focus was on how individuals perceive their past. According to Adler, individuals' interpretations of the past continue to influence their current experiences. In general, Adler presented opposite positions to Freud's approach. For example, Adler proposed that humans are motivated by social relatedness rather than by sexual urges. He also indicated that behavior is purposeful and direction-oriented. Consciousness, rather than unconsciousness, according to Adler, is the main focus in therapy. Different from Freud's pessimism, Adler believed that humans make choices, are responsible, create meanings in life, and strive for success and perfection. Adler and Freud had extremely different childhood experiences, which heavily influenced both theories, and shaped their distinctive perspectives on human nature. Due to Adler's sickness in his childhood, he stressed inferiority feelings, which he saw as a normal condition of almost all people. In contrast to most people's interpretation, Adler stressed that inferiority motivates people to strive for mastery.

Adler also presents a different perspective from Freud regarding what determines human behavior. According to Adler, human behavior is not determined solely by heredity and environment. He believed that what individuals were born with is not as significant as what they choose to do with the ability (and limitations) they possess. Although Adler's position about human nature was not to the extreme that all human behaviors are totally based on choice, he recognized that biological and environmental conditions limit people's capacity to create.

## Theoretical Principles

In general, Adler's theory includes several characteristics: striving with purpose; striving for superiority; birth order, family life, and sibling relationships; social interest; life style; holistic concept and phenomenological approach. Adler believed therapy as teaching, informing and encouraging and therapeutic relationship as a collaborative partnership.

### Striving with purpose

Adler believed that individuals strive with their purposes in life. Indeed, he founded Individual Psychology and one of the basic premises is that personality can only be understood holistically and systematically. According to Adler, human personality becomes unified through a life goal. People's overarching goals in life motivate them to move from positions of inferiority and inactivity to positions of mastery and completion. The nature of people's goals and the approach in which they pursue them are influenced by heredity, socioeconomic and cultural contexts, health, and the family environment. Thus, a critical component influencing human behavior is "attitude toward life" (Adler, 1935, p. 5). Attitude toward life is composed of a delightful combination of individual choice and sense of purpose. Moreover, for Adlerian therapists, everyday behavior can be analyzed with respect to its purpose. For example, when Adlerian therapists notice a maladaptive behavior of their client, they may wonder what causes the problematic behavior and remain interested in the purpose of the maladaptive behavior.

### Striving for superiority

For Adler, striving for superiority and coping with inferiority are critical for human beings. To understand human behaviors, it is important and almost inevitable to grasp the impact of inferiority and compensation. For Adlerian therapists, inferiority can be traced back to people's childhood when they feel helpless and such helplessness is called inferiority. Adler maintains that the goal of superiority contributes to the development of human community, and conceptualizes superiority as a movement from an individual's perceived lower level to a higher level rather than competition with others. Thus, to grow means that people cope with inferiority by striving for competence and mastery. In fact, the process of coping with inferiority reflects Adler's younger days. He reacted to his childhood, which was full of inferiority, with striving for superiority. His personal experiences made him a living example of this aspect of his theory (Carlson & Slavik, 1997).

## Birth order, family life, and sibling relationships

According to Adler, people develop their unhealthy goals during childhood from a confluence of variables such as dysfunctional family environments. Such dysfunctional family environments were discouraging human functioning and worsening psychological problems. These conditions could overwhelm the child's ability to develop a healthy life style and a sense of belonging. Particularly, in these circumstances, children may act out or misbehave as a means to seek attention, power, or withdrawal from a task or interaction. Adults also may develop self-defeating life goals that give rise to physical or psychological symptoms and to interpersonal difficulties. Adlerian therapy seeks to determine the early-in-life causes of unhealthy, self-defeating life goals before reorienting the individual toward healthy life goals.

Since Adler's theory stresses the combination of biological aspects and living environment, family could be a critical environment for children. Children born into their specific birth order may actually perceive their environment in the family uniquely. Based on Adler's observation, the oldest child generally receives a great deal of attention. He/she tends to be dependable and strives to keep ahead of his/her younger siblings. However, he/she may feel that his/her younger siblings would rob the attention and love which he/she enjoys. The second child learns to share the attention with the oldest child, and may feel like always being in a race. The competition between them may set up their life or their relationship in the later course. The middle child may feel squeezed out most of the time. This child may feel unfair, unrecognized, not cared about, and learns to survive by serving the role of a peacemaker. The youngest child is the baby of the family and tends to be the most pampered one. Youngest children tend to go their own way and develop in ways no other family members can think of (Carlson, Watts, & Maniacci, 2006).

## Social interest

In the process of negotiating these goals, Adler contended that all people must address three tasks: (a) how to find a productive work role in life; (b) how to establish and maintain an emotionally close relationship with a life partner and family members; and (c) how to meaningfully contribute to society. Thus, practitioners with an Adlerian approach believe that social interest leads to and is a marker of psychological health. The essence of social interest involves striving to achieve one's life goals while meeting life's tasks in a socially responsible and supportive manner. Some individuals, however, strive single-mindedly after particular goals. Such goals offer only a fleeting sense of efficacy or esteem, life tasks go unmet and other people are viewed as obstacles that must be manipulated or vanished. According to Adler, this approach contradicts healthy functioning in psychology.

### Life style

Adlerian therapy involves four phases. The first phase involves establishing the therapeutic relationship. This is done by enlisting the client's cooperation, addressing and resolving immediate crises, understanding the presenting problem, and identifying the possible goals in therapy. The second phase involves using a semi-structured interview and standardized measures to examine the client's life style (i.e., personality). The life style assessment provides the clinician with essential information and helps the client experience self-discovery. Moreover, a successful life style assessment will also reveal the client's patterns of thoughts, emotions, and behaviors. Such information will help the practitioner and client have more understanding of the presenting problem. Adlerian therapists sometimes use genograms to understand the structure, climate, and emotional expressions of the client's family of origin and to know if the client had any goals before therapy or earlier in his/her life. How the client perceives his/her position in family indicates the relationships between him/her to other family members (Rule & Bishop, 2006).

The third phase involves insights. In this phase, the practitioner helps the client to build a deeper awareness which makes behavior change possible. Adlerian therapists incorporate a variety of techniques into therapy in this phase, such as confrontation, challenge, demonstrating a client's symptoms, and so on. Developing insights to their symptoms could be a client's primary task in this phase. Eventually, this phase culminates with the client's insights into how his or her life goals and subsidiary behaviors lead to problems and dysfunctional relationships.

The final phase attempts to help clients identify their dysfunctional positions in life and then move on to healthy and meaningful life goals. During this phase, practitioners may add some techniques or activities to help clients achieve their new life goals. For instance, the technique of pushbutton helps clients recognize that they choose the particular thoughts they like, along with the ensuing emotions and behaviors that stem from them. Clients are also encouraged to experiment with new life goals by role play or "live" in progressively wider settings outside of therapy. Adlerian therapists then conclude when presenting problems have been resolved and the client is able to identify new life goals.

Currently, Adlerian therapy is widely used to treat a variety of client populations: adults, children, couples, families, and groups. Although many variations of Adlerian therapy exist to fit different client populations, these different variations of Adlerian therapy primarily differ with respect to the duration of therapy, the focus and scope of treatment goals, and the strategies and techniques that are compatible with these goals. Although Adlerian therapy has traditionally been long term and comprehensive in focus, currently practitioners have successfully adapted the approach for short-term therapy. When using Adlerian therapy with couples, practitioners emphasize how compatibility in the life goals and life style of the partners can perpetuate the relational disagreement and unhappiness. Adlerian group therapy provides an active therapeutic forum in which the social manifestations of client's problems (e.g., goals for dominating others, hesitating life style tendencies) can be explored and changed. Adlerian groups accentuate the client's social embeddedness, the interpersonal nature of problems, and ways in which social interest can be cultivated (Carlson et al., 2006).

Adlerian therapy conceptually and clinically is resonant with other theories of classic therapists (e.g., Karen Horney, Abraham Maslow) and is compatible with modern cognitive-behavioral approaches (e.g., those of Albert Ellis, Aaron Beck). Moreover, mental health professionals continue to find Adlerian therapy and individual psychology highly useful to their work. In scholarship, the *Journal of Individual Psychology* is the primary forum for disseminating the conceptual and clinical scholarship of the field. Books summarizing the Adlerian literature or focusing upon specific topics continue to appear regularly.

## An Integration: Positive Psychology and Adlerian Therapy

Adler shifted the grounds of his therapy from a Freudian standpoint to focus on the individual evaluation of the world. He gave special prominence to societal factors. According to him a person has to combat or confront three forces: societal, love-related, and vocational. Adlerian psychology shows parallels with the humanistic psychology of Maslow, who acknowledged Adler's influence on his own theories. Both individual psychology and humanistic psychology hold that the individual human being is the best determinant of his or her own needs, desires, interests, and growth. Although Adler's approach in therapy was less pessimistic than Freud's, he based his theories on the pre-adulthood development of a person. He laid stress on such areas as hated children, physical deformities at birth, birth order, and so on. There are several ways that positive psychology can contribute to Adlerian therapy.

### Compensation integrated with happy ending

Adler stressed that achievements come from individuals' compensation for their inferiority, and weaknesses could motivate individuals to strive for excellence. However, positive psychology brings a new perspective that working toward success could come from individuals' enjoyment of learning rather than compensation for inferiority. From the perspective of positive psychology, the journey of moving forward itself could be a memorable process, even though the ending might be a failure. Thus, by integrating the Adlerian focus on striving for success and positive psychology, therapists can help clients see that being successful does not need to be based on inferiority or defects. In contrast, hard work itself could be a joyful journey regardless of the success or failure.

### Resignation integrated with persistence

According to Adlerian therapy, there are those who give in to their disadvantages and become reconciled to them. Such people are in the majority. The attitude of the world toward them is of a cool, rather uninterested sympathy. However, positive psychology may appreciate persistence and encourage individuals not to give up their goals (Eisenberger & Selbst, 1994). Persistence is defined as a "voluntary continuation of a goal-directed action in spite of obstacles, difficulties, or discouragement" (Peterson & Seligman, 2004, p. 229). Just as fear is a prerequisite for courage, disadvantage is a prerequisite for perseverance.

Simply measuring how long someone sticks with a task does not adequately capture the essence of perseverance because continuing to perform something that is fun or easy does not involve the overcoming of obstacles or disappointment.

If people reconcile with disadvantage based on Adlerian therapy, people may get a temporary relief by reconciling to disadvantages, however, they are still unable to solve their problems. Perseverance may make a different story to different people. For example, we know that Thomas Edison did not invent the light bulb on his first try. Rather, he put more than 6000 substances to the test before he discovered that carbonized cotton thread makes a nice filament for the electric light bulb. If he reconciled with his disadvantages, perhaps we would still live in a world of darkness.

Taken together, Adlerian therapy which describes most people's tendency, reconciliation with disadvantage, may give people some short-term relief. Whether people take such reconciliation as a brief break or the end of work, what is important is to persist through difficulties and challenges and succeed. In general, people with higher self-esteem are more likely to persist on a difficult task than people with lower self-esteem. Thus, individuals with high self-esteem may take reconciliation as a break from their next endeavor. Persistence may inspire individuals to perceive reconciliation as a period of transition rather than failure. By integrating reconciliation into the mindset of persistence, individuals may be persistent at practice or in preparation for a major task. If one reconciles and fails to persist in a task, then failure can be explained by blaming the failure on lack of persistence.

## Striving with purpose integrated with engaged life

While Adlerian therapy emphasizes on striving for purposes, positive psychology stresses on how an engaged life can enhance the well-being of individuals' lives. Both approaches aim to help individuals create a meaningful life. Adlerian therapy believes that people's pursuit of their overarching life goals motivates them to move from positions of inferiority, inactivity, and inertness to positions of mastery and completion. In contrast, positive psychology proposes that people possess an intrinsic motivation to have an engaged life (Peterson, 2006). Rather than judging which proposition is correct, the intent is to find an integrative appreciation of Adlerian therapy and positive psychology to develop a useful approach for individuals and counselors. According to Csikszentmihalyi (1990), engagement in life overlaps with the concept of flow or optimal experience, and flow is defined as a psychological experience in which one is fully immersed in what he or she is doing, rather than moving from inferiority. Flow is not an abstract concept; in fact, there are concrete and clearly defined characteristics or conditions of flow (Csikszentmihalyi , 2008). In order to have an engaged life, one must see a challenge as an opportunity to activate one's existing skills and strengths. When individuals endeavor to conquer a challenge, flow becomes more likely when such challenging activities require concentration, and individuals have clear goals followed up with immediate feedback on progress. Under these conditions, people may enter into a state in which there is joy in the process of accomplishing a goal. The flow may also require the merging of action and awareness, deep involvement in the task at hand, intense focus in the moment, and even the feeling that time seems to stop or pass more quickly than normal (Diener & Biswas-Diener, 2008).

Taking Adlerian therapy's "striving for purpose" and positive psychology's "engaged life" together, counselors may help clients appreciate the importance of striving for purpose while helping clients savor the process of accomplishing a goal or task. When clients learn to single-mindedly concentrate on the purpose they strive for, they can find meanings in their life and enjoy the rewarding experience of accomplishing a task. Moreover, such positive feelings can facilitate well-being and may reduce their psychological problems (Seligman, 2006).

## Strive for superiority integrated with character strengths

Adler proposes that individuals strive for superiority and cope with their inferiority. However, coping with inferiority might not be a primary focus in positive psychology. In positive psychology, building clients' character strengths and virtues (Peterson & Seligman, 2004) in the change process is a primary focus for counseling and psychotherapy. In positive psychology, to succeed in a task needs the development and fulfillment of an individual's character strengths and virtues. A key aspect to fulfilling a client's character strengths is more than Adler's striving for superiority – the process requires a counselor's understanding that the cultivation of character strengths requires collaboration between counselor and client. In this approach, counselors do not serve as experts who provide information to clients; rather, clients and counselors work together to make meaning of client experiences (Peterson & Seligman, 2004). Over the course of integration between striving for superiority and character strengths, counselors do not let clients find out how to strive for superiority, instead, they work with clients to develop new meanings for client experiences and to expand client strengths. Clients also learn to attach their life experiences to that which is positive and adaptive. Thus, the integration expands the coverage of strengths which include striving for superiority. With a scientific focus, counselors can work with clients to cultivate their strengths on a weekly or bi-weekly basis. During a period of weekly sessions, counselors can help clients go through four phases of cultivating strengths such as explicitizing, envisioning, empowering, and evolving (Wong, 2006).

## Birth order and family life integrated with harmony

Adler believes in the importance of family life and birth order. For example, he claims that unhealthy goals developed during childhood arise from a confluence of variables such as dysfunctional family environments. Such environments discourage and disempower untreated psychological or medical conditions. These conditions overwhelm the child's ability to develop a healthy life style and a sense of belonging. Particularly, in these circumstances children may act out or misbehave as a means of seeking attention, becoming more powerful, exacting revenge, or withdrawing from a task or interaction. However, positive psychology embraces different types of interpersonal relationships and family environment; importantly, it focuses on how interpersonal relationships/family environment relates to well-being. Indeed, it is universally accepted that significant social relationships are crucial to individuals' well-being and happiness. Furthermore, positive psychology suggests that each stage of life span contributes to individuals' growth and people can make positive changes in various family environments. Ryff and Singer (1998) indicate that an important goal for the future is to promote healthy interactions and relationships while the family environment is moving toward varied situations. That is, while Adlerian therapy may argue that individuals struggle with dysfunctional family relationships, positive psychology emphasizes that the family also needs to go through different levels of evolvement and growth and each stage provides unique opportunities to individuals. For Adlerian therapists, the negative experiences in childhood may push individuals to compensate for feelings of inferiority later in adulthood, positive psychology proposes that individuals have the resilience to "bounce back" from negative environments.

When integrating Adlerian therapy and positive psychology regarding the family environment, it is important to remember that negative family environments may relate to negative experiences later in life. Positive psychology encourages people to see each transformation of the family cycle as an opportunity to reflect on the meanings of family and life. According to Vaillant (2000), it is impossible to describe positive psychological processes without taking a life span, or at least a longitudinal approach. Although Adlerian therapy assumes that parental divorces could hurt children's feelings and decrease their sense of security, positive psychology encourages people to take this negative experience (i.e., divorce) as an opportunity to reflect on marriage, to mourn the lost intimate relationships, and even to forgive those who hurt us.

### Social interest integrated with positive psychology at an institutional level

Social interest has been a primary focus in Adler's principles, and he contended that all people must address tasks in life, relationships, and society. These tasks may be appreciated by positive psychology, which also focuses on institute and society. Yet, positive psychology also proposes collective well-being to promote the quality of life and levels of well-being of general populations. Thus, for positive psychology, well-being involves several levels, from individuals to society.

While Adler used the concept of social interest to highlight that people live in a social context and it is people's tendency to contribute to society, positive psychology seems to seek a balance between individual and collective well-being. Seligman and Csikszentmihalyi (2000) indicated that some hedonic rewards tend to be zero-sum when viewed from a systemic perspective. For example, if someone's happiness is the cost of another person's pain, which person's well-being will the counselors support? Or, if running a noisy motorcycle for an hour provides the same amount of happiness to individual A as reading a novel provides to person B, yet the noisy motorcycle disturbs a quiet neighborhood, should counselors weigh the two experiences (i.e., riding a motorcycle and reading a novel) equally? Will a social science of positive community and positive institutions arise?

Putting Adlerian therapy and positive psychology together, it is important to know that both social interests and collective well-being deserve understanding from counselors. Social interests may focus on how social context impacts on client's mental problems, but collective well-being encourages counselors and clients to keep others' well-being in mind and demonstrate the spirit "you are OK, and I am OK."

### Life style integrated with measures in positive psychology

Adler was a pioneer in creating measures to assess life style, which provides the counselor with essential information and helps the client experience self-discovery. A successful life style assessment will also reveal the client's patterns of thoughts, emotions, and behaviors; such information will help the practitioner and client have more understanding of the presenting problems. Adlerian therapists sometimes use genograms to understand how the problem develops through the client's family.

Many decades after Adler's life style assessment, positive psychology also stresses the importance of assessment and measures. Indeed, for positive psychology, good intervention comes from accurate understanding, which is developed through measures. As positive psychology grows into its own discipline, the attention from researchers, educators, and counselors has turned to interventions to cultivate positive experiences and a good life. Useful interventions may be based on rigorous measures and empirical evaluation. Positive psychology combines new theoretical approaches with rigorous research; this combination may provide positive psychology a cutting-edge position. The most critical tools for positive psychologists interested in evaluating interventions include methods to test what a good life is and assessment strategies to examine its components. In the past decade, there has been more attention on positive traits such as kindness and hope.

By integrating life style assessment and positive psychology, counselors can facilitate their clients in various areas. For example, counselors can use clients' life style assessments to enhance their appreciation of their character strengths in addition to solving problematic behaviors. In the life style assessment, counselors explore clients' character strengths such as hope, optimism, and resilience. Peterson and Seligman (2004) listed six types of characteristics: wisdom and knowledge; courage; humanity; justice; temperance; and transcendence. While Adlerian therapists sometimes use life style assessment to understand how the problem develops through the client's family, counselors can also integrate the life style assessment with character strengths and explore if clients use these strengths to overcome any problems. Specifically, counselors can use life style assessment to explore with clients their experiences of using courage to conquer their problems.

## Multiculturalize the Integration

Even though Adler's counseling theory included family and social interests, his theory is still based on a Western mono-training approach. To date, many scholars and trainers question the effectiveness of traditional counseling approaches and techniques when applied to multicultural clients (Sue & Sue, 2008). It is apparent that the major reason for counseling ineffectiveness on multicultural clients lies in the mistaken direction in training mental health professionals (Sue, Akutsu, & Higashi, 1985). Currently, although most counseling psychology programs require at lease one course on multiculture-related issues, the ideology, importance, and concepts of multiculturalism are still treated as separate topics, and multicultural courses are often taken as an ancillary, not an integral part of counseling. Many counseling theory courses solely focus on traditional theories, which rarely integrate multicultural understanding. Based on these concerns, this section multiculturalizes this integration of Adlerian therapy with positive psychology.

### Multiculturalizing integration between compensation and happiness

Compensation is an essential concept in Adler's theory. He believed that achievements come from individuals' compensation for their inferiority; positive psychology indicates that working toward success can come from individuals' enjoyment. This integration must be multiculturalized when working with multicultural clients.

Moreover, cultural-sensitive counselors are aware of their own cultural biases. For example, they know that both Adler's theory and positive psychology originated in Western culture, and counselors themselves may have also been raised and educated with a Western perspective. With this awareness, counselors realize that seeking achievements, whether because of inferiority or joy of learning, is based on individualism in Western culture. As we know, many multicultural clients come from collectivistic cultures, seeking achievements perhaps due to family expectation, school requirement, and/or social climate.

For example, over thousands of years, Confucius shaped the Chinese definition of success. Asians believe that education is the most important way to success (Ayres & Mahat, 2012). Thus, culturally effective counselors are able to differentiate the role of achievements and their reasons between their own culture and their clients'. Culturally skilled counselors have knowledge of multicultural clients' family structures, hierarchies, values, and beliefs. They understand multicultural clients' community characteristics. For example, for multicultural clients, seeking achievements could originate in cultural value, as Asian culture expects people to pursue superior performance. Thus it requires counselors' cultural sensitivity to apply the integration between compensation and positive psychology to multicultural clients.

### Multiculturalizing integration between resignation and persistence

Adler believed that sometimes people give in to their disadvantages and become reconciled to them; in contrast, concerning inferiority or disadvantages, positive psychology still encourages people to persist instead of giving up on their goals (Eisenberger & Selbst, 1994). Although such integration may strengthen clients' will to fulfill their dreams in life, it requires counselors' cultural awareness, knowledge, and skills when working with multicultural clients with such integration. Counselors are aware that multicultural clients are resigned to disadvantages or reconciled with them due to lack of family support or of interpersonal harmony. Culturally sensitive counselors also have knowledge that multicultural clients may put others' (e.g., family members, friends, co-workers) interests as their priority despite it being to their disadvantage. Thus, their behavior seemed to fit with Adler's "resignation" because they reconcile with personal disadvantages or are against "persistence" in positive psychology. However, for multicultural clients, their behavior may reflect their cultural values. The challenge for counselors is how to culturally sensitively deliver this integration to multicultural clients to enhance their strengths and well-being in their own cultures.

To meet the above challenges, counselors must know that multicultural clients have their culturally unique ways of demonstrating their persistence. For example, Asians may find themselves having to give up their personal dreams (e.g., becoming a writer) in order to follow parents' decision on their career (e.g., be a doctor). They may end up working as a doctor, adding various volumes of writing to their profession. In Adler's theory, these people appeared to give in to parental decision (doctor) with personal disadvantages (sacrificing dream to be writer). They did not persist in their goal to be writers; their failure seems to go against the principles of persistence in positive psychology.

Yet, from an Asian cultural perspective, they did not give in to disadvantages or reconcile with failures; instead, they maintained family harmony by following parental decision, and treasured their own dreams by becoming prolific writers in the medical profession. This example further reinforces how indispensable it is for counselors to be multiculturally aware, to acquire relevant knowledge and skills to work with multicultural clients. Culturally sensitive counselors should demonstrate their persistence to be familiar with the most recent findings regarding the mental health of multicultural groups. Without persistently seeking educational opportunities, counselors may end up finding it difficult to work with multicultural clients.

### Multiculturalizing integration between striving with purpose and engaged life

Counselors may notice that multicultural clients' striving with purposes appears to echo Adler's theory. Yet, culturally sensitive counselors are aware of the cultural differences in "purposes." For example, Adlerian therapy believes that people's pursuit of overarching life goals motivates them to move from positions of inferiority, inactivity, and inertness to positions of competence, mastery, and completion. Taking together, Adlerian therapy's "striving for purpose" and positive psychology's "engaged life," counselors can help clients appreciate the importance of striving for purpose (from the Adlerian therapy) while enabling them to savor the process of accomplishing a goal or task. However, "purposes" for multicultural clients may focus on their family members, relatives, friends, neighborhood, churches, or people in need. Positive psychology proposes that people have an intrinsic motivation to lead an engaged life (Locke, 2002a), and counselors should be alert to how such Western-based concept of engaged life fits multicultural clients' cultures.

Confucius said, "Wherever you go, go with all your heart" (Dawson & Mukoyama, 2012). An African American best-seller writer Delany said, "Life is short, and it's up to you to make it sweet" (Delany, Delany, & Hearth, 1994). Latina/o people say, "dum vita est, spes est (While there's life, there's hope)" (Morwood, 1998). Thus, multicultural clients' cultures demonstrate culture-specific ways of leading an engaged life. Culturally sensitive counselors need to be aware of culturally different ways in which striving with purpose and engaged life are integrated.

### Multiculturalizing integration between strive for superiority and character strengths

Adler proposed that individuals strive for superiority as they cope with their inferiority, but positive psychology encourages people to build their character strengths and virtues

(Peterson & Seligman, 2004). Over the course of integration between striving for superiority and character strengths, counselors work with clients to develop new meanings for client experiences and to expand client strengths to reach their superiority. Although striving for superiority by one's character strengths is an excellent way to promote well-being, culturally sensitive counselors must be aware that different cultures may have their specific definitions of superiority and character strengths.

### Multiculturalizing integration between birth order and family and harmony

Birth order plays a significant role in Adler's theory at least partially due to his personal experiences in childhood. For multicultural clients, both birth order and gender represent important implications to individuals and the family. For example, in Asian families, the oldest child assumes major responsibility. Also, implications of birth order interweave with gender. In poor Asian families, boys will have favorable chances to receive better education than girls even if boys are younger, because boys will carry the family name onto next generations. For girls who are older siblings, they need to take care of younger siblings, share financial responsibility, and so end up having less chances for education. Thus, it is important not to miss the cultural implications of birth order in multicultural clients' families without considering gender.

Adler stressed the importance of birth order and family life, while positive psychology focuses on harmony among people. However, culturally effective counselors have knowledge that family in Adler's theory may have a different meaning in non-Western cultures (e.g., Asian). For example, Adler claimed that unhealthy goals developed during childhood from a confluence of variables such as dysfunctional family environments. In contrast to focusing on family dysfunction, many cultures regard family as the place to nurture and support an individual's growth and development. Thus, counselors respect the meanings of "family" in non-Western clients' various cultures.

Integration of Adler's concept of family with harmony in positive psychology may help people to understand how interpersonal relationships, family environment, and social relationships are crucial to individuals' well-being and happiness. When working with multicultural clients, culturally sensitive counselors have knowledge that collectivistic societies may focus on harmony more than individualistic societies do. Harmony in a collectivistic society means that an individual should restrain his or her personal interests to promote intrapersonal and interpersonal harmony.

### Multiculturalizing integration between social interest and positive psychology at an institutional level

In Adler's theory, all people must address three tasks: find a productive work role in life; establish and maintain an emotionally close relationship with a life partner and family members; and meaningfully contribute to the society. Positive psychology shares these principles and expands them to collective well-being. Social interests may help clients understand how social context has impacts on their mental problems, but that it is still mostly on the individual's level of well-being. Collective well-being encourages people to keep others' well-being in mind and demonstrate the spirit of "you are OK, and I am OK." Despite this, counseling may still begin with an individual's feelings and then expand to others' experiences. This approach could be different from multicultural clients' worldview which focuses on relationships and sometimes emphasizes others' benefits more than one's needs.

Applying this integration to multicultural clients, culturally sensitive counselors respect clients' religious beliefs and/or spiritual values about physical and mental well-being. For example, some multicultural clients refer their mental well-being to the physical health and energy of themselves and family members. To maintain positive relationships with partners and family members, some multicultural clients may seek help from religious or spiritual leaders. In other words, multicultural clients have their culture-specific ways of connecting to people.

Specifically, Asians may connect to others through mutual friends, people from hometowns, and relatives. African Americans may maintain close relationships through churches, neighborhoods, or multi-parenting. Thus, culturally sensitive counselors respect the culture-specific connections, indigenous patterns of helping, and their internal networks of help. Because of culture-specific connections and contributions to society, culturally sensitive counselors understand that there are potential biases in assessment usage, procedures, and interpretations made concerning multicultural clients. Thus, it is essential that multiculturalizing the integration begins with cultural awareness and knowledge regarding multicultural clients' specific cultures.

### Multiculturalizing integration between life style and measures

Although Adler was a trail blazer at using life style assessment and genograms to understand the client's thoughts, emotions, behaviors, and family patterns in the issues discussed in counseling, it requires cultural sensitivity when applied to multicultural clients. Decades later, positive psychology also stresses the importance of assessment and measures. Recently, there have been numerous assessments in life style, emotions, positive affects, and character strengths.

Yet, the problem remains on how these Western assessment instruments fit multicultural clients' various cultures, interpretations, and language usage. Counselors must be aware that multicultural clients' life style is closely related to their cultural and perhaps immigrating or refugee experiences. From the life style assessment, culturally skilled counselors have knowledge that the character strengths multicultural clients demonstrate may differ from those in a Western culture. For example, a refugee may give up his or her benefits for the younger siblings to receive them. This personal character of self-sacrifice may be inconsistent with Western individualism, but it could imply a praiseworthy unselfishness in the refugee's culture.

Life style assessments for multicultural clients may also reveal the long and difficult journey of immigration. Moreover, in this journey, culturally competent counselors are sensitive to the racial, language, or cultural barriers, stereotypes, and discriminations experienced by multicultural clients.

## Application in Counseling: Case Study

John is a freshman; he was referred to a university counseling center by his professor in mathematics. John reported that he argued with a few classmates, and felt discriminated against. His professor tried to intervene in their argument, but John felt more isolated because he thought he was an "outsider" to the class. When John was 16 years old, he immigrated to the United States with his family from South Korea. His father kept telling him of the enormous efforts just to bring John and his younger siblings to the States. His mother had limited English and stayed at home. In South Korea, she was an executive manager with an astonishing salary. She kept reminding John of the importance of English because "Americans despise you if you cannot speak English."

John felt stressed living in his family with cultural and language barriers. He had to spend hours on end studying to maintain all, so as to meet his parents' expectation. He was close to a loner in class, and the places he went to were classrooms, library, and home, and no other. In the math class, he struggled with a question, and his classmates teased him, saying that "you are a math genius, how could you not know the answer?" Feeling frustrated and stereotyped, he confronted these classmates and argued with them. Their argument escalated and then the professor had to intervene. However, John felt that his professor was not fair because "it was they who start the fight while I was working on my question," but the professor did not punish them, just asked everyone to calm down.

### How to help John

It is important to understand that John's problems have been a long time brewing since he immigrated to the United States when aged 16. His counselor also needs to be aware of his/her own racial attitudes, values, and worldview. The counselor should understand how such race-related stress (e.g., oppression, racism, discrimination, stereotyping) affects John mentally, behaviorally, and deeply personally, added to possible institutional barriers. When talking with John, the counselor must possess appropriate skills to engage him in a variety of verbal and nonverbal give-and-take in helping responses. The counselor can work with John on seven tasks.

*Compensation vs. happiness* First, the counselor can explore with John how he can cope with inferiority in his Korean culture. Because he immigrated to the United States just a few years ago, the counselor needs to be cautious about the acculturative stress he has undergone so far. The counselor explores if his discriminative experiences are related to his motivation for success. The other focus is on whether he enjoys working in his journey toward success (e.g., to become an all As student). From his report, it looks like he has been striving for achievements to reduce pressure from family and school. To promote his well-being, the counselor explores what interests he has that can apply to his journey of striving for achievements.

*Resignation vs. persistence* When working with John, it is important to keep in mind that after his immigration to the United States, he might give in to the life and/or environmental disadvantages. For example, he might give in to all types of course works and stop playing his favorite guitar, he might be busy with adjusting to his new school, new teachers, and new assignments so much that he stopped talking to his best friends in Korea. Of course, working hard in his study is as important as pursuing his interests in music, and combining them is crucial. Continuing in his dream as an amateur guitarist may help him discover joy in study and doing school assignments. Thus, the counselor normalizes John's tendency to reconcile with disadvantage, by helping him see how persistence can make a difference in his life. The counselor also explores with John how Koreans see persistence and to understand its meanings in John's personal life.

*Striving with purpose vs. engaged life* Both Adlerian therapy and positive psychology focus on helping individuals create meaningful lives: Adlerian therapy emphasizes striving for purposes, while positive psychology focuses on how engaged life can enhance the individual's well-being. By integrating these two approaches, counselors can assist John to appreciate the importance of striving for purpose (e.g., what he needs to accomplish in his life) while helping him savor the process of accomplishing it. Being an immigrant from South Korea, John has been able to compare and enjoy different foods in Korea and the United States. He keeps reading books from South Korea while he works hard to maintain good grades. Thus, being a bilingual student has actually brought him a number of special opportunities for valuable experiences.

He was selected by his university to be an exchange student to Korea with a prestigious scholarship. His bilingual ability has also inspired and widened his career choices; he now plans to be a medical doctor to serve the immigrants who have no insurance or suffer with language barriers. He mentioned this career dream to his parents a few times because this is what makes his life meaningful. When talking to his friends about his plan to be a medical doctor, his friend challenged him "So why did you still get angry and fight with classmates in the math class? If you want to help those underserved immigrants, your personal experiences of discrimination could deepen your empathy toward your future immigrant patients!" At first, John felt misunderstood, but later he somewhat agreed with his friend's comment. He learned that as he pursues his purpose in life, he need not sacrifice his joy in life. His fighting with classmates in math class could inspire him and prepare him to understand those suffering from discrimination. Later, he tried to talk to his math professor about his anger. He said "I did not mean to make troubles in your class, but I felt lonely when my classmates teased me. So that's why I was so angry." John felt relieved and understood by this conversation with his math professor. Thus, his willingness to reflect on his fight and negative affect in that class inspired him to have new insights which eventually helped him better manage his stress.

*Strive for superiority vs. character strengths* When counseling John, the counselor helps him explore why he strives for superiority. At first, John believed that his parents kept telling him that an immigrant family had to tolerate all kinds of discrimination and the only way to succeed is to get good grades. His parents also believed that they were inferior to others because English is not their primary language. After talking about his cultural background, the counselor explores John's character strengths and virtues and discussed which personality characters are rooted in Korean culture, and which are not.

The counselor also believes that, according to positive psychology, to succeed requires John's awareness, appreciation, and development of his character strengths. John listed his character strengths as commitment, perseverance, and faithfulness. The counselor explored how such character strengths could help him fulfill his goal and life excellence. John noticed that he was happy when he was committed to a project or helped people, and this is how he successfully completed his work. He also appreciated that over the course of integration between striving for superiority and character strengths, his counselor did not let him struggle alone, they worked together to find strategies to help John develop his character strengths while he pursued excellence. His counselor also respected John's Korean background and was interested in character strengths in Korean culture. Thus, the integration for John served two purposes: expanding the coverage of strengths to include striving for superiority. Working with John, his counselor encouraged him to keep a weekly journal to track his development of character strengths.

*Birth order and family life vs. harmony* In Adlerian therapy, birth order contributes to current problems. As the oldest son, John felt stressful most of the time. In Asian culture, being the oldest son implies that he will carry his family name to his children and take the major responsibility of caring for his parents. He is expected to be the role model for his younger siblings.

Understanding the implication of birth order in Adlerian therapy and Asian culture, his counselor helped him to be aware that, although different birth orders have the respective pressure, he still can pursue his own goal in life. His family had been going through different stages, from Korea to the United States, and struggled to provide a stable and healthy environment for each family member. From the perspective of Adlerian therapy, the negative experiences in John's childhood may push him to compensate for feelings of inferiority. Despite sometimes feeling inferior, his counselor helped him see his resilience and achievements, to thrive in his struggle against cultural difficulties as an immigrant child in an alien culture.

During counseling, the counselor encouraged John to see that each transformation of his family is an opportunity for him. For example, moving to the United States made him a bilingual person and competent in two different cultures. Although being an immigrant child experiencing almost endless struggles, through positive psychology in counseling, he learned to take his negative experiences (e.g., being isolated from his classmates, feeling lonely in school) as an opportunity to reflect on his different identities (e.g., being Korean American).

*Social interests vs. positive psychology at an institutional level* John's counselor also helped him see his problem as a reflection of his sensitivity to social interests. His sensitivity to his classmates' racial comments also demonstrated his eagerness to "protect" other immigrant students from being hurt. John's counselor recognized his interests in promoting others' well-being and encouraged him to reflect on three topics: (a) What is a productive work role in his life? (b) How would he establish an emotionally close relationship with his family members? and (c) How would he meaningfully contribute to the society? These three questions shed a light on John's living struggles, and he explored how his future career as a medical doctor could answer them. Coming from an Asian culture based on collectivism, John's commitment to promote people's well-being seemed to echo institutional well-being proposed by positive psychology. Given his intention to contribute to society, John's counselor challenged him on what would happen if someone's happiness is the cost of another person's pain. John replied that he wanted to become a medical doctor to serve all people, so he would explore to find a solution that works best for most people.

*Life style vs. measures* John's counselor also applied life style measures to facilitate John's self-awareness regarding his patterns of thoughts, emotions, and behaviors. Such life style assessment further strengthened his intention to serve sick people by working as a doctor. With the integration of positive psychology, his counselor then introduced a few measures such as the altruism personality scale (Rushton, Chrisjohn, & Fekken, 1981) to advance his self-awareness about why serving others was so important for him. Although this counseling experience did not teach him how to increase altruistic behaviors, John felt that his interests to serve others were understood and supported by his counselor. He further confirmed to himself that being an altruistic person would be his goal in life.

At the end of the counseling, both John and his counselor agreed that John came to the university counseling center due to his math professor's referral. John's presenting problem in the intake session included anger, isolation, racism, and discrimination, and acculturative stress of being an immigrant child. Through the integration of Adlerian therapy and positive psychology, John was very excited that he and his counselor had a better understanding of why he was so angry at his classmates and how he could transform his immigration experience into an opportunity to serve others. Through the counseling, John recognized that his life could be full of barriers and hurdles, but what is important is how he would manage the challenges in life. He also understood that, living in at least two cultures (e.g., Korean, American) could imply numerous struggles but also suggest that he could appreciate various resources from different cultures.

### Follow-up: You continue as John's counselor

Consider how you would help John if you were his counselor. Here are a series of questions to provide some structure in your thinking about his case:

- How much interest would you have in John's cultural background? What are some ways you would help him strive for success and increase his well-being?
- Consider birth order in Adlerian therapy, positive psychology, and Korean culture. How would you continue addressing this issue with him?
- In working with John, would you recommend him to participate in a group counseling to enhance his interpersonal skills?
- What is the role of cultural difference between you and John? Would you help John see the potential benefits of living in two different cultures (i.e., Korean and American)?

## Concluding Remarks

When talking about Adler, it is inevitable to mention Freud. From being invited by Freud and recognized as President of the Vienna Psychoanalytical Society to resigning from this prestigious position, Adler actually lived this own theory. This theory, Individual Psychology, presents an optimistic view of people while resting heavily on the notion of social interest. Different from Freud's reduction of all motivations to sex and aggression, Adler's individual psychology stresses a feeling of oneness with all humankind. Additionally, Adler argued that human behavior is determined by expectations about what we hope to achieve in the future, not by what we have done in the past.

Perhaps related to Adler's experiences in his childhood, Adlerian theory includes striving with purpose; strive for superiority; holistic concept and phenomenological approach; social interest; birth order and sibling relationships; personal logic; and life style. However, despite his emphasis on overcoming feelings of helplessness and inferiority, Adler's therapeutic approach may still concentrate on difficulties and distresses. This is why positive psychology can complement Adlerian therapy to promote clients' well-being.

Positive psychology can be integrated into Adlerian therapy to benefit clients in many ways. First, while Adlerian therapy believes that weaknesses could motivate individuals to strive for excellence, positive psychology can inspire people that to pursue success could be a joyful experience instead of feeling inferior. Second, when encountering stress, to reconcile with disadvantages may neglect the other side, i.e., persistence, of the human mind. In reality, many clients may have a strong character of persistence and counselors need to conceptualize such a personality to encourage clients to fulfill their goals. To recognize stress in life is one thing, and to persist through struggles is quite another. The first half of task may be accomplished by Adlerian therapy, but the second half will rely on positive psychology (i.e., persistence) to accomplish.

Third, the integration between Adlerian therapy and positive psychology can help clients strive for purposes which do not limit to only overcoming inferiority. People do not need to pursue superiority due to their weaknesses and inactivity. In other words, enjoying the journey of pursuing excellence might be as critical as conquering difficulties. Fourth, although it is inevitable to be aware of the influences of family life and birth order, what is important is to help clients shift the negative impacts into opportunities to promote health. Thus, promoting harmony in family instead of only focusing on competition could strengthen people's ability to promote their well-being. Finally, life style assessment could be a tool to track character strengths throughout the family. With such awareness provided, people could develop new insights regarding themselves and their family, from negative complaints to positive appreciation.

Living in an increasingly diverse society, counselors encounter the challenges of being culturally effective mental health professionals. To meet the increasing demand of service to multicultural clients, it is critical to multiculturalize this integration between Adlerian therapy and positive psychology and be aware that these two approaches originated in Western culture. Specifically, in addition to being self-aware of cultural values and biases, counselors need to possess knowledge about multicultural clients' family structures, hierarchies, and beliefs. For example, although both Adlerian therapy and some multicultural clients (e.g., Asian clients) stress family environment and birth order, counselors should be aware that birth order has different roles in Adlerian therapy and non-Western cultures. Finally, this chapter addressed the necessity of applying the integration to the case study about John, s an immigrant student from Korean. This section of case study highlighted the integration and cultural sensitivity when working with a racial/ethnic minority client.

## Review Questions: What Do You Think?

1. What relationship do you think there is about Adler's childhood and his theory? If he had no physical issues during his childhood, do you think he would still develop his theory in the way he has? Please provide your rationale.
2. Adler believed that inferiority or weakness is a necessary condition for people's striving for superiority. Do you agree with him? How does positive psychology disagree with this theoretical principle?
3. Make a life style assessment about your family. What positive emotions are most significant in your family? How do these positive emotions help your family work through their difficulties?
4. Adlerian therapy proposed that a dysfunctional family environment negatively influenced children's development and growth. Can you think of any examples to dispute this principle? For example, Abraham Lincoln's education consisted of little more than a total of 18 months throughout his early life, and was mostly from itinerant teachers. Yet, he was one of the greatest presidents in American history. Why is Adlerian theory limited in explaining Lincoln's experience? How can positive psychology complement Adlerian therapy to provide a comprehensive interpretation to Lincoln's experience?

# 7

# Existential Therapy

**Learning Objectives**

- Learn about existential therapy, its historical background, and theoretical principles.
- Describe the role of Viktor Frankl in existential therapy.
- Define freedom, responsibility, choice, search for meaning, and anxiety in existential therapy.
- Learn about integrating wisdom into freedom to make good choices.
- Learn about how courage can enhance people's self-awareness.
- Describe how sense of purpose can guide the journey of searching for meaning.
- Multiculturalize the integration between existential therapy and positive psychology.
- Apply the integration to a case study.

Existential psychology arose in the 1940s and 1950s as part of a larger movement in psychology that also included humanism and phenomenology (a focus on individuals' subjective experiences). This larger movement was the third force, so-called by American psychologist Abraham Maslow, a reaction to the two leading paradigms in psychology at the time: Freudianism and behaviorism. The proponents of the third force saw Freudianism and behaviorism as highly deterministic, dehumanizing, and that it is important to seek different ways of viewing human beings and psychology.

Existential therapy is a kind of psychotherapy that promotes self-awareness and personal growth by stressing current reality and by analyzing and altering specific patterns of esponse to help a person realize his or her potential. This process may be facilitated in a

*Counseling Psychology: An Integrated Positive Psychological Approach*, First Edition. Ruth Chu-Lien Chao.

individual counseling or group setting where additional aspects of problems are revealed through interaction with others (Van Deurzen, 2012).

## Historical Context

Existential psychology is rooted in existential philosophy, particularly the writings of Søren Kierkegaard (1813–1855), Martin Heidegger (1889–1976), and Jean-Paul Sartre (1905–1980), among others. The first existential psychotherapist was Swiss psychiatrist Ludwig Binswanger (1881–1966) (Lanzoni, 2004), a student of Carl Jung and close friend of Sigmund Freud. Binswanger (1958) described different levels of existence and modes of interpersonal relations. According to him, the highest level is *Eigenwelt* – individuals operating at this level are self-aware and self-actualizing. They experience life in relation to their own personal meanings; the norms of society and opinions and judgments of others are secondary to the individual's own values and perspectives. Binswanger believed that most people crave purpose in their lives, but many do not know their purpose. Many people, in their search for meaning and direction, make decisions without thinking, such as following an organized religion or joining a political cause. This lack of authenticity causes suffering (May, Angel, & Ellenberger, 1958).

Other existential therapists came after Binswanger, including Austrian psychiatrist Viktor Frankl (1905–1997), who was also a Holocaust survivor. He lost almost all his immediate family members in Nazi concentration camps, only a sister survived. A number of years after being liberated, he published a world-famous book, *Man's Search for Meaning* (Frankl, 1962). In this book, he describes the life of an ordinary concentration camp inmate from the objective perspective of a psychiatrist. Frankl eloquently explains his philosophy, in addition to his experience as a captive in a number of concentration camps in World War II. It was Frankl's contribution that he transformed painful suffering to meaning for search in life. That is, it was due to his and other people's suffering in these camps that he validated his hallmark conclusion that even in the most severe torture, life has its own potential meaning and perhaps, even suffering itself could be meaningful. This statement set a strong foundation for his famous logotherapy (*logos* = "meaning" in Greek). In logotherapy, the client is encouraged to find his or her own meaning in life. Frankl describes a number of ways that people experience meaning, including creating or accomplishing something, giving to others, and loving another. When practicing Frankl's logotherapy, the therapist presents the client with alternative ways of looking at events, in an attempt to reveal the client's unique meaning or purpose in life.

American psychiatrist Irvin Yalom (b. 1931) is also an important existential psychotherapist. Yalom sees existential anxiety as the root of most neurosis. In his book *Existential Psychotherapy* (Yalom, 1980), he describes four causes of existential anxiety: fear of death; human freedom (which means that we are responsible for our choices); isolation (humans enter and exit this existence alone); and meaninglessness. Yalom is also well known by his group therapy, where he applies his existential principles. Existential psychotherapy exists in the present day; however, it is not nearly as popular as other forms of psychotherapy such as cognitive-behavioral or behavioral psychotherapy. Additionally, existential psychotherapy is difficult to test empirically for a number of reasons, including that it assumes individual meanings rather than general laws of human nature. However, some research lends support to the fundamental principles of existential psychology or psychotherapy. For instance, research indicates that most people value meaning in life more than they value wealth. Additionally, therapy is more effective if the therapist recognizes the client's phenomenological perspective (e.g., Walsh, Perrucci, & Severns, 1999).

## View of Human Nature

A fundamental idea behind existential psychology is free will which refers to the freedom to choose. For existential therapists, everyone has the freedom to make his or her own decisions. Of course, there is no free lunch. Existential therapists believe that an individual's freedom to choose comes with responsibility for the decision this person makes. Existentialists and others representing the third force argue that neither psychoanalysis nor behaviorism make allowances for free will. Indeed, according to Freudians, human behavior is largely controlled by unconscious factors; yet, according to behaviorists, much of human behavior is almost always caused by external circumstances only (May et al., 1958).

Another assumption on existential therapy is that life has no intrinsic meaning, and individuals must search for their own meaning. Life may be experienced as meaningful through many, diverse routes, and each person chooses his or her unique meaning, which may transform from moment to moment. Deriving from existential philosophy, another assumption of existential therapy is the importance of phenomenology, an individual's particular perception or experience. Each of us has our own and subjective way of viewing experiences. In other words, two individuals may have totally different perceptions of a loving relationship. Person A may believe that having a trusting relationship is essential to love, while person B may perceive secure life and wealth are priorities in love. These differences in perspectives come from the unique phenomenology of persons A and B. To completely understand one another, people must be aware that life is experienced by each individual through his own, unique, selective filter.

## Theoretical Principles

### Freedom and responsibility

Freedom and responsibility are essential to existential therapy. Individuals are totally free to choose among alternatives and therefore individuals can shape their life based on their choice. Totally opposite to other psychologists such as Freud who proposed that biological aspects contributed to human behavior, existential therapists believe that the manner in which we live and what we become are the results of our choices. However, the choices people make come with responsibility, though it is possible to avoid the reality of choice responsibility by making excuses. Sartre believed that not accepting responsibility reveals the inauthenticity of individuals. Because people are responsible for their lives, responsibility ranges from actions people make to failures they have made. Living inauthentically includes two scenarios: the first is not to take responsibility and the second is to allow others to define people's lives or let others make choices for them. If living inauthentically means that people avoid responsibility for their lives and passively assume that their lives are controlled by external forces, living authentically means that people live true to themselves (Corsini & Wedding, 2013).

For existential therapists, being free and being human are identical. In fact, choice and responsibility go hand in hand, and the assumption of responsibility is a basic condition for change. People who refuse to accept responsibility by blaming others for their problems make themselves unhappy. A primary task for existential therapists is to assist clients in seeing how they are avoiding responsibility and the consequential outcomes of such avoidance. The therapists then help clients to discover the importance and meaning of assuming responsibility. For existential therapists, people seek counseling because their lives are out of control. Being out of control may come from avoidance of taking responsibility.

### Self-awareness

In addition to making choices and the consequential responsibility, individuals also have an awareness of choice and responsibility. The greater self-awareness the individuals have, the more capacity they possess. For existentialists, the increased capacity is reflected as more self-awareness in the areas below. Nobody is going to live forever. So people are finite and do not have unlimited time to do what they want to do. Individuals have the potential to decide to take action or not. Even no action is one type of decision. Individuals create their own destiny and lives by making their own choices. Individuals are subject to loneliness, meaninglessness, guilt, and emptiness.

Existential anxiety basically is a component in our consciousness. Such anxiety is an essential part of living. People are basically alone, but they are able to make connections to others. Seeking relationships or staying alone is one choice people make. For existential therapists, increasing self-awareness means that individuals have more awareness of alternatives, freedom, choices, responsibility, and goals (May et al., 1958).

### Striving for identity and relationship with others

Freedom to make choices may make every individual different from others, and this process may make each person unique and even lonely. For existential therapists, being unique or searching for identity is not an easy task; in contrast, it takes courage to seek identity. However, according to existentialists, people can choose to stay alone or seek relationships with others. Each choice may come with responsibility and potential outcomes which shape people's lives. Existentialists take the meaning of aloneness differently from most psychologists. For existentialists, being alone could be a good opportunity to look into ourselves rather than being denied or rejected by others. Being alone could add strengths to people while sensing their separation from others and this experience may help them further search for their uniqueness and identity (Binswanger, 1958).

The opposite of aloneness could be relationship with others. Existentialists welcome the paradox that being human includes both aloneness and relationships. It is natural for individuals to want to be significant in another person's world. Thus, for existentialists, when individuals can stand alone and dip within themselves for their own strengths, their relationship with others is based on fulfillment, not deprivation or competition. Developing relationships with others differs from being overly dependent on others. For existentialists, the development of relationships with others is based on an equal position between two independent individuals. Neither party dominates the other; that is, neither is overly dependent on the other one.

### Search for meaning

Human beings are characterized by the struggle for a sense of significance and purpose in life. Some typical questions related to search for meaning include "Who am I?" "What do I want to have from my life?" and "Where is the source of meaning for me in life?" Transferring the search for meaning into practical questions for clients in counseling includes "Do you like the direction of your life? How pleased are you with what you are now? What is the most meaningful experience in your life?"

When individuals cannot find meanings in their lives, they may be struggling with low self-esteem, emptiness, and meaninglessness in life. Meaninglessness leads clients to experience anxiety or psychological distress. Thus, search for meaning could be connected to a person's basic worldview and beliefs. The belief that people are meaning-creating creatures assumes that they are able to create or search for meaning in their lives. It is important for existential therapists to be aware of this assumption and the assumption of their clients in regards to this issue in order not to impose their values upon others. According to existential therapists, meaning can be organized into at least three different types: false meaning; transitory meaning; and ultimate meaning. It should be emphasized that what constitutes each of these types of meaning is highly personal and may vary from person to person. False meaning is typically destructive because it may help people copy but cannot help people to address the existential issues. For example, money or sex could be a part of false meaning to some people. These may have some positive utility, but in and of themselves are lacking. Sex, when part of a loving, intimate relationship has tremendous power for connection. Transitory meaning can help us cope, but cannot help us to transcend. Again, transitory meaning lacks the ability to address existential issues. However, such meanings are not as destructive in nature as false meanings can be. Transitory meaning may facilitate growth and lead to ultimate meaning, but is not ultimately meaningful. Examples include work, service, leadership, self-growth, and self-awareness. All these can be positive, healthy values, but are not good ends. Ultimate meaning is a type of meaning that aids in transcending the existential issues of death, isolation, freedom, and meaninglessness. According to existential therapists, this type of meaning makes relationships necessary. However, the assumption that ultimate meaning necessitates relationships does not, in this conception, include relationships with self (Yalom, 1980).

### Anxiety

The concept of anxiety is essential to existential therapists. Existential therapists define anxiety more broadly than and perhaps differently from other psychotherapeutic groups.

For existential therapists, anxiety arises from our personal need to survive, to preserve our being, and to assert our being. Anxiety shows itself physically in faster beating of the heart, rising blood pressure, preparation of the skeletal muscles for fighting or fleeing, and a sense of apprehension. Rollo May defines anxiety as "the threat to our existence or to values we identify with our existence" (1977, p. 205).

Anxiety is more basic than fear. In psychotherapy, one of our aims is to help the patient confront anxiety as fully as possible, thus reducing anxiety to fears, which are then objective and can be dealt with. But the main therapeutic function is to help the patient confront the normal anxiety that is an unavoidable part of the human condition. Normal anxiety has three characteristics. First, it is proportionate to the situation confronted. Second, normal anxiety does not require repression: We can come to terms with it, as we come to terms with the fact that we all face eventual death. Third, such anxiety can be used creatively, as a stimulus to help identify and confront the dilemma out of which the anxiety arose. Neurotic anxiety, on the other hand, is not appropriate to the situation. For example, parents may be so anxious that their child will be hit by a car that they never let the child leave the house. Second, it is repressed, in the way most of us repress the fear of nuclear war. Third, neurotic anxiety is destructive, not constructive. Neurotic anxiety tends to paralyze the individual rather than stimulate creativity. The function of therapy is not to do away with all anxiety. No person could survive completely without anxiety. Mental health is living as much as possible without neurotic anxiety, but with the ability to tolerate the unavoidable existential anxiety of living.

## An Integration: Positive Psychology and Existential Therapy

### Freedom (responsibility) integrated with wisdom

Existential therapy believes that freedom and responsibility are essential to human beings. Individuals are free to shape their life based on their choice and should be responsible for that choice. Positive psychology looks at life from a different perspective. Although positive psychology respects individuals' freedom to choose, it also encourages people to utilize their wisdom before their choices are made. Wisdom in this section refers to an insightful understanding about personal and interpersonal issues. Wisdom also relates to judgment to differentiate different concepts and prioritize topics based on the sequence of significance. Wisdom also includes the abilities to learn, evaluate, and give advice to maintain people's well-being. According to Sternberg's balance theory of wisdom (2000), wisdom is the application of practical intelligence, and the tacit knowledge that such intelligence involves, to develop problem solving to achieve a common good. Additionally, to achieve the common good among multiple interests is based on ethical principles. These multiple interests include intrapersonal interests such as personal wishes, interpersonal interests which include things good for relationships and even others' well-being, and extra personal interests (e.g., things that are good for everyone affected by the problem). Wisdom also involves applying knowledge to problem solving in a way that achieves a balance among responses to environmental contexts. Thus, the outcome of wisdom refers to a judgment on how to solve a complex problem involving varied competing interests or perspectives.

By integrating freedom/responsibility with wisdom in positive psychology, individuals learn when to exert their judgments and how to claim their freedom. While it is essential that individuals can choose whatever they want to do, it might be beneficial that they learn from wisdom to make wise choices. Thus, individuals can shape their life based on their choice, via the integration with wisdom. Individuals have abilities regarding (a) how to balance their freedom to choose and others' well-being and (b) how to balance personal freedom and social interests.

### Self-awareness integrated with courage

In addition to making choices and the consequent responsibility, individuals also have an awareness of choice and responsibility. The greater self-awareness individuals have, the more capacity they possess. For existentialists, the increased capacity is reflected as more self-awareness in the areas below. People's courage may further enhance people's self-awareness and strengthen their willingness to take responsibility for their choices. Based on positive psychology, courage here is defined as the will to accomplish goals in the face of opposition, external or internal. Courage also includes characteristics such as bravery, perseverance, industry, diligence, and integrity. As existential therapy says, people may avoid being responsible for their choices and such difficult awareness of responsibility may result in anxiety. Courage in positive psychology may facilitate individuals' willingness and awareness of taking responsibility, since courage helps individuals persist through their goals in awareness despite oppositions. Thus self-awareness can be integrated with courage in positive psychology to enhance individuals' perseverance in finishing the journey of self-awareness.

### Search for meaning integrated with sense of purpose

According to existential therapy, individuals are characterized with searching for the purpose in life. Individuals may question themselves "What do I want to have from my life?" and "Where is the source of meaning for me in life?" Transferring the search for meaning into practical questions for clients in counseling includes "Do you like the direction of your life? How pleased are you with what you are now?" Existential therapists believe that individuals' mental health problems stem from their inability of finding the meanings in their lives and have presenting symptoms such as low self-esteem, emptiness, and meaninglessness in life. Worse, meaninglessness leads clients to experience anxiety or psychological distress.

Positive psychology may perceive meanings in life with a different perspective. Positive psychology suggests that people have coherent beliefs about the purpose and meaning of the universe and know where they fit within the larger scheme. They also have beliefs that shape their thoughts and provide support and values. Although both existential therapy and positive psychology agree on the importance of searching for meanings in life, they approach the search with different perspectives. Existential therapy claims that being unable to find the meaning is a source of psychological symptoms, but positive psychology proposes that such journey of search may enhance individuals' sense of direction in life. By integrating these two approaches into a synthetic understanding of meanings in life, individuals may appreciate the struggles of meaning search and joy in each discovery in the purpose of life. The integration of searching for meaning and sense of purpose will reinforce individuals' pursuit of life purpose.

### Anxiety integrated with vitality

The concept of anxiety has been important in existential therapy which believes anxiety arises from our personal need to survive, to preserve our being, and to assert our being. Thus, anxiety is conceptualized as a presentation to the need to survive. Anxiety is also a warning sign that individuals may struggle with searching for meaning and identity in their life. Anxiety also indicates that individuals have uncertainties and insecurity in their life or living environment.

Although positive psychology does not deny the existence of anxiety and the relationship between anxiety and needs in life; to some extent, positive psychology may agree that anxiety could be one of presentations to the need to survive, but there are other presentations involved. According to positive psychology, vitality represents an individual's energy and enthusiasm for life, the capacity to live and grow, and the power to survive. Vitality is demonstrated in several dimensions of human life, for example, in the physical or mental energy and the ability to continue to live and grow.

Looking at how people express their needs to survive with these two different approaches, existential therapy and positive psychology, we can see that the need to survive presents a significant issue to human beings. Yet, different approaches focus on their respective ways of presentation. Specifically, while existential therapy believes that anxiety is the presentation to people's need to survive because people are caught between freedom to choose and responsibility, positive psychology focuses on human strengths rather than the tension described by the existential therapy. This is why positive psychology believes that, despite encountering various difficulties in life, people still pursue their goals, keep energized and optimistic, and maintain aliveness.

By integrating these two approaches, counselors can help clients recognize that it could be a natural reaction of feeling anxious about needs in life. Counselors can also help clients accept such anxiety and understand that the anxiety could be a reminder of our needs in life. Beyond such acceptance, what could be more important is to see the need in life with a different perspective such as vitality. That is, clients can learn to appreciate their energy and power in life and promote their capability to live and growth while recognizing their anxiety.

## Multiculturalize the Integration

### Multiculturalizing integration between freedom/responsibility and wisdom

Existential therapy believes that freedom and responsibility have been essential since time immemorial to all human beings across different cultures, and positive psychology proposes that wisdom can help people make better choices in taking responsibility to improved daily living. Still, these laudable proposals originated from Western perspectives, and so these two disciplines come from individualism.

Working with multicultural clients, culturally sensitive counselors realize that some cultures focus on responsibility more than freedom. Thus, the existentialist belief that individuals are free to shape their life based on their choice may sound incompatible with the values and beliefs of some multicultural clients. Confronted by the integration of freedom/responsibility with wisdom, some multicultural clients may take "wisdom" to mean that their best prudence is to take good care of *others* rather than enriching their lives. Thus, culturally sensitive counselors are aware of distinctive meanings of wisdom in clients' culture as different from Western definitions.

Therefore, counselors should respect multicultural clients' judgments and prioritize tasks under freedom/responsibility in line with their own cultural values, not according to the Western assumption of individualism. For example, an African American single mother's top priority could be raising children and finding a job; a culturally effective counselor respects this decision in understanding "wisdom" to be embedded in one's own culture such as American individualism.

Culturally skilled counselors use their counseling skills and cultural sensitivity to assist multicultural clients to facilitate the task of prioritizing according to clients' peculiar cultural values, so as to make choices and be responsible in their own cultural ways. Because wisdom involves applying knowledge to solve problems, culturally skilled counselors have knowledge about how multicultural clients' problems relate to their cultural contexts, and so counselors assist the clients in resolving the clients' problems in line with the clients' own cultural values, not in American values.

Some multicultural clients may suffer race-related stress which negatively affects their self-esteem, and so counselors assist those cultural clients to cultivate their positive well-being and self-esteem in their own ways by helping them exert their judgments when and how to claim their sort of freedom. While it is essential that individuals can choose whatever they want to do, counselors have knowledge that some marginalized clients are not even sure that they have such privileges to make choices in their life. Multicultural clients must manage their daily life rife with various stresses to compose barriers in their struggles, and culturally effective counselors know well that the clients' choices in their freedom often relate to the basic needs in daily living. In helping them struggle for better living, counselors respect these clients' culturally specific definition of freedom, responsibility, and wisdom, to adequately orient their struggles in ways different from American culture.

### Multiculturalizing integration between self-awareness and courage

For existentialists, people's increased capacity may harvest higher self-awareness, and their courage further strengthens willingness to take on the responsibility. Still, when promoting this insight among multicultural clients, these clients may think self-awareness and courage to be too far away, too abstract to fulfill. They may have to laboriously actualize "self-awareness" and "courage" in concrete behaviors. For example, as a Latina gets married, raises a family, makes an income, and fulfills parental duties, she may not have heard of self-awareness and courage, for they are too abstract to even see their meanings. What is important for this person is that it is her single most important responsibility to raise a family by taking care of children, and help all family members to succeed. She never realizes that these behaviors of hers actually exemplify the meanings of self-awareness, choices, responsibility, and courage.

In such a manner as this, culturally sensitive counselors understand that people in cultures different from the West have their culture-specific ways to convey the meanings of freedom, responsibility, and courage. To take another example, in Taiwan, a train driver sacrificed himself to save more than 300 lives. He made an extremely brave choice, being responsible for customers in his duty as a train driver, in the face of overwhelming barriers, external and internal. Still, he and Taiwanese people may not realize that this driver's acts are those of freedom, responsibility, and courage, all so abstract so far. Here and elsewhere, culturally sensitive counselors would feel and respect the clients' cultural heritage and its implications for their thoughts, emotions, and behaviors. Culturally sensitive counselors have culture-specific knowledge about the multicultural living and are aware of the life experiences and historical/cultural background of the multicultural clients, while working with them.

## Multiculturalizing integration between search for meaning and sense of purpose

From the Western perspective, the integration of search for meaning (in existential therapy) and sense of purpose (in positive psychology) promotes a synthetic understanding of meanings in life. Individuals may also appreciate the struggles of meaning search and joy in each discovery in the purpose of life. All is fine while working within the context of Western culture.

In working with multicultural clients, however, counselors may notice, strangely, that some people enjoy their life without searching for meaning or pursuing the sense of purpose. Those people enjoy and savor every single moment of life, as they appreciate the simple things, e.g., raising a family, having friends, and so on.

For example, Chuang-Tzu's *wu-wei*, is not "do," not "not do," but "no do," meaning "acting without purposeful action, without conscious effort, or without manipulative control." This *wu wei* is also expressed in the paradoxical "*wei wu wei*" "acting without action" or "effortless effort." The practice of *wu wei* and the efficacy of *wei wu wei* are fundamental tenets in Chinese thoughts and praxis.

Since "do" and "not do" exhaust logical possibilities, a story can hit "*wu wei* no-do" on the head. Tommy shouts, "I don' wanna nap!" His scream of protest precisely shows his need of a nap. But Mom cannot "do" his nap, pushing him forcefully into bed; it would be a disaster. Nor can Mom "not do," just to let her boy go out to play; it would be another disaster of having him stumble and get terribly hurt. Instead, Mom calmly steers between "do" and "not do." She says, "OK, Tommy. Don't nap. Just sit here on your bed; Mom will read you your favorite story, OK?" Tommy nods. "Once upon a time," and Tommy hits his pillow. All is now quiet at the front; Tommy satisfies his need for a nap without protest, as Mom smilingly soft-covers a blanket over him, with a kiss. That is, Mom's spontaneous "*wu wei*, no do" that "*wei wu wei* acts without acting" so marvelous.

*Wu wei* is a spontaneous display of one's behavior in life while accepting agents for who they are, released from conscious control over living. Thus, Asians may define meaning in life as enjoying and appreciating every living moment as life is too short. For Latino/a immigrants, the meaning in life could be that they work hard to give their children better lives. African Americans may define their meaning in life as fighting against injustice, discrimination, in pursuit of equality. Native Americans may define their meaning in life as renewing their cultural heritage and connecting to their native spirituality. Therefore, culturally skilled counselors respect multicultural clients' exciting culture-specific meanings in life and their particular journeys in pursuit of them.

### Multiculturalizing integration between anxiety and vitality

In existential therapy, anxiety is a warning sign that individuals are struggling with their search for meaning and identity in life, but for positive psychology, anxiety shows life's problems, how to manage the person's life power to survive. Their integration shows that people's vitality is demonstrated in their physical and/or mental energy, in their persistence to continue living and growing.

Counseling multicultural clients in this integration, culturally sensitive counselors possess knowledge that different cultures have their culturally prescribed definitions on anxiety. Because different cultures have their respective meanings in life, freedom, and responsibility, it is not surprising that the causes of the anxiety are different across cultures. Asian culture focuses on interpersonal harmony, and so Asian anxiety might well be related to caring for others. Counselors respect these culture-related definitions of anxiety and work with them accordingly.

With this knowledge about anxiety related to clients' culture, culturally skilled counselors would then appreciate their various manifestations of vitality as clients' background differ. Positive psychology is convinced that, as people encounter various difficulties in life, they still continue to pursue their goals. With knowledge about clients' culture, counselors learn about various cultural implications on vitality and adjust the way of promoting it in *their* cultural contexts. Some multicultural clients use meditation, relaxation, or qigong to boost their energy to manage daily hassles. In such cultural situations, culturally sensitive counselors do not deprive clients of their culture, instead, counselors work with clients to see how such integration can variously benefit clients in line with their cultures, values, and beliefs.

## Application in Counseling: Case Study

Bob was required to complete a 12-session court-mandatory counseling in a mental health center. Bob is a 25-year-old European American male with a history of violent behavior toward men and verbal abuse toward women. He was recently released from jail and given 3 years of probation. He has served 4 years of a 3- to 7-year prison sentence for assault. He was sentenced after beating and hitting a man almost to death in a drunken brawl following a basketball game. This was Bob's first time in jail; however, he had been arrested 3 years earlier for participating in a bar fight. Being raised in a violent home where he witnessed domestic violence, Bob was a victim of child abuse. He is presently involved in a relationship with 19-year-old Alice. In his past, Bob's romantic relationships have never lasted more than 6 or 7 months. He met his girlfriends in bars and the relationships developed very fast. And then, very soon, he would have violent fights or arguments with his girlfriends. He reports that he has a very violent temper and tends to get angry easily. During his time in jail, Bob realized that he was tired of having one girlfriend after another, and wanted to settle down and raise a family with Alice.

Currently, Bob is unemployed and reports that it is very difficult to find a job during his probationary period. Despite having a Bachelor degree in computer science, his criminal record has prevented him from gaining a stable job in his field. Although he now tries to be friendly with others, he has been very anxious about job interviews which may expose his past criminal record. Although there have been no aggressive or assault episodes in past months, his probation officer still believes that Bob will relapse eventually and continues to meet with him on a weekly basis.

## How to help Bob

*Freedom (responsibility) vs. wisdom* Existential therapy believes that Bob is free to shape his life and should be responsible for his choices, but positive psychology has a different perspective on his current problem. From positive psychology, some questions may be raised, "Does he use his wisdom to make his best choices? What would have happened if Bob had an insightful understanding about personal and interpersonal issues?" Although Bob's previous violent behaviors and assaults shows his poor insight, what is important is that he currently wants to change. Counselors can help him see how his previous choices of violent behaviors resulted in his jail sentence, and how his present wisdom may help him make better choices to result in a better life. With wisdom, Bob can acquire abilities to learn, evaluate, and give advice to himself to maintain well-being. As he currently wants to have a stable job and relationship with Alice, Bob's multiple interests include intrapersonal needs and interpersonal interests. Through counseling, he can learn how to prioritize his various needs. To deepen his wisdom, he can also apply knowledge to solve his problems such as job searching. Thus, the outcome of his wisdom suggests a direction in which he judges on how to solve his problems involving varied needs with various perspectives. Thus, Bob's counselor can help him advance his wisdom to exert his judgments on how to claim his freedom and assume his responsibility.

Having learned lessons from his past behaviors, Bob felt that he needed to learn to use wisdom to make wise choices. For example, he asked his counselor what choices he could make when people isolate him due to his probationary status. He mentioned that he used to fight with people to deal with others isolating him. Now he wanted to exert his wisdom to make better choices to manage people's isolation. His counselor explored several choices he had used before and other choices he could use now. From this exploration, Bob understood the close relationship between choices and responsibility and, more importantly, how wisdom can help him make wiser choices to result in better reasonable outcomes.

*Self-awareness vs. courage* In addition to being aware of making choices and consequent responsibility, Bob also learned that the greater self-awareness he develops, the more capacity he would possess. However, he also felt anxious over some choices. For example, he said that sometimes people never gave him a chance to improve. Many people disconnected from him when they learned of his probationary status. Or else, prospective employers declined his job application when he told them of his criminal record. At those moments, he would almost lose himself to another anger or fighting. In addition to expressing empathy, his counselor introduced the concept of courage defined as the will to accomplish goals in the face of opposition, for making a good choice sometimes costs people a huge price. His counselor also explained that sometimes it takes courage such as bravery, perseverance, industry, diligence, and integrity just to make choices. Specifically, Bob said that his job application was rejected two days ago due to his criminal record, but nobody wanted to listen to his explanation. His counselor further comforted him by confirming that it was difficult not to fight with people when they did not listen. His counselor also highly recognized that Bob did something correct himself by simply leaving the situation instead of initiating another fight. Bob's willingness and awareness of taking responsibility demonstrated that he learned to persist on self-improvement despite being confronted with oppositions. His insistence of not initiating another fight enhanced his perseverance to change his previous violent behaviors to initiate leading a new life.

*Search for meaning vs. sense of purpose* According to existential therapy, Bob's mental health problems stem from his inability to find meaning in his life, and meaninglessness leads to experiencing anxiety or psychological distress. This interpretation explains only a part of Bob's search for meaning in life. He mentioned that he grew up in a violent family and thought that being aggressive would be an effective way to solve problems. During childhood, he thought that being tough showed his importance in his life and others. Thus, later when encountering conflicts, he believed that he just needed to repeat what he learned in his violent family. Unfortunately, his previous choices did not bring him recognition by people around him. During the counseling, his counselor indicated that he could develop his sense of purpose in life. He replied that he only wished to have a stable job and raise a family with Alice. After knowing his sense of purpose in life, his counselor encouraged him to set up a sense of direction in his life. Bob would need to deliberate on the meaning of a stable job and how to reach this goal. For example, does a stable job imply that he will receive a high salary? Or does Bob mean that a stable job is a tool for him to raise a family? His ultimate question for himself is "what is my goal in life?" If his primary goal is to raise a family, can he find another job with steady income and then develop his dream career later?

Moreover, his counselor reminded him that no matter which choice Bob makes, he must take responsibility for his choice. Integrating existential therapy and positive psychology appears to provide Bob a synthetic understanding of meaning in life. He also appreciates the journey and joy in search for the purpose in his life. This integration of search for meaning further helps him discover that having a family is more important than a job with high salary. Growing up in a violent family made him lose opportunities to connect to family members, and this is why he was eager to build his own family with support and gratitude.

*Anxiety vs. vitality* From the approach of existential therapy, Bob learned that anxiety could arise from his personal need to survive, to preserve his being, and to assert his being. Thus, especially in his past violent life, anxiety could be a presentation to him of his need to survive. He then learns to view anxiety from a different perspective, to wit, anxiety was a warning sign to him that he was searching for his meaning and identity or felt uncertain and insecure in his living environment.

However, for Bob, his current task should focus on how to live his life meaningfully, and find ways to promote his energy and enthusiasm for life. While understanding the reasons behind anxiety, he wondered if there is available capacity to help him live and grow more purposely. To promote his enthusiasm and energy for life, his counselor introduced the concept of vitality to be demonstrated in his physical and/or mental energy and the ability to continue living to grow.

Through the counseling, Bob learned that having vitality is totally different from being aggressive. Vitality means that he can persist in doing his best to pursue his dream (e.g., raise a family with Alice), develop his career, and renew his relationships with others. Vitality does not mean that he needs to fight with people; in contrast, vitality means that he could persist to enjoy his life with people he cares for, help those in need, and plan his future. After learning the meaning and function of vitality, Bob noticed that he could "redo" his past by not initiating fights or arguing with others. He understood that there are numerous other ways to solve problems and he does not need to limit himself to violence. He could use humor to solve conflicts, he could use acceptance to replace argument, and he could just leave an unpleasant situation.

The integration of existential therapy and positive psychology was mainly to help Bob to have deep understanding about his past behaviors and then develop new insights in his new life. While there are numerous ways to survive, and anxiety could be a reminder of his needs to survive, through the counseling, Bob noticed that he learned to appreciate his anxiety in his past, though the anxiety cost him a big price (e.g., being arrested, lost friends, being jailed). What is more important for him now is that he learned to see his anxiety with a different perspective to instill vitality to his current life. That is, he agreed that anxiety is presentation of his need to survive, but it is vitality that keeps him moving on and become a stronger person. This is why he noticed that, despite encountering various difficulties in his current life, he is able to still focus on his goal with energy and optimism.

Bob's counselor was pleased that Bob learned to accept his anxiety and understand that his anxiety could be a reminder of his needs in life. They then explored that beyond acceptance, what would be more important is to see the need in life with a different perspective such as vitality. That is, Bob now learned to appreciate his energy and power in life to enhance his capability to live and grow on.

*Follow-up: You Continue as Bob's Counselor* Please consider how you would help Bob if you were his counselor. Here are a series of questions to provide some structure in your thinking about his case:

- How much interest would you have in helping Bob build meaningful relationships with Alice and others? What are other insights would you help him see patterns of his relationships with people?

- Can you help Bob see the messages from his anger or violence? Does his anger attempt to reveal his loneliness and/or eagerness to get people's attention?
- When Bob mentioned that he wanted to settle down and raise a family with Alice, how would you strengthen his awareness of choice and responsibility? What strengths do you think he might demonstrate in this decision?
- Consider helping Bob see the meaning of his journey, from easily getting violent to wanting to raise a family. Which characters did he demonstrate in this journey? How could he maintain his well-being in the future when he encounter difficulties?
- Can you help Bob transfer his anger, violence, problems, and weaknesses into opportunities to grow? What lessons do you think he has learned from his previous problematic behaviors?
- If Bob told you that he came from a family with a low social economic status, would you include this as a part of multicultural counseling? Please provide your rationale. When he was planning to be the first person to attend a college in his family, how would you advocate his needs in seeking more education?

## Concluding Remarks

Closely connected to humanism and phenomenology in the 1940s and 1950s, readers need to be aware that existential therapy presents a rigorous thinking and philosophy about the meanings of life. Although most people today criticize the emptiness and abstractness of existential therapy, this therapeutic approach actually awakened our quest for meanings in life and self-actualizing. For example, a Holocaust survivor Viktor Frankl integrated his personal experiences into existentialism to develop logotherapy and transform painful suffering to meaning for search in life. Thus, the impact of existential therapy appears to be underestimated. Research also indicates that most people value meaning in life more than wealth, and therapy is more effective if counselors recognize client's phenomenological perspectives (e.g., Walsh, Perrucci, & Severns, 1999).

Positive psychology can strengthen existential therapy in several ways. First, although people are free to shape their life based on their choice and should be responsible for that choice, wisdom (in positive psychology) may enhance people's ability to make more meaningful choices. Second, although self-awareness is essential for people to search for meaning in life, courage can strengthen such self-awareness which results into better capacity. Third, positive psychology suggests that those who have coherent beliefs about the meaning of life have a sense of purpose. Thus the sense of direction from positive psychology can guide people's journey of search for meaning. Fourth, although anxiety is essential for living and is a presentation of survival, positive psychology indicates that vitality can advance people's survival. Vitality represents an individual's energy and enthusiasm for life, the capacity to live and grow, and the power to survive.

Culturally sensitive counselors tailor the integration between existential therapy and positive psychology to benefit multicultural clients. Because existential therapy and positive psychology might be new to multicultural clients, counselors need to contextualize this integration to fit clients' values, beliefs, and backgrounds.

## Review Questions: What Do You Think?

1. Compare and contrast existential therapy and positive psychology. What do you think existential therapy misses in understanding the human mind?
2. Because some philosophical positions between existential therapy and positive psychology are similar to each other, do you think that integrating two approaches with similar philosophical positions would be easy or redundant? Justify your answer.
3. What do you feel about multiculturalizing the integration between existential therapy and positive psychology? What challenges could you encounter?

# 8

# Person-Centered Therapy

**Learning Objectives**

- Learn about person-centered therapy, including the historical background and Roger's perspective on human nature.
- Differentiate person-centered therapy from existential therapy.
- Define nonjudgmental climate, unconditional positive regard, congruence, genuineness, and accurate empathic understanding in person-centered therapy.
- Learn about six conditions in person-centered therapy.
- Know the roles of counselors in both person-centered therapy and positive psychology.
- Learn about how scientific research contributes to person-centered therapy and positive psychology.
- Multiculturalize the integration between person-centered therapy and positive psychology.
- Apply the integration to a case study.

Person-centered therapy is also known as person-centered counseling, client-centered therapy, and Rogerian psychotherapy. Person-centered therapy is a form of talk psychotherapy majorly developed by Carl Rogers in the 1940s and 1950s. The goal of person-centered therapy is to provide clients with an opportunity to develop a sense of self-concept and help them realize their attitudes, feelings, behavior, and potential. Person-centered therapy proposes that human minds are being negatively affected and so this approach tries to find

*Counseling Psychology: An Integrated Positive Psychological Approach*, First Edition. Ruth Chu-Lien Chao.

individuals' positive potentials. In person-centered therapy, practitioners and counselors create a comfortable, nonjudgmental environment by showing congruence, genuineness, empathy, and unconditional positive regard toward their clients while using a nondirective approach. This aids clients in finding their own solutions to their problems. Although person-centered therapy has been criticized by behaviorists and empirical researchers for lacking structure and by psychoanalytic therapists for providing a conditional and perhaps superficial relationship, person-centered therapy has been proven to be a useful and popular treatment.

Person-centered therapy, now considered a founding work in humanistic counseling, began formally with Carl Rogers. Indeed, "Rogerian psychotherapy" is identified as one of the major approaches in counseling and therapy, along with psychodynamic psychotherapy, psychoanalysis, Adlerian therapy, existential therapy, and cognitive behavior therapy.

## Historical Context

Person-centered therapy was mostly developed by Carl Rogers. To best understand his system, readers must know Rogers first. Rogers was born in Oak Park, Illinois. His parents devoutly ascribed to the beliefs of fundamentalist Protestantism and accordingly encouraged pragmatic and Christian values. Rogers initially entered the University of Wisconsin to study agricultural science, however, following an influential trip to China, his interests shifted from practical pursuits to intellectual ones. Rogers received a BA degree in history and entered the Union Theological Seminary in New York City before transferring to Columbia University Teacher's College to study clinical psychology. While at Columbia, Rogers specialized in the treatment of children. His dissertation, "Measuring personality adjustment in children nine to thirteen years of age" (Rogers, 1931), offered an objective test of children's attitudes toward their abilities and relationships. He obtained his Ph.D. in 1931 from Columbia University.

In his first book, *The Clinical Treatment of The Problem Child* (1939), Rogers critiqued the major approaches of psychotherapy and presented original thoughts concerning psychotherapist skills that would later become fundamental concepts of person-centered therapy.

Rogers introduced the concept of person-centered therapy during a presentation at the University of Minnesota in 1940. Soon after, he wrote *Counseling and Psychotherapy: Newer Concepts in Practice* (Rogers, 1942) to emphasize the use of humanistic principles in psychotherapy. Rogers referred to this new approach as "nondirective." The nature of nondirective psychotherapy greatly contrasted with the dominant approaches of behaviorism and Freudian psychoanalysis. Like many groundbreaking achievements, nondirective techniques were initially ignored, then met with heated criticism.

In 1945, Rogers left a professorship at The Ohio State University to direct a new counseling center at the University of Chicago. The counseling center was conducive to the cultivation of nondirective techniques, and Rogers published another book on client-centered therapy (Rogers, 1951). Rogers asserted that person-centered or client-centered therapy empowers clients to achieve greater self-understanding through the therapist's ability to employ unconditional positive regard, empathy, and genuineness. Much of Rogers' subsequent work sought to refine and promote client-centered therapy, as well as supporting its efficacy by conducting controlled outcome research. Late in his career, Rogers addressed the fields of education and conflict resolution. Rogers published 16 books and more than 200 articles. The American Psychological Association awarded Rogers the first Distinguished Scientific Achievement Award in1956 and the first Distinguished Professional Contribution Award in 1972.

## View of Human Nature

Rogers strongly believes that people are trustworthy, resourceful, capable of self-understanding, able to make constructive changes, and able to live effective and productive lives. When psychoanalysts, particularly Freud, appeared to take the view that human beings are never free from the primitive passions originating in their childhood fixations and are solely the product of powerful biological drives, Rogers believes that individuals are able to be resourceful and feel positively. Although some psychoanalysts emphasize the dark side of human nature with its destructive impulses, Rogers suggests that in psychoanalysis, human beings were seen to have no choice and no control over themselves, that individuals are inherently bad or weak, and are likely to get "broken," and will need the help of the counselor as an expert who could "mend" the broken individual. Because of the negative view of psychoanalysis on human nature, the counselor would assess and diagnose what was wrong with the client and identify the goals for change which the client needed to achieve. Being almost in a position opposite to psychoanalysis regarding human nature, Rogers disagrees with the approach which assumes people as being passive, needing guidance, and being determined by external forces.

Although individuals do have potentials of growth, Rogers claims three therapeutic attributes facilitate a self-promoting growth climate in which individuals can move forward. These three attributes are: (a) congruence, genuineness, or realness; (b) acceptance, caring or unconditional positive regard; (c) accurate empathic understanding. According to Rogers, if therapists communicate with clients using these attitudes, clients will be less defensive and more open to themselves, others, and the world. That is, individuals will move toward health if they feel that they are free and understood. Individuals will engage in self-exploration if the climate sets them free and people (e.g., therapists) show their sincerity, genuineness, and positive regard. When individuals feel and are free, they will be able to find their own way and even flourish in life.

According to Rogers, the position of human nature in person-centered therapy is different from psychoanalysis which assumes individuals as passive and determined by external force. Yet, Rogers' perspective about human nature might be subtly different from existential therapy as well. Existentialists assume that individuals should have freedom to choose and do not consider influence from biological issues or external force. Although Rogers' perspective overlaps with existentialism in that both theories focus on people's potential and self-awareness, he also claims that individuals experiencing a growth-promoting climate (i.e., a supportive environment) will move forward to health, self-actualization, and fulfill their potentials.

For person-centered therapists, individuals have an internal source of healing which comes from their directional process of striving toward self-actualization and fulfillment.

According to Rogers, such an internal source of healing does not exclude individuals from connecting to or socializing with others. Rogers' positive view of human nature creates significant implications for counseling and practice. It also implies that clients have a primary responsibility toward health since the individual has an inherent tendency of moving away from maladjustment and toward health. Because individuals possess such ability and internal source of healing, person-centered therapists reject taking on the role of "expert" or "authority" who knows best and put clients in a passive role to follow therapists' direction. Due to the positive view of human nature, therapy in the person-centered approach is rooted in providing a nonjudgmental climate where clients develop their own self-awareness and self-directed change in attitude and behavior.

Rogers' perspective on human nature focuses on the constructive side of human beings or what's right within individuals, though he also emphasizes the importance of the climate in which therapists' attitudes contribute to. Thus, from Rogers' perspective, it is important to recognize conditions which block or facilitate individuals' growth. These conditions include how individuals act in their world with others, how they move forward toward or distract from their life directions, and how they manage obstacles. Through providing a climate with genuineness and positive regard, person-centered therapists encourage individuals to make changes that will lead them to living fully and authentically. For person-centered therapists, life is dynamic and lively rather than static, so individuals continue to be involved in the process of self-actualization.

## Theoretical Principles

Many practitioners and scholars acknowledge Rogers' broad influence on counseling with his person-centered approach. According to Rogers, three areas require attention: (1) the client-centered view of disturbance; (2) the therapeutic conditions of personality change; and (3) the process of therapeutic change.

### The client-centered view of disturbance

Rogers believes that clients who come for counseling experience some type of disturbance. This disturbance is the product of conflict, tension, and distress, which result from client's dishonesty with self. At its most fundamental level, Rogers views disturbance as coming from an individual losing trust in his or her "self." When people lose trust in self, he or she begins to distort or deny their own experience of the world, over time they increasingly separate themselves from fully freshly experiencing of self and the world. Rogers used the term "incongruence" to capture this idea of the discrepancy between one's self and one's experience. As incongruity emerges, it may increase further in magnitude and becomes incorporated into daily functioning. The individual would thus operate more on a basis of "what I should be" or "what I must be" instead of "who I am."

Rogers had a clear belief in humanity which is positive, optimistic, and proactive. He believed that an individual possesses an inherent tendency to fully develop his or her capacities, a process Rogers termed self-actualization. Though life experiences can derail this tendency, everyone still holds to the call of great upward striving. Clients may express this in various ways such as "I don't like it when I do that," "I don't believe that I'm being true to myself," and "I think something doesn't feel right." When clients experience that something is wrong (e.g., disturbance, conflict, or distress), they sense that this experience involves a compromise of self (e.g., incongruity or discrepancy). The antidote for these disturbances lies in reconnecting clients with their authentic selves; reestablishing the process of their listening to, valuing, and trusting their innermost selves; and setting them on the path to becoming fully genuine persons.

## The therapeutic conditions of personality change

For Rogers, the key issue in the therapeutic relationship was whether the counselor can provide a relationship helpful for the client's personal growth. Based on Rogers' conviction, a counselor provides a helping nurturing relationship that has the potential to liberate a client from his or her incongruous or unactualizing way of being. When a counselor provides such a facilitative relationship, clients will use it to help themselves grow. Clients are capable of personal growth in a counseling relationship characterized by three core conditions: empathic understanding, unconditional positive regard, and genuineness.

Empathic understanding establishes a climate for a client's self-initiated experiential learning. Empathetic understanding is often defined by the ability of a therapist accurately and sensitively to understand a client's experiences and feelings and the meaning of such experiences to the client. Rogers also advocated a counselor (metaphorically) crawls into the skin of a client, to see as the client sees, to think as the client thinks, and to feel as the client feels. By deeply understanding the client, communicating understanding, and facilitating further exploration, a counselor can help the client to begin listening to and understanding themselves. For Rogers, being empathic was the core facilitative condition that freed the client to use counseling to grow.

Unconditional positive regard is also referred to as warmth, respect, and acceptance. According to Rogers, unconditional positive regard is an appreciation of clients for who they are, and is a step to complete self-acceptance. It also involves a positive respect for and acceptance of the client's immediate experiencing. In the words of Thomas Harris' popular 1969 book, *I'm OK—You're OK*, positive regard involves a therapist's genuine communications to the client that he or she is OK.

Rogers referred genuineness to realness, congruence, and transparency. Genuineness entails honestly being oneself in the counseling relationship. It involves honesty, expressed with sensitivity, compassion, and appropriateness. Although genuineness is difficult to define concretely, when present in a counseling interview, its salience is incontrovertible and its presence is palpable.

## Six conditions in person-centered therapy

Rogers affirmed individual personal experience as the basis and standard for living and therapeutic effect. Rogers identified six conditions which are needed to produce personality changes in clients: relationship; vulnerability to anxiety (on the part of the client); genuineness (the therapist is truly himself or herself and incorporates some self-disclosure); the client's perception of the therapist's genuineness; the therapist's unconditional positive regard for the client; and accurate empathy. This emphasis contrasts with the dispassionate position which may be intended in other therapies, particularly the more extreme behavioral therapies. Living in the present rather than the past or future, with deep trust, naturalistic faith in your own thoughts and the accuracy in your feelings, and a responsible acknowledgment of your freedom, with a view toward participating fully in our world, contributing to other people's lives, are hallmarks of Rogers' person-centered therapy. Rogers also claims that the therapeutic process is essentially the accomplishments made by the client. The client having already progressed further along in their growth and maturation development, only progresses further with the aid of a psychologically favored environment. According to Rogers, the six necessary and sufficient conditions required for therapeutic change are:

1. The contact between therapist and client: This is a relationship between client and therapist; in this relationship, Rogers focused on each person's perception of the other.
2. The incongruence between the client's experience and awareness. Furthermore, the client is vulnerable to anxiety which motivates them to stay in the relationship.
3. The therapist accepts the client unconditionally, without judgment, disapproval or approval. This facilitates increased self-regard in the client, as they can begin to become aware of experiences in which their view of self-worth was distorted by others.
4. The therapist expresses an empathic understanding of the client's internal frame of reference. Accurate empathy on the part of the therapist helps the client believe the therapist's unconditional love for them.
5. The client perceives the therapist's unconditional positive regard and empathic understanding.
6. The client is willing to use the therapeutic relationship to facilitate his or her personal growth. The client is motivated to work through the incongruence between his or her distorted perception and true self.

## The process of therapeutic change

The concept of the therapeutic change process has been likened to peeling an onion one layer at a time. The process cannot be rushed. Therapeutic change takes time. Each client's needs must be considered and respected, and a program of change must be charted accordingly. Clients should be allowed to proceed at the pace that promotes optimal growth and learning. Generally, personal growth involves the development of the self from more general and undifferentiated to more specific and differentiated; from blocked to unblocked; from less open to more open; from more distant to more immediate; from less responsible to more responsible; and from limited functioning to full functioning.

For Rogers, the therapeutic process involves seven stages. Clients in the first stage refuse to acknowledge that a problem exists and are unwilling to talk about anything other than external generalities. This is typical of involuntary clients. In stage two, clients perceive problems to be of external origin and fail to recognize their own personal contribution. A limited acceptance of their feelings and some freer self-expression occurs in stage three. In the next stage clients become more present focused, further accept and own their feelings, and begin to evidence some self-responsibility; self-acceptance and self-responsibility are further enhanced in stage five. The clients' internal communications are clear, their perceptions of their experiences are sharp, and their focus is present oriented in the penultimate stage. The final stage of counseling is characterized by the highest levels of immediacy and openness to experience, and by the emergence of self-acceptance and self-responsibility.

## An Integration: Positive Psychology and Person-Centered Therapy

In general, positive psychology and person-centered therapy share similar perspectives in therapy and theoretical assumptions. Both approaches emphasize empathy and focus on therapeutic relationship and process. Moreover, today's trend shifts from deficit approach to enhancement quest. This is a very important shift. In recent years, Western psychologists have turned their attention to positive human functioning to inquire how psychologists can help individuals achieve an optimal level of health and well-being (e.g., Linley & Joseph, 2004; Seligman & Csikszentmihalyi, 2000; Snyder & Lopez, 2002).

Positive psychology aims to promote people living to their fullest potentials, no matter where they are along the spectrum of human functioning, from illness and disorder to health and well-being. This perspective of positive psychology also contrasts with client-centered therapy using the deficit model, which simply tries to reduce distress by providing a nonjudgmental environment. In contrast, positive therapy aims to change how counselors think about what they are doing and how they can help clients, so that counselors come to realize that they should not only help alleviate distress and various dysfunctions, but also promote well-being in the optimal functioning of clients.

According to positive psychology, counselors in the know have many choices on how to respond to what and how clients express themselves. Different from person-centered therapy, which sees clients as themselves "experts" in counseling, positive psychology believes that counselors are in a position to give advice, ask questions, make diagnoses, reassure clients, listen to them expertly, administer tests, as long as these interventions can reduce distress *and* promote wellness.

Still, positive psychology would partially agree with the person-centered approach. For example, a new client arrives and sits down opposite a counselor. What do we do next? Person-centered therapy may focus on the client's experience and provide an unconditionally supportive environment; the positive psychologist will do all and this but may also incorporate therapeutic techniques or scientific tools such as tests.

Integrating these two approaches, counselors can now help clients by differentiating when to see clients as the "experts," and when to provide advice or suggestions of tests. Of course, clients deserve to be the "experts" since they are the ones living with their problems for weeks, years, or even decades. The use of other techniques in counseling does not mean that positive psychology proposes to deprive client's experiences. To utilize other techniques mainly attempts to reach the goal of alleviating distress and promoting well-being of the client. Counselors and clients can collaborate to seek the most appropriate solutions that originate in respecting the clients' expert role as counselors to take advantage of therapeutic techniques and scientific research.

## The role of scientific research

The role of scientific research may receive different attention from person-centered therapy and positive psychology. However, it is inaccurate to assume that these early pioneers of person-centered therapy or humanistic psychologists as not scientific enough. In their day, they were at the forefront of scientific psychology. This is particularly true of Carl Rogers.

Rogers' approach has been mistakenly criticized for the looseness of his language and vagueness of his concepts as incapable of lending themselves to empirical testing. These critics neglect that Carl Rogers had produced high quality scientific works of peer reviewing. In fact, person-centered therapy has a rich history in science. It is Rogers who is most often credited with introducing scientific research into the field of psychotherapy, recording his interviews, and then transcribing the interviews verbatim, and publishing the transcripts for subsequent reviews and examinations.

In addition to pioneering psychotherapy research, Rogers' theoretical statements about the necessary and sufficient conditions for personality change were precisely presented as empirically testable hypotheses (see Rogers, 1957, 1959). Unfortunately, despite his contribution to empirical testing regarding person-centered therapy, the common impression among many scholars remains that person-centered therapy is not well grounded in science.

In this prevalent context, the emphasis of empirical research in positive psychology may strengthen the therapeutic principles in person-centered therapy. Specifically, half a century ago, these ideas of humanistic psychology or person-centered therapy were unable to be tested with today's methodological and statistical sophistication. The theories of Rogers could now turn more challenging by being put to the test. We have sophisticated techniques to conduct advanced statistical analyses in seconds that would have previously taken weeks and months. We can now test with complicated multivariate models to examine the summative and interactive effects of many different variables at once.

In other words, positive psychology has begun to develop an empirical research consistent with the principles of person-centered therapy. This is an integration of person-centered therapy into the focus of scientific research in positive psychology. This integration can help mental health professionals to be scientific consumers to incorporate research evidence to enhance their work with clients.

## Uses of assessment and measures

In addition to strengthening person-centered reduction of distress by positive psychological enhancement of personal well-being, and solidifying person-centered therapy with empirical scientific research of positive psychology, the third integration between these two approaches lies in redefining the role of assessment and tests in counseling. Many person-centered mental health professionals object to the use of tests and measures, fearing such use to be conflated with objective diagnosis and missing personal understanding (Rogers, Lyon, & Tausch, 2014). Positive psychology acknowledges that psychologists should be cautious in using tests and measures lest they label clients objectively. Still, positive psychology research also offers mental health professionals a different repertoire of assessments that provide counselors with more information to better understand their clients.

According to positive psychology, there are various types of assessments for various purposes. On the one hand, positive psychology is still concerned with and objects to the diagnoses and assessments in purely medical physiological models. On the other hand, positive psychologists recognize that we do have some assessments that measure clients' psychological distress, some others that measure their well-being, and some other tests and measures that clients may test themselves with, to find them useful in self-knowledge, such as assessing their strengths and happiness, to help collaboration with counselors in counseling sessions. Thus positive psychology is open to tests and measures as long as care is taken in using them.

Person-centered therapy does not require counselors to take case histories, or assess, or diagnose the clients, for counselors do not assume that there are specific treatments for specific problems. Person-centered therapy also assumes that psychological problems result from internalization of feeling worthless. Accordingly, dismissing the necessity of tests and measures, person-centered therapists instead provide the best intervention, supplying the core conditions to the clients, a social environment that serves to spontaneously dissolve the client's basis of feeling worthless.

Positive psychology would also endorse the importance of providing a supportive environment to clients. Yet, positive psychology could also contribute to person-centered therapy with a rigorous assessment and testing, so that mental health professionals can better evaluate and understand clients' progress. For example, while person-centered therapists facilitate clients' self-actualization, positive psychology may further enhance counselors' and clients' "seeing" self-actualization with weekly data of progress and empirical evaluation, so that they can cooperate to chart future progress in well-being.

## Multiculturalize the Integration

### Multiculturalizing person-centered counseling and positive psychology

Although both positive psychology and person-centered therapy emphasize empathy and focus on therapeutic relationship and process, both approaches originate in the perspective of individualism of the West. Despite the focus on client's well-being and the nonjudgmental climate from the client-centered counseling, without multicultural sensitivity, counselors may still continue to impose Western-styled counseling. For example, multicultural clients may be concerned about family members and such worries may be acceptable in their cultures. However, without appropriate multicultural knowledge, some counselors may not realize that some cultures may overtly or covertly encourage people to care for others in interpersonal relationships. Such other-caring is supremely important in such cultures.

Thus, when talking about individual well-being and self-actualization, a female Asian client may continually focus on her care for elderly parents and younger siblings. This is typical of Asian culture, stressing filial piety as a virtue of respect for parents and ancestors, as the prime virtue and basis of all correct personal relations. Without such cultural knowledge of Asians, counselors may perceive this Asian female client as avoidant or resistant to her own well-being. Thus, culturally skilled counselors would respect this Asian client's interpretation of well-being and self-actualization, and proceed counseling accordingly.

Although positive psychology believes that counselors can give advice, ask questions, make diagnoses, reassure clients as they listen attentively to clients, and also administer tests, all these counseling behaviors have one ultimate goal, to reduce clients' distress and promote their wellness – specifically based on the unique culture of each cultural client. Thus, the integration of positive psychology and person-centered therapy should be further tempered with minute sensitivity to multicultural clients' cultural values and beliefs. The unconditionally supportive environment should include respecting clients' definition of "unconditionally supportive environment," never only explaining the definition from Western culture and expecting clients to understand it.

Additionally, originating in Western culture, while positive psychologists incorporate scientific tools such as tests, culturally sensitive counselors would understand that assessment instruments themselves could be culturally biased. For example, using a scale on assertiveness to assess the above Asian female's ability to formulate and communicate her own thoughts, opinions, and wishes in a clear and direct way, this Asian female's answers and goals could be focused on her parents instead of herself. When being asked about fulfilling her potentials, she might be hesitant because Asian culture prescribes others' well-being on top of oneself. From the perspective of Asian culture, she is a daughter with deep filial love. Her focus on her parents, not on herself, might lead her to be misunderstood as "unable to fulfill her personal goals." Thus, culturally sensitive counselors need to be aware of the cultural biases inherent in assessments and tests.

### Multiculturalizing scientific research to serve diverse clients

Carl Rogers' theory was at the forefront of scientific psychology, and positive psychology attempts to utilize scientific methodology to discover empirical evidences and to promote well-being. To effectively help multicultural clients, it is a welcomed idea to integrate practice with empirical evidences. Unfortunately, in the process of applying evidence-based practice to multicultural clients, the issues on culture tend to be neglected, not addressed, or even assumed nonexistent. Despite the fact that empirical research may strengthen the therapeutic principles in person-centered therapy, without considering cultural implications, counselors may be unaware of multicultural clients' cultural heritages and of respecting the differences between themselves and their clients. Such culture-blindness simply makes self-assured scientific evidence misfire. We would be falsely assured, out of touch with cultural realities.

### Multiculturalizing the use of assessments and measures

Integration of person-centered therapy into positive psychology redefines the role of assessment and tests in counseling, provides a new perspective on person-centered therapy, and promotes a common understanding of psychological distress and well-being by both clients and counselors.

These potential benefits regarding using assessments and measures would be severely negated, even turn counterproductive, unless these assessments and measure are multiculturalized. Uses of assessments and measures require counselors' extreme caution and sensitivity on cultural interpretations of these measures. This is because assessments and measures, are specifically developed for white persons, and applying these white-centered measures to multicultural clients could produce problems (Kearney, Draper, & Barón, 2005; Lucas & Berkel, 2005).

For example, in black psychology, without knowing the worldviews or cultural context of African Americans, clinicians may unintentionally misdiagnose or even psychopathologize African Americans (Anderson, 2003). Moreover, mental health measures, including those measures in positive psychology, may inaccurately assess African Americans' mental health status if white-centered scales are used to evaluate them. If measures were developed with whites as the norm, whether current mental health measures in person-centered approach or positive psychology, these measures would lack cultural sensitivity and the assessment would misfire.

The U.S. Surgeon General's (2001) supplement, *Mental Health: Culture, Race, and Ethnicity*, warns that the measures, and also mental healthcare, provided to African Americans and other multicultural populations are inadequate. Moreover, the absence of an adequate assessment of multicultural clients' mental health contributes to a misunderstanding of them and worsens their counseling (Clark, Anderson, Clark, & Williams, 1999; Landrine & Klonoff, 1996). Even though positive psychology emphasizes measures and tests and person-centered therapy focuses on unconditional acceptance, there are very limited measures assessing how multicultural populations contribute to this society.

The fact is, despite a long list of adverse conditions and centuries of marginalization in the socioeconomic mainstream, multicultural populations (e.g., Asian Americans, African Americans, Latina/o, Native Americans) try to manage to contribute to American society, by for example work ethics, cultural independence, and a legacy of social activism (Anderson, 2003). And such encouraging historical facts are simply bypassed and ignored. All this ignorance stems from inadequate measures to assess multicultural clients on their positive contributions and their unspoken distresses.

Culturally sensitive counselors are aware that there are potential biases of measures on multicultural clients, and such biases may put these underrepresented people in very disadvantaged or vulnerable positions. Counselors also have knowledge that there are numerous culture-specific strengths, well-being, and contributions that are simply not measured or neglected even in current days.

## Application in Counseling: Case Study

Mary is a 27-year-old Latina female who was raised by a very restrictive father and a powerless mother. Her father sometimes had aggressive expressions of anger and aggressive or neglectful problem solving. Either Mary's parents ignored how she was behaving or what was happening to her, or else they overreacted to her mistakes and developmental struggles, and her father sometimes used abusive punishment. Mary survived this history by developing a people-pleasing style and left her parent's house when she was 17 years old.

She has also carefully observed the people around her and tried to meet their needs so that they would accept her and not hurt her. Her passive approach to her own needs led to an early pregnancy outside marriage. In her culture, it was a shame that she was having a child without marriage. As she raised her son alone, she sought to be a "better parent" than she had had herself. She strove to attend to all of her son's needs and deny him nothing. As she had no role models for effective parenting, her simple wish to be loving led her to overindulging the desires of her son. Her desire to avoid abusive parenting practices has led her to avoid setting limits on her son's behavior.

Mary's strengths lie in her sincere desire to be a good parent, her ability to observe and predict the moods of others, and her average level of intelligence that allows her to understand the consequences of her son's present behavior. At this time, Mary is very aware that she and her son are having serious difficulties, but she is not aware of how her permissive and people-pleasing style is related to these difficulties.

## How to help Mary

*Person-centered approach and positive psychology* Both person-centered therapy and positive psychology emphasize empathy and focus on therapeutic relationship and process. For Mary, it is crucial to understand and accept her past experiences of living in an abusive environment. Although Latina culture gives fathers much power and authority and respect their fatherly care for the family, it does not mean that Mary has to tolerate his abusive parenting. Moreover, Mary's mother appeared powerless to protect Mary from fatherly abuses, and motherly powerlessness may add a disappointing impact to Mary's childhood. Now Mary is a mother to her son. Because of Mary's Latina background, the counselor asked her the definition of being a good mother in her culture. In Latina culture, women are expected to be good wives and good mothers by cooking and cleaning.

Yet, to be a good mother to her son, Mary needs to learn from scratch her positive functioning, caring for her son's health and well-being (e.g., Linley & Joseph, 2004; Seligman & Csikszentmihalyi, 2000; Snyder & Lopez, 2002). Through counseling, she learned that she might not be a happy mom for her son if she herself did not live to her fullest potentials. Although she was providing a very supportive and nonjudgmental environment for her son, she was unable to *guide* him when he made mistakes such as bullying other children.

With her counselor, Mary re-learned the meaning of a great person and a good mother in Latina culture. With an unconditionally supportive climate, her counselor assisted her to reduce her frustration, her hurt of being abused, and her painful breakup with her son's father. Importantly, her counselor further assisted her to see her strengths in her own culture. Some typical questions from her counselor include: "What does a happy person look like in Latina culture?" "What roles do Latina/os expect women to play in work and families?" "How do Latina mothers guide their children when they make mistakes?"

Her counselor also recognized the cultural differences between them and the counselor was willing to share her own worldview. Through counseling, Mary has further confirmed that she is the "expert" in her life and counseling has been the experience to assist her to become a person with great characters such as resilience in addition to managing her hurt sustained in childhood.

To facilitate her development of insights, her counselor introduced various techniques in addition to providing a nonjudgmental climate. Her counselor was attending sensitively to her, thereby demonstrated empathy to her. Moreover, Mary asked questions, was reassured, was listened to, and now was open to other techniques as long as these interventions can reduce her distress and promote wellness.

Providing a multicultural counseling has been a focus in Mary's counseling. Her counselor was honest admitting to having little experience with Latina culture. Still, her counselor was eager to learn from Mary about here culture. From Mary's perspective, her counselor's eagerness to be familiar with Latina culture was the best way to show her care. Her counselor's interests also ignited her pride and refreshed her sense of cultural heritage.

Her counselor integrated these two approaches of person-centered therapy (learn from Mary) and positive psychology (enhancing Mary's cultural pride), and Mary noticed that her counselor believed that Mary was the "expert" of her own life. When appropriate, her counselor introduced some assessments or tests to strengthen her self-awareness. Through such counseling, Mary learned to collaborate with another person (her counselor) to reach her personal goal. The usage of techniques may be new to Latina/os, but she also understood that tests may help her reach her goal of alleviating distress and promoting well-being. Collaborating with her counselor was a brand new experience for her. Yet, she was pleased to use such collaboration to seek the most appropriate solutions that respect her expert role and take advantage of therapeutic techniques and scientific research.

## The role of scientific research

Despite both person-centered therapy and positive psychology appreciating and supporting a scientific approach in counseling, the emphasis of empirical research should be aligned with the client's culture. As the earlier section described, Mary's counselor sometimes introduced assessments and tests to enhance Mary's insights, self-awareness, and development of her positive characters. However, there are at least two challenges in using assessments and tests: (a) How culturally appropriate is it to conduct tests for Mary who is a Latina woman? Should the counselor find tests in Mary's language? How did the counselor manage some potential biases in tests? (b) When is the best time to conduct a test? How should the counselor conduct the assessment in appropriate ways to Mary's culture?

Some researchers suggest that Latina culture is characterized by family-ism (prioritizing unity of the family), *respecto* (having respect for elders), *personalismo* (valuing warm and caring relationships over formal partnerships), collectivism (valuing the group over the individual), religion and spirituality (traditionally important for Latina families). Thus, Mary's counselor explored, based on Latina culture, the potential impacts of assessments on her presenting problems and well-being.

For example, would the assessments diminish the focus of family and only address Mary's individual needs? Or would the process of testing make Mary feel that her needs of warm and supportive interactions were neglected? Mary was also curious about how the counselor would manage the potential conflicts between her spiritual orientation and the test items. Her counselor acknowledged the inherited limitations of assessments and tests which were primarily developed in Western culture. Thus, the counselor appreciated Mary's inputs on the test items, assessment results, and cultural interpretation. Her counselor also highlighted that the focus of the counseling was on Mary as a person, client, and mother in her culture, not about the tests or assessments.

Similarly, the purpose of incorporating empirical studies into the counseling was to promote Mary's self-awareness and well-being, in addition to reducing her frustration. Without discounting the importance of Latina culture on Mary's parenting, Mary's counselor noticed that Mary appeared hopeless whenever she talked about her son's behavior problems such as violence or bullying other kids in school.

Through her counseling, her counselor also introduced a parent training which might be helpful for altering the developmental trajectories of Mary's son with behavior problems or at risk for them. Mary believed, like other Latina mothers, that the causes of her son's misbehavior were bad tempers or peer pressure. However, research showed that Latina/o students' acculturative stress may play a significant role to their behavior problems (Pérez Benítez, Sibrava, Zlotnick, Weisberg, & Keller, 2014). Specifically, the less connected to their cultural heritage, the more vulnerable Latina/o youth would be to acculturative stress (DeVylder, Oh, Yang, Cabassa, Chen, & Lukens, 2013). After learning the findings from empirical studies, Mary recognized that she rarely talked to her son about Latina culture, much less sharing with him how much she felt supported by her Latina background.

Taken together, she learned that, despite her past negative and abusive trauma in childhood, what she needs now is to recover from her traumatic childhood, reconnect to her culture, and provide appropriate guidance for her son. Her counselor also appreciated the opportunity of working with Mary, a Latina female client. In addition to learning to providing counseling from person-centered therapy and positive psychology, the counselor also learned how to provide such integration in a culturally appropriate way. Because Latina culture focuses on collectivism and family, Mary frequently talked about her son when the counselor asked for Mary's personal feelings. When the counselor understood the high emphasis of family in Latina culture, the counselor noticed that the Western individualistic approach might culturally clash with Mary's Latina focus on family. When the counselor shifted focus from Mary as an individual to her multiple roles, a woman, mother, a daughter, and so on, their collaborative counseling turned more beneficial to Mary.

The other challenge Mary's counselor encountered was the role of evidence-based or empirical studies. At first, whenever the counselor interpreted the findings from the empirical findings, Mary was suspicious. For example, Mary thought that those empirical studies were too abstract and distant to her. Her problems were about her daily frustration with how to parent her son. However, when the counselor connected the empirical studies with Latina youth or contextualized the evidence-based therapy in Latina culture, Mary started to consider the implication of studies to her son. She also discovered that she was desperately trying to discard her Latina root due to her abusive childhood. Unfortunately, when she repressed her childhood trauma by discarding her Latina culture, she also threw away her cultural heritage and support. This could be a reason why her son felt strange to Latina culture and used bullying to show his pride.

Over a few sessions of counseling, both Mary and the counselor had their respective challenges and learning. For Mary, she learned to look at her problem with a new perspective. Additionally, her counselor examined the counseling with an integration between person-centered therapy and positive psychology in the Latina culture perspective. Both of them also appreciate when and how to incorporate empirical or scientific approach of counseling into their sessions. Thus, for Mary and her counselor, the integration of person-centered therapy and the focus of scientific research into positive psychology helped them be science consumers who incorporate research evidence to promote well-being.

*The use of assessment and measures* The third integration between person-centered therapy and positive psychology is to redefine the role of assessment and tests in counseling and to tailor such integration to Mary's Latina culture. Although practitioners recognized the necessity not to use tests and measures to label clients, with multicultural clients such as Mary, it is inevitable to contextualize the integration to clients' cultural background. Thus, in addition to acknowledging that both person-centered therapy and positive psychology originated in Western culture, this section focuses on how to provide the integration in a culturally appropriate way.

Applying assessments and tests to Latina/o population, it is crucial to realize that one size does not fit all. As the US's largest ethnic minority, Latina/o population's lives reflect a wide spectrum of cultural, language, and social factors. Traditionally, assessment has paid scant attention to such variables, but now culturally sensitive counselors are increasingly aware of linguistic and acculturation issues that can influence how psychological problems present themselves, and that skewed test results can lead to misdiagnosis, inappropriate and ineffective treatment, and potentially devastating consequences. This is why Mary's counselor frequently discusses with Mary the usage, potential biases, and interpretations of assessments and tests.

This evolving challenge of applying assessments to the Latina population should consider outlining the necessary cultural considerations and recommending specific culturally adjusted measures. For example, because Mary had a traumatic childhood and such negative experiences pushed her away from her Latina culture, her counselor needs to be aware how Latina culture positively and negatively influenced her.

Additionally, neither person-centered therapy nor positive psychology welcomes the approach of diagnosis or a disease-based model. Mary's counselor was cautious about considering diagnosis toward Mary. Such cautious consideration would also fit Latina culture because cultural differences imply different interpretations about mental problems.

The other challenge inherent in the usage of assessment for a Latina population was the focus of measurement. Traditional assessment appeared to emphasize problematic behavior, mental illness, internalization of being worthless, or personality problems. It is questionable how much of such negative approach to mental health reflects Latina culture and worldview. For example, Mary's counselor may find it difficult to find a scale to measure Mary's strengths in the Latina culture. According to positive psychology, what we need to measure is the client's distress and their strengths, happiness, and positive characters to compose well-being.

Unfortunately, person-centered therapists believe that the best intervention is not to assess client's problems and difficulties, but to provide the core conditions of a social environment to their clients, to serve to dissolve the client's conditions of feeling worthless. The integration of person-centered therapy and positive psychology was to evaluate the benefits of assessments based on Mary's perspective. Thus, when conducting assessment with Mary, the counselor will present an empathic approach to measuring the agreed assessment areas. It is thus that positive psychology can also contribute to person-centered therapy with a rigorous assessment and testing, so that mental health professionals can better evaluate and understand clients' progress. While person-center therapists facilitate clients' self-actualization, positive psychology may further enhance counselors' and clients' "seeing" self-actualization with weekly data of progress and empirical evaluation.

*Implications for culturally competent care* In providing a culturally sensitive integration of person-centered therapy and positive psychology, there are at least eight implied requirements when considering conducting assessments to Latina (and other) populations. There must be more, but this is enough to show how much cultural sensitivity is required in treating multicultural populations, the most sensitive of which is using assessment measures developed primarily in the Western culture of individualism.

*First*, there is a great need for increased numbers of bilingual and bicultural service providers to competently evaluate, diagnose, and treat Latina. *Second*, there is a need to develop effective, affordable models of assessment and therapy to address the mental health and service needs of Latina in both urban and rural communities. Such services should be community based and available before severe distress is experienced. *Third*, there is a need to better train primary service providers and mental health specialists to accurately recognize symptoms of emotional distress in Latinas. *Fourth*, Latina populations embrace what has become known as the "mestizo" perspective, a dynamic process that strives for harmony with one's physical and social surroundings, recognizes the value of every person by encouraging respect for and acceptance of all individuals, an openness to new experiences, and a strong sense of spirituality. Males may have higher power and authority than females in Latina families. This perspective results in deference to elders and accepting their guidance, especially senior males.

*Fifth*, Latina population's strong family orientation and collective sense extends to medical care. Many Latina will involve the entire family rather than only an individual or a child's parents in decisions about treatment. *Sixth*, Latina' adherence to "personalismo" may cause them to develop strong ties to their provider rather than the care setting. It also may result in the expectation that their service provider will interact in a caring manner and provide a more constant presence of support and assistance. *Seventh*, Latina/os' expressions of emotion may be more intense than what is typically experienced among the more reserved white Americans. It is important to interpret these expressions within the context of cultural norms rather than automatically interpreting such behaviors as reflecting pathology. *Eighth*, there are strong religious beliefs and practices combined with family or community support for folk remedies. Such beliefs may affect the Latino's willingness to seek mental health services. Mental health problems may have to be framed as spiritual concerns.

*Follow-up: You continue as Mary's counselor* Consider how you will help Mary if you were her counselor. Here are a series of questions to provide some structure in your thinking about her case:

- How much interest would you have in Mary's experiences with her father? What patterns would you see between her experiences with her father and her own parenting skills to her son?

- Consider the gender role in Latina culture. That is, males may have more power than women, but person-centered therapy might propose no power differences between men and women. When you work with Mary, would you accept her according to Latina culture or person-centered therapy? Why?
- When working with Mary, which of her strengths would you want to highlight?

## Concluding Remarks

Being mainly developed by Carl Rogers in the 1940s and 1950s, person-centered therapy set up a different therapeutic direction from psychoanalysis and behavior therapy. The goal of person-centered therapy is to provide clients with an opportunity to develop a sense of self-concept wherein they can actualize their attitudes, feelings, behavior, and potential. Person-centered therapy focuses on three attributes: congruence; acceptance; and accurate empathic understanding. Additionally, this approach includes six conditions in counseling: the contact between counselor and client; the incongruence exists between the client's experience and awareness; counselor's acceptance of the client unconditionally; counselor's understanding of the client; client's perception of counselor's unconditional positive regard; and client's willingness to use the therapeutic relationship to facilitate his or her personal growth.

When integrating with positive psychology, three components could enrich person-centered therapy: refusal of the "expert" role in counseling; scientific or empirical research evidence in practice; and incorporation of assessment in counseling. Importantly, when applying this integration to multicultural clients, counselors should be aware of their own cultural biases and that these two approaches originated in Western culture. Thus, counselors possess knowledge that different cultures have their respective expectations regarding the role of counselors. Counselors are also aware that scientific research and assessments might be new to some multicultural clients.

## Review Questions: What Do You Think?

1. What are the roles of counselors in person-centered therapy and positive psychology?
2. What are your thoughts on scientific research in person-centered therapy and positive psychology?
3. What is the person-centered perspective with regard to psychological assessment? What is the positive psychology perspective with regard to psychological assessment?
4. What are your challenges when applying the integration of person-centered therapy and positive psychology to multicultural clients?

# 9

# Gestalt Therapy

**Learning Objectives**

- Explain the historical background of Gestalt therapy.
- Explain the Gestalt understanding of the nature of people and the process of change.
- Describe the necessary conditions under which psychological growth and behavioral change occur in Gestalt therapy.
- Demonstrate specific procedures and techniques from Gestalt therapy.
- Learn about holism in Gestalt therapy and positive psychology.
- Know how the perspectives regarding unfinished business in Gestalt therapy and positive psychology.
- Integrate Gestalt therapy and positive psychology.
- Multiculturalize the integration between Gestalt therapy and positive psychology.
- Apply the integration to a case study.

Gestalt therapy is an experiential form of psychotherapy that emphasizes the holistic perspective in counseling, including an individual's experience in the present moment, personal responsibility, the therapist–client relationship, the environmental and social contexts of an individual's life, and the self-regulating adjustments people make as a result of their overall situation. Developed by Fritz Perls, Laura Perls, and Paul Goodman in the 1940s and 1950s, Gestalt therapy includes two central ideas. One, Gestalt therapy indicates that the most helpful focus of psychotherapy is the experiential present moment. Two,

*Counseling Psychology: An Integrated Positive Psychological Approach*, First Edition. Ruth Chu-Lien Chao.

everyone is caught in webs of relationships. It is only possible to know ourselves against the background of our relationship to the other. Expanded, these two ideas support the four chief theoretical constructs (i.e., phenomenological method, dialogical relationship, field-theoretical strategies, and experimental freedom) that comprise Gestalt theory. Moreover, these constructs also guide the practice and implementation of Gestalt therapy.

## Historical Context

Gestalt therapy is based on theories and techniques developed in the 1940s by Friedrich (Fritz) Perls (1893–1970), a German-born psychiatrist. Later, Laura Perls (Fritz's wife) and Paul Goodman worked with Fritz to refine the ideas and techniques of Gestalt therapy. Other theorists further developed the model in the 1970s, especially Joen Fagan and Irma Lee Shepherd (Gladding, 2004). Gestalt therapy sprang from the early twentieth-century Gestalt movement founded by Czech psychologist Max Wertheimer, German psychologist Kurt Koffka, and German psychologist Wolfgang Köhler. The Gestalt movement was based on the theories of Johann Wolfgang von Goethe, Immanuel Kant, and Ernst Mach.

The meaning of Gestalt is "the whole figure." The main idea of Gestalt is that the whole defines the parts of which it is composed. A Gestalt perspective maintains that the whole objects (and people) are more than the sum of their separate parts. That is, objects are perceived within an environment according to all their parts taken together.

Gestalt therapy arose largely in reaction to what Fritz Perls perceived as the reductionist emphasis of other therapies at that time (e.g., psychoanalysis [Freudian psychotherapy] and behaviorism). Gestalt therapy operates on the premise that people strive for wholeness and completeness in their lives, that is, people have a tendency in self-actualization; Gestalt therapy also emphasizes how people function in their totality. The self-actualizing tendency emerges through self-awareness and personal interaction with the environment. The Gestalt view places trust in people's inner wisdom and a belief that people seek to live in an integrated fashion and strive toward a healthy, unified whole. People are actors in the events around them, not just reactors.

## View of Human Nature

The Gestalt view of human nature is rooted in phenomenology, existential philosophy, and field theory. To Gestalt therapists, therapy aims not at analysis but at contact and awareness with the environment. The environment, based on Gestalt therapy, consists of both the internal and external worlds. Thus, "contact" includes interactions with both internal and external worlds. The internal world includes the parts of self or disowned parts, and the external world includes other people or environment.

Similar to existentialism, Gestalt therapy claims that individuals have the capacity to self-regulate in their environment when they are aware of what happens in and around them. A primary function of therapy is to provide opportunity and setting for individuals to increase their awareness and support the contact process with internal and external worlds. Gestalt therapy also believes that the more individuals try to be or not to be what they are, the more they remain the same. In fact, according to Breshgold (1989), it would be impossible to change oneself just by trying to be different without awareness. Therefore, Gestalt therapy indicates that problems begin when a person tries to be who or what he or she isn't. Living with "masks" and being inauthentic does not promote change. In fact living an inauthentic life or with a "mask" only promotes stagnation of the personality. It is a paradox that individuals change because of their increasing awareness of what they are opposed to what they attempt to be. What makes individuals change comes from being fully aware of their internal and external worlds rather than striving for what they "should be." Putting this perspective into therapy, therapists' role is not to direct, suggest, or propose change, but to assist the clients to increase their awareness which leads to reintegration of their disowned parts or reconnecting to their alienated parts of self.

Fritz Pearls believed that individuals have to grow up, stand on their own feet, and take care of their own life problems. Pearls' understanding of human beings is that people can deal with their problems, especially if they become fully aware of what is happening within oneself and outside of oneself. Moreover, for Pearls, change happens in a person's life when he or she can reintegrate a disowned part of the self back into the mix of identity. Pearls' work involved two personal agendas: first, individuals move from environmental support to self-support; second, reintegrate the disowned parts of the self. The process of reowning parts of oneself and the unification process proceeds step by step until individuals are strong enough to carry on their own growth. Growth, according to Gestalt therapy, will make individuals more aware of their external and internal worlds. More awareness will lead to people's ability to make informed choices and live meaningfully.

Contemporary Gestalt therapy continues Pearls' view on human nature, but with a different way of working. Contemporary Gestalt therapy stresses dialogue between therapist and client. Therapists have no agenda and no direction. They perceive the relationship between client and environment as interdependent rather than independent. This interpretation of the relationship between individuals and environment creates ground for contact and experiments that are spontaneous and moment-to-moment dynamic of the therapeutic engagement.

## Theoretical Principles

In general, Gestalt therapy is an existential, phenomenological, and experiential therapy that emphasizes the present moment. According to the existential perspective, individuals create their lives by the decisions they make, and thus individuals are responsible for the actions they choose. A phenomenological perspective maintains that a person's perception of reality or an event is more important than the event itself. Experiential learning is that which is derived from experience. Gestalt therapy utilizes an individual's life experiences, exercises, and experiments in therapy to help develop insight. The focus of Gestalt therapy is on discovering different aspects of the self through experience rather than just talk. Gestalt therapy suggests that extreme dependency on intellectual exploration diminishes the importance and experiences of emotions and the senses. Eventually, such heavy reliance on intellectual understanding of self will result in limiting an individual's ability to respond to situations.

## Holism

Since Gestalt therapy stresses the holistic perspective of understanding and awareness, the basic goal is to attain awareness through self-knowledge, taking responsibility for choices, contact with the environment, and self-acceptance. Gestalt therapy does not aim to analyze internal conflicts; it strives to integrate these conflicts into new self-awareness. Conflicts include unfinished business – earlier thoughts, feelings, and reactions that still affect personal functioning and interfere with current living and present life. An example of unfinished business is not forgiving a loved one for his/her mistakes such as abandonment. The identification and resolution of conflicts allows an individual to grow and move forward in life.

Gestalt therapists in counseling aim to create an atmosphere that promotes a client's exploration by being honest, exciting, energetic, fully human, and intensely and personally involved (Gladding, 2004). Maintaining focus on "here-and-now" moments allows the therapist to help clients recognize the (negative and even maladaptive) patterns in their lives. Recognition of the immediacy of experience, a focus on verbal and nonverbal communication (e.g., body language), and focus on the concept that life includes making choices all help the client to resolve the past and become integrated.

Gestalt therapists believe that deep awareness comes from a holistic appreciation of varied avenues of experiences such as action. With an emphasis on action beyond the analysis or interpretation, Gestalt therapists utilize techniques, exercises, and experiments to deepen clients' awareness and insights. Exercises in Gestalt therapy are designed to evoke certain responses from the client such as anger or frustration and thus include the enactment of fantasies, role playing, psychodrama, and dream work. Different from the dream work in Freudian psychoanalysis, the Gestalt therapist does not interpret dreams. Clients recount dreams and are directed to experience what it is like to be in each part of the dream. One Gestalt exercise is the empty chair, in which clients talk to various aspects of their personality. This exercise helps clients deal with the dichotomies and conflicts related to the personalities in the "empty chair." Moreover, Gestalt experiments are unplanned activities that grow out of the interaction between client and therapist. Perls challenged clients to see how they avoided responsibility or feelings by using a confrontational, abrasive, and theatric style in therapy. Corey (2008) introduced a newer version – relational Gestalt therapy – which shows more support, kindness, and compassion than Perls' original Gestalt therapy style. Although Gestalt therapy has been adapted for use in a group format, it was originally developed for use in individual therapy.

While helpful for various mental health problems, Gestalt therapy is found to be most effective for individuals with mood disorders (e.g., depression), adjustment disorders, somatoform disorders (e.g., physical complaints with unknown causes), and interpersonal difficulties (Gladding, 2004). It is not a recommended treatment for individuals with severe mental illnesses (e.g., schizophrenia, psychotic disorders). Gestalt therapy provides a useful direction that helps people integrate all aspects of their lives. It considers the whole individual and puts the presenting problems in a holistic perspective so clients can gain more insights. Gestalt therapy helps clients focus on the present moment and perceive their problems within the context of their environment and relationships.

Unsurprisingly, critics say that Gestalt therapy lacks a strong theoretical base and empirical evidence. Some people criticize Gestalt therapy as too focused on techniques or exercises and clients may lose opportunities to explore their thoughts. Another criticism is Gestalt therapy's emphasis on the present experience which may work better for some people than others. For some clients, visiting their past experiences (e.g., trauma) may help them work through their negative feelings and rebuild positive experiences. Others have said that Gestalt therapy is self-centered, focusing solely on feelings and personal discovery. Finally, Gestalt therapy does not utilize diagnosis or assessment techniques (Gladding, 2004). This makes it difficult to monitor progress and change and could result in an individual receiving an inappropriate type of therapy. It is crucial for Gestalt therapists to be properly trained and supervised, lest they cause harm to clients (Gladding and Cox, 2008).

## Now

In Gestalt therapy, the present is the most significant and strongest, and individuals' power is in the present. Gestalt therapy stresses on appreciation and full experience of the present moment because nothing exists except the "now." Dwelling on the past, to Gestalt therapy, can be seen as a way to avoid coming to terms with the present. Gestalt therapy does not focus on the future, either, because the past is gone and the future has not yet arrived. Thus, a primary task individuals can do is to be fully aware to live in the here and now. By reliving the past or worrying about the future, individuals cannot be authentic and cannot come to terms with who they are.

For many people the power of the present is lost because they may focus on their past mistakes or engage in endless resolutions and plans for the future. Therapists will focus on the "what" and "how" of a person without asking the "why" questions to assist clients to stay in the present moment and to promote an awareness of the moment. Gestalt therapists also use questions such as "What is happening now?" or "What are you feeling in this moment?" to intensify the experience of the present and create awareness. In Gestalt therapy, "why" questions lead only toward rationalizations and drifting away from the immediacy of the moment to the past.

Most individuals can only stay in the present moment for a short while and tend to find ways of interrupting the flow of the present. This tendency may make individuals talk about rather than experience their feelings and then they become detached from feelings. A Gestalt therapist helps a client live their feelings rather than talk about them. They aim to assist clients to make contacts with their experiences with immediacy. Gestalt therapy proposes that people need to live the moment rather than describe it in a detached way, though the past is recognized as having an important influence on a person's present attitudes and behavior. But what is in the past is either brought into the here and now ("As you talk about this issue, what are your feeling now?"), so that a client can experience the feelings of the present moment. Therapists encourage the present time by inviting the client to bring the past into the present by reenacting it in the present. For example, a female client imagines her father across from her in a chair and tell him how she feels when he ignores her. Gestalt therapists recognize the impact of the past on the present moment mostly because of some lack of completion of the past experience.

### Unfinished business

When experiences are not completed and unresolved, individuals are left with unfinished business. The unfinished business can be manifest in unexpressed feelings such as resentment, rage, hatred, pain, anxiety, grief, guilt, and abandonment. The feelings in the past are not totally experienced in awareness, they linger in the background and are carried into the present life in ways that interfere with effective contact with oneself and others. Gestalt therapists maintain that these unfinished experiences seek completion with varied formats such as distinct memories, fantasies, preoccupation, compulsive behavior, wariness, oppressive energy, and self-defeating behavior. Unexpressed feelings can result in physical symptoms, so Gestalt therapists emphasize paying attention to the bodily experience. The effects of unfinished business are often demonstrated by some blockage in the body in the forms of physical symptoms, emotional disturbances, and so on.

Because the effects of unfinished business may create emotional disturbances which interfere with the present-centered awareness, the unfinished business prevents individuals from contacts with the present moment. The impasse is the time when the external support is not available, In Gestalt therapy, therapists' role is to accompany clients to work through this impasse without feeling frustrated. Therapists also assist clients by providing situations that encourage them to fully experience their condition of being at an impasse. By completely working through the impasse, individuals can further contact with their frustrations, accept whatever the frustrations are, and fully live in the present moment. If individuals can accomplish this task, they would not wish to be different from themselves. Moving toward self-acceptance of whatever individuals are fulfills the therapeutic principles of Gestalt therapy.

## An Integration: Positive Psychology and Gestalt Therapy

### Holism in positive psychology

Gestalt therapy stresses the holistic perspective in understanding and awareness. Gestalt therapists also attempt to help clients attain awareness through self-knowledge, take responsibility for choices, and have contact with their environment. Gestalt therapists do not analyze internal conflicts; instead, they strive to integrate these conflicts into a holistic self-awareness. In all, Gestalt therapy proposes that a natural system (i.e., a human being) and its properties (i.e., physiology, sensation, feelings, emotions, cognition, etc.) should be viewed as a whole, not as a collection of parts. This often includes the view that systems always function as wholes and so their functioning cannot be understood solely in terms of their component parts. Thus, individuals' feelings should be viewed in their holistic context involving cognition, physiology, and the like.

Positive psychology devotes itself to proactive building of personal strengths and competencies, by seeking to make people stronger and more productive thereby to actualize all their potentials. Thus, positive psychology welcomes the perspective of holism in Gestalt therapy.

Gestalt therapists may confront or challenge clients to help them gain new awareness, and therapists may take a strong stance to urge clients to be responsible for their choices. Yet, in positive psychology, counselors believe that the client is their own great expert and possesses within them an internal developmental tendency toward growth and fulfillment. And so the therapist would follow the client's agenda, seeking to promote their tendency in self-actualization, rather than considering counselors as the "expert," imposing their "expertise" on the client. Based on this perspective of help, positive psychologists welcome a broad range of therapeutic techniques, and accept the view that a person may work to facilitate the growth of another.

## "Now" in positive psychology

In Gestalt therapy, the present is the most significant, intense, and strongest point in people's life, the individuals' controlling power is in the present, and so Gestalt therapy stresses appreciation of the present moment to fully experience it, because nothing exists except the "now." Dwelling on the past is seen as a way to avoid coming to terms with the present. Gestalt therapy does not focus on the future either, because the past has gone and is nowhere, and the future has not yet arrived and is also nowhere.

In contrast, positive psychology focuses on promoting people's strengths and well-being more than the present, past, or future. Thus, for example, positive psychology welcomes people's reflections on how they worked through difficulties and thrive in the present. In positive psychology, as long as people are able to enhance their well-being, it is fine to recollect the history of how people used resilience or other characteristic strengths to motivate themselves to thrive. According to positive psychology, learning from past success to solve present problems is a character demonstrating people's persistence and wisdom. Thus, no matter whether past, current, or future issues, what is important is to increase clients' strengths toward well-being.

Integrating these two approaches, counselors can focus on the here-and-now principle of Gestalt therapy, and are at the same time be open to the issues and experiences in the past or future, when such exploration can facilitate clients' growth to develop further. Counselors incorporate positive psychology so as to facilitate clients' optimal functioning (Linley & Joseph, 2004) and plan how to solve problems and enhance strengths; all this is an application of positive psychology (Linley & Joseph, 2003).

With this integration, positive psychology now strengthens Gestalt therapy by reframing the focus of the problems, in past, present, or future. The role of a counselor, from a positive psychological perspective, is not only to serve to harvest skills to alleviate distress, treat illness, and repair weakness, but also to facilitate building strengths, promoting health, to achieve overall well-being.

For example, counselors can facilitate clients' strengths toward happiness and well-being in the "here-and-now" Gestalt framework. Counselors can promote the optimal experiences of depressed clients, rather than simply seeing them as clients in need of resolving depression. Integrated counselors can also work with angry clients in ways that recognize their needs and aspirations, thereby significantly reducing anger by redirecting sources of anger to energy toward new projects (Ward & Mann, 2004).

With the therapeutic principle of here-and-now in Gestalt therapy, counselors can apply positive psychology to balance individuality and community in order to achieve good lives for all people (Myers, 2004), and take advantage of the opportunity of preventing disorder and promoting well-being through population-based approaches (Huppert, 2004). These integrations can make Gestalt therapy and positive psychology work together for the clients' benefit.

### Unfinished business

According to Gestalt therapy's view, individuals are often trapped by struggles with unfinished business; in general, Gestalt theory tends to see such unfinished business as a negative burden on the present, which manifests in unexpressed feelings of resentment, rage, hatred, pain, anxiety, grief, guilt, and abandonment. Gestalt therapists maintain that these unfinished experiences seek completion in various forms such as peculiar memories, fantasies, preoccupations, compulsive behaviors, wariness, weariness, oppressive energy, and self-defeating behaviors. Unexpressed feelings can result in painful physical symptoms, so Gestalt therapists emphasize paying attention to bodily experience.

Positive psychology may see the unfinished business as a neutral experience. Whether there is a negative impact of the unfinished business in the past may depend on individuals' strengths or well-being. Some questions important for positive psychology are: How could people promote their strengths toward well-being despite their unfinished business? What characters of individuals may be able to manage the unfinished business?

Integrating Gestalt therapy with positive psychology, we see three points emerging. *First*, it appears that the unfinished business in Gestalt therapy mostly relates to negative impacts on the present. In contrast, positive psychology sees how there might be positive unfinished business.

For example, a moment toughing things out that had changed an individual's life could always linger in life. A stranger's smile or words of comfort may have saved someone from committing suicide, and that turning point may create a long-term impact on both people who were two strangers. Or a sweet and tender gesture of a friend may motivate people to persevere, despite various hurdles in career or life. In our daily life, such examples could form a long list, but they are mostly forgotten or taken for granted. However, if people remind themselves of those positively experienced moments, whether finished or not, they would be able to promote their strengths and well-being (Todd, 2010).

*Second*, Gestalt therapists often perceive people as passive entities being impacted negatively with unfinished business. Human beings have resilience, hope, and optimism. When encountering an unfinished business, they may be provoked and motivated to develop more resilience and perseverance to manage the unfinished business and move on in life. Or people may take the unfinished business as an important lesson, thanks to which they now reconsider life in a new way toward taking a different approach. In other words, the relation between unfinished business and people's current problems may not be linear, as proposed by Gestalt therapy. The relationship could be changed, controlled, or moderated by people's strengths and overflowing well-being.

## Multiculturalizing the Integration

### Multiculturalizing integration between holism and positive psychology

Gestalt therapy proposes that a natural system and its properties should be viewed as a "whole," and positive psychology devotes itself to a proactive buildup of personal strengths and competencies. Their integration could be to treat conflicts, positive affect, and strengths as one whole. That is, people have positive and negative experiences, and they can be viewed in the perspective of holism as components of one whole person.

Counseling multicultural clients with this integration, culturally sensitive counselors are aware that Gestalt's holism originated in Western culture and may or may not reflect world-views of multicultural clients. Thus counselors respect potential differences between holism and collectivism in which some multicultural clients live. In general, collectivism describes any moral, political, or social outlook that stresses human interdependence in a collective perspective. Collectivistic culture focuses on family, community, and society, giving priority to group goals over individuals' goals (Ponterotto, Utsey, & Pedersen, 2006).

In contrast, holism in Gestalt therapy views that the whole is greater than the sum of its parts, but the main focus is still on individual, not family or community. Thus, culturally sensitive counselors are aware of the differences of these two worldviews and respect clients' cultures and their values (Ponterotto, 2010).

To help multicultural clients gain new awareness in this integration, counselors collaborate with multicultural clients to explore what counselor roles work best for them. For example, different cultures may have different expectations of counselors. Specifically, working with Native Americans, counselors are aware of the importance of consultation with spiritual or tribe leaders. In such a way as this, culturally skilled counselors are sensitive and respect how multicultural clients' culture and value define the therapeutic relationship between clients and them.

Moreover, Gestalt therapy may incorporate some techniques such as empty chair, and positive psychology may welcome a broad range of therapeutic techniques to promote clients' strengths and well-being. However, incorporating techniques or not, counselors are aware of clients' level of readiness or comfort with their effects. Some multicultural clients may recognize counselors as "experts" and may accept incorporation of techniques in counseling, and yet others may prefer counseling with as few techniques as possible. Instead of expecting clients to follow the best therapy based on the counselor's own perspective, culturally sensitive counselors possess the awareness that different cultures have their respectively different interpretations on using techniques in counseling, and adjust the usage of techniques accordingly.

### Multiculturalizing "now" in positive psychology

In Gestalt therapy, the present is the most significant and strongest concept. Integrating with positive psychology may reinforce the importance of the present moment "here-and-now." At the same time, therapists must be aware that different cultures have respectively different time orientations due to their history and cultural backgrounds. For example,

Asian cultures tend to be oriented toward a more distant future. Mexicans and many Latin cultures, on the other hand, are more heavily influenced by the past.

Part of the difference may be related to cultural concepts of control over environment, which may in turn be related to various religious traditions. Mexico, for instance, is usually taken as a fatalistic culture where the past is in firm control of the present and future. Thus, without knowledge of the time orientation in clients' culture, counselors may miss understanding cultural differences in time. The counselors' task would be how to counsel multicultural clients with cultural sensitivity when applying the integration between Gestalt therapy and positive psychology.

Integrating these two approaches also involves the presenting problems (e.g., psychological distress, interpersonal conflict, etc.) as closely related to differences in cultural perceptions of these problems. Culturally sensitive counselors are aware that multicultural clients may need help related to their family, job, or living environment. Cultural counselors understand that some cultures have stigma on counseling itself which could be a reason for low utility of counseling among some multicultural populations.

Counselors also possess the knowledge that some cultures present mental health difficulties via physical problems. Or some cultures expect people not to reveal too much about their emotions. For example, Japanese culture expects women to be calm and gently smiling even while feeling excited. Thus, when counselors incorporate positive psychology into Gestalt therapy to facilitate multicultural clients' optimal functioning (Linley & Joseph, 2004), they are aware that different cultures have culture-specific time orientation and understanding of presenting problems in counseling.

## Multiculturalize the unfinished business

According to Gestalt therapy, individuals may be trapped by struggles with unfinished business which can manifest in unexpressed feelings of resentment, rage, hatred, pain, anxiety, grief, guilt, and abandonment. With the integration with positive psychology, there might be new or positive implications from the unfinished business. However, despite the potential help from integration, counselors still need to be cautious when counseling multicultural clients.

*First*, counselors must be aware of their own reactions toward the unfinished business and be willing to explore the meanings of the unfinished business with their culturally different clients in a nonjudgmental fashion. For example, Latin cultures are heavily influenced by the past, and so their unfinished business may be based on historic issues. It might not be surprising that clients from Latin cultures feel pain, grief, guilt, and/or abandonment due to unfinished business. Culturally skilled counselors understand the connection between Latin cultures and unfinished business and provide counseling appropriate for such cultures.

*Second*, different cultures may present unfinished business in different fashions, so counselors should actively seek information regarding how unfinished business is interpreted in their clients' culture. That is, culturally sensitive counselors take advantage of opportunities in education, training, and consultation to enhance their understanding of the unfinished business in the many cultures of their clients. They are also willing to explore the meanings and implications of the unfinished business with their specific multicultural clients.

*Third*, when exploring the meanings of the unfinished business in clients' culture, culturally skilled counselors are open to varied possibilities, including inquiring about possible positive impacts of the unfinished business in the client's culture. They thus demonstrate their openness, flexibility, and interests in the client's culture, and many topics in counseling (e.g., unfinished business). For example, when exploring the issues of unfinished business with Asian clients, counselors may use the concept of "yin-yang" to explore the impacts of unfinished business; yin represents one side (negative) of the implications of unfinished business and yang represents the other side (positive) of the implications. With such cultural knowledge, counselors can blend positive psychology into clients' culture to provide culturally appropriate intervention.

## Application in Counseling: Case Study

Betty is a 51-year-old Caucasian white woman who recently felt anxious and fearful for no specific reasons. She wanted to talk about her fear, but she could not identify what to talk about, or what was connected to "it." She had recently resigned from a job she had held for 20 years, and was in a transition period. Having been married to her husband for 15 years, they have 2 daughters. During the intake session, Betty appeared uneasy and restless. She felt anxious most of the time, though people around her envied her perfect life and perfect family, and she also denied any marital problems and reported feeling secured with her husband.

Sill, according to Betty, most of the time she felt constant worrying or obsession about small or large concerns, restlessness and keyed up, or on edge, fatigued, irritable, and had difficulty concentrating and sleeping. Betty described her typical day. In the morning, she tended to worry about things for no apparent reason. She may feel intensely worried about her husband and daughters' safety, or sometimes she may have a vague general sense that something bad is about to happen. Her husband then suggested she see her family doctor because she felt like she was worrying constantly, and these worries were interfering with her daily life. She went to see her family doctor and had a few medical tests. Her doctor did not find any physical problems to cause anxiety and fears. Her doctor referred her to a counselor to seek mental health counseling.

### How do we help Betty?

*Holism in positive psychology* Gestalt therapy stresses enhancing Betty's holistic perspective on understanding and awareness and attempts to help her attain awareness through self-knowledge. Specifically, Gestalt therapy focuses on her current experiences as a primary topic in counseling. Her counselor also explained that each and every person, including her, is linked to all things. So her knowledge that she was in relation with all things and people would help her understand who she was. During the counseling, she was introduced techniques to provide insight into ways in which she can alleviate her current anxiety and fears, and also aspire to her maximum potentials.

Later, Betty was asked if she would take responsibility for her choices of feeling anxious. At first, she was confused about taking responsibility for her fears. Her counselor explained that her anxiety or fears were not an isolated incident or just happened overnight. Instead, her fears may reflect how her feelings were in relationship with things around her. With the new self-awareness about her fears, she would understand that properties of her fears should be viewed as wholes. In other words, individuals' feelings should be viewed in their holistic context.

Despite the fact Betty may have learned of the holistic perspective about her fears, she still wanted to feel relaxed and enjoy her life. With Gestalt therapy, Betty may be only able to reduce her distress, anxiety, and fears. The symptoms-free status does not mean that she will feel happy and excited with her life. According to positive psychology, what Betty can do through counseling includes the proactive building of her personal strengths and well-being. Through positive psychology, she would be able to cultivate her character strengths and be more productive.

To help Betty gain new awareness and cultivate her strengths, her counselor used various techniques to help her meet her therapeutic goals of managing her fears and promote her positive affects. Her counselor incorporated techniques such as confrontation and challenges. Her counselor also questioned Betty's role in maintaining her anxiety and fears. At first, Betty felt it was almost impossible to be responsible for her anxiety. Yet, her counselor mentioned that without taking responsibility, it would be difficult to move on to gain new awareness about her problems. In other words, when Betty was willing to reflect on her role in her anxiety and how such anxiety relates to her life, she had taken her first step to gain new insights to manage her distress.

Through positive psychology, Betty's next step in counseling was to learn and acknowledge that she could be her own best expert and possess an internal tendency to live her fullest life. Collaborating with her counselor, Betty noticed the significant role of taking responsibility for her choice. For example, her general worry could be the choice she made and the anxiety could indicate that she needed to take responsibility. With this awareness, she felt more ready to pursue her positive affect. This means in practice that her counselor would collaborate with her on her own agenda which could be an opportunity to set up her own goals and directions in counseling. When Betty learned to own her counseling, she noticed that her self-confidence and self-esteem also increased. Instead of continuously worrying about many things, she learned to refocus her attention on herself.

Because Betty's primary goal was to promote her strengths and well-being, according to positive psychology, she might benefit from a broad range of therapeutic techniques such as "use your signature strengths," "three good things," "list of gratitude," and so on. "Use your signature strengths" refers to a habit that Betty learned to identify her top five strengths and try to use them in some new way daily. Her top strengths include caring, being sincere, resilient, and hopeful. She also tried to write down three good things that happened that day and think about why they happened. About a few times a week, she renewed her list of gratitude. This list includes writing a letter or note to someone explaining why she felt grateful for something that the person has done. Or she may send a card to her friend to appreciate her care and friendship. She also expressed her gratitude to her husband, daughters, and other family members. During each session, she shared techniques or activities with her counselor and planned if she wanted to explore new techniques in positive psychology.

*"Now" in positive psychology* When counseling Betty, her counselor explained that in Gestalt therapy the present is the most significant and strongest concept, and people's power is in the present. Instead of regretting the past, Betty can fully focus on her current experience of the present moment because nothing exists except the "now." That means that the focus of staying in the present moment facilitated Betty's awareness of the feelings and emotions associated with the moment, including her worries, anxiety, and fears, with or without reason.

Instead of forming conjectures or assumptions as to the unknown past, Betty learned to stay with her present feelings. In addition, staying at the "here-and-now" moment, Betty was able to learn how to define what is truly experienced versus what is merely an interpretation of the events. When she became fully aware of this difference, she was ready to identify which patterns, thoughts, emotions, and behaviors that she wanted to change, as days go by.

On the foundation of focusing on the present moment, Betty further learned to build her strengths to manage her anxious feelings. Yet, positive psychology appears open to different time orientations, past, present, and future since it stresses promoting people's well-being. Even though these two approaches may have distinct time orientations, Betty felt comfortable to rebuild her strengths in the present moment. She would continue the techniques of positive psychology she learned during the counseling sessions, one at a time.

With emphasis on "now," she learned to be responsible for her choice. For example, she learned to choose to reverse her focus from negative worries, fears, etc. to positive affects, relaxation, belief, etc. Whenever she regressed back to her negative thoughts, her counselor showed her a coin telling her that things have positive and negative aspects, and it is up to her to focus on the positive side.

Within the orientation of the present moment, Betty now learned to develop a language of strength to promote her positive affect. Recognizing the new pattern of thinking, her counselor incorporated the practice of language of strength into the counseling. For example, when Betty said "I am a failure" more than a few times, her counselor reminded her of switching the focus to the language of strength such as "I will finish it." To enhance the usage of language of strength, Betty invited her husband and daughters to remind her of herself when she fell into her negative pattern of talk.

Integrating with Gestalt therapy, Betty noticed that she could take responsibility for her good as well as bad choices. Many people feel angry when Gestalt therapists mention taking responsibility for choices they made. However, such one-sided reaction demonstrates that people forgot that they would also be responsible for choices which resulted in positive outcomes. Thus, to be responsible for choices means a true acceptance. Similarly, positive and negative thoughts, emotions, and behaviors are part of being human. Although positive psychology stresses cultivation of strengths, it does not mean to diminish our negative thoughts. Instead of dismissing negative aspects of ourselves, people might need to accept their negative aspects and listen to their message, the need to launch out in a positive direction directed by negative affects.

Within the "here-and-now" position, Betty learned to build strategies that foster hope. She began with finding ways to foster her hope in managing her anxiety. She was thankful for the new insight that she needed to be responsible for her choices. In accepting that her anxiety should be her responsibility, such true acceptance appeared to reduce her symptoms. She then identified skills and coping mechanisms that would enable her to overcome her constant worries. She now felt comfortable requesting people's help rather than perceiving herself as a failure.

*Unfinished business* According to Gestalt therapy, Betty was struggling with unfinished business. Such a struggle could be a reason for her negative experiences at the present. Worse, her unfinished business can manifest in unexpressed feelings such as resentment, rage, hatred, pain, anxiety, grief, guilt, and abandonment. Thus, her constant worries may be a result of her struggle with unfinished businesses. Or else, her unfinished businesses were presented in various forms of preoccupation, overly worries, compulsive behaviors, fatigue, oppressive energy, and self-defeating behaviors.

As she recognizes her unfinished businesses, Betty might be able to gain a better understanding of how connected emotional and physical responses are. For example, before seeking counseling, she tended to feel anxious, fearful, physically fatigued, and had difficulty concentrating. With the understanding of her internal self, Betty gained the key to understanding actions, reactions, and behaviors. Thus this awareness of her unfinished businesses and understanding of their impacts can promote Betty's acceptance of these patterns.

With the acceptance of unfinished businesses and their impacts, Betty can now learn to move beyond the unfinished businesses. That is, with a new perspective, she would now learn to appreciate those unfinished businesses and impacts. For example, because of her unfinished businesses, she learned that she has not completed her journey on particular topics. With positive psychology, she now learns to see her unfinished businesses with positive as well as negative perspectives. She could also reflect on some important questions, "How could I promote my strengths or well-being despite the unfinished business?" "What characters of mine can be used to manage the unfinished business?" "What did I learn from my unfinished businesses?"

Taken together, four points emerge out of integrating Gestalt therapy with positive psychology in counseling Betty. *First*, as Betty learned various techniques in positive psychology, she could also apply those techniques to unfinished businesses. For example, she might have not written a note to appreciate her friend who came to visit her two weeks ago. Or she may remember that she has not finished her conversation with a church member who was struggling with a new job. That is, with positive psychology, Betty might find that she has various *positive* unfinished business that she can enjoy finishing. When she reminded herself of these unfinished businesses, she felt very grateful that she has the energy and time to help others. Now in her daily life, such examples could make a long list and could replace her list of worries.

*Second*, in Gestalt therapy, Betty may be conceptualized as a passive entity being impacted negatively with unfinished businesses, but this approach cannot assist Betty to develop her *positive* affects. Indeed, Betty has various dimensions of mentality, anxiety, distress, as well as positive feelings such as happiness, hope, and optimism. When encountering her unfinished business, Betty learned to accept them and develop more resilience and perseverance to manage them. Betty could also take these unfinished businesses as a reminder to build her strengths and well-being. Or else, she could take her unfinished business as a lesson and in its light consider her life with a new different approach. In other words, the relationship between her unfinished businesses and her current mentality may not be linear (negative), as proposed by Gestalt therapy. The relationship could be managed by her strengths in a positive direction toward well-being.

### Follow-up: You continue as Betty's counselor

Consider how you will help Betty if you were her counselor. Here are a series of questions to provide some structure in your thinking about her case:

- How would you continue encouraging Betty to focus on thoughts and feelings being experienced in the moment?
- Would you shift your focus to help Betty solve her issues in the past? What are the pros and cons if you do so?
- Would you consider applying holism in Gestalt therapy and positive psychology to increase Betty's awareness and well-being?
- Would you consider using several language, game, and fantasy methods in order to maintain the focus on the here and now? Would you use some exercises to increase Betty's positive emotions?
- Based on your understanding about Betty, what strengths would you help her develop?

## Concluding Remarks

According to Fritz Perls, what is most important is the thoughts and feelings people are experiencing in the moment. Viewing the person as a total organism, Perls believed that full awareness of self could be curative. With a high level of concentration, most healthy people can solve problems and resolve conflicts with others. In Gestalt therapy, the key to successful adjustment is the development of personal responsibility – responsibility for one's life and response to one's environment. Gestalt therapists facilitate clients' ability to attend and to be in touch with the present by using direct experiences. Thus, the deeper awareness promotes a sense of living fully in the here and now. Moreover, positive psychology goes beyond Gestalt therapy and welcomes people's reflections on how they worked through difficulties and thrive in the present. Gestalt therapy advises people not to dwell on unfinished businesses, but positive psychology proposes to help clients reframe their unfinished businesses into new opportunities for growth. Positive psychology also believes that unfinished conflicts with others could be opportunities for new relationships. What is important is to find a reasonable balance between choices, freedom, and responsibility in their lives.

To serve multicultural clients, it is inevitable to multiculturalize this integration, which could begin with counselors' awareness of their values, beliefs, and biases. Counselors also possess knowledge whether this integration between Gestalt therapy and positive psychology fits with clients' cultures. Culturally skilled counselors are also competent in exploring how different cultures present awareness, here-and-now focus, and responsibility.

## Review Questions: What Do You Think?

1. Some Gestalt therapists focus solely on the here-and-now. Explain the benefits and the disadvantages of this approach. How important are the past and the future? Does this approach miss something in not focusing on them?
2. Would you discuss the unfinished business with clients?
3. How would you promote clients' well-being if they refuse to take responsibility for their decisions?
4. Different cultures have their respective time orientations. How would you connect their preferred time orientations with Gestalt therapy's "here-and-now"?

# 10

# Behavior Therapy

**Learning Objectives**

- Explain the historical background of behavior therapy.
- Identify four major models within behavior therapy.
- Learn about the assumptions regarding behavioral disorders.
- Demonstrate specific therapeutic methods in behavior therapy.
- Learn about the deterministic model in behavior therapy and how positive psychology can complement this model.
- Learn about how positive psychology can help manage behavioral disorders.
- Multiculturalize the integration between behavior therapy and positive psychology.
- Apply the integration to a case study.

Behavior therapy includes a spectrum of behavior modification techniques applied as therapy, such as operant conditioning, aversion therapy, extinction, desensitization, and modeling. Behavior therapy incorporates assessment, evaluation, and treatment, and it has been used successfully with a variety of populations (e.g., adults, children, adolescents) in diverse settings (e.g., hospitals, psychiatric facilities, mental health centers, schools). Behavior therapy has been used to treat various problems (e.g., depression, addiction, anxiety, social skills difficulties, interpersonal problems, academic skills), and behavior therapists feel comfortable addressing a wide range of human behaviors. While other approaches in psychotherapy such as psychoanalysis probe a client's recollected history, behavior therapy focuses mainly on immediate behavior and aims to eliminate undesired

*Counseling Psychology: An Integrated Positive Psychological Approach*, First Edition. Ruth Chu-Lien Chao.

behavior and produce desired behavior. Such behavior change derives from methods instilled by the experimental analysis of behavior and from reinforcement theory. Behavior therapy is more mechanical, creating systems of reinforcement and conditioning that may work to help clients reduce their undesired behaviors.

Compared with other therapeutic approaches in counseling, behavior therapy has the broadest sense in that its methods focus on behaviors, not on the thoughts and feelings that might be causing them. To date, behavior therapy breaks down into two disciplines: one is a more narrowly defined sense of behavior therapy and the other is behavior modification. Within the psychological theories of learning and conditioning, behavior therapy generally treats psychological disorders with Pavlovian or respondent conditioning, while behavior modification makes use of operant or instrumental conditioning. These distinctions are not absolute with some crossover occurring in practice (Kazdin, 1979).

## Historical Context

Since the early 1960s, behavior therapy has appeared in several important publications. Related terms, such as behavior modification, also began to be used more frequently during the 1960s. In 1963, the first scientific journal devoted to behavior therapy (*Behavior Research and Therapy*) was published, and in 1966, the Association for Advancement of Behavior Therapy (AABT) was formed, with Cyril Franks as the founding president. Since its inception, a number of terms, with somewhat different connotations, have been used almost interchangeably to denote the field (Cautela & Kearney, 1986). In addition to behavior therapy, some practitioners and therapists use terms such as behavior modification, applied behavior analysis, social learning theory, and clinical behavior therapy. Attempts to clarify or standardize the meaning of the various terms based on the populations served (e.g., individual or group), techniques used (e.g., systematic desensitization, contingency management), methodologies (e.g., single-subject designs), or theoretical bases (e.g., classical conditioning, operant conditioning) have failed to gain wide acceptance. In this book, we will use "behavior therapy" and exchange it with other terms when necessary.

Historically, several formal definitions of behavior therapy have been proposed. For example, Wolpe (1982) defined behavior therapy as "the use of experimentally established principles and paradigms of learning to overcome [maladaptive] habits" (p. 1). Moreover, Wolpe and Lazarus (1966) wrote:

> While the modern behavior therapist deliberately applies principles of learning to this therapeutic operation, empirical behavior therapy is probably as old as civilization – if we consider civilization as having begun when man first did things to further the well-being of other men. From the time that this became a feature of human life there must have been occasions when a man complained of his ills to another who advised or persuaded him of a course of action. In a broad sense, this could be called behavior therapy whenever the behavior itself was conceived as the therapeutic agent. Ancient writings contain innumerable behavioral prescriptions that accord with this broad conception of behavior therapy (p. 1).

Whereas Wolpe and Lazarus's definition emphasizes a theoretical basis of behavior therapy, other definitions stress the methods of inquiry used by behavior therapists. For example, Ross (1985) believed that behavior therapy is "the empirically controlled application of the science of human behavior to the alleviation of psychological distress and the modification of maladaptive behavior" (p. 196). This definition reflects the growing acceptance of methodological behaviorism, which focuses on the methods used in obtaining psychological information. Such a definition, however, does not delineate behavior therapy from other construct systems that might also use methods of empirical inquiry.

According to Kazdin and Wilson (1978), it is a difficult process to reach a common definition useful for most practitioners and researchers:

> Contemporary behavior therapy is marked by a diversity of views, a broad range of heterogeneous procedures with different theoretical rationales, and open debate about conceptual bases, methodological requirements, and evidence of efficacy. In short, there is no clearly agreed upon or commonly accepted definition of behavior therapy (p. 1).

Despite the difficulties in reaching a commonly accepted definition in behavior therapy, there are at least four major models within behavior therapy that can be identified: (1) applied behavior analysis; (2) neobehavioristic mediational model; (3) social learning theory; and (4) cognitive-behavior therapy (Kazdin, 1979). The models differ on the bases of theories, fundamental principles, and therapeutic procedures.

## Applied behavior analysis

Applied behavior analysis draws heavily from the Skinner tradition of operant conditioning. Behavior is assumed to be under the control of environmental stimuli. These controlling stimuli include the consequences of behavior as well as the antecedent events that are associated with differential consequences. Intervention involves the manipulation of the controlling environmental stimuli in order to modify overt behavior. Therapeutic procedures are based on principles derived from operant conditioning such as reinforcement, punishment, extinction, and stimulus control. The token economy, in which appropriate behaviors earn tokens that later can be exchanged for desired activities, consumable goods, and privileges, is a procedure representative of applied behavior analysis.

## Neobehavioristic mediational model

The neobehavioristic mediational model is based primarily on the principles of classical conditioning derived from the learning theories of Pavlov, Hull, and Mowrer (Wolpe, 1982). The model emphasizes the role of anxiety as a conditioned emotional response. For example, the anxiety response can be elicited by previously neutral stimuli as a result of pairing those neutral stimuli with noxious stimuli. Therapeutic procedures such as systematic desensitization and flooding are designed to reduce the anxiety underlying behavioral disorders by exposing the individual to the conditioned, feared stimulus in the absence of the noxious stimulus.

### Social learning theory

This model, social learning theory (Bandura, 1977a, 1977b) includes three interacting systems to regulate behavior. The first system is external stimulus control, which regulates behavior either through the association of stimuli, as in classical conditioning, or through antecedent stimuli reliably predicting differential consequences of behavior. Response feedback, primarily in the form of reinforcing consequences, provides a second regulatory system. Finally, cognitive processes mediate the effect of external events by influencing which events are attended to and how those events are perceived and interpreted. An important cognitive mediator of behavior change is self-efficacy, the expectation that the behavior required to produce an outcome can be performed. Social learning theory further posits that human functioning is a result of the reciprocal interaction among behavior, the environment, and a person's cognitions (Bandura, 1981). That is, not only does the environment influence behavior, but a person's behavior also influences the environment. Modeling of the desired behavior by the therapist, either with or without the client's subsequent performance, is a therapeutic procedure derived from social learning theory's emphasis on cognitive processes such as the capacity to learn through observation.

### Cognitive-behavior therapy

A fairly recent development in behavior therapy is the emergence of cognitive-behavior therapy (Beck, 1976; Mahoney, 1974). According to this model, it is the perception of events rather than the events themselves that most influence behavior. Further, adaptive and maladaptive patterns are acquired through cognitive processes. Thus irrational beliefs, errors of logic, faulty self-talk, dysfunctional attributions, and mental representations of one's self and one's world contribute to behavioral and emotional disorders. Cognitive restructuring, in which clients are taught to examine and change faulty cognitions, is a representative procedure used in cognitive-behavior therapy. Cognitive-behavior therapy has become the treatment of choice for several adult and childhood disorders, including panic, phobic, and obsessive-compulsive disorders. It has also dominated outcome research on psychological therapy (Wilson, 1997). Because of its significant influence in psychology and counseling, we will describe the cognitive-behavior therapy in detail in the next chapter.

## View of Human Nature

Behavior therapy is based on a scientific view of human behavior that suggests a systematic and structured approach to counseling and therapy. This view of human nature does not rest on the deterministic assumption that humans are merely a product of their social conditions. Rather, behavior therapy claims that an individual is the producer and product of his or her environment. Kazdin (1984) argues that the major characteristics of behaviors include the primacy of behavior, especially a concentration or overt concentration in particular. Behavior therapy also emphasizes the importance of learning and that all behaviors adaptive or maladaptive are learned. Behavior therapy maintains the necessity of developing procedures that give control to individuals and to increase their sense of freedom. Behavior therapy aims to increase individuals' skills to have more options for responding. According to behavior therapy, as behavior therapy is applied, it will increase individuals' freedom.

Theoretically, behavior therapy is the opposite of existential therapy. Behavior therapy claims a strict stimulus-response or response-consequence relationship of behavior model. This strict relationship has been criticized by existentialism that focuses on freedom to choose. For example, Bandura (1986) rejects the deterministic and mechanical model of behavior therapy which fails to take into account people's capacity to affect their environment. Behavior therapy's view of human nature includes three features. First, it describes individuals as being asked to act rather than passively reflect on environmental conditions. Individuals are assisted to take specific actions to change their lives. Second, more and more behaviorists are concerned about how environmental conditions are mediated through individuals' cognitions or thoughts. Third, increasing emphasis is placed on the role of responsibility for an individual's behavior. In other words, more focus is put on individuals' choices of specific behaviors rather than the other behaviors, and learning can be an effective means of changing.

Based on a scientific approach, behavior therapists believe the necessity of directive and active nature of treatments and highlight the importance of assessments and evaluation. For behavioral therapy, adaptive or maladaptive behavior mostly comes from learning, and maladaptive behavior itself is seen as the problem that needs to be changed, rather than looking for some elusive underlying cause Behavior therapy also suggests that therapeutic goals are well defined and rigorous and behaviorists stress the importance of obtaining empirical evidence and support for the techniques.

## Theoretical Principles

Despite the diversity of models in the behavioral construct system and the inability to provide a single definition of behavior therapy, a number of characteristics and assumptions can be delineated (Agras, 1997; Groth-Marnat, 2009; Kazdin & Hersen, 1980). No one of these characteristics is definitive of the field, nor does any one necessarily differentiate behavior therapy from other systems. Nevertheless, taken together, they represent the common core of behavior therapy. By nature, behavioral therapies are based on empirical (data-driven) evidences, contextual (focused on the environment and context), functional (interested in the effect or consequence of a behavior), statistically predictable, and focusing on relationship between stimuli and effects.

Overall, there are a few assumptions in behavior therapy regarding methods of inquiry: One, there is a commitment to empiricism and scientific methodology as the primary basis for developing and evaluating concepts and therapeutic techniques. Two, there is a commitment to an explicit, testable, and falsifiable conceptual foundation. Three, the therapeutic procedures and hypotheses with sufficient precision to make evaluation, replication, and generalization possible are specified. Four, there are close ties to the experimental findings of the science of psychology. Five, there is a low level of inference about data so as to minimize biases.

Regarding the behavioral disorders, behavior therapy also has its assumptions (Kazdin, 1979):

One, there is a deterministic model of behavior in which environmental antecedents and consequences are assumed to have the greatest impact on behavior. Recently, interactional models have been introduced in which behavior, the environment, and the person (most notably cognitive events and physiological conditions) are all presumed to influence one another.

Two, there is an emphasis on current determinants of behavior as opposed to historical determinants (i.e., early childhood experiences).

Three, the same principles that govern normal behavior also govern abnormal behavior. That is, no qualitative difference separates normal from abnormal behavior.

Four, there are multiple determinants of behavior. The determinants of behavioral disorders may vary from individual to individual, and from one disorder to another.

Five, behavior therapy rejects the disease model that the abnormal behavior is a symptom of an underlying illness. Instead, dysfunctional behavior is construed as a "problem in living" or as learned, maladaptive behavior. Thus the dysfunctional behavior itself is targeted for behavior change.

Six, psychological disorders can be expressed in behavioral, cognitive, and affective modes. These modes can converse to differing degrees owing to situational factors and individual differences.

Seven, there is the relative specificity of behavior to the situation in which it occurs as opposed to the belief that behavior is consistent across situations.

## Therapeutic methods

Based on the principles and procedures of the scientific approach, behavior therapy uses the methods below to facilitate behavior change:

*Systematic desensitization* Systematic desensitization is a method used in behavior therapy to help clients effectively manage phobias and anxiety disorders. More specifically, systematic desensitization is an application of classical conditioning developed by Joseph Wolpe. In the process of systematic desensitization, one must first be taught relaxation skills in order to extinguish fear and anxiety responses to specific phobias. Once the individual has been taught these skills, he or she must use them to manage situations in a hierarchy of fears. The goal of systematic desensitization is that an individual will learn to cope and overcome the fear in each step of the hierarchy, which will lead to overcoming the last step of the fear in the hierarchy. Because of the nature of hierarchy of fears, systematic desensitization is also called graduated exposure therapy.

*Flooding* Flooding in behavior therapy is based on the principles of respondent conditioning. Because of its nature of long-time exposure to stimulus, it is also referred to as prolonged exposure therapy. As a technique in counseling and therapy, it is used to treat phobias and various anxiety disorders such as panic disorders. During the process of flooding, clients are exposed to their painful experiences, with the purpose of incorporating their repressed emotions with their current awareness and control. Flooding was invented in 1967 by Thomas Stampfl (Leitenberg, 1990).

Compared with systematic desensitization, flooding is a faster method of ridding fears. When using flooding in treatment, a psychologist puts a person in a situation where they face their phobia at its worst to show clients how irrational such fear or phobia is. Under controlled conditions and using relaxation techniques, clients attempt to replace their fear with relaxation.

*Covert sensitization* Covert sensitization is a technique in which an undesirable behavior is paired with an unpleasant image in order to eliminate that behavior. Grounded in learning theory, covert sensitization is a treatment based on the principle that all behaviors are learned and that undesirable behaviors can be unlearned under the right circumstances. During the process of covert sensitization, an aversive stimulus in the form of an unpleasant image is paired with an undesirable behavior to change that behavior. It is best understood as a mixture of both the classical and the operant conditioning categories of learning (Kearney, 2006). Additionally, the goal of covert sensitization is to directly eliminate the undesirable behavior itself, unlike insight-oriented counseling that focuses on uncovering unconscious motives in order to produce change. The behaviors targeted for modification are often referred to as "maladaptive approach behaviors," which includes behaviors such as alcohol abuse, drug abuse, and smoking, pathological gambling, overeating, sexual deviations, and sexually based nuisance behaviors such as obscene phone calling. The type of behavior to be changed and the characteristics of the aversive imagery to be used influence the treatment, which is usually administered in an outpatient setting either by itself or as a component of a multimodal program. Self-administered homework assignments are almost always part of the treatment package. Some therapists incorporate covert sensitization with hypnosis in the belief that outcome is enhanced.

*Exposure and response prevention* Exposure and response prevention is a technique for clients with difficulties such as obsessive-compulsive disorder, phobias, and other types of anxiety disorders. Exposure and response prevention is developed from the concept that a treatment is achieved as clients confront their own fears and discontinue using their avoidance as coping. This process is also called Pavlovian extinction or respondent extinction. The therapist will expose clients to their feared stimulus (e.g., leaving stove turned on), and refuses to respond with any safety behaviors. The resolution to refrain from the escape response is to be maintained at all times and not just during practice sessions. Thus, the clients experience habituation to the feared stimulus and practice a fear-incompatible behavioral response to the stimulus.

*Contingency management* Contingency management is a technique in behavior therapy used in the treatment for clients with issues in substance abuse, addition, and/or mental health problems. With the technique of contingency management, clients' behaviors are rewarded when they follow program rules and regulations or their treatment plan. They may be punished if they fail to follow the rules. Contingency management to date produces strong empirical evidence regarding treatment effectiveness.

*Habit reversal training* Habit reversal training is a behavioral treatment package to address a wide variety of repetitive and habitual behavioral problems such as nail biting, skin picking, thumb sucking, and so on. Habit reversal training includes five steps: awareness training; relaxation training; competing response training; contingency management; and generalization training.

## An Integration: Positive Psychology and Behavior Therapy

People may question whether behavior therapy and positive psychology are identical, since both are keen on empirical studies to obtain evidence to support empirical techniques for therapeutic intervention. The answer to this question would be yes and no. First, yes, both are identical in their commitment to empirical exploration in scientific inquiry. Behavior therapy is committed to empiricism and scientific methodology as the primary basis to develop concepts and evaluate them. Positive psychology also shares reliance on scientific study and empirical research to support statements and techniques. Further, both approaches strive after clear conceptual foundations. Behavior therapy is committed to an explicit, testable, and falsifiable conceptual foundation; positive psychology welcomes rigorous analysis to support its propositions.

However, both are not wholly identical concerning empirical exploration; the answer to the question whether both approaches are scientifically identical is no. This is because the primary goal of behavior therapy is to treat and repair problems, while positive psychology aims at promoting individuals' well-being by enhancing their strengths. Thus, both behavior therapy and positive psychology thoroughly take advantage of scientific methodology, but they differ completely on areas in which scientific inquiries are used.

For behavior therapy, the therapy begins with a client's problems and ends in successfully treating the client's problem, all by using scientific methodology. In contrast, for positive psychology, while pursuing empirical evidence, treatment and problem-free are not equivalent to good quality of life, well-being, and internal joy of the client. What is important is to utilize the rigorous scientific methodology to assess how far the clients have advanced in well-being, to help further plan on promoting their strengths toward well-being.

### Deterministic model and positive psychology

In behavior therapy, behavioral disorders are assumed to be influenced by environmental antecedents, even though determinants of behavioral disorders may vary from individual to individual and from one disorder to another. Moreover, behavior therapy emphasizes the present moment such as the current determinants of behavior as opposed to historical determinants (i.e., early childhood experiences).

In contrast, for positive psychology, the above linear relationship proceeding from environmental antecedents to behavior problems appears rigidly limited and not appropriate to reality. Worse yet, importantly, such a one-dimensional deterministic relationship cannot explain why some people thrive under so many various and serious traumas, continuing to maintain their well-being. Besides, this linear rigid relationship cannot answer many questions such as why some people choose to forgive those who hurt them, why some people persevere and work harder toward their goals while facing numerous failures. For example, Thomas Edison failed countless times before he succeeded in inventing a single light bulb. If people actually behave as predicted by the linear relationship between previous negative antecedents and equally negative behavioral consequences, Edison should never have invented the light bulb! Thus, this simple relationship of behaviorism fails to give a rationale as to why people defy failures, oppositions, pressure, and difficulties to persist in their work to succeed in attaining their dream.

Since positive psychology focuses on people's strengths more than weaknesses, it would help practitioners and researchers to understand why the behavioral linear relationship from antecedents to consequences cannot explain how people thrive against difficulties. Elimination of the behavioral lineal model would encourage counselors and clients to proceed scheming toward using the clients' many varied strengths to struggle with presenting problems to work hard to promote well-being and maintain it. Counselors would now be free to help clients be aware of their strengths and proudly recognize their inherent strengths independent of clients' environmental antecedents responsible for their current affects, negative and positive.

This point is worth emphasizing again. Behavior therapy may focus on how environmental antecedents influence behavioral consequences (A --> C). Although environmental issues could significantly impact behavior or emotional outcomes, it is still limited at justifying why some people succeed despite various barriers or why some people enjoy life despite having a low income. The "B" as belief that includes strengths and well-being stressed in positive psychology must be added to "A --> C" to explain why some people are able to maintain low psychological distress due to their strengths or feelings of well-being.

In counseling, while it is impossible to change environmental antecedents or external factors which contribute to psychological disturbances, Figure 10.1 also demonstrates that when clients learn to recognize and use their strengths, they may have better management over the impacts of environmental antecedents on their disturbances, emotional or psychological. In this way, integration of behavior therapy with positive psychology would

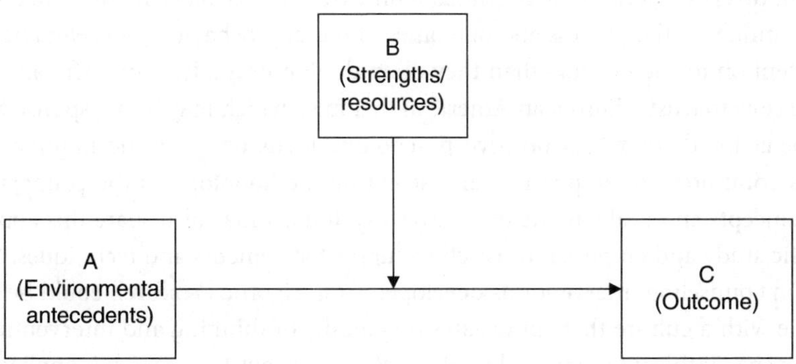


**Figure 10.1** The role of strengths/resources in the environmental antecedents-outcome relationship.

help counselors and clients understand the impact of antecedents on mentality while, more importantly, further highlighting that clients' strengths and/or well-being may buffer against or even reduce the impacts of antecedents.

### The role of dysfunctional behavior

In behavior therapy, psychological disorders or behavioral problems are construed as learned and can be explained with learning theories. And so, behavior therapy usually applies learning theories or principles to explain maladaptive behaviors and treat dysfunctional activities by targeting and effecting behavior change. Moreover, psychological disorders can be expressed in behavioral, cognitive, and affective modes. Such interpretation demonstrates two points. *First*, if psychological disorders or behavioral problems are the outcomes of learning, clients can also learn to cultivate positive affects, positive thoughts, and positive behavior. That is, while counselors attempt to "treat" or "fix" clients' dysfunctional behaviors, it is equally important for counselors to promote clients' positive behaviors. When clients learn to develop positive affects into functional behaviors, these positive changes would in turn become positive "stimuli" or "antecedents" to other positive reactive consequences.

*Second*, based on learning principles, behavior therapists attempt to fix clients' maladaptive behaviors. Now, when such approach integrates with positive psychology, mental health professionals can also "fix" strengths, celebrating inherent strengths clients have demonstrated or learned in counseling. "Fixing" thus goes both ways, negative and positive, inter-enhancing. Taken together, the integration of behavior therapy and positive psychology by no means implies minimizing the importance of behavior therapy but, on the contrary, such integration would enrich behavior therapy with a focus on clients' strengths toward enhancing their efforts to promote their well-being and maintain it consistently.

## Multiculturalizing the Integration

In general, behavior therapy has been criticized of lacking multicultural sensitivity. In other words, behavior therapists need to become more responsive to specific issues pertaining to all forms of diversity. Because race, gender, ethnicity, and sexual orientation are critical variables that influence the process and outcomes of therapy, behavior counselors need to pay greater attention to such factors than they often do. For example, some African American clients are slow to trust a European American therapist, which may be a response to racism.

Both behavior therapy and positive psychology focus on scientific inquiry. Behavior therapy is committed to empiricism and scientific methodology as the primary basis to develop concepts and evaluate them; positive psychology may also share this appreciation of scientific study and empirical research to support statements and techniques. Scientific inquiries in counseling interventions developed from rigorous research could be rendered compatible with a culture that appreciates this model of thinking and intervention. But it might hit a snag if this intervention based on Western scientific research is applied to those clients in non-Western cultures who have no exposure to such modes of thinking.

Thus, culturally sensitive counselors are well aware that while some cultures can easily connect to scientific inquiries and scientific thinking mode, other cultures may have their preferred thinking styles based on their history that differs from science in the West. Counselors also are aware that for some multicultural clients, indigenous healing might work best for them, and respect this approach and follow it.

According to behavior therapy, the primary focus in counseling is to treat and fix problems, but positive psychology endeavors to promote individuals' well-being. Integration of these two approaches may enable counselors to use behavioral techniques to enhance people's strengths toward well-being. However, for multicultural clients, counselors are aware that behavioral techniques could be new or even strange to them. In other words, counselors have to move from being culturally unaware to being aware and sensitive to different ways of accepting behavioral techniques by clients, and thereby to adjust those techniques appropriately.

In addition to the manners of acceptance of behavioral techniques, the other issue is what topics should be covered in behavior therapy. While behavior therapy operates on a deficit model, proposing to treat problems, positive psychology, on the opposite end, suggests that counselors need to promote positive affects and strengths of clients. As counselors put these approaches together to counsel multicultural clients, it is important to explore with clients their priority in counseling.

Multicultural clients may find themselves strapped with varied sorts of struggles (Cole, Piercy, Wolfe, & West, 2014) as related to their backgrounds. For example, even in our twenty-first century, African Americans are still facing age-old discrimination. They are still suffering under various injustices of discrimination and stereotypes. An example can easily be given. Unemployment among black people is double that of white people with identical qualifications, as some companies still hire predominantly white people. Racial discrimination is also a serious problem in the US judicial system. About 98 percent of the judges are white. Black men are eight times more likely to be put in prison than white men; 74 percent of death sentences are meted out to black men. Living in overwhelming experiences of discrimination, African Americans would understandably be vulnerable to stresses, as almost all comments and impressions they get from others could be negatively deteriorating.

Culturally skilled counselors have knowledge about how oppression, racism, and discrimination affect people personally and in the midst of their work. So, different from comments these discriminated people usually heard, positive intervention from counselors may promote their self-esteem, strengths, and well-being. Moreover, although the integration between behavior therapy and positive psychology can clearly provide treatment to reduce symptoms and promote clients' good quality of life, such integration should be provided in a culturally appropriate manner.

## Deterministic model and positive psychology in multicultural context

In behavior therapy, behavioral disorders are assumed to be influenced if not determined by environmental antecedents, but such assumption may not be shared by multicultural cultures. For example, some cultures believe that behavior disorders are related to physical discomfort, or spiritual problems as religious issues.

Moreover, importantly, many underrepresented and marginalized clients endure various environmental limitations, and yet they still thrive against environmental, language, and/or cultural barriers. Thus, the straight linear relationship between environmental antecedents and behavioral disorders would be unable to understand multicultural clients. Therefore, culturally skilled counselors recognize that, although the deterministic model in behavior therapy can provide some rationale for the behavior problems of multicultural clients, this model insufficiently reflects the role of cultures on behavioral disorders. Culturally sensitive counselors are aware that behavior therapy originating in Western culture can at most only provide very limited explanations on culturally different clients' behavioral disorders. Culturally skilled counselors appreciate other culturally relevant explanations, so as to incorporate these different cultural explanations into their specific counseling with multicultural clients.

Although, environmental antecedents, such as difficulties to access mental health facility, may not invariably result in behavioral disorders, counselors are aware that multicultural people may have their culture-related resources that may protect them from environmental limitations, and even help them thrive despite numerous problems. How multicultural people thrive against various barriers or hurdles can be explained by positive psychology.

For positive psychology, the linear relationship from environmental antecedents to behavior problems appears rigid and limited. For example, an African American teenager may have to contemplate dropping out of school due to her pregnancy. However, her support from family and church may serve as her buffer and help her continue her schooling and then become a successful manager. Thus, the behavioral linear relationship is insufficient in this situation, as this linear relationship is unable to take into consideration an extra factor of support and culture-specific resources.

Another example is Asian culture that endorses perseverance under repeated failures and endurance through difficulties. When Asians suffer from ordeals, they may choose to silently tolerate the ordeals and to grit their teeth to finish difficult projects. In the behavioral deterministic model, Asians would have given up working on their extremely difficult project. Culturally sensitive counselors have knowledge about such culture-specific resources these multicultural clients possess. Culturally skilled counselors possess knowledge about clients' cultural heritage and culture-specific resources, and how such culture-specific resources can be utilized to help multicultural clients survive through difficulties.

Thus, although environmental issues could understandably make an impact on behaviors or emotions, this straight model of environmental causation is still limited, unable to give adequate rationale on how some multicultural people succeed despite various barriers or why some people enjoy life despite living at the poverty level. How environmental antecedents influence behavioral consequences (A--> C) can only very limitedly explain how multicultural people thrive against various barriers. What is missing here is their culture-specific resources, shown as "B" (see Figure 10.2). The "B" for multicultural people includes resources related to their culture such as their culture-specific social network, energizing foods, festivals, family support, culturally relevant coping with support of friends.

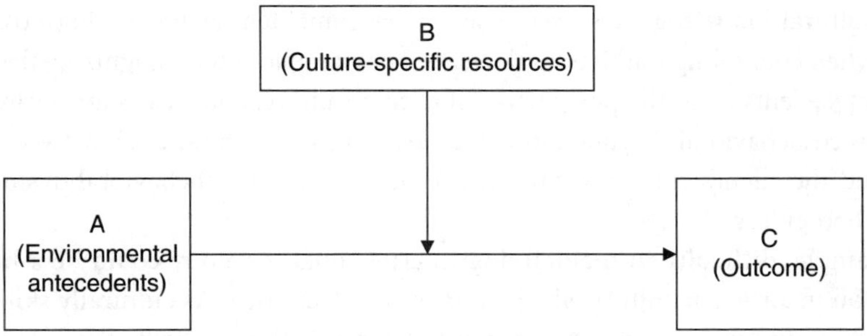


**Figure 10.2** The role of culture-specific resources in the environmental antecedents–outcome relationships among multicultural people.

When counseling multicultural clients, in addition to recognizing the environmental antecedents that multicultural clients encounter, culturally sensitive counselors are aware that multicultural clients have their cultural heritage and other resources to support them. Figure 10.2 demonstrates that when multicultural clients have opportunities to use their culture-related resources and strengths, they may have better management over the impacts of environmental antecedents (e.g., discrimination, life stress) on their emotional or psychological disturbances. It is in this way that multiculturalizing the integration of behavior therapy and positive psychology may well be a crucial step to understanding the impact of antecedents on multicultural clients' psychological distress.

## The role of dysfunctional behavior and positive psychology in multicultural context

From behavior therapy we learn that psychological problems or behavioral disorders are construed as learned and can be explained with learning theories. However, as the appropriateness of applying linear relationships to multicultural clients is questioned above, so simply applying the learning principles to explain and treat the dysfunctional behaviors without cultural considerations may well result in misunderstanding clients' issues, to worsen the outcome.

Culturally sensitive counselors understand that dysfunctional behaviors may well have different presentations in different cultures. Western culture emphasizes individualism, directness, and activity. Living with parents during adulthood and being quiet most of the time may be perceived as not independent, shy, or having behavior dysfunction. However, the same behavior patterns are quite normal and usually accepted in other cultures such as Asian and especially Chinese.

In fact, Asian culture recognizes living with parents as a presentation of filial love and caring fidelity as elderly parents may need care from their adult children. Being quiet in Asian culture shows this individual's respect for others. Thus, culturally skilled counselors recognize that normal behaviors in other cultures may be misunderstood as "behavior dysfunction" in Western culture, if they have no knowledge about culturally appropriate behaviors.

With cultural knowledge, counselors are more competent at integrating positive psychology when counseling multicultural clients. For example, after recognizing the environmental antecedents from the perspective of clients' culture, counselors are aware that the usually called behavioral dysfunction could result from a cultural clash between Western culture and the client's culture. Or the client may report some behavioral dysfunction in terms of their culture.

For example, difficulty in maintaining interpersonal harmony could be a behavioral dysfunction in an Asian culture which cherishes collectivism. As culturally skilled counselors possess cultural knowledge regarding the multicultural clients they counsel, they would be competent in assisting clients to cultivate their culture-specific strengths to manage their behavioral dysfunction.

Taken together, while multiculturalization of the integration between behavioral dysfunction and positive psychology by no means minimizes the principles of behavior therapy and positive psychology, on the contrary, multiculturalization would hope to expand the appropriate application of behavior therapy and positive psychology to multicultural clients with appropriate sensitivity on their culture.

## Application in Counseling: Case Study

Tim came to a university counseling center to resolve his social anxiety. He has been extremely anxious about what he needs to say or do in front of people and/or in class. His problems include public speaking and day-to-day social situations. He felt so anxious that he did not interact with others. In class, he asked his professors if he could submit a paper instead of an oral presentation in class. If his professors did not allow him to change the assignment, he experienced fears, weeks or months in advance of the presentation. When he has to talk to people, he felt a fast heartbeat which made it hard to focus and breathe.

Tim also understood that this problem affected his daily life. He felt so stressed or afraid that he avoided public situations, even so far as to miss classes or appointments. Tim reported that he felt nervous, sad, sweaty, shaky and/or easily upset before or during a social event. He worried a lot or was afraid that something bad would happen. People also commented that he blushed quite often. During the intake session, Tim's counselor conducted a mental health assessment and asked about his symptoms, emotions, interpersonal relationships, and others.

### How to help Tim

Tim's presenting problem, social anxiety, might benefit from a behavioral therapy to treat specific behavioral issues, phobias, panic disorder, and so on. Behavior therapy is designed to help Tim understand how changing his behavior regarding presentations in class can lead to reducing his distress. Accordingly, Tim's anxiety when he made a presentation should be explained with current determinants as opposed to historical determinants (i.e., early childhood experiences). Additionally, the behavior therapist would reject the assumption that Tim's behavior problem resonates with symptoms of an underlying illness. That is,

Tim's dysfunctional behavior or anxious reactions are targeted for *behavior* change. Because Tim's anxious responses almost always happened when he had to conduct oral presentations in class or speak in public, the treatment would be target-specific situations (e.g., in class) which triggered anxiety.

Despite articulate conceptualization by behavioral therapy, Tim may at most learn to reduce his symptoms or reactions during his presentations. Because the focus of behavior therapy is to treat or repair symptoms, it still remains doubtful whether the behavioral improvement could enhance Tim's strengths and well-being. Since positive psychology focuses on positive emotions and personal strengths, it could complement traditional psychotherapy such as behavioral therapy to promote Tim's positive affects, strengths, and well-being. Importantly, techniques in positive psychology provide a much-needed balance to the traditional deficit model of counseling. Thus, the following paragraphs will describe the application of the integration of behavior therapy and positive psychology to benefit Tim.

*Systematic desensitization and positive emotions* Systematic desensitization is a method in behavior therapy to help Tim manage his social anxiety when making presentations in class. Before the application of systematic desensitization, Tim's counselor needs to demonstrate and teach Tim the relaxation skills in order to extinguish his fear and anxiety when working on his class presentation. Once Tim is familiar with relaxation skills, he will learn to use them to manage his fears in a hierarchical way. With systematic desensitization, it is hoped that Tim would learn to manage his anxious responses step by step and then eventually he could deal with his whole presentation in the last step in the hierarchy.

Together with the step-to-step desensitization, the counselor can also introduce to Tim on promoting his positive emotions in a hierarchical manner. Tim can learn to cultivate his well-being by reflecting on his positive reactions after he finished each step of managing his fears. For example, after he has managed his lowest level of anxiety regarding his presentation, he also reflected on his positive emotions (e.g., happiness) that came from the beginning level. When he completed his training at the highest level of managing his fears, he would also be ready to harvest his most happiest moment.

*Flooding and posttraumatic growth* Flooding in behavior therapy is based on respondent conditioning, as the client is exposed to their painful experiences. Flooding could be a faster method of treatment for fears, compared with systematic desensitization. Yet, due to the pain of exposure to painful experiences, caution is recommended in using this radical method. Before applying the technique of flooding to Tim, his counselor would suggest he conducts a presentation and see how irrational his anxious responses would be. Because Tim would have learned to use relaxation skills by now, he would attempt to replace his anxious responses with relaxation.

Based on positive psychology, it is crucial to continue growth even after anxious responses or traumatic experiences have subsided (Bonanno, 2004). After being exposed to an extremely painful experience in presentation, in addition to encouraging Tim to use his relaxation skills, Tim's counselor could help him grow and develop positive psychological changes as a result of his exposure to the highly challenging situation (i.e., presentation).

*Convert sensitization, self-efficacy, and optimism* Covert sensitization involves in pairing undesirable behavior with an image to make the client uncomfortable. The purpose of the pairing here was to eliminate Tim's maladaptive behavior during the presentation. His counselor would also explain that since all behaviors, including maladaptive ones, were learned, so these maladaptive behaviors can be unlearned.

Moreover, the goal in covert sensitization was to change behavior rather than uncover Tim's internal conflicts, so Tim's behavior change would be an index to a successful treatment. The maladaptive or dysfunctional behavior regarding his presentation was his avoidance of presentation. The aversive imagery paired with his avoidance of presentation could be a super oily cake which usually made him feel nauseous. Tim was also guided on how to practice and finish homework assignments to learn to pair the aversive stimulus with his dysfunctional behavior.

Because covert sensitization may cause unpleasant feelings or discomfort for Tim due to the inclusion of aversive stimulus, it is important to highlight his efforts and commitment after each practice of this technique. During its application, Tim would need to have self-efficacy and optimism to support him to finish the elimination of his maladaptive behaviors. With self-efficacy, Tim can learn to increase his belief in his own ability to complete his task of reducing anxiety in presentation. After each session, the counselor would highlight his progress and celebrate his "small" success. Optimism is a disposition or tendency to look on the more favorable side of events or conditions and to expect the most favorable outcome. With optimism, an admirable quality, Tim could consistently interpret situations in the best possible light, or simply not blame himself when his progress was not as fast as he expected. When he is able to add optimism to the reality of his behavior changing, he may be on the right track to building up his resilience and achieving his goals.

*Exposure and response prevention and persistence* Exposure and response prevention is another technique in behavior therapy, and is developed from the concept that a treatment is achieved as Tim confronted his own fears as he discontinues using his avoidance as coping. Thus, with this technique, he would stop asking his professor to give him alternative assignments to avoid his presentations in class. Here, his counselor would expose him to his feared stimulus (e.g., in front of a group of people), and would not respond with any stopgap safety behaviors. During the process of this technique, Tim would be expected to completely refrain from his escape response. The underlying purpose of this technique was to make Tim live with the stimulus that used to make him afraid as it encourages him to develop a behavioral response to manage the stimulus such as class presentation.

Positive psychology stresses the character trait of persistence which refers to a firm or obstinate continuance in a course of action in spite of difficulty or opposition. According to this perspective, Tim definitely used persistence to help him live with his feared stimulus (e.g., presentation) with no use of ways of escape. He would feel anxious, nervous, self-doubt, and fatigued; however, despite these negative reactions, he still made it through the tough process. During the process, he and his counselor would continually stress such important character traits demonstrated by Tim. In the technique of exposure and response prevention, Tim would also understand that this could be the best timing for him to cultivate his persistence.

*Contingency management and well-being* With the technique of contingency management, Tim's behaviors would be rewarded if he followed the rules and regulations, or his counseling plan. He might be "punished" (e.g., no praise) if he did not follow the rules. For example, if Tim's behavior (e.g., completed a 3-minute mini presentation) is reinforced or rewarded, it is more likely that he would make a presentation in his class. Thus, the counselor's challenge in helping Tim would be defining "reward," "rule," and even "punishment." Additionally, the counselor can also use examples in everyday life to enhance Tim's understanding of contingency management.

According to positive psychology, how to promote client's well-being has constantly been a primary focus. Well-being refers to a state of being healthy, happy, and/or prosperous. Well-being also suggests the satisfactory condition of existence, and a status characterized by psychological, financial, and physical health. The counselor can regularly discuss with Tim ways to explore (e.g., connect to friends, have hobbies, volunteer) the promotion of his well-being.

*Habit reversal training and hope* Habit reversal training is part of a behavioral treatment package mostly used to apply to a wide variety of repetitive and habitual behavioral problems such as nail biting, skin picking, thumb sucking, and so on. This technique could be helpful for Tim. Habit reversal training includes five steps: awareness training; relaxation training; competing response training; contingency management; and generalization training. These techniques can be used to help Tim eliminate his maladaptive behaviors and learn new functional ones to complete his presentation.

Positive psychology believes that hope inspires people to move on. Snyder, Irving, and Anderson (1991) say that "hope is a positive motivational state that is based on an interactively derived sense of successful (a) agency (goal-directed energy), and (b) pathways (planning to meet goals)" (p. 287). Through the counseling, counselor can facilitate Tim's hope to successfully change his behaviors. Thus hope is the essential key to inspire him to continue and move on in his behavior change.

## Concluding Remarks

To date, behavior therapy contributes to counseling with innovative techniques and assessments. It has been used successfully with a variety of populations (e.g., adults, children, adolescents) in diverse settings such as hospitals. Moreover, behavior therapy has been used to treat various problems. Behavior therapy focuses mainly on immediate behavior and aims to eliminate undesired behavior.

Despite various benefits, behavior therapy has been criticized with limits in appreciating deep psychological changes. Specifically, behavior therapy may change behaviors, but it does not change feelings. Behavior therapy does not provide insight or causes of problems. To increase clients' insights and positive emotions, counselors can incorporate positive psychology in counseling. Positive psychology can also promote clients' strengths when they change their behaviors.

Because both behavior therapy and positive psychology are the products of Western culture, culturally sensitive clients are aware that some multicultural clients may be new to these two approaches. Moreover, counselors are knowledgeable about whether clients' cultures and values are compatible with these two approaches. Counselors should also be skilled in tailoring the integration of behavior therapy and positive psychology to fit clients' cultures.

## Review Questions: What Do You Think?

1. Compare and contrast the four models: applied behavior analysis, neobehavioristic mediational model, social learning theory, and cognitive behavior therapy. What are the similarities and differences between these four models?
2. What therapeutic methods are used in behavior therapy? What criticisms do you have for these therapeutic methods?
3. Based on the integration between behavior therapy and positive psychology, it shows that if psychological disorders are the outcomes of learning, clients can also learn to cultivate positive affects, positive thoughts, and positive behavior. Would you agree with this statement? Explain your answer.
4. Find someone with a different cultural background from yours, and explain the integration between behavior therapy and positive psychology to him or her. Ask what is new or unfamiliar according to his or her culture. Reflect on his/her observation regarding the "mismatch" between the integration and that person's culture. What do you feel?

# 11

# Cognitive-Behavior Therapy

**Learning Objectives**

- Explain the historical background of cognitive-behavior therapy.
- Explain the human nature and the process of change from the perspective of cognitive-behavior therapy.
- Describe the necessary conditions under which psychological growth and behavioral change occur in cognitive-behavior therapy.
- Demonstrate four attributes in cognitive-behavior therapy.
- Learn about Ellis's and Beck's views of human nature.
- Know the ABC model and ABCDEF model in Ellis's REBT.
- Describe in Beck's cognitive-behavior therapy how people's negative beliefs relate to their emotional disorders.
- Learn about the strategies used in cognitive-behavior therapy.
- Learn about the integration between cognitive-behavior therapy and positive psychology.
- Multiculturalize the integration between cognitive-behavior therapy and positive psychology.
- Apply the integration to a case study.

Cognitive-behavior therapy (CBT) is based on three assumptions: an individual's behavior is mediated by cognitive events (e.g., beliefs, thoughts); a change in mediating events results in a change in behavior; and people actively participate in their own learning. As behavior

*Counseling Psychology: An Integrated Positive Psychological Approach*, First Edition. Ruth Chu-Lien Chao.

therapy has broadened and moved in a direction of CBT, it can be seen as an extension of behavior therapy. To date, three primary theories include Albert Ellis's Rational Emotive Behavioral Therapies (REBT), Aaron Beck's Cognitive Therapy (CB), and Donald Meichenbaum's Cognitive-Behavior Therapy (CBT). There are more than 20 different types of therapies labeled as "cognitive" or "cognitive therapy" (Mahoney & Lyddon, 1988). CBT, which combines cognitive and behavior principles and methods in a session-limited therapy, has produced more empirical research than other counseling theories.

Although cognitive-behavior therapies are diverse and have various approaches, there are four common attributes: (a) a collaborated relationship between client and therapist; (b) maladaptive thinking or disturbance in cognition play a critical role in psychological distress; (c) the change of cognition produces the desired effect on changing emotion and behavior; and (d) time-limited sessions combined with a psychoeducation component work together on specific problems (Dobson & Block, 1998). Almost all approaches of CBT are based on or related to a psychoeducation model, emphasize the importance of homework, expect the client to take responsibility of change, the therapist is a collaborator, and apply a variety of cognitive and behavior strategies.

These assumptions recognize the reciprocal relationships among an individual's thoughts, behavior, and environment. CBT is different from behavior therapy (see the previous chapter) regarding the behaviorist's rigid unidirectional view of the individual and treating people as passive recipients of environmental influences. Also different from psychoanalysis which helps clients gain insights regarding their presenting problems, CBT recognizes and remedies dysfunctional thought patterns and focuses on changing the behaviors and cognitions that are thought to be currently maintaining a problem. CBT is used to treat various disorders such as depression, anxiety, low self-esteem, and is often used in combination with medication. Evidence shows that there is strong treatment effectiveness when CBT is used with medication.

## Historical Context

CBT has its roots in the 1950s and 1960s, when several psychologists and psychiatrists, working in South Africa and the United States, began to study the use of interventions based on principles of learning theory. A growing dissatisfaction with psychoanalysis, as well as increased interest in learning theory among basic scientists in psychology, set the stage for the development and proliferation of behavior therapy and later CBT. Before long, thanks to the work of pioneers such as Hans Eysenck, Cyril Franks, Arnold Lazarus, Isaac Marks, S. Rachman, G. Terence Wilson, and Joseph Wolpe, behavior therapy became an established form of treatment that included techniques using exposure, modeling, contingency management, and other strategies.

From the 1960s to the 1970s, several authors and pioneers began to incorporate cognitive explanations for understanding phenomena with learning theories. This development had a profound influence on the development of specific treatments designed to change negative patterns of thinking and information processing. Among a number of pioneers who had played important roles in the early advancement of CBT, Beck and Ellis are most often credited with the development of these treatments. Both of these individuals were originally trained as psychoanalysts, and both described their dissatisfaction with traditional psychoanalysis as fueling their decision to develop a new approach to treating psychological problems such as depression, anxiety, and related problems. Ellis called his form of treatment "rational-emotive therapy" (later changed to "rational-emotive behavior therapy"), and Beck called his form of treatment "cognitive therapy." Both treatments were focused on helping clients to shift their beliefs, assumptions, and predictions from being negative and dysfunctional to being realistic and adaptive.

Later in the 1970s and 1980s, researchers began to develop protocols that included strategies from both forms of treatment. It was during this period that CBT began to be used more frequently as a way of describing treatments that included both cognitive and behavioral techniques. For most psychological disorders, there are now structured treatment protocols based on CBT principles. For example, Barlow and his colleagues developed a series of treatment manuals on anxiety disorders (e.g., Craske, Anthony, & Barlow, 2006; Hofmann, 2014).

In the workbook authored by Craske and Barlow (2008), they include exposure-based strategies, breathing skills, and thinking skills for individuals who suffer from anxiety and panic disorders. In their workbook, exposure is used to reduce avoidance behavior, which, in turn, leads to improved management of psychological and physical symptoms and also helps to change anxious thinking when confronting a feared situation. The cognitive strategies used during panic and agoraphobia control treatment are designed to help a client to recognize that the psychological and physical symptoms he or she experiences during panic attacks are neither dangerous nor unmanageable. Finally, breathing skills and relaxation are included to help clients with panic and agoraphobia disorders to slow down their breathing, thereby reducing the frequency and intensity of panic symptoms that may be triggered by stimuli.

## View of Human Nature

Albert Ellis, the founder of REBT, maintains that individuals are born with a potential for both rational and irrational thinking. Individuals have predispositions for self-preservation, happiness, growth, thinking, loving, communication with others, and self-actualization. Yet, Ellis also indicated that individuals have a tendency for self-destruction, self-defeating, and irrationality. However, Ellis believes that this duality (or opposites) of self-actualization and self-destruction coexisting within individuals is biological and thus is perpetuated unless a new way of thinking is learned. Because Ellis focuses on irrationality or rationality of human nature, he may not take age into his consideration regarding counseling and psychotherapy. Although Ellis does not deal with developmental stages, he does think that children are more vulnerable to outside influences and irrational thinking than adults. In other words, he assumes that people are gullible and highly suggestible and are easily disturbed. People have within themselves the ability to control thoughts, feelings, and behavior; but they must first become aware of their self-talk. Ellis believes that individuals are self-talking, self-evaluating, and self-sustaining, but individuals often sabotage their movement toward growth due to self-defeating patterns they have learned (Ellis, 2000).

Aaron T. Beck is well known for his development of cognitive therapy. In his research on depression, he observed that depressive patients have a negative bias in their interpretations of life events, which contributed to their cognitive distortions. Beck's view on human nature focuses on the role of cognition. He believes that the way people feel and behave is determined by how they perceive and structure their experience. Thus, his perspective on human nature is not passive like Freud nor only focusing on freedom of choice as existentialists do. Instead, Beck maintains the key role of people's cognition. He further elaborates his assumptions into three parts: (a) individuals' internal communication is accessible to introspection, (b) that clients' beliefs have highly personal meanings, and (c) these interpretations can be discovered only by individuals themselves not by therapists (Weishaar, 1993).

## Theoretical Principles

### REBT

In general, REBT focuses on (a) examining irrational beliefs which may lead to unhealthy negative emotions and (b) helping individuals replace them with more productive rational alternatives. Ellis believes that individuals learn irrational beliefs from significant others during childhood. Moreover, individuals create irrational dogmas and superstitions by themselves. Individuals then reinforce their irrational beliefs by repeating their pattern of behavior and thoughts. Thus, for Ellis, if individuals can stop repeating their early-indoctrinated irrational thoughts, they would develop rational beliefs. Ellis also indicates that individuals do not need to be loved and accepted.

*ABC model* REBT employs the "ABC model" to describe the relationship between events, individuals' beliefs, and the consequences of beliefs. Ellis specifies that "A" means the activating events; "B" means individuals' beliefs about these events; and "C" includes the cognitive, emotional, or behavioral consequences of individuals' beliefs.

Although the ABC model in Figure 11.1 is also used in some conditions or by therapists of CBT, REBT frequently uses this model to clarify the role of mental activities or predispositions in mediating between experiences and emotional responses. In addition to the ABC model, REBT also emphasizes that while negative emotions are the consequences of individuals' irrational beliefs, people can also have healthy emotions if they have rational beliefs. For Ellis, REBT employs three primary insights. One, while external events are of undoubted influence, psychological disturbance is largely a matter of personal choice in the sense that

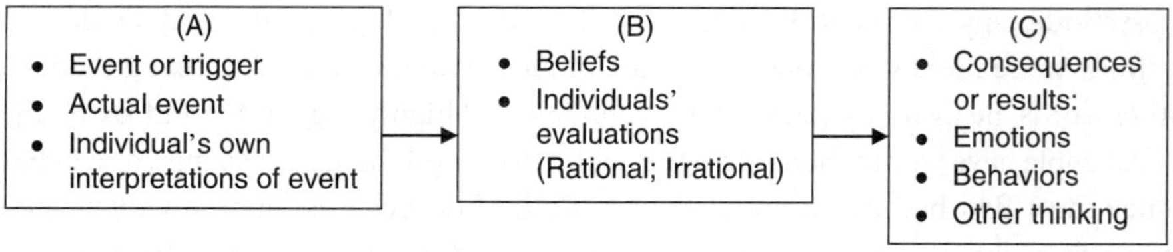


**Figure 11.1** *ABC model.* Adapted from Ellis, 1957.

individuals consciously or unconsciously select both rational beliefs and irrational beliefs at (B) when negative events occur at (A). Thus, the beliefs individuals have when encountering an external event, they can choose irrational or rational beliefs to interpret the event. Two, it is the individual's negative responses which disturb them which results from his or her choice of irrational beliefs. If the individual chooses a rational belief to respond to the event, he or she may have a positive emotional consequence. Three, modifying the irrational beliefs in addition to being aware of irrational and rational beliefs requires persistence and hard work, but according to Ellis, it can be done.

*Goals and change in REBT* The ABC model explains the development and reasons why individuals have negative or unhealthy emotions. Yet, for Ellis, the main purpose of REBT is to help individuals to replace absolutist beliefs which are full of "musts" and "shoulds." According to REBT, there are several ways to achieve this goal. First, REBT encourages individuals to accept that all human beings (including themselves) are fallible, so individuals need to learn to increase their tolerance for frustration while aiming to achieve their goals. Although both REBT and Rogers' person-centered counseling accept that human beings are fallible, REBT does not emphasize unconditional positive regard and counselors' genuineness in counseling. Instead, REBT views these conditions as neither necessary nor sufficient for therapeutic change to occur. During the process of change, REBT attempts to facilitate individuals with the client acknowledging the existence of a problem and identifying any disturbances about that problem (i.e., concerns about the problem, feeling guilty about being depressed). REBT counselors then help clients identify the underlying irrational belief which caused the original problem and to understand both why it is irrational and why a rational alternative would be preferable. The client challenges their irrational belief and employs a variety of cognitive, emotive, and imagery techniques to strengthen their conviction in a rational alternative.

Because the primary goal of REBT is to help individuals develop rational thinking or change irrational beliefs to rational ones, for Ellis, it is essential for individuals to challenge their irrational beliefs. Thus, after the ABC model, there comes disputing (D). In REBT, the disputing process includes three components: detecting, debating, and discriminating. In REBT, detecting mainly refers to individuals' sensitivity to their irrational beliefs. For example, individuals may use "must," "should," "totally," "always," and other extreme expressions in their irrational beliefs. Sometimes individuals just automatically use these extreme expressions (e.g., "always") without awareness. The purpose of detecting in REBT is to increase individuals' sensitivity whenever they use these terms which contribute to their irrational thinking. In other words, "musts" and "shoulds" can be important indexes for individuals' irrational beliefs.

The second component, debating, of the dispute means that individuals learn how to logically and empirically question their dysfunctional thinking and vigorously argue with themselves out of the dysfunctional thinking. The final component, discriminating, indicates that individuals can differentiate irrational or dysfunctional beliefs from rational or self-helping beliefs. Being able to discriminate irrational beliefs from rational ones, Ellis suggests that individuals can choose the rational beliefs which result in positive or healthy emotions.

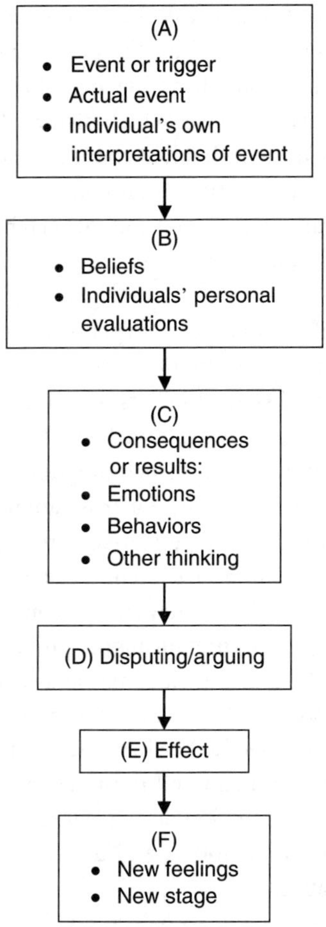


**Figure 11.2** *ABCDEF model*. Adapted from Ellis, 1999.

For Ellis, dispute can be used in counseling and everyday life as well. Although REBT utilizes various strategies such as cognitive, emotive, and behavioral approaches to minimize the impacts of irrational beliefs, dispute still plays an important role in changing individuals' beliefs and helping individuals move to the stage of "E" (effect). When individuals dispute their irrational beliefs or dysfunctional thinking, they arrive at new effective philosophy which results in new feeling or the stage of "F."

From the ABC model to the ABCDEF model (Figure 11.2), REBT indicates several points regarding the change of behaviors, affect, and personality. One, REBT stresses that individuals are responsible for their own emotional or behavioral problems. Two, because individuals are responsible for creating their problems, they also have the ability to change their problems. Three, according to the ABC model, most emotional or behavioral disturbances come from individuals' irrational beliefs. Four, although there are various approaches to change irrational beliefs, based on the concept of REBT, dispute might be an essential strategy to target the irrational beliefs by detecting, debating, and discriminating them. Five, after disputing irrational beliefs or dysfunctional thinking, individuals may experience a new effective philosophy about themselves and events and then experience new feeling. Finally, it is important to practice REBT in daily life to uproot the disturbing thinking or beliefs for the rest of life.

## CBT

Counselors and therapists who work within a CBT framework assume that psychological problems experienced by clients are caused and maintained by a number of factors, as outlined below (Beck, Brown, & Henriques, 2002; Beck & Steer, 1989).

*Negative beliefs, assumptions, predictions, and interpretations* Beck (1967) indicated that depression and other emotional disorders occur when individuals hold negative beliefs about themselves (e.g., "I am stupid"), the world (e.g., "People are generally nasty"), and the future (e.g., "I will never find a job") and when they engage in errors or biases in thinking, such as interpreting events in a negative way despite a lack of evidence supporting such thoughts.

*Patterns of reinforcement* An individual who receives considerable praise and rewards for being detail oriented and hardworking may begin to overvalue the importance of his or her work and may feel devastated when he or she is unable to meet certain arbitrary standards. Similarly, an individual who is criticized and teased frequently while growing up may develop a fear of socializing and of developing intimate relationships.

*Behavioral deficits* Sometimes individuals lack functional behaviors to the point of causing disruptions in day-to-day functioning. Specifically, individuals who suffer from phobias typically avoid encountering the objects of their fears, unfortunately, lacking confrontation with fears reinforces these fears over time.

*Skills deficits* Individuals with negative beliefs and thoughts about themselves, the world, and the future tend to lacks assertiveness skills which results in feeling being taken advantage of by others, thereby leading to problems with anxiety, depression, or other difficulties.

### Strategies used in CBT

*Cognitive restructuring* Cognitive restructuring involves teaching clients to be more aware of their negative thoughts, to evaluate evidence of the extent to which thoughts are accurate, and to replace unrealistic thoughts with more balanced interpretations, predictions, and assumptions. Clients are encouraged to question their beliefs rather than automatically assuming the thoughts are true. Monitoring forms are used to help clients to identify and challenge the thoughts that lead to problems with anxiety, depression, and other negative emotions.

*Strategies for challenging negative thinking* There are a few strategies used in CBT to help clients challenge their negative thinking:

One, clients can learn to become educated about relevant facts (e.g., learning about the actual risks of dying in a plane crash in an effort to overcome a fear of flying). Two, clients work with therapists to examine the evidence (e.g., "The fact that my friend often invites me to socialize is evidence that he or she enjoys spending time with me, despite that fact that I believe otherwise when my mood is low").

Three, clients learn to examine one's previous experiences (e.g., "Given that I have never fainted before during a panic attack, the odds of my fainting during my next panic attack are minimal") and self-question the current situation (e.g., "In what ways I am handling this problem better than I used to?").

Four, clients can perceive different perspectives (e.g., "My expectations for my own performance are much higher than the expectations I hold for others or the expectations that others hold for me").

Five, clients can learn to manage catastrophic thinking by asking "So what. . .?" (e.g., a client who is convinced that not getting a job he or she has just applied for might be encouraged to ask questions such as "What if I don't get the job?" "How could I cope with not getting the job?" "Does not being offered this job mean that I will never find a job?").

Six, clients will benefit from behavioral experiments (also called hypothesis testing) which involve testing out the validity of a particular belief or prediction by conducting an experiment and evaluating the outcome. For example, an individual who is convinced that being the center of attention will lead to horrible consequences might be encouraged to purposely draw attention to him or herself (e.g., speaking in public, dropping keys, spilling a glass of water, etc.) to learn that the actual consequences are quite mild. In reality, it is often quite difficult to get the attention of others.

*Social skills and communication training* Social skills and communication training involve therapists' teaching individuals particular strategies for increasing the effectiveness of his or her social behaviors. Examples of areas that may be the target of intervention include: increasing eye contact when talking to people; developing assertiveness skills; managing conflicts effectively; enhancing nonverbal communication skills; and so on. Particularly, social skills involves identifying particular social skills deficits, discussing alternative ways of behaving, modeling appropriate social behaviors, allowing the client to practice alternate behaviors, and providing feedback on the client's performance. Communication training involves how to clearly express one's needs and negotiate with others especially to solve conflicts. During the counseling with CBT, these skills are often useful for clients with social anxiety, depression, marital distress, psychotic disorders, and a variety of other problems.

Finally, problem solving is another technique therapists use to help client develop. Problem-solving training in CBT involves psychoeducating clients a structured, systematic method of solving problems that arise, as an alternative to solving problems impulsively, focusing on the wrong problems, or avoiding dealing with problems all together (e.g., procrastination). Clients tend to have difficulty solving problems because the problems seem overwhelming, amorphous, or vague. Problem-solving training helps to get around both of these barriers to the effective resolution of a problem. Problem-solving technique includes assessing, defining, and understanding the problem; generating and creating solutions; evaluating solutions, selecting the best or most appropriate solutions. To date, problem-solving skill has been used to effectively treat a number of psychological problems, including depression.

## An Integration: Positive Psychology and Cognitive-Behavior Therapy

REBT mainly employs the ABC model to describe the relationship between events, individuals' beliefs, and consequences of beliefs. As we know, "A" means the activating events, "B" means individuals' beliefs about these events, and "C" includes the cognitive, emotional, or behavioral consequences of individuals' beliefs. Although REBT addresses individuals' beliefs about the events which trigger peoples' emotions or response, its main focus remains on how to fix problems rather than how to promote strengths and well-being (Frisch, 2005).

Unfortunately, various disputes favored by REBT could easily meander off track into minutiae relatively removed from the individuals' primary concern, and the mental gymnastics required to keep client and therapist on the same track could easily eat up time better spent on more productive activities. The counselor's and client's estimations of relative importance could diverge rather profoundly, particularly if the client's outlook really embodies significant irrationalities. Having said all that, each preceding sentence includes the qualifier "could," and with a great deal of skill, each pitfall can undoubtedly be avoided.

Because individuals' strength would be their resource to manage the triggering events and their consequences, it is important to add individuals' strengths to "B" of the ABC model. Thus, instead of only talking about beliefs of triggering events, counselors and clients can evaluate what strengths (e.g., resilience, hope, optimism, etc.) can help clients manage adverse effects of events. Thus while there is no need to disregard the ABC model in REBT, it would enrich REBT if clients learn how to use their strengths to manage their problems.

The integration between REBT and positive psychology may well solve a dilemma for counselors. It is crucial to realize that although some clients do appreciate exactly this REBT sort of disputing, not all clients do so, and some others may well prefer not to dispute. On the counselors' side, some counselors are unwilling to provide the disputation approach while others may see its benefits; such discrepancy may unnecessarily disrupt the therapeutic relationship. However, if clients' strengths can be added to the ABC model, both counselors and clients can explore how to promote clients' strengths and how clients' strengths can help clients deal with such events. Therefore, the integration can solve this dilemma created by disputes (Frisch, 2005).

The integration of REBT and positive psychology may also increase empirical support to REBT, which is much less empirically supported than some other approaches. Positive psychology is a discipline where science meets people's strengths, and has consistently been advocating rigorous scientific research to support its therapeutic intervention. To date, there are plenty of empirical evidences that individuals' strengths (e.g., coping, well-being, resilience, perseverance, etc.) do help people manage their stress, traumatic experiences, and other negative events. The integration between REBT and positive psychology would launch an evidence-based counseling practice in which the ABC model (specifically "B" taken as clients' strengths) will obtain support from empirical research.

Integration of these two approaches does not mean that positive psychology would replace any component of REBT. On the contrary, the integration seeks to enrich REBT, as both look for ways to benefit clients, with the integration that joins forces and includes clients' strengths, to increase clients' and counselors' active participation in the process of identifying irrational beliefs, recognizing strengths, and incorporating well-being. Clients fully realize that their collaboration with counselors working with them in many diverse ways will enhance their strengths by challenge, dispute, and clarification, they recognize and appreciate their strengths, and highlight their efforts to grow and maintain their well-being. These diverse multiple ways of working with clients in the integration aim to fulfill one mission – to promote clients' awareness of their strengths and to advocate their struggles in strengths toward happy well-being.

## CBT and positive psychology

Founded by Beck, the principle in CBT is that depression and other emotional disorders occur when individuals hold negative cognitive beliefs about themselves (e.g., "I am stupid"), the world (e.g., "People are generally nasty"), and the future (e.g., "I will never find a job"). According to CBT, when people engage in errors or biases in thinking, their emotional affect is influenced and becomes negative, problematic, and they continue to interpret events in a negative way despite lack of evidence to support such thoughts. In all, with various techniques, the CBT works on how to fix problems rather than how to promote strengths (Taylor & Armor, 1996).

The introduction of positive psychology brings a positive direction into CBT. Positive psychology is convinced that it is vital to understand one's inherent strengths, and build from one's strengths to persist in skillfully managing (rather than focusing on repairing) weaknesses or mental problems (Hall & Nelson, 1996). In other words, it is fine with positive psychology that counselors help clients promote their strengths as they help the clients manage problems.

Unfortunately, such an integrated and balanced approach seems contrary to most counseling theories, including CBT. Indeed, many teachers, parents, and leaders work from the following unwritten rule: "Let's fix what's wrong and let the strengths take care of themselves" (Clifton & Nelson, 1996, p. 9). Examining current theories, we see that this rule or attitude is shared by many therapists and counseling theories, consistently failing to practice from a strengths-based point of view that is positive psychology. CBT shares therapeutic assumptions of working on what needs to be improved, rather than what the clients have been doing successfully. In CBT, what needs to be fixed include clients' negative emotions, negative beliefs that are negative thoughts about themselves, and negative worldviews, honing in on what is wrong with a client, rather than what is going right.

In this negative context of therapies and CBT, its integration with positive psychology serves overall enrichment. This integration does not minimize much less neglect the contributions in treatment by CBT. On the contrary, the integration attempts to use positive psychology to enrich CBT. As CBT addresses mutual relations among negative thinking (e.g., "I am a failure"), negative emotion or disturbed affect (e.g., "I feel sad"), and a negative worldview (e.g., "No one likes me"), positive psychology can add strengths-based thinking, insisting that there is another way to promote clients' positive emotions toward well-being. Accordingly, a new relationship between thinking/belief, affect, and expectation about future can be built by positive thinking (e.g., "I am hopeful in managing this event though it could be challenging"), positive affect (e.g., "I feel peaceful now"), and positive expectation, hope for a bright future (e.g., "I am hopeful").

*Deficits in behavior/skills and strength-based counseling* CBT insists that deficits in behavior and skill relate to emotional disturbances. For example, individuals who suffer from phobias (emotional disturbance) typically avoid encountering the objects of their fears (deficit behavior). Unfortunately, lacking confrontation in fear reinforces these fears over time. Individuals with negative beliefs and thoughts about themselves, the world, and the future tend to lack assertive skills which results in feeling being taken advantage of by others, thereby leading to emotional problems such as anxiety, depression, or other negative feelings.

CBT thus focuses on the deficit aspects of behaviors and emotions, and develops plans to treat and repair these deficit problems, so as to restructure individuals' thoughts and beliefs to prevent such deficits in the future. While some studies demonstrate the effectiveness of CBT's strategies, it is important to know that exclusively focusing on deficits could push counselors into neglecting clients' strengths. Strengths might not be magic pills, but when clients recognize their strengths, they feel more self-esteem and self-confidence to handle their problems, and resolve the problems without too much help from outsiders such as counselors.

In order to capitalize on strengths, clients must be nurtured by counselors' cultivating techniques in a balanced and comprehensive way. For example, students who do well in English but struggle with music are often assisted with their music skills while their English ability is ignored. While their music skills may get better, their English will likely only slightly improve, at most, if not deteriorate due to negligence. Instead, educators and parents should help manage weakness while simultaneously promoting English skills. This example enables us to realize the critical difference in perspective between CBT and positive psychology. CBT focuses on treating problems while positive psychology attempts to promote strengths in reducing symptoms, in balanced and comprehensive ways.

The integration may resolve some misunderstanding. Because strengths and weaknesses are different domains in human life, individuals do not learn about strengths by studying weaknesses. For example, after counseling or psychological treatment, clients may be "symptom-free" or have "reduced symptoms," but this state of affairs is not equivalent to positive mentality such as "happiness," "hopefulness," or "optimism." It is quite significant to note that repairing problems alone may not promote well-being, but promoting strengths toward well-being would involve defeating problems to resolve them.

## Multiculturalizing the Integration

### Multiculturalizing REBT and positive psychology

REBT uses the ABC model to describe the process from the activating events to individuals' beliefs about these events, and then the result in emotional or behavioral consequences of these beliefs. Culturally sensitive counselors are further aware that multicultural clients' activating events could be beyond counselors' experiences in their own culture and values. For example, an African American male client may describe his racial discrimination as an antecedent for his emotional outcomes (e.g., sadness, hopelessness, tiredness, etc.), and yet his antecedent-outcome experience could be *different* from his counselor's.

Additionally, although REBT addresses the existence of individuals' beliefs about the events which trigger their emotions or behavioral response, what is important is how to integrate positive psychology to promote strengths and well-being, and even here multicultural clients manifest varieties of situations beyond the counselors' cultural expectations. Multicultural counselors must possess knowledge about multicultural clients' distinct beliefs, values, and opinions regarding the antecedents resulting in their respectively different emotional, cognitive, and behavioral outcomes.

It is in this way that culturally skilled counselors would respect clients' culture-specific resources, strengths, religion, and spirituality, and coping. For example, to manage the impact of the antecedent, some multicultural clients may believe that it is important to request guidance from their religious or spiritual leaders, practice religious rituals, or follow a special diet. Culturally sensitive counselors respect these multicultural beliefs and explore with them how their cultures view the antecedent. Importantly, counselors respect the culturally specific strengths, resources, and coping that clients feel comfortable with. Thus, instead of only exploring straight "beliefs and thoughts" that trigger events, culturally skilled counselors assist clients to reflect on what culture-specific strengths can help these specific multicultural clients managing the effect of the events. It would multiculturalize REBT to make it effective when multicultural clients learn how to use their culture-specific strengths to manage their problems.

As practitioners have observed and indicated, the process of dispute can be confusing and cause the primary focus to go off track. Multicultural clients who are new to the disputes favored by REBT could feel confused. Counselors must be aware of the clients' specific cultural background and thinking process. For example, a senior Asian client may feel confused about the process of dispute, especially if REBT is his/her new experience. Culturally skilled counselors understand their confusion and explain the process of dispute in the language understandable to this client. The content and strategy of dispute should also be specifically tailored to the client's own culture and thinking mode.

To multiculturalize the integration between REBT and positive psychology enriches REBT with culturally appropriate intervention to specific multicultural clients. The integration of culture-specific strengths would increase multicultural clients' progress by counselors' cultural knowledge to identify irrational beliefs as defined by the client's own background. Culturally sensitive counselors recognize that processes in dispute are based on Western culture and would invite multicultural clients to explore how to process dispute in their culturally appropriate way. In Western culture, counselors may utilize techniques such as challenge, dispute, or clarification to facilitate dispute, and add the clients' strengths to promote their own specific well-being. In order to do so, counselors must be aware of cultural differences and respect clients' cultural heritages, with utmost sensitivity, inviting those special clients to design together a culturally appropriate strategy to utilize REBT's various techniques, to highlight and promote multicultural clients' culture-specific strengths to enhance their well-being.

## Multiculturalizing CBT and positive psychology

CBT has possibly received the most attention of the psychotherapies. Now, according to CBT, when people engage in errors or biases in thinking, their emotional affect becomes negative or problematic and they continue to maintain their interpretation of events in a negative way despite a lack of evidence supporting such thoughts. The introduction of positive psychology brings people's strengths to counseling (Clifton & Nelson, 1996).

And then the situation gets complicated. When counseling multicultural clients with the integration of CBT and positive psychology, culturally sensitive counselors are aware that both CBT and positive psychology are Western products. It requires counselors' cultural awareness, knowledge, and skills to use both approaches culture-appropriately to counsel multicultural clients. For example, culturally skilled counselors are aware of their own attitudes and experiences toward CBT and positive psychology, not noticing how counselors' "comfort" with these two approaches may create invisible biases in counseling. CBT proposes that the cognitive negative triad is made up of the negative schemata and cognitive biases of the person, and it is important to restructure the cognitive distortions to reduce psychological problems.

Now, culturally skilled counselors possess knowledge about how to culture-appropriately match the concepts of cognitive triad and cognitive distortions with clients' specific culture and its values. CBT routinely focuses on people's thinking (e.g., cognitive triad, cognition distortion, etc.) and explores how cognitive distortions contribute to people's psychological distress.

Sucha regular CBT approach turns complex, in need for further adjustments, when working with multicultural clients. Culturally sensitive counselors would recognize that multicultural clients encounter daily problems struggling with financial, educational, language, acculturative, and/or housing stress, all quite practical problems. These multicultural clients may feel that "cognitive distortions" discussed in CBT are too abstract and powerless to solve their daily stress.

With the infusion of positive psychology which includes culture-specific coping, multicultural clients may well turn capable of better understanding how to respond to and solve stress. For example, an Asian student wants to run a marathon, though with no experience in running. Her motto, "Thousand miles of walk begins with the first step," may become her culture-specific resource to challenge her cognitive distortion such as "I am a failure" and "If I do not win, I am a loser." With her motto, she may develop new and worry-neutral thoughts and change her cognitive distortion such as "I cannot complete running a marathon" into "I am making progress everyday, one step at a time."

Thus, multiculturalization of the integration between CBT and positive psychology has three requirements. *First*, we say, "Counselors, counsel thyself!" Counselors must turn culturally sensitive by becoming aware of their own cultural heritage and how their values may influence their attitudes toward this integration. For example, the thinking-frame in counseling, including CBT, has been dominated by the deficit-based model, and positive psychology has been known to focus on scientific inquires. Being aware of these ideologies of CBT and positive psychology could well be the crucial step to multiculturalizing their integration.

*Second*, culturally sensitive counselors must possess cultural knowledge regarding rebuilding or restructuring distorted thoughts to culture-appropriately promote multicultural clients' well-being. Counselors must be knowledgeable about cultural strengths which refer to the strengths produced or developed by a given cultural group. Some cultural groups that appreciate autonomy would value strengths based on individualism, and other cultural groups that focus on collectivism would value strengths based on relationships.

*Third*, different cultures differently present their specific "distorted thoughts." For example, some cultures have standards that prescribe people to be active and assertive, and being humble could be taken as lack of self-esteem. Culturally sensitive counselors must have sensitivity enough to differentiate different impacts of different cultures on "cognitive thoughts." Additionally, different cultural groups may differently present their strengths. While some cultures highlight the importance of explicitly expressing in verbal eloquence, other cultures may recognize strengths more in behaviors than verbal eloquence. For example, Asian culture believes that "Sitting and talking are less powerful than actions." Thus, culturally skilled counselors must be able to appreciate that clients' cognitive thinking and strengths are often culturally bound. Moreover, these counselors must engage in a variety of verbal and nonverbal helping responses. Whether they communicate via verbal or nonverbal ways, they are able to understand clients' cognitive thoughts and strengths culture-appropriately.

## Application in Counseling: Case Study

Jane is an Asian female in her mid-70s and arrived in the United States just 2 years ago to live with her daughter. Jane was asked by her daughter to talk about her adjustment to the United States. She expressed a lot of confusion. Knowing completely nothing about English or Western culture, she felt frustrated at her inability even to speak to people. Moving has been a huge change for her. Feeling anxious about her new environment, she stays at home most of the time. She watches lots of TV shows and still feels bored.

In the past month, she had a dental problem which costs her daughter $4,000. Jane felt guilty about her daughter's coverage of her dental fee, but she herself could not afford the cost, specifically because she had no dental insurance. She blamed the enormous cost on herself and believed that she caused many troubles to her daughter. She sometimes felt lonely, miserable, and sad. She lost her husband about 3 years before moving to the United States. She sometimes talked to him, and her daughter wondered if she was still grieving for him.

Last week, she happened to go alone to a grocery store without carrying any ID or cash. With her diabetes, she felt her blood sugar level had dropped too quickly. Being unable to communicate in English, Jane was very anxious about her extremely low sugar level which might result in worse health. The salesperson in the grocery store noticed that she was fatigued, restless, and nervous, and asked her if she needed help. The more the salesperson tried to help, the more anxious Jane felt due to her language barrier and extremely low blood sugar. At this moment, Jane's neighbor happened to shop at this grocery store and kindly took her home.

## How to Help Jane

This section includes two subsections (a) REBT with positive psychology and (b) CBT with positive psychology, to conceptualize how to help Jane. Both approaches require the counselor's cultural sensitivity since Jane is an Asian woman in her mid-70s. Because Jane comes from an Asian culture and does not speak English, culturally sensitive counselors must consider ways to overcome the language barrier, such as working with a bilingual counselor or Jane's family member. Either way, culturally sensitive counselors would respect Jane's cultural values, attitudes, and decisions.

*Applying REBT* In applying REBT to help Jane, her counselor needs to be aware that they both have their respective cultural heritages. To effectively counsel Jane, her counselor must explore their cultural differences regarding the rationale and usages of assessment, practice, and intervention. For example, Jane's counselor would acknowledge that there could be cultural differences in awareness regarding the purposes and goals of counseling, in addition to incorporating REBT to help Jane.

Since Jane has never received any counseling or mental health intervention, her counselor may need to begin with explaining REBT's "ABC model" in a culturally appropriate way. For Jane, her activating events, "A", could refer to her loss of husband and relocation to a new environment. Her beliefs, "B", about these events could be mixed with sadness, confusion, acculturative stress, and hope. Finally, her outcomes, "C," regarding the cognitive, emotional, or behavioral consequences of her beliefs could include grief, feeling challenged to adjust a new environment, and excitement at living with her daughter.

Moreover, the "disputes" favored by REBT could make her confused. For Jane, her positive affects depended on her children's prosperity, health, and success. Additionally, in Asian culture, mental health counselors are perceived as medical doctors or teachers always accorded with the highest respect. With such cultural values, Jane's counselor would notice that she usually agreed with the counselor's suggestions and advice rather than disputing with the counselor. The counselor may need to explore what "dispute" means in Asian culture and process dispute in a perspective understandable to Jane.

In addition to helping Jane with REBT's "ABC model" in her Asian cultural perspective, a culturally sensitive counselor needs to explore how she has managed her life events. The counselor would also respect for her culture-specific resources such as chatting with friends, neighbors, and relatives, seeking guidance from gods, and discussing her difficulties with children. The counselor must also respect her wisdom in life, with knowledge about the roles of seniors in Asian culture. To facilitate Jane's awareness of her strengths, it would be helpful to incorporate culturally appropriate interventions such as story-telling by asking Jane to talk about her life journey. These culturally specific interventions may well help her reflect on how she has managed past problems.

Additionally, the counselor could expand the REBT's "ABC model" into the "model" with additional factors of positive affects and strengths. Specifically, in Asian culture, living with family (e.g., her daughter in the United States) means harmony and mutual support. Thus, for Jane, her "A," environmental event (e.g., living in her daughter's house), in Asian culture represents her daughter's loving piety toward her. Her "B" or belief about this event could include "she has great kids," "she needs to help her kids with housework and to cook for them," and so on. In such a way as this, according to her Asian value, she would feel very satisfied, grateful, and happy. She would thank gods most of the time and remind herself of cherishing whatever she has had so far. Thus, by integrating REBT and positive psychology, and tailoring such integration to Jane's Asian culture, the counselor would help her recognize her strengths (e.g., resilience, hope, optimism, etc.) and realize that she can facilitate her new insights regarding how she can manage the effect of her events to steer her new life through to maximum well-being.

It is in this way that, for Jane, learning to appreciate the integration between REBT and positive psychology from her cultural perspective, would promote her well-being. A culturally sensitive counselor would also realize that, even within multicultural clients, different clients have their specific cultural values and beliefs. Different multicultural clients may have distinctive different reactions toward REBT's "A–B–C model" of Jane's. Culturally sensitive counselors would respect each client's cultural background, beliefs, and values and provide culturally appropriate intervention to *each* client. That is, the case example of Jane cannot be treated as the recipe for *all* multicultural clients.

Each culture in each client has its culturally specific environmental events or antecedents, beliefs, strengths, resources, and interpretations of emotions. This subtle issue in specific cultures, each different for each person, highlights the importance and necessity of subtle cultural sensitivity to use general cultural knowledge to serve each multicultural client.

In addition to understanding the cultural implications in the application of the integration of REBT and positive psychology, the counselor would also respect that different clients have their preferred way of integration, as the culturally sensitive counselor respects various clients' definitions of their environmental events, beliefs, and outcomes. These counselors would also understand and respect that each client has their respective culturally individual strengths.

When working with multicultural clients such as Jane, it is important to be flexible with the variations of this integration. For example, for Jane, due to her being new to Western culture, REBT, and positive psychology, she may feel comfortable spending more time on her beliefs than on other categories (e.g., environmental antecedents and outcomes), and so the culturally sensitive counselor would respect her decision and facilitate her insights based on the process she chose. That is, despite Jane's barriers in language, culture, and other issues, the therapeutic relationship would still remain amicable and collaborative.

To help Jane with the integration of these two approaches, the counselor would not focus only on either REBT or positive psychology. Jane may feel benefited by the counselor balancing and combining these two approaches while tailoring this integration to Jane's culture.

## Applying CBT

Similar to REBT, CBT also originated in Western culture. Thus the thought-frame and rationale of CBT would be new to Jane, a mid-70 year-old Asian woman. The principle here is that Jane's emotional problems such as sadness occur when she holds negative beliefs about herself (e.g., I am a failure), the world (e.g., People do not care for me), and the future (e.g., I will never succeed). According to CBT, when she engages in errors in thinking, her emotional affect would also be negative and then she would use such negative emotions to interpret things around her in a negative way. Thus, to help Jane understand the principles of CBT, the culturally sensitive counselor could incorporate Jane's life experiences into the explanation of CBT. For example, she might have acculturative stress due to having moved to the United States. Based on Jane's acculturative stress, the counselor could explore her beliefs about herself, her worldview, and her perception about her future.

Positive psychology brings Jane's strengths and well-being into CBT during the counseling. Positive psychology believes that it is vital to understand and build on one's strengths while managing (rather than focusing on or repairing) weaknesses or mental health problems (Clifton and Nelson, 1996). With this principle, the counselor could explore with Jane if she has engaged in positive thinking in the past even while encountering stress. She may well describe how she has overcome lots of ordeals in life and succeeded at raising her kids. With her positive attitudes and beliefs toward her stress, she even thrived against various difficulties in life and felt satisfied.

With CBT, Jane may only learn how to fix her negative emotions, negative beliefs about herself, and negative worldview. Yet, such a deficit-based model may not appear necessarily incompatible with Jane and her culture. Jane's counselor would discuss with Jane regarding her Asian culture, how people manage stress and enhance their strengths.

For Jane, to multiculturalize the integration of CBT and positive psychology serves two purposes. *First*, without intention to minimize or neglect the contribution of CBT, positive psychology would complement CBT by facilitating Jane's well-being. Such integration of these two approaches may echo Jane's Asian culture which stresses balance without pursuing extremes.

*Second*, only focusing on negative aspect may well amount to missing a comprehensive understanding of Jane. In her life stories, she demonstrates numerous positive character traits such as resilience, gratitude, caring, and open-mindedness. Because CBT addresses the relationship between Jane's negative thinking (e.g., "I can't speak English"), negative emotion (e.g., "I feel stupid"), and negative worldview (e.g., "I would make troubles to my daughter if I stay here"), positive psychology would add strength-based thinking to the CBT. For example, a new relationship between thinking/belief, affect, and expectation about the future can be built up as follows: positive thinking (e.g., "I can cook for my daughter") relates to positive affect (e.g., "I feel happy") and positive expectation on future (e.g., "I can help and I am useful").

In Asian culture, they are all very important values, such that a mother puts her children as her top priority; similarly, Jane believes that her children are the most important persons in her life. Culturally sensitive counselors could beneficially add the client's cultural values and beliefs into counseling. It is in this way that cultural sensitivity should be a part of the application of the integration of CBT and positive psychology to multicultural clients.

## Follow-up: You continue as Jane's counselor

Consider how you would help Jane if you were her counselor. Here are a series of questions to provide some structure in your thinking about her case:

*A. You continue as Jane's counselor in REBT*

- How much interest would you have in Jane's childhood?
- Would you add the ABCDEF model of REBT to help Jane? What does such addition of the ABCDEF model mean to her, a senior Asian woman who has no experiences in counseling?
- Would you consider using Jane's experiences and Asian culture to explain the ABC model? Why?

*B. You continue as Jane's counselor in CBT*

- In working with Jane, what negative beliefs would you notice? How would you help her reduce her negative beliefs with CBT?
- After Jane reduces her negative emotions, would you consider helping her promote positive affects? What would you feel if you notice that you do not understand Jane's expression of her positive emotions?

## Concluding Remarks

Based on the assumption that people's behavior is mediated by cognitive events, cognitive-behavior therapy is now one of the most popular approaches in counseling. CBT has been supported by various empirical studies and shows significant treatment effects to numerous clients. As two major figures in cognitive-behavior therapy, Ellis and Beck may share different views on human nature, but they agree that people's beliefs and thinking are crucial for emotions and behaviors. They also highlight the importance of assessments and scientific research in counseling.

While Ellis frequently used the ABC model, Beck developed many strategies such as cognitive restructuring. However, both approaches are still focused on treating problems rather than promoting well-being. Thus, it is critical to introduce positive psychology to enhance clients' positive affects, strengths, and well-being. Both REBT and CBT seem to be limited in multicultural application. Thus, culturally sensitive counselors may need to help multicultural clients be familiar with the principles of these two approaches.

## Review Questions: What Do You Think?

1. Compare and contrast Ellis's REBT and Beck's CBT, the historical backgrounds, views on human nature, and theoretical principles.
2. Practice explaining REBT and CBT to a culturally different person. Which one is easier to be understood by him or her? Why?

# 12

# Reality Therapy

**Learning Objectives**

- Explain the historical background of reality therapy.
- Explain how reality therapy views the human nature of people and the process of change.
- Understand the relationship between choice theory and reality therapy.
- Describe the necessary conditions under which psychological growth and behavioral change occur in reality therapy.
- Demonstrate specific procedures and techniques from reality therapy.
- Learn about choices and responsibilities in reality therapy and positive psychology.
- Integrate reality therapy and positive psychology.
- Multiculturalize the integration between reality therapy and positive psychology.
- Apply the integration to a case study.

Reality therapy believes that people can decide on their behavior to meet their basic needs. It teaches directing life, making effective decisions, and dealing with stressors, as the client's living becomes more focused and evaluated. Established by William Glasser in 1965, reality therapy is a method of counseling which is firmly based on choice theory and its successful application is dependent on a strong understanding of choice theory. The goal of reality therapy is to help people reconnect because there are unsatisfactory or nonexistent

*Counseling Psychology: An Integrated Positive Psychological Approach*, First Edition. Ruth Chu-Lien Chao.

connections with people we need and such poor quality of connections is the source of almost all human problems. Thus, reality therapy aims to create or recreate a connection between people.

## Historical Context

William Glasser (1925–2013), a physician, developed the theory of reality therapy over a period of years beginning with his psychiatric training. Both Glasser's reaction against traditional psychoanalytic psychotherapy and his experiences in working with delinquent youths at a California school for girls probably played major roles in the development of reality therapy (Belkin, 1975). Glasser (1965) sees the individual as motivated internally by the need to belong, to be loved, and to be a successful, worthwhile person. Control is seen as a major element in the human system: the individual works to control the environment so that internal, personal needs can be met. The individual's interface with the reality of his or her current life situation is the arena of action. Therefore, reality therapy stresses personal commitment, change in behavior, responsibility, and the here and now. The individual's past history is not seen as particularly significant, and the medical model or orthodox concept of mental illness has no place in this approach (Corey, 1986).

Glasser has promoted the acceptance of his approach by numerous presentations and publications. In *Reality Therapy: A New Approach to Psychiatry* (1965), *Stations of the Mind* (1981), and *Take Effective Control of Your Life* (1984), Glasser develops his theoretical approach to psychotherapy and demonstrates its application to clinical cases. Glasser's *Schools Without Failure* (1969) applies the concepts of reality therapy to the school setting. *Positive Addiction* (1976) treats a different, but related, theme; it has also met with wide public acceptance.

To date, reality therapy has grown in popularity and influence. It is particularly well received in schools and the criminal justice system, and with counselors who work to rehabilitate handicapped individuals. This psychotherapeutic approach lends itself to short-term, direct, and active therapy.

## View of Human Nature

Glasser's reality therapy is based on choice theory which posits that individuals are not born with blank minds waiting to be influenced by external forces. Instead, the essence of reality therapy is that individuals are completely responsible for what choices they make. Because individuals are responsible for their choices, they may be the product of their past and their choices, but they are not victims of the past unless they choose to be. Choice theory focuses on internal force thus it is a part of internal psychology, and assumes that all behaviors come from within, rather than being forced or shaped by external influences. Moreover, choice theory suggests that individuals are born with five internal or genetic needs: survival; love and belonging; power and achievement; freedom and independence; and fun. These internal forces drive individuals to move forward, though these forces vary in strength from individual to individual. When individuals do not meet one or more of these needs, they feel bad. This pain drives them to find a way to feel better, and they may try to fulfill these needs. Thus, individuals need to learn choice theory in order to identify unsatisfied needs and seek to satisfy them. Glasser believes the need to love and to belong is the primary need because individuals need people to satisfy their needs. This perspective of human nature is supported by choice theory which claims that people are social creatures by nature and need to give and receive love. Although important for human beings, Glasser believes that love is the need most difficult to achieve because it requests a cooperative person to fulfill.

Choice theory indicates that individuals do not satisfy their needs directly. From birth, people keep close tack of what makes them feel good. According to choice theory, each individual has what is known as our quality world. In this world, individuals store everything or everyone they encounter in life that makes them feel good or whom they imagine would make them feel good. Pleasurable experiences and beliefs in choice theory refer to whatever makes individuals feel good and these experiences are also stored in their quality world. Individuals' quality world is like a picture album; some pictures are clear and others are blurred. Pictures exist in priority for most people, yet many individuals may have difficulty identifying the priorities. Being unable or feeling it difficult to identify these priorities may cause psychological disturbances. Therapists would use choice theory to assist clients prioritize their needs and decide what is most important for them.

Human beings are the most significant component in individuals' quality world. Human beings that individuals most want to connect with are usually those they are closest with and those who they enjoy being with. According to reality therapy, those who seek counseling means that there is no one in their quality world, or someone in their quality world that individuals cannot connect with in a satisfying way.

Choice therapy indicates that, from birth to death, almost all behaviors come from choices people make. These behaviors are based on the best attempts of choice that individuals take to satisfy their needs. Glasser indicates that behavior occurs to close this gap between needs and wants. Choice theory also explains that total behavior teaches that all behaviors are made up of four distinct components: thinking; acting; feeling; and philosophy. Since behavior comes from the inside of individuals, individuals choose their own destiny.

Being depressed, being anxious, having a headache are expressions which avoid individuals' responsibility in behaving in these ways. According to Glasser, individuals choose to be depressed and hence, when depressed, we are depressing. People choose to have a headache, and hence, when people have a headache, they are experiencing headache. Having experienced headache could result from choice and individuals need to be responsible for choosing headache. This approach of explaining mental disturbance often encounters protesting or questioning from clients. For example, clients are likely to say that they are suffering and that they can't understand how anyone can say that they are choosing to suffer. Glasser and other therapists with choice theory would answer that clients of course don't choose directly to suffer but suffering is part of a total behavior. Glasser would give three possible explanations. One, frustrating relationships usually lead us to choose anger; yet, angry behavior is also dangerous for others and for oneself. Anger does not help individuals satisfy their needs and worse it may cause more dangers to people. So, to reduce that risk, depressing and other psychological symptoms are chosen to replace anger. Two, depressing is one way of getting help without having to beg, work hard, or request. Developing distressed symptoms and feelings enables individuals to retain their self-respect and sense of power. Three, based on choice theory, choosing to develop depressed and other types of mental problems enables individuals to avoid doing what they are required or afraid to do. Losing a job will often be followed by depressed feelings because, in that way, people may receive family's or friends' sympathy.

Depression can do three things to individuals. First, depression helps individuals deal with anger which is an emotion that is more dangerous than the passivity associated with depression. Second, depression gives individuals a measure of control over circumstances that may seem out of our control (e. g., death or illness). Third, depression can assist individuals secure help from friends, doctors, and/or institutions and provides an excuse for not doing what they need to do.

## Theoretical Principles

Reality therapy is a fairly recently developed method of psychotherapy that stresses the importance of clients learning more useful behaviors to deal with their current situations. Reality therapy stresses internal motivation, behavior change, and development of the "success identity." In terms of a philosophical or theoretical stance, reality therapy can be described as strongly cognitive or rational in its approach, appealing to the client's reason and emphasizing the possibility of meaningful change, not just in feelings, but also in behavior. The therapist takes an active, directive role as teacher, but remains supportive and non-punitive.

In reality therapy, the therapist is viewed as a coach or instructor who provides clients with assistance and encouragement in evaluating the usefulness of their current behavior in satisfying their needs. Where the appropriateness of change is recognized, the therapist assists in the development and execution of plans for remediation. Development of the client's strengths and feelings of self-worth leading to a success identity is a key responsibility of the therapist.

Reality therapy is basically a didactic activity, by which the client develops an understanding of reality and learns to act responsibly and effectively in accordance with that reality. A summary of the techniques and procedures of reality therapy is provided by Corey (1986), based on his adaptation and integration of material from several sources. Corey discusses eight steps in therapy: create a relationship; focus on current behavior; invite clients to evaluate their behavior; help clients develop an action plan; get commitment; refuse to accept excuses; refuse to use punishment; and refuse to give up.

*Choice and responsibility* Based on choice theory, individuals choose all the things and behaviors they do, so they must be responsible for their choices. Although choice theory never means that individuals should be punished or blamed because of their choice, it does highlight that counselors need keep in sight that individuals do have the ability to choose and thus individuals do need to be responsible for their choice. Choice theory does not get involved with blaming or finding fault. Individuals cannot control the behavior of others, but they can concentrate on whatever they can control. Particularly, individuals can control their own behavior or their choice of behavior. From the perspective of reality therapy, complaining and blaming are not acceptable as these behaviors are self-defeating. Losing control and feeling suffered by could be what individuals complain of; counselors may assist individuals to understand how individuals' choice contributes to their suffering. Counselors will also respond that life is often unfair and people cannot go through life demanding that it be fair, but individuals can still choose their behavior.

In terms of being responsible for individuals' choices, the outcomes of choice could be positive or negative. For example, when individuals choose ineffective or meaningless activities, they are responsible for negative out comes such as losing others' respect. Yet, when individuals choose meaningful activities such as a job, they can be self-reliable and gain others' respect. Through the meaningful activities, they also fulfill their need of sense of self-control and power. They may also reduce their tendency of choosing self-destructing behavior which results in negative impressions from others.

*Being present* Reality therapy focuses on the present moment, though it respects the impact of the past. Reality therapy believes that the consequences of past traumas cannot be changed, but individuals can choose how to respond to the past trauma. This is why when reacting to the past trauma, some people choose to be stronger and healthier, but others choose to dwell on the negative consequences. According to Glasser, all individuals can do is try to change their present behavior so that they can get their current need fulfilled and get along with those people they want to connect with. From the perspective of reality therapy, it might not be helpful for individuals to visit the past, which may add negative affect to the present, but counselors may still allow individuals to spend some time to peruse that area.

Reality therapy focuses on the present and avoids discussing the past because all human problems are caused by unsatisfying present relationships. Reality therapy also encourages people to avoid discussing symptoms and complaints as much as possible since these are the ways that clients choose to deal with unsatisfying relationships.

Reality therapy focuses on the concept of total behavior, which means focusing on what clients can do, act, and think. Reality therapy discourages people from dwelling on what they cannot do; that is, clients are suggested to change their feelings and physiology. Moreover, it is critical from the perspective of reality therapy to focus on specifics.

*Relationship as a therapeutic tool* In reality therapy, counselors strive to be themselves in their professional work. By being themselves, counselors use the therapeutic relationship to teach clients how to connect with others in their lives. In reality therapy, it is important to maintain people's identities. Glasser contends that transference is a way that both clients and counselors avoid being who they are and disowning what they need to do right now. However, in reality therapy, it is unrealistic for counselors to be anyone but themselves. When counselors maintain who they are, they demonstrate to clients how to be themselves and how to connect to others with real identities.

Relationship in reality therapy plays an important role. Gasser claims the importance of the therapeutic relationship from the beginning and stresses the necessity of being involved in the therapeutic process with clients. Glasser also emphasizes the qualities of being a counselor include being accepting, warm, and understanding; having respect for the client; openness; and being interested to be challenged by others, especially clients. In reality therapy, the significance of counseling is to assist clients to successfully establish relationships with a wide variety of people who would not ordinarily be part of their life. Reality therapy also highlights the problems of criticizing, blaming and/or complaining because these behaviors make clients learn to avoid some extremely harmful external control behaviors that destroy relationships. Reality therapy emphasizes the importance of remaining nonjudgmental and noncoercive, but encourages people to self-critique or self-question all they are doing by the choice theory axiom. A typical question might be: "Is what I am doing getting me closer to the people I need?" If the choice of behaviors is not working for the clients, then the counselor helps them find new behaviors that lead to a better connection so they can maintain good relationships with others.

In the process of counseling, counselors find out as soon as possible who the clients are disconnected from and work to help them choose reconnecting behaviors. If they are completely disconnected, the focus is on helping them find a new connection. That is, counselors help clients create and/or recreate relationships with others and help them make specific, workable plans to reconnect with the people they need. Counselors also help clients follow through on what was planned by helping them evaluate their progress. Accordingly, counselors may suggest plans, but should not give the message that there is only one plan. According to reality therapy, a plan is always open to revision or rejection by the client.

*Avoid emphasizing symptoms* Reality therapy avoids focusing on the nature of the symptoms because asking clients about symptoms will bring them to the past. Rather than like traditional therapy, which spends a big portion of efforts and time on clients' past, reality therapy believes this approach reinforces clients' tendency of avoiding the present and the current problems. Thus, counselors of reality therapy do not ask people how they are feeling because such a question distracts clients' focus from the unsatisfying present relationships to the past. Yet, for reality therapy, symptoms cannot be improved until the quality of relationships is improved. Minimizing time spent on hearing about symptoms and avoiding going into the past assist clients to stay focused on the present. These clients are often so involved in the symptoms they are choosing that they have lost sight of the fact that they need to reconnect. Thus, reality counselors help clients to understand that instead of focusing on symptoms only, reconnection is the best possible solution to their problem.

According to Glasser, counselors would respect clients' decision on visiting the past. If clients believe that counselors want to know the history of symptoms, counselors would comply. However, revisiting the past or discussing the symptoms may result in lengthy therapy. Counselors may need to explain that the more time is spent on symptoms then a longer time would be required to finish counseling. For reality therapy, avoiding focusing on symptoms may be an efficient way of time management in counseling.

*Challenge traditional psychiatry* Glasser disagrees with the traditional perspective that individuals with physical and psychological symptoms are people with mental illness. Although being trained as a psychiatrist, Glasser warns people of being cautious of psychiatry which could be dangerous to physical and mental health. He also criticizes the heavy reliance on the DSM to diagnose and treat clients. Reality therapy also has concerns about the use of medicines to treat clients. Yet, Glasser welcomes techniques in reality therapy. Reality therapy would integrate techniques such as the client's self-evaluation of his/her behavior and developing a contract. Importantly, Glasser's final technique is never give up.

## An Integration: Positive Psychology and Reality Therapy

Both reality therapy and positive psychology have some concerns on the connections between medical issues and psychological disorders. Both approaches also have some disagreements with the DSM. Despite some similarities between these two approaches, there are still lots of potentials that positive psychology can enrich reality therapy, as follows.

### The role of making choices

According to choice theory, individuals choose all the things and behaviors they do, so they must be responsible for their choices. Counselors of reality therapy believe that individuals do have the ability to choose and thus individuals do need to be responsible for their choice. Thus, choice and responsibility are like two sides of a coin; when individuals make a choice, it is inevitable that they need to be responsible for the consequences (McCrae & Costa, 1999).

Applying this relationship between choice and responsibility to clients' presenting problems, Glasser claimed that clients can choose to have depressed feelings or other presenting problems. Or clients can make a choice that results in consequences such as depression. And so, individuals can control their own behavior by controlling their choice of behavior, and they can even control to have negative affects or not. Thus Glasser indicated that complaining and blaming are not acceptable as these behaviors are self-defeating on their self-made choices and disasters.

By focusing on positive aspects of human beings, positive psychology has a different approach toward choice and responsibility. Positive psychology believes that being responsible for choice, rather than escaping from responsibility, could well be seen as a virtue such as courage. Courage is defined as the ability and willingness to take the challenge when encountering uncertainty, fear, or pain. Individuals can choose to avoid, escape, or neglect these uncertainties or other challenges, but instead of escape, individuals are willing to accept responsibility or take on the challenges.

There are subtypes of courage. Specifically, the first subtype is physical courage, which is courage in the face of physical pain, hardship, death, or threat of death. Reality therapy would conceptualize these physical hardships as consequences of choices that individuals made. Positive psychology would perceive such action of *taking* responsibility as itself a part of courage. The second subtype of courage is moral courage, which is the ability to act rightly in face of opposition or discouragement (Locke, 2002b).

To integrate reality therapy and positive psychology on choice and responsibility, it is important to know that the integration does not attempt to evaluate which approach is better than the other. Instead, the integration is to accept two approaches and thereby find a better therapeutic solution to clients. First of all, counselors can assist clients to understand the consequence of choice and the close relationship between choice and responsibility. Counselors can then stress that it is clients' courageous move, which is quite laudable, to decide to be responsible for their choice.

### Being present or not

While recognizing the impact of the past, reality therapy focuses on the present moment because this approach believes that past traumas cannot be changed, and people can only choose how to respond to the past trauma. Reality therapists focus on helping client react to the past trauma. Positive psychology does not limit itself to the past, present, or future.

Despite the negative consequences of past trauma or other disturbances, positive psychology would try to enhance individuals' awareness of their strengths in the past. For example, despite various levels of trauma, mistakes, or negative experiences, counselors with positive psychology would help clients explore "What was right with me in the past?" "Was there anything I did that was right?" or "What did I do that enabled me to survive?" and other strength-based reflections. From such strength-focused exploration and re-examination into the past issues, clients then actually recognize their past in a new positive way. In this way, whether the issues are in the past or present, what is important is strategize on how to help clients explore their past issues to find positive things.

The contrast is quite illuminating. Reality therapy counselors would redirect clients to focus on the present and not to dwell on the past, since there is no way to change whatever has happened. In contrast, positive psychology counselors would help clients explore what they had done that have enabled them to survive, and learn on any strengths clients have neglected because of the overwhelming negative effect of past experiences. Counselors can also assist clients to review in what ways their past strengths have helped them "survive." Or else clients can imagine what present situation they would have been in if they did not have those strengths in the past. In short, although counselors in reality therapy (or other approaches focused on the present) endeavor to help clients not to dwell on the past, it might be more helpful to integrate positive psychology to facilitate clients' awareness of their strengths in the past.

### Relationship as a therapeutic tool

According to reality therapy, counselors use the therapeutic relationship to teach clients how to connect with others in their lives because it is important to maintain people's identities. Positive psychology also endorses transference in a therapeutic relationship. Relationship in reality therapy and positive psychology plays an important role. For example, in reality therapy, counselors build the therapeutic relationship so that clients are involved in the counseling process from the beginning. Positive psychology also appreciates the therapeutic relationship which could facilitate clients' awareness and development of their strengths and well-being.

Integrating these two approaches regarding relationship, counselors can be themselves and thereby share with clients how counselors promote their strengths and well-being.

When counselors maintain their identity and discuss with clients their own journey of re-discovery of their strengths, clients would further appreciate that strengths need to be recognized and cultivated.

## The role of symptoms

Neither reality therapy nor positive psychology focuses on symptoms, though with different reasons. Reality therapy avoids discussing symptoms because asking clients about symptoms would revert them to the past. Positive psychology does not totally embrace "symptoms" due to its philosophical position. Specifically, according to positive psychology, there are three faulty assumptions in the DSM that concentrates on symptoms, following the medical frame.

Positive psychology believes that there are four faulty assumptions in the diagnosis of symptoms. The *first* faulty assumption is that a system of socially constructed categories is presented as a set of facts about the world. In fact, this faulty assumption causes some confusion among mental health professionals because such categories might be not valid in representing the human mind. To describe the world or human mind from the perspective of DSM symptoms-centered is just one of several approaches, and it appears arbitrary if the DSM is presented as the only way to describe the human mind. Using the contents of the DSM as the treatment goal would overly focus on symptoms which only are some parts of the human mind and functioning. Likewise, it would misunderstand the range or coverage of the "human mind" if mental health professionals only focused on symptoms.

The *second* faulty assumption, according to positive psychology, is that the DSM overly focuses on symptoms and neglects the meaning of "normal" psychology. Although it is claimed that "there is no assumption that each category of mental disorder is a completely discrete entity with absolute boundaries dividing it from other mental disorders or from no mental disorder" (American Psychiatric Association, 1994, p. xxii), all 800 pages of the DSM are devoted to descriptions of mental symptoms to undermine the credibility of this claim, because the DSM only describe what symptoms are.

The *third* faulty assumption of a symptom-focused approach is that the diagnostic categories can cloud professional judgments by setting into motion a deficit model and leading mental health professionals to pursue symptom-free in their therapy, neglecting all other aspects of counseling.

The *fourth* faulty assumption is that the development of the DSM misleads mental health professionals into pursuing to meet the system and organization of the DSM as their ultimate goal. Since effective interventions must be guided by theories and concepts, designing effective and helpful interventions requires a conceptualization of human functioning that is grounded in a theoretical framework. Yet, the DSM is purely descriptive and does not conceptualize how patterns of behavior, thought, and emotion develop and how they are maintained. Thus, it could be problematic if counselors or mental health professionals only pursue to meet the criteria listed in the DSM.

Integrating the approaches of reality therapy and positive psychology, counselors would crucially assist clients to strengthen their well-being rather than only exploring the symptoms. Counselors and clients can first explore strengths and well-being in the present.

If clients wish to examine their strengths in the past, counselors would respect their clients' decision, and then help clients re-discover their strengths and well-being in the past, and if clients want to renew those strengths and well-being, counselors would explore with clients on how to promote well-being with their visit of the past.

### Challenging traditional psychiatry

Although Glasser criticizes mental health professionals for heavily relying on the DSM to diagnose and treat clients, reality therapy still focuses on psychological problems or weaknesses rather than strengths. Reality therapy also has concerns about the use of medicines to treat clients. Glasser disagrees with the traditional perspective that individuals with physical and psychological symptoms are people with mental illness. Despite these disagreements on medicines and the DSM that may echo the positions in positive psychology, reality therapy may still share current theories that focus on clients' psychological disturbances more than their well-being.

By integrating reality therapy with positive psychology, counselors can further see that medicines and the DSM present some perspectives on treating clients. What is missed in medicines and the DSM is that they do not consider normal functioning or positive aspects of human beings. Thus the integration of reality therapy and positive psychology will advance counselors' appreciation of strengths and well-being.

## Multiculturalizing the Integration

Counseling psychology has a long history of recommendations concerning the need to develop a multicultural perspective, and so it is critical to multiculturalize the integration of reality therapy with positive psychology; it is important to strive to strategize on how such integration meets the cultural contexts of clients. While positive psychology can enrich reality therapy, how to provide a culture-sensitive counseling with such integration is what we need to focus on in this section.

### Choice and positive psychology for multicultural clients

The integration of reality and positive psychology gives a new perspective on choice and responsibility. According to choice theory, choice and responsibility are like two sides of a coin: when individuals make choices, it is inevitable that they need to be responsible for their consequences. Positive psychology believes that being responsible for choice, rather than escaping from responsibility, could be seen as a virtuous act of courage.

Putting this integration in a multicultural perspective, culturally sensitive counselors respect clients' cultural values, religious and/or spiritual beliefs and values about such integration. For example, Asian clients may perceive responsibility as taking on the chores of caring for their family members, and feel that being responsible in *this* way is a critical part in life. For Asian clients, men spending more than casual hours a day working would expect no special appreciation from family members but see it as a routine task, as Asian culture expects males to be the family breadwinners. Working with multicultural clients, culturally sensitive clients recognize the role of their cultures and highlight the courage and willingness to take responsibility in their culture-specific manners.

Instead of imposing counselors' own interpretation of integration, culturally sensitive counselors would respect culturally indigenous manners of helping practices such as seeking spiritual guidance. In multiculturalizing integration with multicultural clients, the goal of counselor is to promote multicultural clients' well-being with culturally appropriate interventions. In other words, culturally skilled counselors are aware of how clients' cultures may well play a crucial role in clients' understanding of the integration of choice with positive psychology (e.g., courage in culture-specific sense).

## Being present

Before working with multicultural clients while integrating being present and positive psychology, counselors need to be aware that multicultural clients may have different timeframes from Western culture or reality therapy. For example, some multicultural clients believe that "previous life" and "next life" are important to their current problems. Or some clients interpret their current problems in terms of their previous life and believe that human beings will move to the next circle of life after death. Since such a value is different from the focus of reality therapy and positive psychology on the present moment, culturally sensitive counselors must be aware that both reality therapy and positive psychology originated in Western culture, and so may well have potential bias when focusing on the present moment.

Because the ultimate purpose of sharing the integration with multicultural clients is to promote their positive affects such as happiness, counselors need to respect how clients define "being present" based on their cultures and/or spiritual experiences. If multicultural clients emphasize the impact of their previous life on their current problems, counselors have the knowledge that the clients' "previous life" is a significant part of the present moment, and design counseling assistance accordingly.

Additionally, culturally sensitive counselors are aware that some multicultural clients blame their present problems on their previous mistakes because their culture focuses on being humble and self-criticism more than forgiveness. While positive psychology encourages clients to forgive themselves and others to discover new joy, culturally sensitive counselors are not averse to seeking consultation with scholars, practitioners, or religious and spiritual leaders in the treatment of culturally different clients when appropriate.

Consultation with outside experts is in line with American Psychological Association (APA) guidelines. According to the APA's (2003) *Guidelines on multicultural education, training, research, practice, and organizational change for psychologists* and APA's (2002) *Ethical principles of psychologists and code of conduct*, it is ethical to consult with experts or experienced practitioners when counselors notice their potential limitations in understanding clients' values and cultures.

## Relationship in reality therapy and positive psychology

Relationship in interpersonal connection plays a significant role in reality therapy and positive psychology, as reality counselors aim to help clients create connections to people. The integration of reality therapy and positive psychology further highlights the positive outcomes of connecting to others. Maintaining a healthy positive relationship with others appears to be a universal recommendation and a rule across different cultures so as to promote wellness, hope, and optimism.

However, culturally sensitive counselors also recognize that, when encouraging multicultural clients to be proactive in creating connections to others, some multicultural clients may get more benefits by experiencing serenity or aloneness first. Or multicultural clients may benefit by establishing a peaceful inner world before connecting to others. Culturally skilled counselors help multicultural clients establish their culture-appropriate priorities on relationship or connection, by enriching clients themselves first, or asking if clients are ready to connect to people.

In counseling, counselors do not set up the timeline of treatment based on their own values or personal preference. Instead, culturally skilled counselors must move from being monoculturally unaware to being aware and sensitive to their own cultural value and to respect multicultural clients' varied manners and time-frames of readiness to learning how to establish relationships.

## Symptoms in reality therapy and positive psychology

It is widely known that neither positive psychology nor positive psychology appreciate the role of symptoms in counseling. Thus, the integration of reality therapy and positive psychology may further push symptoms outside counseling. Further questions emerge as to how the issue of "symptoms" becomes to counselors when helping multicultural clients. They must ask: What is the role of symptoms in the client's culture? What would happen if we do not talk about symptoms in counseling multicultural clients? To make the integration beneficial for multicultural clients, counselors need to first explore the role and definition of symptoms in the client's culture or experiences.

Some helpful questions include: How does the client's culture interpret symptoms? Will discussion of symptoms deteriorate the client's presenting problem or make counseling motre transparent? What are the possible stereotypes about symptoms in client's culture? Thus, culturally sensitive counselors do not straightly apply the integration to multicultural clients without considering their cultural backgrounds. For example, some cultures have stereotypes on mental symptoms which could be equivalent to "craziness" or "loss of mind." Talking to clients on the technical meaning of symptoms as used by psychology may help them develop an accurate understanding regarding symptoms, though counselors do not need to overly focus on exploring symptoms.

The basic requirement for culturally sensitive counselors is to be aware of how their own cultural background and experiences, attitudes, and values and biases influence counseling processes. Counselors then come out of themselves to respect the possible differences between clients and themselves in the interpretation of symptoms. Instead of just "selling" the interpretation they have been trained and have practiced on, culturally skilled counselors conceptualize the role of symptoms on the integration in this chapter and further, importantly, tailor-made to multicultural client's values of their cultures.

Moreover, neither reality therapy nor positive psychology provide a significant role for the DSM in counseling. Because the DSM could be new and strange to multicultural clients, how to address the DSM culturally appropriately could be a challenge in multicultural counseling. Or multicultural clients may perceive the DSM as a list of labels of various mental illnesses. In addition to understanding that, based on positive psychology, there could be faulty assumptions in the DSM, counselors must be aware as to how the client's culture interprets diagnosis.

Only after having such knowledge would counselors be ready to apply the integration (of reality therapy and positive psychology) to help multicultural clients. Because multicultural clients usually have a lower utility rate of counseling compared to white clients, multicultural clients may be concerned about being over-diagnosed or over-psychopathologized; culturally sensitive counselors have specific knowledge that misdiagnosis could create more harm to clients than benefit.

Moreover, to repeat this essential requirement, counselors must be aware of their own cultural heritage, their assumptions about the DSM, and how their cultural value affects their definitions and biases on the distinction between normality and abnormality that may be quite different from multicultural clients. Unreflectively applying counselors' own impressions and definitions of these matters to multicultural clients would do more harm than benefit.

## Traditional "psychiatry"

Both reality therapy and positive psychology have concerns about traditional psychiatry, which originates in the deficit model. Given this common concern, the integration between reality therapy and positive psychology may push traditional psychiatry further away from counseling. Counselors need to explore the role and function of psychiatry in multicultural clients' cultures. Two possible questions to enhance this exploration are to discuss how a multicultural client's culture describes psychiatry, and what consequences follow when someone sees a psychiatrist. Talking about psychiatry, diagnosis, and the DSM could be a difficult conversation for multicultural clients, as, according to positive psychology, counselors' priority in counseling is to advocate multicultural client's needs so as to enhance their positive affects.

With this requirement of sensitivity in mind, culturally skilled counselors possess knowledge about different styles of communication when exploring such sensitive topics which may trigger race-related negative experiences in the clients. This is quite a sensitive issue since, as counselors are aware how the very style of counseling communication may clash and ruin or facilitate and promote the counseling process with multicultural clients.

Moreover, reality therapy may have its own biases against medicines, as positive psychology appears silent regarding medicines. Despite these apparent concerns about medicines from these two approaches, counselors must still respect how medications are taken in clients' culture. For example, some multicultural clients may have been using herbal medicines all through their lives, and other multicultural clients get relief with alternative treatment such as qigong. Instead of blindly persuading clients to reduce the uses of their preferred medicine, culturally sensitive counselors would respect the function and meaning of medicines for multicultural clients.

## Application in Counseling: Case Study

Mary called a university counseling center to arrange for psychological counseling. Mary had already seen a family doctor and suspected that she had developed some depressive symptoms. She felt sad, lonely, isolated, and had no appetites on most days. She also felt that she might be crazy since she felt fatigued despite lots of sleep. She also felt hopeless and claimed that she would fail all courses. Mary is a 20-year-old, full-time college student with a full scholarship. She lives at home and commutes to campus each day.

Mary reported that although she had been to her university counseling center, she now feels more worried about her symptoms and poor appetites, fatigue, and feeling sad. She wants the counselor to help her explore whether medicine is the right choice for her, though her family doctor declined to prescribe her medicines. She has just completed the fall semester of her sophomore year with all As and two A minuses. She says that she is a loner most of the time and spends her day in the classroom, library, and home. To counsel Mary, who claimed to have depressive symptoms, counselors can apply the integration of reality therapy and positive psychology in the five steps below.

*First*, counselors explain that Mary's symptoms are the result of choices she has made in her life. When she recognizes the responsibility of choosing depressive symptoms, according to positive psychology, the acknowledgment of responsibility is the first step to move toward hopefulness and commitment to new behaviors. For example, Mary can learn that she actually could choose to think, feel, and behave differently. In the same way as she could choose to feel depressed and lonely, she also can choose to feel peaceful and relaxed. As she could choose to isolate herself in library for many hours a day, so she can also choose to meet with friends to finish homework.

When counseling Mary, counselors explain and emphasize Mary's personal responsibility. However, with positive psychology, how to interpret the meanings of taking personal responsibility creates significant impact on Mary. Counselors can take this opportunity of educating personal responsibility with a perspective of courage. Specifically, Mary takes her personal responsibility because of her own courage to face her "symptoms." With courage, she presents a "an acceptance of the consequences of action" (Peterson & Seligman, 2004, p. 214). Hence, at the moment when she takes personal responsibility, Mary is a courageous person, which is commendable, because she takes risks to accept personal responsibility.

The *second* task that counselors would use with Mary is to help her focus on the present. Reality therapy warns people against their tendency to recount what has happened in the past to avoid the present moment. Mary may attribute her depressive symptoms to her negative relationships with family in the past. With the integration of reality therapy and positive psychology, Mary learns to live in the present here-and-now and build her strengths there. For example, despite her depressive symptoms and self-doubts, she has still managed to maintain good grades. This shows that she does have the ability to manage her coursework even though she felt very much concerned. Counselors can help Mary further recognize her strengths which she used to manage her depressive symptoms to obtain good grades.

The *third* task counselors can help Mary with is to teach her how to create connections. According to her description, Mary was lonely and isolated. As loneliness deteriorated her mental well-being, it is not surprising that Mary felt sad, depressive, and exhausted. Making connections, according to reality therapy, could be the best solution for symptoms and problems. Creating relationships also echoes the principles of positive psychology, which would further the meanings of relationships. For positive psychology, relationships include altruism and volunteering. Mary can create relationships with friends, and use relationships as a tool to help those in need. This new change in Mary's relationship, from isolation to meaningful connections, could make a difference in her presenting problems and stimulate her to stay happy in the present moment.

The *fourth* task that counselor can help Mary with is to explore her needs of medicines. According to reality therapy, people often mistakenly choose misery in their best attempt to meet needs, and medicine could be one "miserable choice." Mary requested medicine to help her gain relief from depressive symptoms. Yet, her lack of relationship could well be the root of her symptoms, not lack of medication. Counselors can help her reduce symptoms by creating connections, taking responsibility, and staying courageously in the present moment (see above for details); it is possible that, after these interventions, Mary may not need medicine to reduce her symptoms. Moreover, she may even discover a new insight that she acts responsibly when she meets her needs without medicine.

*Finally*, as the demography of clients is increasingly diversified, it is critical to multiculturalize the above case study for multicultural clients. To be culturally effective counselors for multicultural clients, in addition to considering the above interventions, counselors must examine what role clients' culture plays in these interventions. Counselors are now actively in the process of becoming aware of their own assumptions about human behavior, values, biases, personal limitations, and so forth.

So they would not universally apply identical interventions to all clients, including multicultural clients. Culturally sensitive counselors are also actively attempting to understand the worldviews of their culturally different clients without negative judgments. For example, how the interventions fit in with the worldviews of multicultural clients has been a critical query for counselors. It is crucial that counselors understand their culturally different clients with respect and appreciation. To make the intervention as effective for multicultural clients as for Mary, culturally sensitive counselors actively develop and practice culture-appropriate intervention strategies and skills in working with their culturally different clients.

## Follow-up: You continue as Mary's counselor

Consider how you would help Mary if you were her counselor. Here are a series of questions to provide some structure in your thinking about her case:

- How much interest would you have in Mary's own interpretation of her depression? What are some other ways you would help her see patterns between her choice and depression?

- According to reality therapy, Mary's depression was the outcome of her choice. According to this therapeutic principle, could she choose to have a positive affect?
- In reality therapy, creating connections has been an important task for Mary. Would you recommend her to join a group counseling? Would you assign homework (e.g., talk to people 10 minutes a day, etc.)?
- What is the cultural difference between you and Mary? How would you work through the cultural difference?

## Concluding Remarks

Reality therapy was established by Dr Glasser in 1965 and is mainly based on his choice theory. The goal of reality therapy is to help people reconnect because unsatisfactory connections are the sources of psychological problems. Because people choose to have these unhealthy connections in the past, they are responsible for their current psychological problems or they are the products of their past and their choices. Moreover, in choice theory, people are born with five internal or genetic needs: survival; love and belonging; power and achievement; freedom and independence; and fun. The counselor's job is to help clients attain and satisfy these needs in a healthy way. Counselors also need to help clients learn to make good choices and be responsible. Even though Glasser believed that people should be responsible for their choices, reality therapy still mainly focuses on the present. A tremendous contribution of reality therapy to this field is to challenge the necessity of medicines and diagnosis for treatment. Being a psychiatrist himself, Glasser proposed that if human problems come from poor choices and unhealthy connections, the most efficient treatment would be better decision-making and reconnections, not medicines or diagnosis.

Despite the focus of choices and connections, reality therapy is still positioned at treating problems. Thus, it is critical to expand the choices and connections to promote people's strengths and positive affects. Since relationship is the therapeutic tool in reality therapy and positive psychology, counselors can help clients establish connections with others, rebuild unhealthy clients' relationships in the past, promote strengths, and enhance positive affects via the therapeutic relationship in counseling.

Finally, when applying the integration between reality therapy and positive psychology to multicultural clients, counselors need to be aware of their own cultural biases. Importantly, counselors should also know about clients' cultural values on medicines and diagnoses, though both reality therapy and positive psychology refuse medicines and diagnoses.

## Review Questions: What Do You Think?

1. If people's emotional difficulties come from the choices they make, can you think of any exceptions? A person may be born with a gene-related disease and feel depressed about managing this disease. Can you still use reality therapy to treat him or her? Explain your answer.

2. If socioeconomic or racial issues are taken into consideration in reality therapy, do you believe that racism-related stress is the outcome of choice or unhealthy connections?
3. When working with a multicultural client who has been using herb medicines to treat her migraine, would you suggest her stop using them due to Glasser's position against medicines?

# 13

# Feminist Therapy

**Learning Objectives**

- Explain the historical background of feminist therapy.
- Explain how feminist therapy views the human nature of people and the process of change.
- Understand the key concepts in feminist therapy such as oppression and egalitarianism.
- Describe the therapeutic principles in feminist therapy.
- Learn about the roles of counselors in feminist therapy and positive psychology.
- Integrate feminist therapy and positive psychology.
- Multiculturalize the integration between feminist therapy and positive psychology.
- Apply the integration to a case study.

Feminist therapy is a psychotherapeutic intervention that recognizes the impact of varied social practices on personal well-being. It has its roots in the feminist and equal rights movements of the 1960s, and it embraces the conviction that "the personal is political" – that is, what affects the person represents and ensues from the social-political macrocosm in which persons live and have their being. Feminist therapists practice from a variety of feminist and psychological theoretical perspectives. These counselors include diverse groups of individuals striving to change political and social environments into communities of justice and equality for all peoples (Locke, 2002).

When our life and world are dominated by male chauvinists, feminist therapists notice that women are adversely affected by such socially unjust pressures that damage their

*Counseling Psychology: An Integrated Positive Psychological Approach*, First Edition. Ruth Chu-Lien Chao.

self-identity. Social reformation is then an important agenda in feminist therapy. Feminist therapy is also based on the knowledge that women are innately different from men. Women view their worlds in manners different from men and often struggle with issues that are not relevant to the female psychological construct, and so psychological methodologies that were created by and for men may not quite match women's needs. Circumstances specific to women need specifically tailored treatment methods for women. Therefore, feminist therapy is designed not only to recognize those issues independently of the male perspective, but also to address these specially female issues.

Feminist therapists examine the role of interpersonal relationships in women's lives and take into consideration all aspects of sexual biases in our male-dominated society. The therapists value each woman and her unique experiences as authentic and special. Often these therapists explore the educational and professional disparities between men and women, so that women can be liberated from these barriers to allow them to develop appropriate skills to attain their goals. Specifically, this specialized therapy assists women with issues regarding relationships, career, reproductive concerns, body image, and history of physical or sexual abuse if any. In sum, the primary goal of feminist therapy is to empower women to a higher level of functioning in today's society.

A feminist therapist understands that many women perceive their environment through relationships and a sense of connectedness to those around them, whereas many men see things in the context of competition and power. Interpersonal and intrapersonal relationships are at the core of many psychological challenges for women. A feminist therapist works with a client to help her recognize the dysfunctions within these relationships and to develop tactics to overcome her past experiences and manage any subsequent conflicting relationship issues.

## Historical Context

Feminist therapy has developed in a grassroots manner, responding to challenges and to the emerging needs of women. No single individual can be identified as the founder of this approach, and its history is relatively brief. Feminist therapy can be traced to the women's movement of the 1960s, a time when women began uniting their voices to express their dissatisfaction with the limiting and confining nature of traditional female roles.

A profusion of research on gender bias emerged in the 1970s, which helped further feminist therapy ideas, and organizations began to foster the development of feminist therapy. For example, the Association for Women in Psychology (AWP) has played a critical role in promoting issues related to women. Established in 1969, the AWP is a scientific and educational feminist organization focusing on reevaluating and reformulating the role that psychology and the mental health field generally play within women's lives. This organization seeks to act responsibly and sensitively with regard to women by challenging the unquestioned assumptions, research traditions, theoretical commitments, clinical and professional practices, and institutional and societal structures that limit the understanding, treatment, professional attainment, and responsible self-determination of women and men, or that contribute to unwelcome divisions between women based on race, ethnicity, age, social class, sexual orientation or religious affiliation.

In the 1980s, there were tremendous efforts to define feminist therapy as an entity in its own right, and individual therapy was the most frequently practiced form of feminist therapy work on the different voice of women and the morality of care. In this decade, there was also a launch on the self-in-relation model of women's development which was influential in the development of a feminist personality theory.

Later feminist therapy changed dramatically and became more diverse as it focused increasingly on specific problems and issues such as body image, abusive relationships, eating disorders, and incest and sexual abuse, and the feminist philosophies that guided the practice of therapy also became more diverse.

## View of Human Nature

The feminist view of human nature is one fundamental concept that differentiates feminist therapy from other therapeutic models. While traditional therapeutic approaches were developed on the assumption that social arrangements were assumed to be rooted in biologically based gender, they assumed that men and women possess different personalities and most theories were developed from men's perspectives. To challenge the male-dominated traditional theories, feminist scholars propose that feminist theory perceives humans as being gender-fair, interactionist, and flexible. Rather than assuming biological differences as the true nature, gender-fair feminist theory believes that the differences between men and women are based on socialization processes. The gender-fair theory attempts to avoid stereotypes in social roles and interpersonal behavior, and uses concepts that apply equally to individuals or groups regardless of age, sex, race, culture, class, sexual orientation, social economic status, and ability. Highlighting the perspective of fairness and inclusiveness, feminist theory stresses that concepts regarding humans need to include behavior, thinking, and feeling based on specific context and environment. The inclusiveness of the feminist theory emphasizes that the concepts of humans should include development of all stages rather than being fixed on a specific stage such as childhood.

## Theoretical Principles

Many feminist scholars articulate the principles that provide the foundation for feminist therapy. Although these principles are interrelated and even overlap, they are the foundation to understanding feminist therapy. These core principles are: (a) personal issues are political; (b) definitions of mental illness; (c) integrated analysis of oppression; and (d) egalitarian therapeutic relationship.

## Personal issues are political

According to feminist therapists, no one is isolated because all people live in a society where individuals' personal problems have social and political roots. Feminist therapists aim to not only help clients solve their personal issues but also work on social change. Because personal problems are deeply related to social or political issues, one of the most efficient approaches to manage them is to change society. Feminist therapists claim that their intervention not only helps individuals to deal with their struggles but also advances the transformation of society, since the advancement of social change is a prime responsibility for feminist therapists. Feminist therapists believe that women suffer from oppression in society and social pressure, so suggest that women must actively engage in therapy and examine how social oppression relates to their personal problems. However, feminist therapy does not avoid personal responsibility, even though its stress is on the influence of environment. The purpose of addressing social change is that it may facilitate individual change if personal problems are rooted in the external environment. Thus, rather than justifying personal problems, the goal of feminist therapy is to advance a societal change and promote a new vision of societal organization which frees women and men from the constraints imposed by fixed gender-role expectations.

## Definitions of mental illness

Feminist therapy rejects the disease model of mental illness, and considers the explanation of pain from intrapsychic and interpersonal perspectives as an incomplete conceptualization of psychological distress. Although external factors are influential for individuals, feminist therapy believes that psychological distress is best explained as a presentation of unjust systems. From this perspective, pain should be defined not as a defect or deficit of individuals. Instead, for feminist therapy, pain is an evidence of individuals' resistance to social oppression and will to survive despite various social pressures. Thus, the ultimate goal of feminist therapy is to intervene in a way to promote change in a socially dysfunctional environment.

Within the framework of social context, the dysfunction of environment is a primary reason for individuals' mental illness. Thus, the symptoms should be reframed as strategies for survival. Symptoms could be seen as methods to cope with social or environmental pressures on individuals, particularly women. Thus, feminist therapists believe that counselors should identify the meanings and implications of symptoms which could be clients' methods of survival. Because individuals are living in societal oppression, the expression of pain could be interpreted as the beginning of healing.

## Integrated analysis of oppression

Although oppression exists in various dimensions of a society, gender-related oppression has been one of its earliest topics. Gender is an essential component in feminist therapy and women's experiences of being oppressed is a critical start to examine the impact of oppression on individuals. Men and women living in a society are expected to fulfill different gender roles. According to feminist theory, these fixed gender roles actually create respective restrictions to men and women, and thus, men and women are living gender-related oppression. For example, men have been raised to be tough and never reveal emotions. Showing emotions or revealing vulnerability has been seen as a weakness for men. When men feel sad or experience distress, they are not allowed to express their emotions because of societal expectations. For women, the gender-related expectation creates heavy pressure for their behavior and self-presentation to others. They are expected to be gentle, compliant, kind, warm, and nice. They are expected to manage housework such as cooking meals.

Feminist therapy aims to free men and women from the restriction and constraints of gender-related expectations. Feminist counselors may demonstrate to clients the significance of gender by sharing with clients how he or she perceives the world from his or her gender. Counselors assist clients to understand that, though people are different in gender, such difference cannot be equalized as constraints to restrict people's behavior and attitude. Although feminist therapy may begin with gender-related oppression, counselors may expand the impact of oppression to other dimensions such as race, age, social economic class, disability, and so on. Thus, the ultimate goal of feminist therapy is to challenge all forms of oppression, not just oppression of women.

*Egalitarian therapeutic relationship* Feminist therapy pays attention to the power issue in counseling, and counselors strive to build an equalitarian relationship with clients. Focusing on building a relationship sharing equal power differentiates feminist therapy from other approaches of counseling. For example, in psychoanalysis, the counselor may have more power than the client. Different from other counseling theories, feminist therapists may address the power difference existing in counseling and invite clients to create an equalitarian relationship. The purpose of building an equalitarian relationship is to break the stereotypes of traditional therapy, where the counselor may present as the authority figure, while the client follows the counselor's direction and instruction. The aim of an equalitarian therapeutic relationship is to break all types of hierarchical relationships in society which lead to confinement. With an equalitarian relationship in counseling, the client can freely explore his or her problems without revisiting constraints from social expectations.

The tenets of feminist therapy include, broadly, recognition of diversity in identity and of multiple oppressions, acknowledgment of power differentials inherent in the therapeutic relationship and in society, and responsibility for personal involvement in engendering individual and social changes that equalize power.

*Multiple diversities and oppressions* Feminist therapy acknowledges multiple aspects of human diversity that are likely to affect clients' personal well-being, including but not limited to, sex, heritage, race, class, age, physical ability, religion, and sexual orientation. While each of these aspects alone may create personal difficulties for an individual within society, most individuals suffer from multiple oppressions. In large part, providing didactic experiences that illuminate these inequities provides the framework for the therapeutic process. Additionally, feminist therapists remain aware of the complexity of human diversity and of how their own personal attributes and differences from the client may be affecting the process of healing.

*The therapeutic relationship* Although feminist therapists strive to achieve equality in their therapeutic relationships and to empower their clients, they are continuously aware of the intrinsic power differential, especially early in therapy, that exists in the therapeutic relationship. Throughout the therapeutic process, there is a continuous focus on equalizing the client–therapist relationship and on avoiding taking responsibility for or coercing the client. The intent of this focus is to work collaboratively with clients, who are considered experts relative to their experiences, to achieve goals that are meaningful to them. A strong emphasis is placed on consciousness raising, which assists clients in understanding the context of their psychological distress. Within this relationship, therapists are far more likely to be self-disclosing, especially in relation to their own experiences of oppression and empowerment, than in most formal schools of psychological thought.

*Social change* Practitioners of feminist therapy are active in efforts to bring about change that equalizes social and personal power. Because feminism is multifaceted, the focus of such change efforts may vary greatly; however, personal investment in altering power differentials is considered of primary importance for the therapist and, eventually, for the client. Advocacy requires continuous awareness of both positive outcomes and unanticipated negative consequences of efforts to equalize power and promote justice.

*Developmental issues* While feminist therapy has no formal theory of development, it does view society's construction of what is right and good as having considerable impact on individual identity development. For example, Rayner, Schniering, Rapee, Taylor, and Hutchinson (2013) have suggested that girls develop through connection with their primary caregiver, usually a woman, while boys avoid this connection in favor of autonomy. Girls are expected to adhere to common gender role stereotypes, including nurturance (playing with dolls), sensitivity, and cooperativeness. Boys, conversely, are expected to be sturdy, power seeking, and self-determining. Society, in various forms, stresses similar messages in relation to a plethora of other personal attributes.

*Psychological suffering* Feminist theorists' views of psychopathology, or problems in daily living, are, in some ways, dependent on their theoretical stances. However, there is consistent recognition that psychological distress is engendered by environmental conditions, especially those of disproportionate power and limitations of choice. Thus, as Ballou and Brown (2002) note, it is difficult to label an individual with a "disorder" and to believe that this "disorder" is located exclusively within the person, while ignoring the context of distress. Feminist practitioners maintain awareness that the mental health field has its own discourse that may undermine the well-being of individuals who do not meet the narrow standards of psychological wellness. The historical underpinnings of psychology are based in a white, male-dominated society that emphasizes independence and competition and values instrumental (formerly known as masculine) characteristics. Thus, the profession often ignores the voices and knowledge of the very individuals that they are attempting to serve. Feminist therapists generally have a much broader view of acceptable emotions, cognitions, and behaviors than those that are deemed appropriate in a society that is replete with injustice.

*Consciousness raising* Feminist therapists utilize consciousness raising to examine the role that social power differentials and bias play in personal distress and relationships. Helping clients appreciate the systematic nature of personal constructions and relationships following from cultural constructions and mandates provides a holistic perspective of mental distress and well-being that diminishes self-blame.

*Personal validation* In large part, consciousness raising sets the groundwork for supporting clients' worth and engendering personal empowerment. Feminist therapy is a practice of interdependence and support. Feminist therapy strives to assist clients in finding their own voices to tell their own stories in ways that are self-validating and self-enhancing. It is a therapy of personal esteem and empowerment.

## An Integration: Positive Psychology and Feminist Therapy

As feminist therapy is integrated into positive psychology, the domain of health and well-being is increasingly expanded in our society culture. Also, the integration can make an impact on various people such as mental health professionals, researchers, policy-makers, and social and political movements. In this comprehensive manner, the integration of feminist therapy and positive psychology reflects a new direction toward the conceptualization of mental health which includes personal well-being and positive health in public policies and organizations as well as in intimate personal lives.

### Personal vs. social issues

Both feminist therapy and positive psychology focus on social change. According to feminist therapists, individuals' personal problems have social and political roots, so work on social changes is an essential part of individual therapy. Because personal problems are inextricably involved with social and/or political issues, a most efficient management of personal problems is to change society. To feminist therapists, social conditions are responsible for personal problems.

For example, women clients encounter sexual harassment because society minimizes the importance of females and worse, materializes the role and status of "women." When society minimizes the role of females and degrades the contribution of them, it is not surprising that women encounter numerous barriers in schools, work, and even families.

Emphasizing positive aspects of persons, positive psychology focuses on social changes to promote personal growth in society. Positive psychology insists that positive impact and change should extend to institutional and organizational level, as individuals who are apathetic, alienated, or irresponsible throughout all social strata are numerous examples of unhealthy social pressures. Such human dysfunctions can be observed not only in our mental health clinics but also among the millions who, for hours a day, sit passively and play with their cell phones, watch television nonstop, stare blankly from the back of their classrooms, or wait boringly for weekends to arrive.

These phenomena demonstrate a wide range of reactions to social environment, social climate, and political atmosphere. Specifically, bad social conditions catalyze development and maintenance of personal problems, and, conversely, good social context induces personal strengths. Positive psychology has shown consistent interest in interpersonal empathy and pro-social behavior. Civic virtues and positive social institutions have also been a focus. Thus, positive psychology and social change are intrinsically related not accidentally but in principle, and so positive psychology consistently strives for social change, by serving as a "mechanism" for social change and thereby promotes personal strengths at a societal level.

Integrating feminist therapy and positive psychology, the counseling interventions would include personal counseling combined with social change. In personal counseling, counselors assist clients to develop their strengths such as resilience, hope, and well-being. For social change, counselors should venture beyond their personal supporting roles and become actively involved in setting and promoting various social agenda, such as social support, public trust, safety/security, social tolerance, social promotion of personal competence and its growth, life satisfaction, positive engagement, and lowering negative affect at a social level (Diener & Diener, 2011).

## Definitions of mental illness

Feminist therapy rejects the disease model of mental illness, and considers the explanation of pain from intrapsychic and interpersonal perspectives to be an incomplete conceptualization of psychological distress. For feminist therapy, although external factors are influential to individuals, psychological distress is best explained as a presentation of unjust systems. In a similar fashion, positive psychology also disagrees with the disease or deficit model of mental health, and promotes the importance of strength-based therapy. Peterson and Seligman (2004) developed a classification of human virtues and character strengths to highlight what a deficit-based model missed.

An integration of feminist therapy and positive psychology can be seen in their aversion to disease-based model. Yet, these two approaches have different perspectives on how to change the definition of mental health problems. For feminist therapy, pain is an evidence of individuals' resistance to social oppression, manifesting the personal will to survive despite various social pressures. Since social oppression or pressure is the root of personal problems, the most effective feminist counseling is to intervene in personal problems while pursuing changes in social institutions to change socially dysfunctional environment to induce individual psychological stability.

Positive psychology does not agree with the medicine-centered conceptualization or deficit-based treatment, either. However, its focus is on how to enhance personal well-being by promoting a positive social climate, policy, and environment. For positive psychology, social changes can be fulfilled with several strategies, and confrontation or even challenges of the social system would be just some examples. By focusing on strengths, positive psychologists would attempt to empower policy-making, which increases positive interactions among people and groups.

Mass media can be used to portray positive persons with strong character traits in movies (e.g., *Lincoln*, *The Help*), TV shows, theater, novels, musicals, and many others. Educators can promote educating to instill positive character traits with reforming curricula or education policies. Thus, for positive psychology, social change can be effectively reached by promoting strengths on a large scale, in policies and societal climate, rather than individually fighting or sporadic confrontations.

Integrating these two approaches regarding social changes, mental health professionals will come to have a clear understanding of how intimately social issues are related to personal problems, and, when using the integrated approach to help clients, counselors can help them discover any strengths they have developed despite social oppression. For example, many women thrive in the workforce despite the glass ceiling effect, which often limits women's professional progress. These women have progressed in their careers despite various barriers caused by social stereotypes that turn blind eyes to their ability. Many women are succeeding in math, engineering, technology, and other traditionally male-dominated fields, defying gender-role stereotypes. This integrated approach will help clients understand the root of their personal problem, and importantly, help them find their strengths despite social issues that cause their problems.

## "Oppression" in feminist therapy and positive psychology

Both feminist therapy and positive psychology acknowledge the existence of oppression which widely occurs in various dimensions of a society, visibly or invisibly, and in many formats. However, despite their agreement on oppression, the two approaches have different ways of strategizing on how to manage it.

For feminist therapists, oppression needs to be addressed and solved at a macro-level of intervention to change societal systems, correct stereotypes, and even initiate new policies. For example, it is societal expectation that causes fixed and rigid roles of men and women, and these rigid roles result in personal problems (e.g., a woman feels stressed working as a pilot because of gender-related stereotypes). So, for feminist therapists, it is equally important to provide interventions at both macro and micro levels. At a micro level, mental health professionals can provide individual therapy to treat personal issues (which may be caused by social oppression).

Positive psychology focuses on strengths and well-being, rather than only recognizing negative consequences in culture, society, or individuals caused by social oppression. Thus, the integration of these approaches will help individuals recognize the social oppression while appreciating and promoting their personal strengths and well-being. At a macro level, it is necessary to promote collective well-being by various avenues. For example, in education, school teachers can enhance students' appreciation of pioneers who shifted the directions of our society. These pioneers have often endured suffering under countless difficulties, but they still persisted to fulfill their dreamed missions. On women's rights, there were many important pioneers who were trail blazers in actualizing women's rights to vote, education, work, and others. For example, it took many people's efforts during the late nineteenth century and early twentieth century, to pass the Nineteenth Amendment to the United States Constitution, which refers to "The right of citizens of the United States to vote shall not be denied or abridged by the United States or by any State on account of sex."

Almost 170 years ago in the 1850s, Lucy Stone and the National Woman's Rights Conventions organized campaigns to produce women's suffrage petitions in several states. Ms. Stone became the first person to appeal for woman suffrage before an august body of lawmakers where she addressed the Massachusetts Constitutional Convention in 1853.

Other pioneers such as Susan B. Anthony, Elizabeth Cady Stanton, Judy Ward Howe, and Genevieve Clark worked hard to build support for the federal measure by winning the right of women to vote at the state and local levels, and then at federal voting to win the final victory. These are examples demonstrating the power of an integrated approach to publicly recognize social injustices of gender oppression, but what is crucial in these examples is to highlight the strengths and collective persistence that effected the resounding success in redressing the deep-rooted social injustices. To re-examine these successes and victories may well help individuals re-discover strengths and virtues of these pioneers, which contributed to the success in radically shifting the inveterate social directions.

Conversely, the integrated approach also helps clients promote their personal strengths which in turn results in better management of their problems at social levels. For example, the integrated approach makes it easy to see that, although suffering various oppressions, those pioneers on women rights still persisted in pursuing their dreams as they continued to seek ways to institute equality among women as well as men. Positive psychology stresses persistence as a firm or obstinate continuation of consistent actions in spite of difficulty and/or opposition.

Persistence is defined as "voluntary continuation of a goal-directed action in spite of obstacles, difficulties, or discouragement" (Peterson and Seligman, 2004, p. 229). Just as fear is a prerequisite for courage, challenge is a prerequisite for perseverance. Simply measuring how long someone sticks with a task does not adequately capture the essence of perseverance because continuing to perform something that is fun or easy does not involve the overcoming of obstacles and/or disappointment. In the light of this definition of the concept of persistence, we realize that these pioneers amply demonstrated unlimited persistence.

With the real examples of persistence, demonstrated in history, in the face of continuing social oppression, mental health professionals can promote clients' strengths (e.g., persistence models set up by these pioneers). Clients can be encouraged to reflect on any of *their* experiences in which they "fought" oppression (e.g., inequality in school, workplace, family, etc.) to pleasantly discover their own strengths such as persistence.

Moreover, to fulfill their mission in securing voting rights for women, these persistent ladies had treid many strategies to work through countless unimaginable barriers. They must have gone through so many failures and constantly felt frustrated. Despite all kinds of failures and disturbances, they still resiliently stuck up their noses to finally accomplish their mission, to secure women's voting rights. Resilience refers to the capacity to recover quickly from backbreaking difficulties. According to Petersen and Seligman (2004), resilience includes the ability to bounce back from adversity, work through challenges, and overcome obstacles.

Just think about this. If those pioneer ladies lacked the resilience to work through obstacles they encountered right and left, perhaps there no women's right to vote would exist today, or perhaps such rights would have been indefinitely delayed, as a nice unattainable pie in the sky. Because of their resilience, millions of women can now routinely exercise their right to vote, as a matter of course. Using this example, mental health professionals can help clients find *their* inherent resilience. The clients can be stimulated to ask themselves what they can do to overcome challenges in school, at work, and/or in their family, in the face of oppression and/or stereotypes they suffer now.

## Egalitarian therapeutic relationship in feminist therapy and positive psychology

Feminist therapy pays attention to the issue of power in counseling, as counselors strive to build an equalitarian relationship with clients. So "relationship sharing, equal power" differentiates feminist therapy from other approaches of counseling. For example, in psychoanalysis, counselors have more power than clients. Different from other counseling theories, feminist therapists may often address the power difference existing in counseling and invite clients to create an equalitarian relationship.

Although positive psychology may not disagree with this relationship, it mainly focuses on building clients' strengths. By integrating feminist therapy with positive psychology, counselors can help clients improve their well-being and cultivate their strengths by an equalitarian relationship. Through perceiving equal power between client and counselor, clients may regain their self-confidence and self-esteem.

For feminist therapy, the purpose of building an equalitarian relationship could be just to break the stereotypes of traditional therapy where the counselor often presents as an authority figure while the client follows the counselor's direction and instruction. Yet, with the integration with positive psychology, the question or focus becomes how such breaking of stereotypes can enhance clients' well-being, helping them feel that they are worthy people. Similarly, the focus of an integrated approach between feminist therapy and positive psychology explores how hierarchical relationships and/or equal relations can help clients transfer despair into hope, difficulties into opportunities, and hate/anger into appreciation in a strength-frame.

The tenets of feminist therapy include, broadly, recognition of diversity in self-identity and of multiple oppressions. Sadly, in our current society, numerous people still suffer multiple oppressions, visible or invisible. With the integration of positive psychology, the focus changes to how people survive and even thrive against these multiple oppressions and continually enrich their various self-identities. Why do some people see multiple oppressions as new opportunities for their life identities and/or new possibilities to change the society?

Integrating the concept of multiple oppressions into positive psychology, counselors can explore what factors (e.g., gender, race/ethnicity, sexual orientation, etc.) contribute to client's problems *and,* importantly, what resources (e.g., resilience, optimism, love, etc.) help clients survive these oppressions. For example, Eleanor Roosevelt was the first presidential spouse to hold press conferences, write columns in a syndicated newspaper, and speak at a national convention. On a few occasions, she even publicly disagreed with her husband's policies.

She launched an experimental community for the families of unemployed miners, though later widely regarded as a failure. She advocated expanded roles for women in the workplace, civil rights of African Americans and Asian Americans, and the rights of World War II refugees. In her life, she experienced multiple oppressions such as stereotypes in gender roles. People also criticized her support of civil rights of African Americans and Asian Americans. Despite all oppositions, because of her persistence in passion to make our world better, she kept on improving the collective well-being for so many people.

## The therapeutic relationship in feminist therapy and positive psychology

Both feminist therapy and positive psychology strive to achieve positive impacts via their therapeutic relationships to empower their clients. Yet, feminist therapists are continually aware of the intrinsic power differential, especially early in therapy, that exists in the therapeutic relationship. For positive psychology, counselors use the therapeutic relationship as a strategy to build clients' strengths. Taken these two approaches together, counselors can assist clients to create well-being despite all kinds of oppressions.

Throughout the therapeutic process, clients can learn how an equalitarian relationship promotes their well-being by empowering themselves. A strong emphasis on this integration is placed on consciousness raising and a sense of equalitarianism, which assists clients to accentuate their self-confidence and self-esteem. Within this relationship, counselors may use techniques such as self-disclosure, especially in relation to the counselors' own experiences of oppression and empowerment, to facilitate clients' skills and ability to build their equal relationships with others to promote their own and others' well-being.

## Social change

Counselors of feminist therapy are active at promoting social changes that equalize social and personal powers. As feminist therapy perceives social changes as a necessary condition to solving personal problems, the focus of such change efforts may vary greatly. To date, although positive psychology may focus more on individuals' strengths and well-being, it is critical to expand the concepts of strengths and well-being into various dimensions such as social changes toward an environment that better enhances strengths at social and individual levels. According to Sirgy and Wu (2009), in order to satisfy the full spectrum and dimensions of human survival and growth needs, people have to be involved and actively invest their attention and resources in multiple life domains. Balanced contributions to personal well-being can be included in the agenda of social changes.

Thus, the integration of feminist therapy with positive psychology aims at promoting well-being in various dimensions of society, including personal and interpersonal well-being. This comprehensive ideal of well-being can be achieved through social changes such as developing public policies to promote diverse people's strengths. Or through social changes, the society and/or the entire country should increase social justice toward a community with thorough equality. Thus, such comprehensive advocacy requires both feminist therapy to highlight social changes and positive psychology to inspire well-being on all levels, and this is precisely what integration of both approaches happily achieves. The consequence would be a new environment of our life world with equalized power and true social justice.

## Multiculturalizing the Integration

Positive psychology and traditional psychotherapy are equally criticized as having an excessively individualistic focus, being influenced by middle-class Westerners (e.g. Becker & Marecek, 2008). Multiculturalizing these psychotherapies would ameliorate if not remedy such defect. To multiculturalize the integration of feminist therapy and positive psychology requires familiarity with the clients' various cultural backgrounds. Different from other major counseling theories (e.g., psychoanalysis, existential therapy, CBT), feminist therapy views the experience of oppression as the most salient factor in understanding client concerns. Thus, social justice and awareness of cultural diversity are essential parts of feminist therapy.

The approach of changing social and individual situations in feminist therapy is fully aware that "oppression" is complex and numerous, and it complexly structures and shapes many individuals' reality. The most common of these oppressions are on gender, race/ethnicity, culture, socioeconomic class, sexual orientation, age, and ability. For some, there may be additional and/or other oppressions. According to feminist therapy, almost everyone (e.g., men, women, clients, and counselors) are influenced by these oppressions. It is therapists' responsibility to be aware of their clients' lived experiences of oppression as well as their own lived experiences of oppression.

When counseling multicultural clients in the context of this integration of feminist therapy and positive psychology, culturally skilled counselors must be aware of the differences in gender, social class, and others, to breed social issues in clients' culture. For example, males have higher position and authority than females among the Latino culture, and fathers or male elders have decision power in the family. Indonesian culture in its government has been noted as a concern by advocates of minorities as the root of violent discriminations against religious minorities.

Further, Indian culture has been dominated by the caste system. In fact, India's caste system is nothing more than a formalization of economic class divisions, designed to stabilize and fixate it by making those class divisions hereditary and binding through generations. Caste is identical with class. The upper classes have a vested interest in perpetuating a caste or class system, because its perpetuation establishes the power and privilege of these upper classes. Is this situation socially unjust? The answer depends on whom in which culture the question is asked. It is such a complex matter, because of global cultural diversity.

Taken all this together, when counseling multicultural clients with feminist therapy advocating social justice, culturally sensitive counselors must possess personal knowledge on how social justice is viewed by the client's own culture. The integration of feminist therapy with positive psychology advances the significance of social justice as it faces new directions in various cultures toward the conceptualization of mental health to include personal well-being and positive health in public policies and organizations, but, importantly, in the specific context of the specific cultures of specific cultural clients the counselors must serve.

## Personal vs. social issues in multicultural counseling

We must begin with the important point mentioned above. Although both feminist therapy and positive psychology focus on social change, culturally skilled counselors are aware that different cultures may well have their respective views about social justice and social change. For example, when counseling an international student from China, it might be difficult to talk about social change due to the political climate in China.

Although feminist therapy claims that an individual's personal problems have social and political roots so that to work on social changes is essential for individual therapy, culturally sensitive counselors are aware of the possible sensitive implications for multicultural clients. Some cultures and/or nations may take "social change" as revolution or rebellion and may cause people to be trapped in risky situations. Or some cultures may have negative impressions about the concept of "social change" and such negative values may have unforeseen repercussions in the client's personal or psychological issues.

In this situation, positive psychology introduces the concept of well-being at different levels, from personal to interpersonal and social. Culturally skilled counselors would explore the meanings of personal and social/collective well-being in the client's specific culture. Moreover, counselors would explore how social climatic change would make an impact on the client's well-being and also what specific social or political conditions would facilitate development of strengths. Thus, culturally sensitive counselors must have knowledge about the client's cultural heritage and the role of the client's culture on social change. Importantly, counselors are aware that their own experiences of social change could well be different from their clients' and will respect the difference.

Although counseling multicultural clients with this integration may involve some challenges, as the concept of "social changes" might be taken as too radical in some cultures or nations, counselors can still continue to assist clients to promote well-being at different levels. For example, with knowledge about the client's culture, culturally sensitive counselors can explore how to promote the client's strengths and well-being without involving risks to the client.

Furthermore, culturally sensitive counselors would advocate social well-being compatible with the client's cultural values. Counselors would also recognize the contributions of those pioneers in the client's culture or nation to enhance change for the better. For example, despite various political oppressions, Aung San Suu Kyi, winner of the Nobel Peace Prize in 1991, sought and fought for democracy in Burma. Her bravery in her undaunted acts have awaken her people to pursue a better and stronger country to result in enhancing their personal well-being. Thus, counselors actively develop and exercise sensitively appropriate intervention strategies and skills to work with multicultural clients. The culture-sensitive intervention (i.e., personal well-being and social well-being) would be effective in promoting multicultural clients' positive affect while being compatible with their cultures.

With keen awareness of potential cultural differences between clients and counselors, culturally skilled counselors would explore *with* clients how people in their culture develop their strengths such as resilience, hope, and well-being as defined in their culture. Some possible questions include, "How does your culture define positive affect?" "What is the role of hope in your culture?" "How do people in your culture enhance well-being?" Different cultures have their culturally specific approaches to building hope, resilience, perseverance, and other positive affects or character traits.

Counselors are aware that they themselves have their own racial/cultural heritage and would respect the distinctive cultural heritage of their clients. For social change or social well-being, culturally sensitive counselors would explore the role and meaning of social well-being and social change in the client's culture. Specifically, social change or involvement in social policies might be an intervention at an institutional level in Western culture; however, the same sort of intervention may conflict with a client's culture to invite disasters. Thus, culturally sensitive counselors are aware of the culturally related meaning of social change in the client's culture. With such knowledge, counselors work with people to increase *their* social well-being.

### Definitions of mental illness in a multicultural context

Both feminist therapy and positive psychology reject the disease model of mental illness. For feminist therapy, although external factors are influential for individuals, feminist therapists believe that psychological distress is best explained as a presentation of unjust social systems; positive psychology disagrees with the disease-deficit model of mental health and insists on the importance of strength-based therapy. Despite such shared disagreement with the disease-based model of mental illness, culturally sensitive counselors should respect the definition of mental illness in a client's culture.

Moreover, culturally skilled counselors must be aware of the distinct worldview and its impact on mental illness. While Western culture treats mental illness as a disease, other cultures may view mental illness with stereotype or stigma. Thus, culturally skilled counselors would endeavor to understand the worldview of their culturally different clients and the impact of their worldview on the meaning of "mental illness." It is crucial that counselors understand and regard the worldviews of their culturally different clients with respect, understanding, and appreciation. Importantly, although Western culture appreciates evidence-based treatment, culturally sensitive counselors would respect the clients' indigenous treatment of mental illness in their culture, or counselors would even actively collaborate with tribe leaders or spiritual/religious persons to provide culturally appropriate counseling to clients.

### "Oppression" in a multicultural context

Both feminist therapy and positive psychology acknowledge the existence of oppression; feminist theory believes that oppression needs to be addressed and solved at a macro-level of intervention, as positive psychology focuses on collective well-being. When working with multicultural clients with this integration, culturally skilled counselors should be aware that "oppression" may well be treated differently in different cultures. For example, cultural oppression has been related to high risk to African Americans. Latina/o workers are used to being misunderstood as "cheap laborers," resulting in group-level internalized racism. Asian Americans suffer from the model "minority" stereotype, which is categorization of "positive" characteristics as passivity, docility, and high academic achievements.

Thus, counseling culturally different clients may best begin by exploring the meanings of "oppression" in the clients' respective cultures. The next step after defining "oppression" is to collaborate with clients to work through oppression. Culturally sensitive counselors are aware of the their own assumptions about oppression, cultural values, biases, and so forth. Importantly, counselors respect the different assumptions on oppression and the various ways in which to work through it by cooperating with culturally different clients in the clients' own cultural manner.

In Western culture, to work through oppression requires changes in macro-levels such as policies. With positive psychology, counselors may advocate well-being at macro-levels. Yet, counselors are aware that such Western-based integration may be in conflict with ideologies in other cultures. So counselors must possess knowledge about the macro-level of well-being in their clients' culture. For example, Asian culture may appreciate personal well-being as involved in collective well-being due to its collectivism. Yet, within Asian culture, working against oppression could trigger sensitive risks in China due to its community ideology and conservative political climate. Culturally skilled counselors must have knowledge about between-group and within-group differences on how to work through oppression.

In undertaking the strategies of working through oppression in clients' culture, counselors highlight the positive affect. Some questions to be answered could be, "What could be the positive affect or emotion when oppression is changed in your culture?" "What impact could ensue after oppression is addressed?" Culturally skilled counselors and clients can cooperate to recognize pioneers in clients' culture who worked against oppression.

### The therapeutic relationship in working with culturally different clients

Both feminist therapy and positive psychology strive to achieve positive impacts in their therapeutic relationships to empower their clients. Still, counseling culturally different clients, counselors must constantly respect the client's expectation of the role of counselor. For example, some cultures expect counselors to lead the counseling session while other cultures may endorse equalitarian relationship. Using relationship as a therapeutic tool with multicultural clients serves two purposes. One, it provides a great opportunity for counselors to learn the worldview of the clients and their expectations about therapeutic relationship. Two, when exploring culturally appropriate relationship with client, counselors demonstrate a positive, open-minded, and sincere attitude toward clients, as such positive attitude could well instill hope into counseling. Culturally skilled counselors are well aware of counselors' own biases concerning therapeutic relationship but respect the possible different expectations between themselves and clients.

## Application in Counseling: A Case Study

Selena is an African American female student who performs academically well as a senior college student. She is enrolled in an honors class to work on her undergraduate thesis, and she is a student representative for an on-campus volunteer organization. Her father is an ophthalmologist and her mother is an attorney. Selena and her parents live comfortably in an upper middle-class neighborhood. Although there are several other African American youngsters in her community, most of them are either in their 30s or younger, or they attend private school.

Selena scheduled an appointment with a counselor to request removal from her honors class, and decided not to pursue her thesis. The counselor asked Selena for the details regarding her decision because she has been on the dean's list every semester and even obtained summa cum laude last year. At first, Selena insisted that her decision was related to shifting priorities in student organizations as she is looking for a part-time job.

However, the counselor asked about the student demographics in Selena's honor class and finally asked Selena to what extent her decision might have resulted from her being the only African American student in the class. At that point, Selena felt the counselor truly understood the challenges academically successful African American college students such as herself must endure. Selena wept as she explained to the counselor that her African American friends teased her on working hard to obtain good grades, speaking standard English, participating in the gymnastics team, and living in an affluent community. In essence, in the eyes of her African American friends, she was a coconut, a black "acting white." She confided to her counselor that the stress was overwhelming.

Additionally, her white classmates in her honors class dismissed her good grades as not due to her hard work but to her skin color that even let her into the honor class in the first place. So her white classmates refused to work with her on a group project. Other white students were reluctant to cooperate with her when the professor assigned Selena to the team. They also jokingly questioned on what her parents did to support the family, implicitly insinuating that Selena's parents might have been doing something shady, like selling drugs to afford their life style.

## How to help Selena

At the beginning of the counseling, the counselor, a white female, appropriately validated Selena's frustration and hurt from racial discrimination and shared her experience over the past years' working with other African American females who had expressed similar traumas. The counselor recognized that in many ways Selena was isolated from both her African American friends and white peers and was truly an outsider within two disparate peer groups.

In other words, Selena was suffering from inter-racial and intra-racial discriminations. The counselor was thinking of helping Selena with feminist therapy which could be integrated with positive psychology. Additionally, such integration could be contextualized to Selena's African American culture.

*Personal vs. social issues* According to feminist therapy, Selena's personal problems regarding hurt by racial discrimination have social and political roots. Because Selena's personal problems are deeply related to social and/or political issues, one of the most efficient approaches to manage personal problems is to change the society while helping Selena manage her hurt. When the society tolerates racial discrimination, it is not surprising that Selena encounters numerous unfair treatments by her African American and white peers.

In positive psychology, it is important to promote Selena's well-being and strengths to manage her distress. Recently, a number of scholars and practitioners have indicated that African Americans may benefit by culture-specific copings (Utsey, Ponterotto, Reynolds, & Cancelli, 2000). According to Belgrave and Allison (2010), coping refers to efforts at mastering environmental demands or stress such as racial discrimination. As positive psychology highlights the importance of positive affects, for African Americans such as Selena, culture-specific resources (i.e., internal and external resources) might be more helpful for them to maintain well-being. Internal resources in African American culture refer to individual factors, personality traits, racial identification, social class, and cultural beliefs which are helpful for this population when they encounter stress. External resources refer to family and/or social ties, work relationships, and church affiliations (Belgrave & Allison, 2010).

In addition to helping Selena to work on her personal distress, her counselor could also address the social issues which lead to her personal problems. Positive psychology also focuses on well-being at the social level. Indeed, positive impact and change should extend to the institutional and organizational levels, and positive psychology can also serve as a "mechanism" for social change to promote strengths in a societal level.

A culturally competent counselor would importantly engage in social change. According to Vera and Speight (2003), the counseling should be operated from a perspective of social justice, taking a political stance on social issues. It has been demonstrated that social change can help alleviate persons' mental health issues that many clients such as Selena experience as a result of living in an oppressive society. Thus, Selena's personal problems actually were highly related to social issues requiring social changes.

In order to satisfy various dimensions of growth at a societal and/or national level, counselors have to be actively involved in multiple interventions, from individual to institutional and societal levels. Such involvements are embedded in feminist therapy and positive psychology: feminist therapy advocates social change as positive psychology promotes collective well-being and pursues human growth at societal and/or national level. The consequence could be a new and healthy environment for Selena and others who then would have better personal well-being.

*Definitions of mental illness in feminist therapy and positive psychology* Both feminist therapy and positive psychology reject the disease model of mental illness. Yet, feminist therapy stresses that psychological distress is best explained as a presentation of unjust systems, while positive psychology insists on the importance of strength-based therapy. When applying the integration to Selena, the question remains as to how to tailor such integration to Selena's African American background.

When working with Selena, it is important to know that she suffered multiple external stresses such as white peers' dismissal and African Americans' misunderstanding. These external stresses originated in social oppression and/or public policies – these social factors were the primary causes of Selena's distress. Thus, it is crucial to explore how the client defines her external stresses, which could be culturally specific. With positive psychology, the counselor could explore Selena's strengths such resilience and volunteering to help those in need. Her strengths serves as a buffer against the racial discrimination, as rooted in her African American culture. In other words, when working with African Americans, it is critical to explore strengths and well-being from their cultural perspective, rather than imposing the strengths defined by Western culture. By exploring the strengths from an African American perspective, the counselor can identify factors that contribute to healthy development of Selena and other African Americans. Unfortunately, scholarship and academic practice to date have largely ignored the relevance of racial, ethnic, and cultural factors, nuances, and competencies, particularly as they relate to the resilience and strength of African Americans. The field of psychology's preoccupation with disparity data still fails to inform scholars about attitudes, behaviors, and processes that contribute to the strength of African Americans. Therefore, it is necessary to explore *with* Selena the strength and protective components of resilience in her own culture.

*"Oppression" in feminist therapy and positive psychology* Both feminist therapy and positive psychology acknowledge the existence of oppression which may happen in various dimensions of a society, visibly or invisibly, and in many formats. However, despite the agreement of its existence, what is important is to understand what impacts oppression has made on Selena's mental health. Feminist theory believes that a macro-level of intervention could solve oppression. Only after solving social oppression can Selena enjoy an oppression-free environment. For example, it is a macro-level of stereotype that causes discrimination that made Selena unable to complete her thesis. Thus, the counseling for Selena would need a macro-level intervention (e.g., social justice advocacy) in addition to a micro or personal level of intervention.

Integrating positive psychology into feminist therapy to help Selena would also need to expand well-being to a macro-level in addition to micro-level or individual well-being. At a macro level, the counselor could be an agency to promote multicultural clients' collective well-being by various avenues such as advocacy of policy changes. At a micro-level, the counselor could facilitate the client's (e.g., Selena's) connection to the pioneers in her culture. For example, Selena comes from an African American culture that has numerous African American pioneers (e.g., Martin Luther King Jr., Kenneth and Mamie Clark, etc.) who transformed this nation to a better people-oriented community. These pioneers may well have endured and thrived against numerous racial discriminations. When connecting Selena to these pioneers, she might well be encouraged to learn from them on how to thrive against various stress and/or race-related issues.

## Follow-up: You continue as Selena's counselor

Consider how you would help Selena if you were her counselor. Here are a series of questions to provide some structure in your thinking about her case:

- How much interest would you have in Amy's experiences in growing up as an African American woman in a luxurious neighborhood?
- Would you discuss African American female role models with Selena? Would you use these role models to highlight their defiant of oppression and injustice?

- In working with Selena, what cultural differences do you notice between you and her? What does her cultural background mean to you when you work with her with the integration between feminist therapy and positive psychology?

## Concluding Remarks

Feminist therapy recognizes the impact of varied social practices on personal well-being. Rooted in the feminist and equal rights movements of the 1960s, feminist therapy embraces the conviction about the close relationship between personal problems and the political environment. Feminist therapy contributes to counseling in four ways. First, it conceptualizes personal issues in the political context. Second, it revolutionizes the definitions of mental illness. Third, it integrates analysis of oppression which could be a source of human problems. Fourth, it advocates egalitarian therapeutic relationships.

Positive psychology adds strengths and well-being to the established feminist therapy. Thus, with positive psychology, clients learn to change their sufferings of oppression into opportunities of growth. Clients also appreciate personal well-being and collective well-being. Moreover, with political issues in mind, counselors conceptualize clients' problems with a macro-context and promote social justice to benefit people via social policies.

Although feminist therapy advocates equalitarian relationships between men and women, it is important to know that different cultures may have their respective views on gender differences. Counselors need to be sensitive to the potential contradictions or differences between feminist therapy and clients' cultures. They should respect clients' cultures and facilitate their growth and well-being.

## Review Questions: What Do You Think?

1. What are your personal reactions to feminist therapy? Do you believe it necessary to conceptualize personal problems in the context of the political environment?
2. Describe the relationship between feminism and feminist therapy.
3. What are the therapeutic principles in feminist therapy?
4. Describe personal well-being vs. collective well-being.

# 14

# Family Therapy

## Learning Objectives

- Explain the historical background of family therapy.
- Understand the differences between individual therapy and family therapy.
- Describe the therapeutic principles in family therapy.
- Demonstrate specific procedures and techniques from family therapy.
- Learn about using genograms in family therapy and positive psychology.
- Integrate family therapy and positive psychology.
- Multiculturalize the integration between family therapy and positive psychology.
- Apply the integration to a case study.

The practice of family therapy consists of meetings with all relevant family members. With their full permission, the therapy is usually conducted in a team setting, usually with the therapist in a room with the family and with the rest of the team offering live supervision, watching from behind a one-way screen in an observation room. The supervision team may phone in to make suggestions. Alternatively, in an increasingly popular approach, reflecting team conversation is used, in which the observers join the therapist and the family. The family is then invited to listen while the team have a conversation about the progress of the therapy. The family, in turn, are invited to discuss and reflect back on this discussion. Various activities, such as homework tasks, may also be employed, for example, for members to observe their patterns of interacting at home or to engage in experiments such as the

*Counseling Psychology: An Integrated Positive Psychological Approach*, First Edition. Ruth Chu-Lien Chao.

parents swapping roles. Underlying all these activities is the aim of promoting new patterns of interactions and helping family members to see their problems as interpersonal rather than due to individual deficits (Minuchin & Fishman, 1981).

## Historical Context

Family therapy derives from a view of psychological problems as relational rather than as located within persons. The core theoretical conceptualization is drawn from systems theory in the analogy of a family as like a self-regulating biological system. Family members are seen to interact in such a way that their joint actions serve to produce and maintain problems or symptoms. This is a counter-intuitive view of problems which argues that, despite the typical protestations of family members that they desperately want to be rid of the problems, usually seen to be resident within one of their members, they in fact interact in ways that serve to ensure that the problems are maintained. Typically, the initial stages of therapy are concerned with attempting to understand what the positive functions of the symptoms may be. A core concept is "triangulation," for example, where a child's distress and subsequent symptoms are seen to result from and also serve to detour the parents' conflicted relationship (Minuchin & Fishman, 1981).

Family therapy emerged in the late 1940s and early 1950s as professionals in various parts of the United States began to consider such phenomena as mutual influence, patterns of interaction, and feedback loops between individuals and within systems. Shifting away from an emphasis on the internal states or minds of individuals to a consideration of the dynamics of relationships in families, therapists soon began to develop a variety of family therapy theories and models. The most prominent of the original, or classic, family therapy models include contextual family therapy, created by Ivan Boszormenyi-Nagy; natural systems theory, created by Murray Bowen; the symbolic/experiential approach of Carl Whitaker; the dynamic process model, created by Virginia Satir; strategic family therapy, created by Jay Haley; the brief therapy/communications approach created by the Mental Research Institute in Palo Alto, California; and various behavioral and behavioral/cognitive family therapy approaches.

Although in the early days of the field, professionals tended to align themselves with a particular model or school, by the 1980s there was recognition of the need to be knowledgeable about, and have the ability to integrate information from, all of the family therapy theories. As a postmodern consciousness began to impact the field, several additional approaches to working with individuals and families evolved. These include the reflecting team approach of Tom Andersen; the solution-oriented therapy of Bill O'Hanlon; the solution-focused approach of Steve de Shazer and Insoo Kim Berg; the narrative therapy of Michael White and David Epston; and the therapeutic conversations approach of Harlene Anderson and Harry Goolishian. Each of these approaches attempts to build on lessons learned over the years and to incorporate recent trends emerging across many disciplines (Carlson, Sperry, & Lewis, 2005). They therefore include an emphasis on recognizing the expertise of both clients and clinicians as well as awareness of the importance of facilitating an ethical and respectful process aimed at the achievement of client-defined goals. Many family therapists today use a combination of classic and postmodern approaches. Perhaps most important, a great deal of research has demonstrated the effectiveness of family therapy for dealing with, and resolving, a variety of mental and physical health challenges.

## Theoretical Principles

To understand family therapy, it is important first to understand the basic tenets that underlie family functioning. A family typically involves two to four generations. A family is influenced and facilitated by the opportunities and constraints of its social context. To ensure its own existence, a family adapts available resources to normal and abnormal transitional and crisis stress events. Family resources involve the ability of family members to contribute tangible help such as material support, income, childcare, and household maintenance and nontangible aid such as expressive interaction, emotional support, instruction, and social training and regulation. All families have explicit and implicit rules that govern their interactions, and those rules usually promote robust patterns of interactions. How well a family functions depends on such aspects of family life as the clarity of its communication, rules, and ability to actualize family resources during a time of crisis (Patterson, Williams, Edwards, Chamow, & Grauf-Grounds, 2009).

A family system perspective is central to family therapy. From this perspective, individual problems occur in the broader context of the family. Therefore, family therapy focuses primarily on interpersonal interactions rather than on intrapsychic phenomena. For instance, the goal of family therapy for depression is to change the relationship patterns between a husband and wife to mitigate depressive symptoms, the rationale being that depression can cause relationship problems and that relationship problems can cause depression. This contrasts with traditional cognitive behavioral therapy for depression where the focus is on altering an individual's thoughts and behaviors. Moreover, family therapists have historically understood causality in family interactions through cyclical causal patterns – that is, sequences of ongoing, interactional behaviors that have no clear beginning or end.

Each family system comprises a number of subsystems, which affect one another. "Wholeness" highlights that the whole is more than the sum of its parts, with the implication that there is little point in considering one part of the family system without regard to the rest of the system. Family therapists believe that such properties of systems affect individuals within the system. In earlier views, systems, much as in the context of physics, were seen as homeostatic, that is, moving to reduce change. However, more recent views have seen the family as a source of resilience more than of homeostasis. Today's family therapists believe that families possess the ability to rally their resources to restore healthy family functioning.

Family therapists go about understanding symptomatic behavior in many different ways. Some view symptoms as a result of the family under stress, others look for the meaning or function of the symptom, and still others view symptoms as a result of repeated use of the same flawed solution. Such different ways of understanding symptomatic behavior in one or multiple family members is closely related to the theoretical orientation of the family therapist. Psychodynamic models focus on the family as an integral context in the etiology of adult personality and believe that to solve family problems, it is necessary to understand intrapsychic processes within the individual, to understand early parent–child relationships, and to understand the evolution of family problems across generations. Experiential models focus on increasing the family's sensitivity and sharing of feelings. Structural family therapy focuses on patterns of interaction within the family to understand its basic structure and organization. Strategic models use paradoxes as a technique for changing family patterns and interactions. Therapists using narrative and other postmodern models believe that there is no objective reality; rather, people construct their realities and focus on understanding the family's shared definition of the problems. Cognitive behavioral models use principles from learning theory and social exchange theory to understand family processes. Each of these viewpoints has evolved into a school of family therapy.

Most recently, a movement away from specific theoretical orientations has developed in favor of identifying a set of generic strategies or principles that cut across theoretical orientation. Most family therapy today, in part, uses strategies that work with family structure; strategies that work with cognitions, narratives, or attributions; strategies based in psychoeducation; and strategies for working with affect. Hence, the field of family therapy has moved toward a both/and paradigm rather than an either/or paradigm. Current views of systems theory allow the therapist to examine causal processes, to examine the differential impact of family system processes on different family members, and to examine the impact of intrapsychic processes of individual family members on the larger family system. Although systemic conceptualizations have changed over time, the ultimate goals of successful family therapy remain the same: to resolve the family's difficulties and add to adaptive functioning by rectifying a family's dysfunctional, repetitive interactions, communication, and problem-solving skills (Napier & Whitaker, 1998).

Research on the effectiveness of family therapy shows that the outcomes of this modality are as good as, or better than, those for other psychotherapeutic approaches. Studies have focused on therapy for addictions, childhood conduct disorders, emotional problems, juvenile delinquency, marital problems, relationship enhancement, psychosomatic disorders, physical problems, psycho-education for families with a member diagnosed with schizophrenia, anxiety, depression, child abuse, and spouse abuse. Within each of these categories family therapists have continued to refine their approaches and demonstrate the effectiveness of their work.

Some general conclusions relative to family therapy include the fact that for marital problems, conjoint therapy is twice as likely to be effective than is individual therapy. Further, conjoint therapy is particularly preferred for marriages in which alcohol is a problem. In all cases, improving the ability to communicate effectively has been found to be a significant contributor to successful outcomes in therapy for marital problems.

In addition, research studies have indicated that a variety of family therapy approaches may be effective when working with childhood or adolescent behavior problems. The success rate for family therapy in this realm is approximately 70 percent. For these, as well as many other problems, a relatively brief approach, meaning 20 sessions or less, has proved to be sufficient for the resolution of problems.

Family therapy for clients dealing with physical problems is based on the awareness that when one family member is ill, all members of the family are affected. In addition, the health of the patient may be influenced by what is going on in the family. Thus the ability of family members to work together to shift roles as needed and provide appropriate support for the patient may facilitate his or her healing process. The same also may be said for various emotional and relationship problems. To do effective family therapy, therefore, specialized training is required.

### The process of family therapy

When individuals, couples, or family members go for family therapy, it is likely that they first will be asked to sign an informed consent agreement. The form generally describes what clients can expect as well as the limits of confidentiality. Having agreed to participate, the clients then meet with the therapist, who will begin by becoming acquainted with each person in order to establish a relationship of trust. The therapist will want to know what the clients would like help with and what they would like family therapy to help them achieve (Rasheed, Rasheed, & Marley, 2011).

### The use of a genogram

A tool often used by family therapists is a genogram. This visual mapping of a family over time, including at least three generations, enables both clients and therapist to view patterns and trends that otherwise might be overlooked. Such information may be helpful in understanding the logic of the current problem with which clients are dealing. The family therapist also may create an ecomap, which allows everyone to get a better understanding of other systems – such as work or school – with which clients may be involved that have an impact on the life of the family. Beyond the use of these rather standard tools, the process primarily involves conversations that are consistent with the particular therapist's theoretical orientation. Family therapists may make suggestions for new behaviors or new ways of thinking and perhaps even provide homework assignments. However, the choice to accept or reject what the therapist offers always resides with the client (McGoldrick, Gerson, & Petry, 2008).

### Reasons for family therapy

Family therapy may be helpful in many situations because of its relational, rather than individual, focus. Clients are encouraged to understand that mutual influence is inevitable and that although one person may be showing symptoms, everyone participates in the creation of, as well as the solution to, problems. Rather than judging a person as good or bad, right or wrong, the emphasis is on empathic understanding of the way the problem somehow "makes sense" in that person's context. Keeping in mind previous efforts by the client to solve the problem, the family therapist then can look for and suggest new ways to deal with it, ways that hopefully will be more effective. Such an approach not only accomplishes the client-defined goal but takes the burden off of the so-called identified patient.

Recent research has indicated that there are several common factors that cut across all the family therapy approaches that influence a successful outcome in family therapy. That is, therapists tend to be most effective when, among other behaviors, they are able to build alliances and engage with clients, generate a sense of hope and the expectation of positive outcomes, understand problems relationally, focus on changes in meaning, and meet clients where they are. This speaks volumes about the context of family therapy.

Indeed, family therapy is powerful partly because it is based on a way of thinking that is different from that of Western society in general. For example, a focus on individuals and individualism is one of the most highly cherished values in the United States. Not surprisingly, the strategies Americans generally use to solve problems are logical to this way of thinking. They thus tend to look for a cause and blame the other without considering the possibility that the person pointing a finger or doing the blaming may be participating in both the creation and the maintenance of the problem. When such strategies work, that is wonderful. When they don't work, then something new and different may be exactly what is needed. That is exactly what family therapy has to offer.

## An Integration: Positive Psychology and Family Therapy

Family therapy focuses on the dynamics and interactions among family members, and such relationships among them are the targets of interventions, watching over opportunities and constraints of the social context of family, as the impact of social contexts and family relationships relate intimately to personal problems. Different from other approaches such as psychoanalysis, person-centered therapy, gestalt therapy, and others which focus on individual and private problems, family therapy focuses on relationships and the dynamics among family members in the midst of tacitly agreed-on family rules and regulations. For family therapy, how well a family functions depends on the clarity of its communication, rules, and ability to actualize family resources during the time of crisis. In such as this, family therapists treat family problems, and help family members develop appropriate rules and regulations to repair the concerns of the family.

While positive psychology is open to working with the family as a unit and focus on relationships among family members, positive psychologists constantly keep their eyes on the strengths and well-being of the family and their members more than family problems. Integrating family therapy with positive psychology, mental health professionals can address strengths in the family context and "what's right" in interpersonal interactions among family members.

Let us take a specific example. The goal of family therapy for anger is to change the relationship patterns between family members (e.g., siblings, parents and children) to manage angers that can cause relationship problems that in turn can cause and worsen anger. With the integrated approach, the focus can be on how the relationships among family members can help individuals manage anger. For example, when someone gets angry, other members would show care as the family comes to therapy (Dole, Silbert, & Mann, 2008).

Instead of trying to fix the problematic relationships, the integrative approach highlights the positive interactions among family members. Family members may want to learn how to communicate with each other in a positive and/or an understanding way. Family members also can refresh and/or learn about other members' strengths and remember how each person might have taken care of each other in the past. The integrated approach thus highlights any positive experiences in family interactions in their sequences, from the beginning. For example, the integrated approach may use a family member's birthday as an example to see if there is any positive interaction that the family members have had to enhance amity.

Family therapy sees that each family system comprises a number of unique subsystems affecting one another, and problems of each subsystem affect the whole family. For example, the sisterhood problems in the subsystem may influence the whole family as other members may take sides against one another. In this situation, positive psychologists would continue to stress strengths of each subsystem to result in more strengths of the whole family. Integrating family therapy into positive psychology, the counselors would seek and stress strengths in the context of family dynamics. Instead of solely treating repairing problems, the integrated approach sees the family as a resource for resilience to every family member (Turnbull, Turnbull, Erwin, Soodak, & Shogren, 2010).

## Symptoms in family therapy and positive psychology

Some family therapists view symptoms as a result of the family under stress, others look for the meaning or function of the symptoms, and still others view symptoms as a result of repeated use of the same flawed solution. Positive psychology believes that focusing on symptoms alone would miss understanding of the other side (i.e., strengths) of people and families (Dole et al., 2008). Thus, positive psychology proposes that all the problematic or symptomatic behaviors cannot hide, much less deny, the existence of strengths of individuals and families.

The integration of family therapy with positive psychology uses strategies of promoting strengths that work well in a family structure, and strategies for working with the affect of family members. As the family cultivates its strengths, the power will enable its members to examine their intrapsychic processes in their family. The ultimate goals of integrating family therapy and positive psychology are: to promote family's strengths (e.g., healthy functioning, support to each other, etc.); to increase the adaptability of a family's functioning by increasing positive interactions; and to facilitate the ability of a family to change difficulties into opportunities.

## The genogram in family therapy and positive psychology

The genogram has been a useful tool for family therapy. The visual map of a family across generations enables people to view patterns of problems. Although this technique may facilitate family members' awareness of the pattern of issues with which they are currently dealing, the genogram may also be wrongly used to justify the weaknesses and/or problems and may overlook the strengths of the family. After integrating family therapy and positive psychology, mental health professionals can use the genogram to highlight the pattern of strengths in the family (McGoldrick et al., 2008).

A family is a unit of life that has been through different cycles and crises. By using genograms, the integrated approach can enhance family members' awareness of strengths inherent in the family through generations. For example, members can appreciate that endurance is a main character strength running thorough the family, by reading its genogram, to overcome many crises in its history. For instance, family members could learn that their forefathers had encountered various sorts of discriminations and stereotypes, and their endurance helped them to survive ordeals. Their grandparents thrived against poverty, lack of education, and other crises with persistent hard work. Through the genogram, clients not only recognize the pattern of problems or trends in the family, but also more importantly, further recognize the strengths which have been keeping the family functioning.

From the recognition of the strengths in the family, the integrated approach can encourage family members to continue using their family strengths to solve the problems they are struggling with now, to learn new behaviors or new ways of thinking to maintain and blossom their family, and to develop new rules to help the family grow further.

### Beyond the integration of family therapy and positive psychology

The integration of family therapy with positive psychology may be helpful in many situations because it is a balanced collection of many techniques. Family members will benefit from understanding symptoms and strengths in the family, and everyone contributes to the problem solving by continuing discoveries of their strengths. Rather than blaming the problems on a particular family member, the integrative approach emphasizes empathic understanding of the problems together with family strengths, to enhance the well-being of each and all family members, where harmony is an important goal for the family.

Harmony here means, first, that family members have mutual consensus on family-related issues. Furthermore, harmony implicates happiness of the family members, pleasantly finding themselves as members of their particular family, grateful to have available ready supports from other members, and treasuring the way their family members are to one another. In other words, the integration of family therapy with positive psychology strives to facilitate family members to help each other beyond problem solving to grow to their fullest potentials.

## Multiculturalizing the Integration

Family therapy focuses on the dynamics and interactions among family members, and relationships between them are the targets of interventions, and then together with positive psychology therapists can enhance positive aspects of their communications, relationships, and interactions. However, to effectively provide family counseling with multicultural clients, further research is needed to understand the role of culture in family dynamics among diverse types of family forms (McGoldrick, Giordano, & Garcia-Preto, 2005).

Importantly, culturally sensitive counselors should possess knowledge of the broader ecosystem of cultural factors and worldview of the family. Culture creates a set of implicit norms, values, and beliefs, which influence the attitudes and behaviors of a group of individuals. The cultures of multicultural clients influence behaviors and beliefs as family members as their family cultures determine expectations on their members. The culture of a family affects individual behaviors, race-related experiences, gender roles, career choice, child-rearing practices, discipline, and the importance of education.

Moreover, culture often determines the form and functioning of families including the type of family, family size, hierarchy, interactional dynamics, and patterns of communications. Falicov (1995) defined culture as a set of shared worldviews, attitudes, and behaviors derived from simultaneous membership, culture is alive through family history. Different generations of a family may develop different cultural values and beliefs, and modes of acculturation. The roles of family members (e.g., parents, children, siblings) are determined by family cultures that also determine patterns of manifestations of various stages in the family life cycle. Thus, culturally sensitive counselors must be aware of the impacts of culture on a family and how culture defines problems, resources, and coping. Culturally sensitive counselors should understand the riches and complexity of family cultures and family functioning, as they are sensitive to differences within the same cultural groups (Congress & Gonzales, 2005).

Culturally sensitive counselors are also aware of how their own worldviews influence their assumptions about families. Culturally skilled counselors are also aware that everyone, including themselves, is the product of their cultural conditioning. The old adage "counselor, know thyself" is important for family counselors. With the knowledge and awareness that everyone has his or her worldviews, counselors should not allow their own values to interfere with their work with multicultural clients.

By multiculturalizing the integration of family therapy and positive psychology, counselors can explore, within the cultural context, the strengths in the family and "what's right" in interpersonal interactions among family members. The goal of multicultural family counseling is to change the relationship patterns to manage the presenting problems in this family's cultural context, and assist and guide the family to move from problem-oriented to strength-focused within the appropriate cultural context. For example, culturally sensitive counselors can explore how people express care to other family members (McGoldrick et al., 2005).

Specifically, Asian families are built on hierarchical relationship emphasizing piety, to express their care according to family roles and relationships. Fathers tend to express their care by discipline, worries, and talk; female members (e.g., mothers, sisters) may express their care by supporting comments. Thus, by integrating family therapy and positive psychology in a client's cultural context, the integrative approach highlights the positive interactions among family members in addition to "fixing" problems. Culturally skilled counselors possess knowledge of how multicultural family members communicate with each other positively within their culture, and use this cultural knowledge to enhance positive buildup of strengths.

## Symptoms, family therapy, positive psychology, and cultural context

When providing multicultural family counseling, culturally sensitive counselors should explore the meanings and roles of symptoms in the family in its culture. Because each family has its rules and regulations, counselors are aware of the individual family differences within generally identical cultural groups. For example, Chua (2011) described her parenting experiences in her book, *Battle Hymn of the Tiger Mother*. Many readers believe that her way of parenting represents a typical Chinese style of education: extreme control of children's learning, hobbies, and dating. This book may give Western people an impression that Chinese parents eagerly push their children to become perfect students and then later to have perfect career.

Yet, Chua's tough love strategies with ironclad bans on such Western indulgences as sleepovers may not be completely agreed to by other Asian families. This within-culture difference of family environments highlights the importance of counselors' sensitivity to different climates and environments of families even in the same culture.

With the sensitivity of within and between cultural differences, counselors should also explore the implications of "symptoms" in the family within a culture. Some multicultural families treat symptoms as a family secret, shame, or results of stress; others may believe that the family is "cursed" by bad spirits or is punished by their ancestries for their current wrongdoing (Goldenberg & Goldenberg, 2008).

Beyond symptoms interpreted in various cultural ways, culturally sensitive counselors should explore any potential positive interpretations of symptoms based on the culture in which the family lives. For example, the yin-yang pattern in Asian culture stresses the close connection between crisis and opportunity. Counselors may want to integrate this hopeful cultural implication of "symptoms" to facilitate a positive interpretation in the family. In other words, culturally sensitive counselors apply their knowledge of other cultures to assist the family to look for positive alternative meaning or function of symptoms, and to help the family to manage the impact of symptoms.

While positive psychology believes that focusing on symptoms alone would miss understanding of the other side (i.e., strengths) of people and families, culturally sensitive counselors respect different cultural groups' attitudes toward "symptoms" and adjust sensitively their strategies on how they work through symptoms in the family. For example, counseling Latina families could give an opportunity to re-examine the family bond, which is usually powerful and enduring.

For Latino/as, the family serves as the primary source of support, care, guidance, and healing, and importantly, all difficulties that arise for an individual are surmounted by all family members together. Thus, culturally skilled counselors possess knowledge that "symptoms" could be a reminder for the family to renew the family bond and connection, and to face the individual problem as the whole family affair. Because of the emphasis on resources, connection, and bond, counselors may be welcomed as a member of the family to facilitate the growth and development of the Latina/o family.

For African American families, counselors are aware of and respect mutual help among such families, whether with blood relationships or not. When "symptoms," are encountered, African American families work together to manage the symptoms of an individual. Thus, for African American families, symptoms could also be a reminder to unite, persevere, and help each other. Despite the poverty of some African American families, they assist each other with child care, finances, emotional support, housing, counseling, and so forth, particularly in times of trouble or stress. In addition, African American families, particularly when moving into new communities, may create bonds with nonblood relatives, such as neighbors, babysitters, friends, ministers, ministers' wives, and church family. These bonds are as strong as those in natural family members. Thus, whether with blood or nonblood relatives, what is precious is that African American families work together during stress to solve an individual's symptoms and problems.

Taken together, symptoms or stress may create different impacts on different families in different cultures. Culturally sensitive counselors facilitate the strengths and well-being of the families with approaches appropriate to the family's culture. For example, for Asian families, helping the *families* (not just individuals) create an alternative positive viewpoint related to symptoms could be a culturally appropriate intervention for them. For Latina families, counselors facilitate to renew family connections; for African American families, resources to manage symptoms and/or stress come from various family members who would cope with stress or difficulties by working together. Importantly, the integration of family therapy and positive psychology will design culturally appropriate strategies to promote strengths that work well in a family structure, strategies for working with positive affect of family members to increase the adaptability of a family's functioning.

## The genogram in multicultural family therapy and positive psychology

The genogram used in traditional family counseling is now being considered by scholars and practitioners for use in counseling culturally different families. Culturally sensitive counselors could use genograms to assess culturally different families to determine the patterns running through multiple generations, significant life events, rituals, roles, communication styles, and the nature of relationships among family members. Such knowledge often provides direction for treatment.

Genograms for culturally different families also provide an understanding of worldviews and cultural factors that often influence behaviors, attitudes, and beliefs of family members. For example, for immigrant families, different cultural experiences and worldviews in different generations offer a rich and crucial understanding regarding family conflicts. With such information obtained from studying a genogram, both counselors and family members would gain a deeper appreciation of how and why their culture plays a significant role on family conflicts and problems (McGoldrick et al., 2008).

As cultural factors and within-family differences are complex and interwoven, culturally sensitive family therapists are encouraged to use culturally appropriate skills to work with multicultural families such as telling their life stories in their life journeys. Culturally sensitive counselors actively develop sensitive and culture-appropriate intervention strategies to work with culturally different families. Counseling effectiveness would be enhanced when counselors provide culturally sensitive intervention and goals consistent with the family's values in their cultures.

Thus, with the intervention of genograms, culturally sensitive counselors can explore various significant issues in the family such as "How did the family members communicate with each other?" "Who usually initiated the communication?" "What was the respective role of each family member?" and so on. Counselors should also be aware that some cultural factors will be more salient to different family members and may stimulate the family to lead the discussion of cultural factors. Differences in cultural values between family members should also be included, and counselors should facilitate and enhance communication of diverse views to help families find compromise and negotiation of values, if necessary. With the help of genograms, culturally sensitive counselors can also explore how the family have worked in the past through crises, stress, and enhanced positive affects.

Thus, as counselors integrate multicultural family therapy with positive psychology, culturally skilled counselors can use genograms to highlight the pattern of strengths in the family. Some families may continue their cultural heritages in celebrating culturally relevant festivals and keeping up the foods popular in their family traditions; other families may have a routine by which family members express their gratitude when enjoying their dinners. Within the cultural context, counselors work with families to promote their appreciation of strengths and well-being, in addition to solving their problems. A multicultural family is a unit of life that has gone through different cycles or crises such as managing culturally related stress as they celebrate cultural heritage. All such memorable knowledge is gained by probing genograms.

Through usage of genograms, culturally sensitive counselors can assist family members to advance their understanding of the collective character traits and strengths running through the whole family. For instance, when encountering stress, Latino families may unite together and collaborate to manage the stress. This has been the case throughout Latino history, as found by studying their genograms. With the genogram and intervention strategy of story telling, culturally sensitive counselors can facilitate family members to further appreciate their cultural mode of coping such as strong connection among families and mutual help by united neighbors.

In Asian families, the immigrant great forefathers tolerated various countless discriminations, stereotypes, and risks in work and daily routine to achieve a better life for their subsequent generations. Through the genogram, family members can learn how their grand forebears thrived against poverty and many other crises. Moreover, family members can proudly see how their families, through so many centuries, have maintained their cultural resources and heritage as powers to overcome various unexpected barriers and insufferable difficulties. From the recognition of the strengths manifested in the family genograms, family members can be vastly encouraged and inspired to toughen through, with the strengths found in their family, to resolve the conflicts, stress, or difficulties they face at present and may encounter in the future.

When working with African American families, racism and its related issues might be found. Due to the significant impact of racism on black families, African Americans may be sensitive to the way in which they are approached by counselors. Culturally sensitive counselors are aware that African American families may have various presentations and/or organizational stresses. Their families may have been traditionally two-parent nuclear families, or they may consist of a single parent and a boyfriend or girlfriend, or they may form a complex extended family that includes members from both inside and outside the household, as well as blood and non-blood relatives.

Through studying their genograms, culturally skilled counselors can become aware that counselors' own expectations of family structure may be different from the African American families they work with. Counselors should regrtnspect such diversity of structure in African American families. The extended family kinship system is a cultural legacy and testament to the survival skills of those of African heritage.

Through studying their genograms, culturally sensitive counselors can assist African American families to appreciate various supports available from African Americans' functional kinship networks and other resources in church, friends, and neighbors. By using a genogram as a tool in working with African American families, culturally sensitive counselors may notice that whether complex extended family kinship system, nonblood relatives, or a two-parent family, what is important is how these African American families succeed in managing their race-specific stresses to thrive in the midst of racism, discrimination, and social injustice.

## Multiculturalizing the integration of family therapy and positive psychology: What's next?

Multiculturalizing the integration of family therapy with positive psychology would help multicultural families manage their stress and enhance well-being with a culturally appropriate approach. This is significant because, over the past decades, the US Census has revealed that the United States is fast undergoing some very radical demographic changes. Projections show that by the year 2050, whites, who now account for nearly two-thirds of the population, would become a minority population. If the pace of immigration increases, that benchmark could be reached as early as 2040.

Our current population trend can be referred to as the "diversification of America" and is the result of two notable trends: (a) current and past immigration patterns and (b) differential birth rates among the white and racial and ethnic minority populations (Goldenberg & Goldenberg, 2008).

The changing demographics in the United States would clearly make an impact on family structures and social organizations. For example, since 2000, immigrants have been growing by just under one million immigrants annually. Even if no new immigrants arrived, due to the higher birth rate, the Hispanic share of the population would rise from about 14 percent in 2010 to between 21 percent (with no further immigration) and 31 percent (with the highest projected immigration) in 2050 (Falicov, 1998).

Even without immigration, minorities would still constitute a majority of the population under age five in 2050, because of higher birth rates among Hispanic people already living in the United States. If immigration continues, black, Hispanic, and Asian children will become the majority of young children sometime between 2019 and 2023, according to the latest projections. Moreover, the Asian American population was the fastest growing group in the United States in the 1980s because of the large increase of refugees. While the immigrated families and birth rates of racial minority populations are increasing, white Americans are experiencing a declining fertility and birth rates (1.7 children per mother) and might become an ageing population.

Moreover, these immigrated families from Asia, Mexico, and Latin America also bring their family structure, rituals, organization, values, beliefs, and cultural patterns to the United States. Therefore, it could be expected that in the future, the currently standard nuclear family with two parents could become just one form of family structure among many. As more white Americans become older, there could be radical changes in family structures, such as multiple generations living together as a single family.

Another impact of changing demographics in the United States could be that the deficit model of family therapy may encounter challenges because this disease-based model might be inconsistent with immigrated families' explanation of family problems. Additionally, many immigrant families or non-white families incorporate their religious practice, system of education, of parenting, and pattern of expectations for their children's career into their family structure and dynamics. Such incorporations may change the current dynamics of family interactions. Immigrant families also encounter acculturative stress in addition to bringing their cultural values and heritage to this country.

Taken together, culturally skilled counselors must be sensitive to such demographic changes and their impacts on family structures. To meet the challenges of the changing demographics of families, culturally sensitive counselors need to reflect on the previous models of counseling families used to guide and conceptualize research on multicultural families (Sue & Sue, 2008). These traditional models are three in number.

*First*, the inferiority or pathological model is based on the premise that multicultural families or underrepresented people are more inherently pathological than are their white counterparts. *Second*, due to language and/or other barriers, African American and other marginalized people and families were assumed to be less accomplished and/or lacking in desirable qualities compared to their white counterparts. *Third*, the culturally deprived model blamed "culture" for the problems and difficulties that multicultural people and families encounter. Unfortunately, such a model ironically justified the impoverished environment as correct that multicultural people and families live in, and deprived the motivation to ameliorate the condition.

To correct the above three models on multicultural families, counselors can further explore strengths, contribution, and well-being in multicultural families' cultural context. Multicultural families do not simply change the family structures in a country but further make indispensable contributions to the workforce and economy of that country. With positive psychology, multicultural families would have opportunities to further understand the problems and strengths in their family.

Moreover, in the integrated approach of family therapy and positive psychology, culturally sensitive counselors would assist family members to culturally appreciate everyone's contributions to the problem solving. The strengths and well-being discussed in the family should be consistent with the multicultural family's culture, value, belief, and worldview. Rather than blaming the problems on a particular family member, the integrative approach emphasizes collaboration with all members and support of one another. This integrated approach also parallels favorably with the emphasis of family in various multicultural worldviews (Falicov, 1998) such as Latino families, African American families, Asian families, and Native American families.

Additionally, culturally sensitive counselors further encourage family members to treasure other members and connect to them, as many multicultural families believe in the necessity of gratitude. In all, the multiculturalization of the integration of family therapy and positive psychology goes far beyond problem solving in the deficit model. More importantly, with this integration in the culturally appropriate context, families would thrive against barriers and difficulties to live up to their fullest potentials.

## Application in Counseling: A Case Study

This family at first called their family doctor, being concerned about their daughter's eating problems. After an initial check with the daughter (Becky), the doctor referred the family to contact a community mental health center to receive family counseling. The parents (Tim and Amber) described their daughter's eating problems as disrupting their home life. The intake forms revealed that the daughter had severe academic problems. The presenting problems frequently include the parents and school personnel (e.g., teachers, principal, school counselor) describing the child's problematic behaviors.

The parents arrived at the therapy room expressing feelings of anger, frustration, and directly or indirectly blame the current family dysfunction on Becky's eating problems. Tim and Amber also accused each other. For example, Tim blamed the problem on Amber and believed that she should have quit her job years ago to be a full-time mother to Becky. Amber argued back that Tim just "disappeared" into his work and never showed up for dinner. She also blamed her continuous work on Tim since he was laid off a few years ago and was unable to make sufficient income.

The negative interactions among this couple continue almost nonstop throughout the family system. When the couple blamed each other, Becky looked very uncomfortable and embarrassed, and eventually, she was silent throughout the whole session. The feelings of frustration at being unsuccessful parents or even spouses fuel feelings of shame and doubt. Feeling unable to solve the problem, the parents become even angrier. Anger prompts flight-or-fight options or denies the existence of the problems. Blaming each other may accumulate their misunderstandings and prevent them from solving the problem. None of these choices or behaviors creates good parenting. Worse, the daughter often feels frustrated at failing to gain positive attention as a result of her eating problems.

### How to help this family

To help this family with the integration between family therapy and positive psychology, it is important to address the family problems and strengths during the counseling. While family therapy focuses on the problematic dynamics and interactions among family members, positive psychology is open to working with the family as a unit and focus on relationships among family members. From the perspective of traditional family therapy, this family would be seen as full of problematic interactions: husband (Tim) and wife (Amber), parents (Tim and Amber) and their daughter (Becky), and the daughter's eating disorder. However, even if traditional family therapy were to successfully assist the family in reaching a problem-free situation, this family may still remain unable to cultivate positive interactions among its members.

### "Symptoms" in family therapy and positive psychology

The "symptoms" in this family appeared to be Becky's academic difficulties, eating disorder, and behavioral problems. A family therapist may view the symptoms as a result of the family under stress, their struggle with Becky's development, or their move to the next stage. Unfortunately, such conceptualization may put Becky into the position of "scapegoat," to be the "symptom" of the family. Worse, when Becky's issues became the "symptoms" of the family, her parents may have an opportunity to avoid their own issues (e.g., Tim spent most of time on his work, estranged relationship between the couple, extremely unhappy Amber) and disturb family interactions.

With the integration of positive psychology, the family and their counselor may conceptualize the situation differently. For example, only focusing on "symptoms" (e.g., Becky's academic difficulties, eating problems) would amount to missing an understanding of the other side (e.g., their strengths, the willingness to work together and see the family therapist) of this family. Even the problematic family relationships and symptomatic behaviors of Becky cannot deny the existence of their strengths. That is, in addition to addressing the problems of this family, how to use strategies to promote strengths should be an equally important task, if not a more important one. When the family (e.g., father, mother, and daughter) as a unit is willing to cultivate its strengths, their commitment will enable them to achieve a better quality relationship and each member would gain a clearer definition of his/her family role. Specifically, Tim would reflect on his fatherly responsibility rather than escaping to his work. Amber would change her complaints to understanding the situation with fairness. When the parents provide a warm and accepting environment to Becky, she may well be able to concentrate on her school work and rebuild a healthy life style.

## The genogram in family therapy and positive psychology

A genogram has been a useful tool in family therapy. Through the genogram, the counselor could help this family further understand their negative and positive patterns of interaction. The genogram can also facilitate this family to appreciate its subsystems. For example, Tim could be absent from numerous family interactions, resulting in Amber and Becky becoming intimately close as the mother–daughter relationship develops. If Tim feels neglected by the close mother–daughter subsystem, he might choose to be more absent and hide himself in work. The family's unbalanced dynamics learned from watching the genogram may help family members understand why Amber as a wife and mother felt lonely and isolated most of the time.

Using the genogram can also highlight the positive quality of the family's relationships. That is, the counselor can help them create their genogram by identifying how they have worked together to solve any family crisis in the past, how they helped each other to make their family grow and develop, and how they made efforts to promote each other's happiness. Each member can also identify the other members' strengths through the genogram. For example, the father can identity the strengths of the mother and daughter. When family members shift the conversation into appreciation and support, they develop new insights which might have been forgotten or neglected in the past.

In the recognition of their family strengths, they are actually rebuilding their dynamics and interactions in a positive way. While positive relationships set a great foundation to solve their presenting problems, the family can use this counseling to develop their new regulations and rules to facilitate growth. Rather than blaming the problems on their daughter, this integration of family therapy and positive psychology encourages them to transform these presenting problems into opportunities to grow. In other words, in addition to solving problems, the counselor can help them learn new behavior patterns and new ways of thinking to maintain the life of the family, and to plan how to promote their positive emotions. Ultimately, this family can work together to create new rituals in life styles (e.g., have dinner together every night, writing notes of gratitude to each other) to increase the adaptability of a family's functioning.

### Follow-up: You continue as the family counselor

Consider how you would help this family if you were the family counselor. Here are a series of questions to provide some structure in your thinking about this case:

- How much interest would you have in suggesting Becky has individual counseling for her academic problems and eating disorder?
- Consider using a genogram in this family to highlight each person's strengths. What would happen if you do so?
- A few sessions later, Becky told you that she was pregnant but pleaded with you not to tell her parents. What impact may this issue create on the family dynamics and your counseling? How would you handle it?
- Tim told you that he was immigrated from Mexico and in his culture, he should be the leader of this family. So he expected Amber to stay home to take care of the family and Becky. How would you manage the cultural issue in your counseling?

## Concluding Remarks

In general, family therapy adopts a view of psychological problems as relational rather than as located within individuals. The core theoretical principles treat a family as like a self-regulating biological system. Family members are seen to interact in such a way that their joint actions serve to produce and maintain problems or symptoms. Family members may in fact interact in ways that serve to ensure that the problems are maintained. The initial stages of family counseling are focused on understanding what the positive functions of the symptoms may be and the interactions among all relevant family members. Various activities, such as homework tasks, may also be employed, for example, members observe their patterns of interacting at home or engage in experiments such as the parents swapping roles. Underlying all these activities is the aim of promoting new patterns of interactions and helping family members to see their problems as interpersonal rather than due to individual deficits.

Despite numerous benefits from family therapy, it is important to help family members appreciate each other's strengths. Family members can also learn to develop rules to promote their positive affects and well-being. Thus, counselors can help family members transfer the conflicts into opportunities of new development. Finally, even though some multicultural clients are family oriented, counselors still need to respect clients' cultures and values and be sensitive to cultural differences.

## Review Questions: What Do You Think?

1. Family therapy emphasis is on changing the interaction among family members, would you still attempt to help clients solve family members' individual problems? Please explain your answer.
2. Describe the "family system" in family counseling.
3. Describe how the genogram could be a tool in family counseling.
4. With positive psychology, how would symptoms be transferred into opportunities for growth of the family?
5. When working with a multicultural family, would the family or counselor define "family members"? Explain your answer.

# Appendix

## List of Positive Characters and Strengths (Peterson & Seligman, 2004)

*Category One*: Wisdom and Knowledge – This category refers to the cognitive strengths that entail the acquisition and use of knowledge. Based on Peterson and Seligman's (2004) classification, the category of Wisdom and Knowledge includes five strengths: creativity, curiosity, judgment, love of learning, and perspective.

- **Creativity** [or originality, ingenuity]: Thinking of novel and productive ways to conceptualize and do things; includes artistic achievement but is not limited to it.
- **Curiosity** [or interest, novelty-seeking, openness to experience]: Taking an interest in ongoing experience for its own sake; finding subjects and topics fascinating; exploring and discovering.
- **Judgment** [or critical thinking]: Thinking things through and examining them from all sides; not jumping to conclusions; being able to change one's mind in light of evidence; weighing all evidence fairly.
- **Love of learning:** Mastering new skills, topics, and bodies of knowledge, whether on one's own or formally; obviously related to the strength of curiosity but goes beyond it to describe the tendency to add systematically to what one knows.
- **Perspective** [or wisdom]: Being able to provide wise counsel to others; having ways of looking at the world that make sense to oneself and to others.

*Category Two*: Courage – According to Peterson and Seligman (2004), the category of courage stresses that people use emotional strengths to accomplish goals in the face of

*Counseling Psychology: An Integrated Positive Psychological Approach*, First Edition. Ruth Chu-Lien Chao.

opposition or difficulty. There are four strengths under this category: bravery, perseverance, honest, and zest.

- **Bravery** [or valor]: Not shrinking from threat, challenge, difficulty, or pain; speaking up for what is right even if there is opposition; acting on convictions even if unpopular; includes physical bravery but is not limited to it.
- **Perseverance** [or persistence, industriousness]: Finishing what one starts; persisting in a course of action in spite of obstacles; "getting it out the door"; taking pleasure in completing tasks.
- **Honesty** [or authenticity, integrity]: Speaking the truth but more broadly presenting oneself in a genuine way and acting in a sincere way; being without pretense; taking responsibility for one's feelings and actions.
- **Zest** [or vitality, enthusiasm, vigor, energy]: Approaching life with excitement and energy; not doing things halfway or halfheartedly; living life as an adventure; feeling alive and activated.

*Category Three*: Humanity – This category indicates that individuals have interpersonal strengths that involve tending and befriending others. Three strengths are listed here: love, kindness, and social intelligence.

- **Love:** Valuing close relations with others, in particular those in which sharing and caring are reciprocated; being close to people.
- **Kindness** [or generosity, nurturance, care, compassion, altruistic love, "niceness"]: Doing favors and good deeds for others; helping them; taking care of them.
- **Social intelligence** [or emotional intelligence, personal intelligence]: Being aware of the motives and feelings of other people and oneself; knowing what to do to fit into different social situations; knowing what makes other people tick.

*Category Four*: Justice – This category refers to individuals' civic strengths that underlie healthy community life. It includes three strengths: teamwork, fairness, and leadership.

- **Teamwork** [or citizenship, social responsibility, loyalty]: Working well as a member of a group or team; being loyal to the group; doing one's share.
- **Fairness:** Treating all people the same according to notions of fairness and justice; not letting personal feelings bias decisions about others; giving everyone a fair chance.
- **Leadership:** Encouraging a group of which one is a member to get things done, and at the same time maintaining good relations within the group; organizing group activities and seeing that they happen.

*Category Five*: Temperance – This category focuses on self-control and includes strengths that protect against excess such as forgiveness, humility, prudence, and self-regulation.

- **Forgiveness:** Forgiving those who have done wrong; accepting the shortcomings of others; giving people a second chance; not being vengeful.

- **Humility:** Letting one's accomplishments speak for themselves; not regarding oneself as more special than one is.
- **Prudence:** Being careful about one's choices; not taking undue risks; not saying or doing things that might later be regretted.
- **Self-regulation** [or self-control]: Regulating what one feels and does; being disciplined; controlling one's appetites and emotions.

*Category Six*: Transcendence – This category concentrates on the strengths that forge connections to the larger universe and provide meaning. It includes five strengths: appreciation of beauty and excellence, gratitude, hope, humor, and spirituality.

- **Appreciation of beauty and excellence** [or awe, wonder, elevation]: Noticing and appreciating beauty, excellence, and/or skilled performance in various domains of life, from nature to art to mathematics to science to everyday experience.
- **Gratitude:** Being aware of and thankful for the good things that happen; taking time to express thanks.
- **Hope** [or optimism, future-mindedness, future orientation]: Expecting the best in the future and working to achieve it; believing that a good future is something that can be brought about.
- **Humor** [or playfulness]: Liking to laugh and tease; bringing smiles to other people; seeing the light side; making (not necessarily telling) jokes.
- **Spirituality** [or faith, purpose]: Having coherent beliefs about the higher purpose and meaning of the universe; knowing where one fits within the larger scheme; having beliefs about the meaning of life that shape conduct and provide comfort.

# References


Adler, A. (1935). Prevention of neurosis. *International Journal of Individual Psychology, 1*, 3–12.

Agras, W. S. (1997). Helping people improve their lives with behavior therapy. *Behavior Therapy, 28*, 375–384.

Albee, G. W. (2000). The Boulder model's fatal flaw. *American Psychologist, 55*, 247–248.

Allport, G. W. (1953). The trend in motivational theory. *American Journal of Orthopsychiatry, 23*, 107–119.

Allport, G. W. (1955). Review of realms of value: A critique of human civilization. *Abnormal and Social Psychology, 50*, 154–156.

American Association for Counseling and Development. (1981). *Ethical principles*. Alexandria, VA: Author.

American Association for Counseling and Development. (1988). *Ethical standards*. Alexandria, VA: Author.

American Association for Counseling and Development. (1989). *Bylaws*. Alexandria, VA: Author.

American Counseling Association (2005). *Code of ethics*. Alexandria, VA: Author.

American Psychiatric Association (1994). *DSM-IV: Diagnostic and statistical manual of mental disorders*. Washington, DC: Author.

American Psychiatric Association (2000). *Diagnostic and statistical manual of mental disorders* (4th ed.), Text Revision. Washington, DC: Author.

American Psychological Association. (1981). Ethical principles of psychologists. *American Psychologist, 36*, 633–681.

American Psychological Association (1993). Guidelines for providers of psychological services to ethnic, linguistic, and culturally diverse populations. *American Psychologist, 48*, 45–48.

American Psychological Association. (2002). Ethical principles of psychologists and code of conduct. *American Psychologist, 57*, 1060–1073.

American Psychological Association. (2003). Guidelines on multicultural education, training, research, practice, and organizational change for psychologists. *American Psychologist, 58*, 377–402.

Anderson, H. (2003). On multicultural biases. *Inquiry: Critical Thinking across the Disciplines, 22*, 15–19.

Angers, M. (2011). Summary: Whatever Happened to Mental Health. Nancy McWilliams at Washington Square Institute's 35th Annual Scientific Conference, April 10, 2011. New York: National Association for the Advancement of Psychoanalysis.

Argyle, M. (2008). *The psychology of happiness*. New York: Alpha Books.

Arredondo, P., Toporek, R., Brown, S., & Jones, J. (1996). Operationalization of the multicultural counseling competencies. *Journal of Multicultural Counseling and Development, 24*, 42–78.



*Counseling Psychology: An Integrated Positive Psychological Approach*, First Edition. Ruth Chu-Lien Chao.

Arredondo, P., Toporek, M. S., Brown, S., Jones, J., Locke, D. C., Sanchez, J., & Stadler, H. (1996). *Operationalization of the multicultural counseling competencies*. Alexandria, VA: AMCD.

Aspinwall, L. G., & Staudinger, U. M. (Eds.) (2003). *A psychology of human strengths*. Washington, DC: American Psychological Association.

Ayres, C. G., & Mahat, G. (2012). Social support, acculturation, and optimism: Understanding positive health practices in Asian American college students. *Journal of Transcultural Nursing, 23*, 270–278.

Ballou, M., & Brown, L. S. (2002). *Rethinking mental health and disorder: Feminist perspectives*. New York: Guilford Press.

Bandura, A. (1977a). *Social learning theory*. Oxford, England: Prentice-Hall.

Bandura, A. (1977b). Social-efficacy: Toward a unifying theory of behavioral change. *Psychological Review, 84*, 191–215.

Bandura, A. (1981). In search of pure unidirectional determinants. *Behavior Therapy, 12*, 30–40.

Bandura, A. (1986). The explanatory and predictive scope of self-efficacy theory. *Journal of Social and Clinical Psychology, 4*, 359–373.

Batson, C. D., Ahmad, N., Lishner, D. A., & Tsang, J.-A. (2002). Empathy and altruism. In C. R. Snyder and S. J. Lopez (Eds.), *Handbook of positive psychology* (pp. 485–498). New York: Oxford University Press.

Beck, A. T. (1967). *Depression*. New York: Harper & Row.

Beck, A. T. (1976). *Cognitive therapy and the emotional disorders*. Boston: International Universities Press.

Beck, A. T., Brown, G. K., & Henriques, G. R. (2002). *Cognitive therapy for suicide attempters*. Distinguished Lecturer Series, National institute of Mental Health. Bethesda, MD: National institute of Mental Health.

Beck, A. T., & Steer, R. A. (1989). Clinical predictors of eventual suicide: A five to ten year prospective study of suicide attempters. *Journal of Affective Disorders, 17*, 203–209.

Becker, D., & Marecek, J. (2008). Positive psychology history in the remaking?, *Theory & Psychology, 18*, 591–604.

Belar, C. D., & Perry, N. W. (1992). The National Conference on Scientist-Practitioner Education and Training for the Professional Practice of Psychology. *American Psychologist, 47*, 71–75.

Belgrave, F. Z., & Allison, K. W. (2010). *African American psychology: From Africa to America* (2nd ed.). Thousand Oaks, CA: Sage.

Belkin, G. S. (1975). *Practical counseling in schools*. Dubuque, IA: Brown.

Benvenuto, S., & Molino, A. (Eds.). (2008). *In Freud's tracks: Conversations from the Journal of European Psychoanalysis*. Lanham, MD: Jason Aronson.

Binswanger, L. (1958). The existential analysis school of thought. In R. May, E. Angel, and H. F. Ellenberger (Eds.), *Existence: A new dimension in psychiatry and psychology* (pp. 191–213). New York: Basic Books.

Biswas-Diener, R. (2006). From the equator to the north pole: A study of character strengths. *Journal of Happiness Studies, 7*, 293–310.

Bolt, M. (2004). *Pursuing human strengths: A positive psychology guide*. New York: Worth.

Bonanno, G. A. (2004). Loss, trauma, and human resilience: Have we underestimated the human capacity to thrive after extremely aversive events? *American Psychologist, 59*, 20–28.

Breshgold, E. K. (1989). Resistance in Gestalt therapy: An historical theoretical perspective. *Gestalt Journal, 12*, 73–102.

Brown, L. S., & Ballou, M. (Eds.). (1992). *Personality and psychotherapy: Feminist reappraisals*. New York: Guilford Press.

Bryant, F. B., & Veroff, J. (2007). *Savoring: A new model of positive experience*. Mahwah, NJ: Lawrence Erlbaum.

Caldwell-Colbert, A., Parks, F. M., & Eshun, S. (2009). Positive psychology: African American strengths, resilience, and protective factors. In H. A. Neville, B. M. Tynes, and S. O. Utsey (Eds.), *Handbook of African American Psychology* (pp. 375–384). Thousand Oaks, CA: Sage.

Calhoun, L.G. & Tedeschi, R. G. (2004). The foundations of posttraumatic growth: New considerations. *Psychological Inquiry, 15*, 93–102.

Cautela, J., & Kearney, A. (1986). *The covert conditioning handbook*. New York: Springer.

Callander, T. (1922). The hope of the future. *North American Review, 215*, 403–411.

Carlson, J., & Slavik, S. (Eds.) (1997). *Techniques in Adlerian therapy*. New York: Routledge.

Carlson, J., Sperry, L., & Lewis, J. A. (2005). *Family therapy techniques: Integrating and tailoring treatment*. New York: Routledge.

Carlson, J., Watts, R. E., & Maniacci, M. (2006). *Alderian therapy: Theory and practice*. Washington, DC: American Psychological Association.

Carlyle, T. (1929). *Best of Carlyle: Selected essays and passages*. New York: Thomas Nelson.

Cartwright, B. Y., Daniels, J., & Zhang, S. (2008). Assessing multicultural competence: Perceived versus demonstrated performance. *Journal of Counseling and Development, 86*, 318–322.

Chan, Wing-tsit (Trans.) (1963). *A source book in Chinese philosophy*. Princeton, NJ: Princeton University Press.

Chao, R. C.-L., & Green, K. E. (2011). Multiculturally Sensitive Mental Health Scale (MSMHS): Development, factor analysis, reliability, and validity. *Psychological Assessment, 23*, 876.

Chua, A. (2011). *Battle hymn of the tiger mother: This is a story about a mother, two daughters, and two dogs*. New York: Penguin Press.

Chun, C., Moos, R. H., & Cronkite, R. C. ( 2006). Culture: A fundamental context for the stress and coping paradigm. In P. T. P. Wong & L. C. J. Wong ( Eds.), *Handbook of multicultural perspectives on stress and coping* (pp. 29–53). New York: Springer.

Clark, R., Anderson, N. B., Clark, V. R., & Williams, D. R. (1999). Racism as a stressor for African Americans: A biopsychosocial model. *American Psychologist, 54*, 805–816.

Clifton, D. O., & Nelson, P. (1996). *Soar with your strengths: A simple yet revolutionary philosophy of business and management*. New York: Dell.

Cloninger, R. C. (2004). *Feeling good: The science of well-being*. New York: Oxford University Press.

Cokley, K., Caldwell, L., Miller, K., & Muhammad, G. (2001). Content analysis of the *Journal of Black Psychology* (1985–1999). *Journal of Black Psychology, 27*, 424–438.

Cole, E. M., Piercy, F., Wolfe, E. W., & West, J. M. (2014). Development of the Multicultural Therapy Competency Inventory – Client Version. *Contemporary Family Therapy: An International Journal, 36*, 462–473.

Compton, M. T. (2004). Considering schizophrenia from a preventive perspective. *American Journal of Preventive Medicine, 26*, 178–185.

Compton, W. T. (2012). *Introduction to positive psychology*. Belmont, CA: Wadsworth.

Confucius (2008). *The Analects*. Tran. by R. Dawson. New York: Oxford University Press.

Congress, E. P., & Gonzales, M. J. (Eds.) (2005). *Multicultural perspectives in working with families*. New York: Springer.

Constantine, M. G., & Gloria, A. M. (1999). Multicultural issues in predoctoral programs: A national survey. *Journal of Multicultural Counseling and Development, 27*, 42–53.

Constantine, M. G., & Sue, D. W. (Eds.). (2006). *Addressing racism: Facilitating cultural competence in mental health and educational settings*. Hoboken, NJ: John Wiley & Sons.

Corey, G. (1986). *Groups: Process and practice*. Independence, KY: Brooks/Cole.

Corey, G. (2008). *Theory and practice of counseling and psychotherapy*. Monterey, CA.: Brooks/Cole.

Corey, G. (2012). *Theory and practice of counseling and psychotherapy* (9th ed.). Belmont, CA: Brooks/Cole.

Corsini, R. J. (1995). Putting the "B" in RET: It has to be. *Journal of Rational-Emotive & Cognitive-Behavior Therapy, 13*, 5–7.

Corsini, R. J., & Wedding, D. (2013). *Current psychotherapies* (10th ed.). Itasca, IL: F. E. Peacock.

Craske, M. G., Anthony, M. M., & Barlow, D. H. (2006). *Mastering your fears and phobias: Therapist guide* (2nd ed.). New York: Oxford University Press.

Craske, M. G., & Barlow, D. H. (2008). Panic disorder and agoraphobia. In D. H. Barlow (Ed.), *Clinical handbook of psychological disorders: A step-by-step treatment manual* (4th ed.) (pp. 1–64). New York: Guilford Press.

Csikszentmihalyi, M. (1990). The domain of creativity. In M. A. Runco and R. S. Albert (Eds.), *Theories of creativity* (pp. 190–212). Thousand Oaks, CA: Sage.

Csikszentmihalyi, M. (2004). *Good business: Leadership, flow, and the making of meaning*. New York: Penguin.

Csikszentmihalyi, M. (2008). *Flow: The psychology of optimal experience*. New York: Harper.

Daly, A., Jennings, J., Beckett, J. O., & Leashore, B. R. (1995). Effective coping strategies of African Americans. *Social Work, 40*, 240–248.

Davidson, C. L., Wingate, L. R., Slish, M. L., & Rasmussen, K. A. (2010). The great black hope: Hope and its relation to suicide risk among African Americans. *Suicide and Like-Threatening Behavior, 40*, 170–180.

Dawson, J., & Mukoyama, M. (Eds.) (2012). *Global strategies in retailing: Asian and European experiences*. London: Routledge.

Delany, S. L., Delany, A. E., & Hearth, A. H. (1994). *Having our say: The Delany sisters' first 100 years*. New York: Dell.

Dendy, W. C. (1853). *Psychē; A discourse on the birth and pilgrimage of thought*. London: Longman, Brown, Green, and Longmans.

DeVylder, J. E., Oh, H. Y., Yang, L. H., Cabassa, L. J., Chen, F., & Lukens, E. P. (2013). Acculturative stress and psychotic-like experiences among Asian and Latino immigrants to the United States. *Schizophrenia Research, 150*, 223–228.

Diener, E. & Biswas-Diener, R. (2008). *Happiness: Unlocking the mysteries of psychological wealth*. Oxford, England: Wiley-Blackwell.

Diener, E., & Diener, C. (2011). Monitoring psychosocial prosperity for social change. In R. Biswas-Diener (Ed.), *Positive psychology as social change*. New York: Springer.

Diener, E., Sapyta, J. J., & Suh, E. (1998). Subjective well-being is essential to well-being. *Psychological Inquiry, 9*, 33–37.

Diener, E., Suh, E. M., Lucas, R. E., & Smith, H. L. (1999). Subjective well-being: Three decades of progress. *Psychological Bulletin, 125*, 276–302.

Dobson, K. S., & Block, L. (1998). Historical and philosophical bases of the cognitive-behavioral therapies. In K. S. Dobson (Ed.), *Handbook of cognitive-behavioral therapies* (pp. 3–38). New York: Guilford Press.

Dole, D. C., Silbert, J. H., & Mann, A. J. (2008). *Positive family dynamics: Appreciative inquiry questions to bring out the best in families*. Chargrin Falls, OH: Taos Institute Publications.

Driscoll, M. W., & Torres, L. (2013). Acculturative stress and Latino depression: The mediating role of behavioral and cognitive resources. *Cultural Diversity and Ethnic Minority Psychology, 19*, 373–382.

Easterbrook, G. (2001, March 5). I'm OK, you're OK. *The New Republic*, 20–23.

Easterbrook, G. (2003). *The progress paradox: How life gets better while people feel worse*. New York: Random House.

Eid, M., & Diener, E. (2006). (Eds.). *Handbook of multimethod measurement in psychology*. Washington, DC: American Psychological Association.

Eisenberger, R., & Selbst, M. (1994). Does reward increase or decrease creativity? *Journal of Personality and Social Psychology, 66*, 1116–1127.

Ellis, A. (1957). Rational psychotherapy and individual psychology. *Journal of Individual Therapy, 13*, 38–44.

Ellis, A. (1980). Rational-emotive therapy and cognitive behavior therapy: Similarities and differences. *Cognitive Therapy and Research, 4*, 325–340.

Ellis, A. (1984). Expanding the ABCs of RET. *Journal of Rational-Emotive Therapy, 2*, 20–24.

Ellis, A. (1999). Why rational-emotive therapy to rational emotive behavior therapy? *Psychotherapy: Theory, Research, Practice, and Training, 36*, 154–159.

Ellis, A. (2000). A critique of the theoretical contributions of nondirective therapy. *Journal of Clinical Psychology, 56*, 897–905.

Ellis, A., & Dryden, W. (2007). *The practice of rational emotive behavior therapy* (2nd ed.). New York: Springer.

English, O. S. (1946). The sense of well-being and its relation to clinical improvement. *Bulletin of the Menninger Clinic, 10*, 137–144.

Falicov, C. J. (1995). Training to think culturally: A multidimensional comparative framework. *Family Process, 34*, 373–388.

Falicov, C. J. (1998). *Latino families in therapy: A guide to multicultural practice*. New York: Guilford Press.

Frankl, V. E. (1959). The spiritual dimension in existential analysis and logotherapy. *Journal of Individual Therapy, 15*, 157–165.

Frankl, V. E. (1962). *Man's search for meaning*. Boston: Bacon.

Fredrickson, B. L. ( 2001). The role of positive emotions in positive psychology: The broaden-and-build theory of positive emotions. *American Psychologist, 56*, 218–226.

Fredrickson, B. L. ( 2003). Positive emotions and upward spirals in organizations. In K. S. Cameron, J. E. Dutton, and R. E. Quinn ( Eds.), *Positive organizational scholarship: Foundations of a new discipline* (pp. 163–175). San Francisco, CA: Berrett-Koehler.

Fredrickson, B. (2008). *Positivity: Groundbreaking research reveals how to embrace the hidden strength of positive emotions, overcome negativity, and thrive*. New York: Crown.

Fredrickson, B. L., & Branigan, C. (2005). Positive emotions broaden the scope of attention and thought-action repertoires. *Cognition and Emotion, 19*, 313–332.

Fredrickson, B. L., & Joiner, T. (2002). Positive emotions trigger upward spirals toward emotional well-being. *Psychological Science, 13*, 172–175.

Fredrickson, B. L., & Losada, M. F. (2005). Positive affect and the complex dynamics of human flourishing. *American Psychologist, 60*, 678–686.

Freud, A. (1935). *Psycho-analysis for teachers and parents: Introductory lectures*. Trans. by B. Low. New York: Emerson Books.

Freud, S. (1926). *The question of lay analysis*. London: Hogarth Press.

Freud, S. (1930). Civilization and its discontents. In J. Strachey (Ed. & Trans.), *The complete psychological works of Sigmund Freud – The future of an illusion, civilization and its discontents, and other works*. London: Hogarth Press.

Freud, S. (1932). The anatomy of the mental personality (Lecture 31). In *New introductory lectures on psychoanalysis*. London: Hogarth Press.

Freud, S. (1953). The project for a scientific psychology. In J. Strachey (Ed. & Trans.), *The complete psychological works of Sigmund Freud, vol. 1*. London: Hogarth Press.

Freud, S. (1957a). Five lectures on psycho-analysis. In J. Strachey (Ed. & Trans.), *The complete psychological works of Sigmund Freud* (pp. 3–55). London: Hogarth Press.

Freud, S. (1957b). Leonardo Da Vinci and a memory of his childhood. In J. Strachey (Ed. & Trans.), *The complete psychological works of Sigmund Freud* (pp. 63–137). London: Hogarth Press.

Freud, S. (1959). Beyond the pleasure principle. In J. Strachey (Ed. & Trans.), *The complete psychological works of Sigmund Freud* (pp. 3–64). London: Hogarth Press.

Freud, S. (1962). *The ego and the id*. Trans. by J. Riviere. New York: W.W. Norton.

Frijda, N. H. (1994). The *lex talions*: On vengeance. In S. H. M. van Goozen, N. E. van de Poll, and J. A. Sergeant (Eds.), *Emotions: Essays on emotion theory* (pp. 263–289). Hillsdale, NJ: Lawrence Erlbaum.

Frisch, M. B. (2005). *Quality of life therapy: Applying a life satisfaction approach to positive psychology and cognitive therapy*. Hoboken, NJ: Wiley.

Galassi, J. P., & Akos, P. (2007). *Strengths-based school counseling: Promoting student development and achievement*. New York: Taylor & Francis.

Gallagher, M. W., & Lopez, S. J. (2007). Curiosity and well-being. *Journal of Positive Psychology*, *2*, 236–248.

Gandhi, M. K. (1965). *Collected works*. India: Publications Division, Ministry of Information and Broadcasting.

Gandhi, M. K. (1993). *Gandhi, an autobiography: The story of my experiments with truth*. Trans. by M. H. Desai. Boston: Beacon Press.

General, S. (2001). *Mental health: Culture, race, and ethnicity. Supplement to mental health: A report of the Surgeon General*. Washington, DC: Government Printing Office.

Gilbert, D. (2009). *Stumbling on happiness*. New York: Random House.

Gladding, S. T, (1996). *Community and agency counseling*. New York: Prentice Hall.

Gladding, S. T. (2004). The potential and pitfall of William Glasser's New Vision for Counseling. *The Family Journal*, *12*, 342–343.

Gladding, S. T., & Cox, E. (2008). Family snapshots: A descriptive classroom exercise in memory and insight. *The Family Journal*, *16*, 381–383.

Glasser, W. (1965). *Reality therapy: A new approach to psychiatry*. New York: Harper & Row.

Glasser, W. (1969). *Schools without failure*. New York: Harper & Row.

Glasser, W. (1976). *Positive addiction*. New York: Harper & Row.

Glasser, W. (1981). *Stations of the mind*. New York: Harper & Row.

Glasser, W. (1984). *Take effective control of your life*. New York: Harper & Row.

Goldenberg, H., & Goldenberg, I. (2008). *Family therapy: An overview* (8th ed.). Belmont, CA: Brooks/Cole.

Goodman, L. A., Liang, B., Weintraub, S. R., Helms, J. E., & Latta, R. E. (2004). Warts and all: Personal reflections on social justice in counseling psychology. Reply to Kiselica, Palmer, Thompson and Shermis, and Watts. *The Counseling Psychologist*, *32*, 886–899.

Groth-Marnat, G. (2009). The five assessment issues you meet when you go to heaven. *Journal of Personality Assessment*, *91*, 303–310.

Guyer, M. F. (1931). The internal secretions and human well-being. *Science*, *74*, 159–166.

Haidt, J. (2006). *The happiness hypothesis*. New York: Basic Books.

Hall, C. B., & Nelson, G. (1996). Social networks, social support, personal empowerment, and the adaptation of psychiatric consumers/survivors: Path analytic models. *Social Science & Medicine*, *43*, 1743–1754.

Harris, T. A. (1969). *I'm ok you're ok: A practical guide to transactional analysis*. Oxford, England: Harper & Row.

Hartmann, G. W. (1934). Personality traits associated with variations in happiness. *Journal of Abnormal and Social Psychology*, *29*, 202–212.

Haybron, D. (2008). *Pursuit of unhappiness: The elusive psychology of well-being*. New York: Oxford University Press.

Helms, J. E. (1990). *Black and White racial identity: Theory, research, and practice*. New York: Greenwood Press.

Heredia Montesinos, A. (2015). Precipitating and risk factors for suicidal behavior among immigrants and ethnic minorities in Europe: A review of the literature. In D. D. van Bergen, A. Heredia Montesinos, & M. Schouler-Ocak (Eds.), *Suicidal behavior of immigrants and ethnic minorities in Europe* (pp. 27–43). Boston, MA: Hogrefe.

Hofmann, S. G. (2014). Interpersonal emotion regulation model of mood and anxiety disorders. *Cognitive Therapy and Research*, *38*, 483–492.

Huppert, F. A. (2004). A population approach to positive psychology: The potential for population interventions to promote well-being and prevent disorder. In P. A. Linely and S. Joseph (Eds.), *Positive psychology in science* (pp. 693–709). Hoboken, NJ: John Wiley & Sons.

Huppert, F., Baylis, N., & Keverne, B. (2005). *The science of well-being*. New York: Oxford University Press.

Jacobs, T. (2001). Reflections on the goals of psychoanalysis, the psychoanalytic process, and the process of change. *Psychoanalytic Quarterly, 70*, 149–181.

James, W. (1902). *The varieties of religious experience*. New York: Longmans, Green & Co.

Jones, E. (1953). *The life and work of Sigmund Freud*. New York: Basic Books.

Jung, C. G. (1939). On the psychogenesis of schizophrenia. *Journal of Mental Science, 85*, 999–1011.

Kazdin, A. E. (1979). Unobtrusive measures in behavioral assessment. *Journal of Applied Behavior Analysis, 12*, 713–724.

Kazdin, A. E. (1984). Integration of psychodynamic and behavioral psychotherapies. In H. Arkowitz and S. B. Messer (Eds.), *Psychoanalytic therapy and behavior therapy: Is integration possible?* (pp. 139–170). New York: Plenum Press.

Kazdin, A. E., & Hersen, M. (1980). The current status of behavior therapy. *Behavior Modification, 4*, 283–302.

Kazdin, A. E., & Wilson, G. T. (1978). *Evaluation of behavior therapy: Issues, evidence, and research strategies*. Oxford, England: Ballinger.

Kearney, A. J. (2006). A primer of covert sensitization. *Cognitive and Behavioral Practice, 13*, 167–175.

Kearney, L. K., Draper, M., & Barón, A. (2005). Counseling utilization by ethnic minority college students. *Cultural Diversity and Ethnic Minority Psychology, 11*, 272–285.

Keyes, C. L. M. (1998). Social well-being. *Social Psychology Quarterly, 61*, 121–140.

Keyes, C. L. M. (2002). The mental health continuum: From languishing to flourishing in life. *Journal of Health and Social Behavior, 43*, 207–222.

Keyes, C. L. M. (2005). Mental illness and/or mental health? Investigating axioms of the complete state model of health. *Journal of Consulting and Clinical Psychology, 73*, 539–548.

Keyes, C. L. M., & Haidt, J. (2002). *Flourishing: Positive psychology and the life well-lived*. Washington, DC: American Psychological Association.

Keyes, C. L. M., Shmotkin, D., & Ryff, C. D. (2002). Optimizing well-being: The empirical encounter of two traditions. *Journal of Personality and Social Psychology, 82*, 1007–1022.

Landrine, H., & Klonoff, E. A. (1996). The schedule of racist events: A measure of racial discrimination and a study of its negative physical and mental health consequences. *Journal of Black Psychology, 22*, 144–168.

Lanzoni, S. (2004). Existential encounter in the asylum: Ludwig Binswanger's 1935 case of hysteria. *History of Psychiatry, 15*, 59–62.

Layard, R. (2005). *Happiness: Lessons from a new science*. New York: Penguin.

Leitenberg, H. (Ed.) (1990). *Handbook of social and evaluation anxiety*. New York: Plenum Press.

Linley, P. A., & Joseph, S. (2003). Trauma and personal growth. *The Psychologist, 16*, 135.

Linley, P. A., & Joseph, S. (Eds.) (2004). *Positive psychology in practice*. Hoboken, NJ: John Wiley & Sons.

Locke, E. A. (2002a). Setting goals for life and happiness. In C. R. Snyder and S. J. Lopez (Eds.), *Handbook of positive psychology* (pp. 299–312). New York: Oxford University Press.

Locke, E. A. (2002b). The dead end of postmodernism. *American Psychologist, 57*, 458.

Lopez, S. (2014). *Making hope happen: Create the future you want for yourself and others*. New York: Atria.

Lucas, M. S., & Berkel, L. A. (2005). Counseling needs of students who seek help at a university counseling center: A closer look at gender and multicultural issues. *Journal of College Student Development, 46*, 251–266.

Lyubomirsky, S., Sheldon, K. M., & Schkade, D. (2005). Pursuing happiness: The architecture of sustainable change. *Review of General Psychology, 9*, 111–131.

Mahoney, M. J., & Lyddon, W. J. (1988). Recent developments in cognitive approaches to counseling and psychotherapy. *The Counseling Psychologist, 16*, 190–234.

Mahoney, M. J. (1974). *Cognition and behavior modification*. Oxford, England: Ballinger.

May, R. (1977). *The meaning of anxiety (rev. ed.)*. New York: W. W. Norton.

May, R., Angel, E., & Ellenberger, H. F. (Eds.) (1958). *Existence: A new dimension in psychiatry and psychology*. New York: Basic Books.

McCrae, R., & Costa, P. T. (1999). Introduction to the empirical and theoretical status of the five-factor model of personality traits. In T. A. Widiger and P. T. Costa (Eds.), *Personality disorders and the five-factor model of personality* (3rd ed.) (pp. 15–27). Washington, DC: American Psychological Association.

McGoldrick, M., Gerson, R., & Petry, S. (2008). *Genograms: Assessment and intervention* (3rd ed.). New York: W. W. Norton.

McGoldrick, M., Giordano, J., & Garcia-Preto, N. (2005). *Ethnicity and family therapy* (3rd ed.). New York: Guilford Press.

McMahon, D. M. (2006). *Happiness: A history*. New York: Grove Press.

McRae, M. B., & Johnson, S. D. (1991). Toward training for competence in multicultural counselor education. *Journal of Counseling and Development, 70*, 131–135.

Mencius (2005). *Mencius*. Trans. by D. C. Lau. New York: Penguin.

Minuchin, S., & Fishman, H. C. (1981). *Family therapy techniques*. Boston, MA: Harvard University Press.

Molino, A. & S. Benvenuto, E. (Eds.). (2009). *Freud's Tracks: Conversations from the Journal of European Psychoanalysis*. Lanham, MD: Jason Aronson.

Moore, B. E., & Fine, B. (1995). *Psychoanalysis: The major concepts*. New Haven, CT: Yale University Press.

Morawska, E. (2008). Research on immigration/ethnicity in Europe and the United States: A comparison. *The Sociological Quarterly, 49*, 465–482.

Mother Teresa (1989). *No greater love*. Novato, CA: New World Library.

Morwood, J. (1998). *A dictionary of Latin words and phrases*. New York: Oxford University Press.

Murphy, M. C., Wright, B. V., & Bellamy, D. E. (1995). Multicultural training in university counseling center predoctoral psychology internship programs: A survey. *Journal of Multicultural Counseling and Development, 23*, 170–180.

Murray, C. (2009). *Human accomplishment: The pursuit of excellence in the arts and sciences, 800 B.C. to 1950*. New York: Harper-Collins.

Muzak, J. (2009). Trauma, feminism, and addiction: Cultural and clinical lessons from Susan Gordon Lydon's Take the long way home: Memoirs of a survivor. *Traumatology, 15*(4), 24–34.

Myers, D. G. (2006). *Pursuit of happiness*. New York: Harper-Collins.

Myers, D. G., & Diener, E. (1995). Who is happy? *Psychological Science, 6*, 10–19.

Myers, R. E. (2004). Review of TV or no TV? A primer on the psychology of television. *Journal of Child and Family Studies, 13*, 511–513.

Napier, A. Y., & Whitaker, C. (1998). *The family crucible: The intense experience of family therapy*. New York: Harper & Row.

Nathan, P. E., & Gorman, J. M. (2002). Efficacy, effectiveness, and the clinical utility of psychotherapy research. In P. E. Nathan and J. M. Gorman (Eds.), *A guide to treatments that work* (2nd ed.) (pp. 642–654). New York: Oxford University Press.

Neff, K. D., & Costigan, A. P. (2014). Self-compassion, well-being, and happiness. *Psychologie in Österreich*, 114–117.

Nietzsche, F. (1990). *The twilight of the idols and the anti-Christ: Or how to philosophize with a hammer*. Trans. by R. J. Hollingdale. New York: Penguin.

Norcross, J. C., Sayette, M. A., Mayne, T. J., Karg, R. S., & Turkson, M. A. (1998). Selecting a doctoral program in professional psychology: Some comparisons among PhD counseling, PhD clinical, and PsyD clinical psychology programs. *Professional Psychology: Research & Practice, 29*, 609–614.

Okazaki, S., & Sue, S. (2000). Implications of test revisions for assessment with Asian Americans. *Psychological Assessment, 12*, 272–280.

Olson, R. P. (Ed.). (2002). *Religious theories of personality and psychotherapy: East meets West*. New York: Haworth Press.

Ong, A., & Van Dulmen, M. (Eds.) (2006). *Oxford handbook of methods in positive psychology*. New York: Oxford University Press.

Osho International Foundation. (1999). *Courage: The joy of living dangerously*. New York: St. Martin's Press.

Park, N., & Peterson, C. (2003). Early intervention from the perspective of positive psychology. *Prevention & Treatment, 6*, 1–8.

Patterson, J., Williams, L., Edwards, T. M., Chamow, L., & Grauf-Grounds, C. (2009). *Essential skills in family therapy: From the first interview to termination* (2nd ed.). New York: Guilford Press.

Pérez Benítez, C. I., Sibrava, N. J., Zlotnick, C., Weisberg, R., & Keller, M. B. (2014). Differences between Latino individuals with posttraumatic stress disorder and those with other anxiety disorders. *Psychological Trauma: Theory, Research, Practice, and Policy, 6*, 345–352.

Perls, F. S., Hefferline, R. F., & Goodman, P. (1994). *Gestalt therapy: Excitement and growth in the human personality* (9th ed.). Gouldsboro, ME: The Gestalt Journal Press.

Peterson, C. (2006). *A primer in positive psychology*. New York: Oxford University Press.

Peterson, C., & Seligman, M. E. P. (2004). *Character strengths and virtues: A handbook and classification*. Washington, DC: American Psychological Association.

Pettigrew, T., Tropp, L. R., Wagner, U., & Christ, O. (2011). Recent advances in intergroup contact theory. *International Journal of Intercultural Relations, 35*, 271–280.

Ponterotto, J. G. (2010). Multicultural personality: An evolving theory of optimal functioning in culturally heterogeneous societies. *The Counseling Psychologist, 38*, 714–758.

Ponterotto, J. G., Alexander, C. M., & Grieger, I. (1995). A multicultural competency checklist for counseling training programs. *Journal of Multicultural Counseling and Development, 23*, 11–20.

Ponterotto, J. G., Utsey, S. O., & Pedersen, P. B. (2006). *Preventing prejudice: A guide for counselors, educators, and parents* (2nd ed.). Thousand Oaks, CA: Sage.

Pressman, S. D., & Cohen, S. (2012). Positive emotion word use and longevity in famous deceased psychologists. *Health Psychology, 31*, 297–305.

Prilleltensky, I. (1989). Psychology and the status quo. *American Psychologist, 44*, 795–802.

Prochaska, J. O., & Norcross, J. C. (2010). *Systems of psychotherapy: A transtheoretical analysis*. Belmont, CA: Brooks/Cole.

Quintana. S. M., & Bernal, M. E. (1995). Ethnic minority training in counseling psychology: Comparisons with clinical psychology and proposed standards. *The Counseling Psychologist, 23*, 102–121.

Ramirez, M., III. (1999). *Multicultural psychotherapy: An approach to individual and cultural differences* (2nd ed.). Needham, MA: Allyn & Bacon.

Rasheed, J. M., Rasheed, M. N., & Marley, J. A. (2011). *Family therapy: Models and techniques*. Thousand Oaks, CA: Sage.

Rayner, K. E., Schniering, C. A., Rapee, R. M., Taylor, A., & Hutchinson, D. M. (2013). Adolescent girls' friendship networks, body dissatisfaction, and disordered eating: Examining selection and socialization processes. *Journal of Abnormal Psychology, 122*, 93–104.

Ridley, C. R. (2005). *Overcoming unintentional racism in counseling and therapy: A practitioner's guide to intentional intervention* (2nd ed.). Thousand Oaks, CA: Sage.

Rogers, C. R. (1939a). *The clinical treatment of the problem child*. Oxford, England: Houghton.

Rogers, C. R. (1939). Review of psychological foundations of personality. *Journal of Educational Psychology, 30*, 473–475.

Rogers, C. R. (1942a). The use of electronically recorded interviews in improving psychotherapeutic techniques. *American Journal of Orthopsychiatry, 12*, 429–434.

Rogers, C. R. (1942). *Counseling and psychotherapy; newer concepts in practice*. Oxford, England: Houghton Mifflin.

Rogers, C. R. (1951). *Client-centered therapy: Its current practice, implications, and theory*. Oxford, England: Houghton Mifflin.

Rogers, C. R. (1957). The necessary and sufficient conditions of therapeutic personality change. *Journal of Consulting Psychology, 21*, 95–103.

Rogers, C. R. (1959). The essence of psychotherapy: A client-centered view. *Annuals of Psychotherapy, 1*, 51–57.

Rogers, C. R., Lyon, H. J., & Tausch, R. (2014). *On becoming an effective teacher: Person-centered teaching, psychology, philosophy, and dialogues with Carl R. Rogers and Harold Lyon*. New York,: Routledge.

Ross, A. O. (1985). To form a more perfect union: It is time to stop standing still. *Behavior Therapy, 16*, 195–204.

Rothstein, A. (1999). Some implications of the analyst feeling disturbed while working with disturbed patients. *Psychoanalytic Quarterly, 68*, 541–558.

Roudinesco, E. (2003). *Why psychoanalysis?* New York: Columbia University Press.

Routh, D. K. (2000). The field of clinical psychology: A response to Thorne. *Journal of Clinical Psychology, 55*, 275–286.

Rule, W. R., & Bishop, M. (2006). *Adlerian lifestyle counseling: Practice and research*. New York: Routledge.

Rushton, J. P., Chrisjohn, R.D., & Fekken, G. C. (1981). The altruistic personality and the self-report altruism sale. *Personality and Individual Differences, 1*, 292–302.

Rusk, H. A., & Taylor, E. J. (1949). *New hope for the handicapped*. Oxford, England: Harper.

Ryan, R. M., & Deci, E. L. (2001). On happiness and human potentials: A review of research on hedonic and eudaimonic well-being. *Annual Review of Psychology, 52*, 141–166.

Ryff, C. D. (1989). Happiness is everything, or is it? Explorations on the meaning of psychological well-being. *Journal of Personality and Social Psychology, 57*, 1069–1081.

Ryff, C. D., & Keyes, C. L. (1995). The structure of psychological well-being revisited. *Journal of Personality and Social Psychology, 69*, 719–727.

Ryff, C. D., & Singer, B. (1998). The contours of positive human health. *Psychological Inquiry, 9*, 1–28.

Sandell, R., Blomberg, J., Lazar, A., Carlsson, J., Broberg, J., et al. (2000). Varieties of long-term outcome among patients in psychoanalysis and long-term psychotherapy. *International Journal of Psychoanalysis, 81*, 921–942.

Sandhu, T., & Moosa, F. (2013). Mental health of children of immigrants and ethnic minorities in Europe. *Adolescent Psychiatry, 3*, 30–33.

Scheidlinger, Z. (1999). Education calls for a new philosophy. *Educational Technology & Society, 2*, 119–126.

Scheier, M. F., & Carver, C. S. (1992). Effects of optimism on psychological and physical well-being: Theoretical overview and empirical update. *Cognitive Therapy and Research, 16*, 201–228.

Schwartz, B. (2005). *The paradox of choice: Why more is less.* New York: Harper Perennial.

Seligman, M. E. P. (1995). The effectiveness of psychotherapy: The consumer reports survey. *American Psychologist, 50*, 965–974.

Seligman, M. E. P. (2001). Comment on "priorities for prevention research at NIMH". *Prevention & Treatment, 4*, 1–3.

Seligman, M. E. P. (2002). *Authentic happiness: Using the new positive psychology to realize your potential for lasting fulfillment.* New York: Simon & Schuster.

Seligman, M. E. P. (2006). *Learned optimism: How to change your mind and your life.* New York: Vintage.

Seligman, M. E. P., & Csikszentmihalyi, M. (2000). Positive psychology: An introduction. *American Psychologist, 55*, 5–14.

Seligman, M. E. P., Reivich, K., Jaycox, L. & Gillham, J. (2007). *The optimistic child.* New York: Houghton Mifflin.

Seligman, M. E., Steen, T. A., Park, N., & Peterson, C. (2005). Positive psychology progress: Empirical validation of interventions. *American Psychologist, 60*, 410–421.

Sheldon, K. M. (2004). *Optimal human being: An integrated multi-level perspective.* Mahwah, NJ: Lawrence Erlbaum.

Sheldon, K. M., Kashdan, T., & Steger, M. (Ed.). (2011). *Designing positive psychology: Taking stock and moving forward.* New York: Oxford University Press.

Shenk, J. W. (2006). *Lincoln's melancholy: How depression challenged a president and fueled his greatness.* New York: Mariner Books.

Simoni, J. M., Martone, M. G., & Kerwin, J. F. (2002). Spirituality and psychological adaptation among women with HIV/AIDS: Implications for counseling. *Journal of Counseling Psychology, 49*, 139.

Sirgy, M. J., & Wu, J. (2009). The pleasant life, the engaged life, and the meaningful life: What about the balanced life? *Journal of Happiness Studies, 10*, 183–196.

Snyder, C. R. (1994). *The psychology of hope: You can get there from here.* New York: Free Press.

Snyder, C. R. (2002). Hope theory: Rainbows in the mind. *Psychological Inquiry, 13*, 249–275.

Snyder, C. R., Harris, C., Anderson, J. R., Holleran, S. A., Irving, L. M., Sigmon, S. T., et al. (1991). The will and the ways: Development and validation of an individual-differences measure of hope. *Journal of Personality and Social Psychology, 60*, 570–585.

Snyder, C. R., Irving, L. M., & Anderson, J. R. (1991). Hope and health. In C. R. Snyder and D. R. Forsyth (Eds.), *Handbook of social and clinical psychology: The health perspective* (pp. 285–305). Elmsford, NY: Pergamon Press.

Snyder, C. R., & Lopez, S. J. (2002). *Handbook of positive psychology.* New York: Oxford University Press.

Snyder, C. R., & Lopez, S. J. (2010). *Positive psychology: The scientific and practical explorations of human strengths* (2nd ed.). Thousand Oaks, CA: Sage.

Sommers-Flanagan, J. & Sommers-Flanagan, R. (2004). *Counseling and psychotherapy theories in context and practice: Skills, strategies, and techniques.* Hoboken, NJ: John Wiley & Sons.

Speight, S. L., Thomas, A. J., Kennel, R. G., & Anderson, M. E. (1995). Operationalizing multicultural training in doctoral programs and internships. *Professional Psychology: Research and Practice, 26*, 401–406.

Stephens, P. (Ed.) (2007). *Altruism and health: Perspectives from empirical research.* New York: Oxford University Press.

Sternberg, R. J. (2000). Wisdom as a form of giftedness. *Gifted Child Quarterly, 44*, 252–260.

Sternberg, R. J., & Grigorenko, E. L. (2001). Unified psychology. *American Psychologist, 56*, 1069–1079.

Stoner, G., & Green, S. K. (1992). Reconsidering the scientist-practitioner model for school psychology practice. *School Psychology Review, 21*, 155–166.

Sue, D. (2004). Whiteness and ethnocentric monoculturalism: Making the "invisible" visible. *American Psychologist, 59*, 761–769.

Sue, D. W., Arrendondo, P., & McDavis, R. J. (1992). Multicultural counseling competencies and standards: A call to the profession. *Journal of Counseling & Development, 70*, 477–486.

Sue, D. W., Bernier, J. E., Durran, A. A., Feinberg, L. L., Pedersen, P. P., Smith, E. J., & Vasquez-Nuttall, E. E. (1982). Position paper: Cross-cultural counseling competencies. *The Counseling Psychologist, 10*, 45–52.

Sue, D. W., Carter, R. T., Casas, J. M., Fouad, N. A., Ivey, A. E., Jensen, M., & ... Vazquez-Nutall, E. (1998). *Multicultural counseling competencies: Individual and organizational development*. Thousand Oaks, CA: Sage.

Sue, D. W., & Sue, D. M. (1977). Barriers to effective cross-cultural counseling. *Journal of Counseling Psychology, 24*, 420–429.

Sue, D. W., & Sue, D. M. (2008). *Foundations of counseling and psychotherapy: Evidence-based practices for a diverse society*. Hoboken, NJ: John Wiley & Sons.

Sue, D. W., & Sue, D. M. (2012). *Counseling the culturally diverse: Theory and practice*. (6th ed.). Hoboken, NJ: John Wiley & Sons.

Suzuki, L., & Ponterroto, J. G. (Eds.) (2008). *Handbook of multicultural assessment: Clinical, psychological, and educational applications*. San Francisco, CA: Jossey-Bass.

Taylor, S. E., & Armor, D. A. (1996). Positive illusions and coping with adversity. *Journal of Personality, 64*, 873–898.

Todd, K. (2010). *Curious? Discover the missing ingredient to a fulfilling life*. New York: Harper Perennial.

Torres, L., Driscoll, M. W., & Voell, M. ( 2012). Discrimination, acculturation, acculturative stress, and Latino psychological distress: A moderated mediational model. *Cultural Diversity & Ethnic Minority Psychology, 18*, 17–25.

Turnbull, A., Turnbull, H. R., Erwin, E. J., Soodak, L. C., & Shogren, K. A. (2010). *Families, professionals, and exceptionality: Positive outcomes through partnerships and trust* (6th ed.). Upper Saddle River, NJ: Pearson.

Vaillant, G. E. (2000). Adaptive mental mechanisms: Their role in a positive psychology. *American Psychologist, 55*, 89–98.

Van der Zee, K., & Van Oudenhoven, J. P. (2001). The multicultural personality questionnaire: Reliability and validity of self- and other ratings of multicultural effectiveness. *Journal of Research in Personality, 35*, 278–288.

Van der Zee, K., & Van Oudenhoven, J. P. (2013). Culture shock or challenge? The role of personality as a determinant of intercultural competence. *Journal of Cross-Cultural Psychology, 44*, 928–940.

Van der Zee, K. I., & Van Oudenhoven, J. P. (2014). Personality and multicultural effectiveness. In V. Benet-Martínez, & Y. Hong (Eds.), *The Oxford handbook of multicultural identity* (pp. 255–275). New York: Oxford University Press.

Van Deurzen, E. (2012). *Existential counselling and psychotherapy in practice* (3rd ed.). Thousand Oaks, CA: Sage.

Van Gogh, V. (1963). *The letters of Vincent Van Gough*. New York: Penguin.

Vera, E. M., & Speight, S. L. (2003). Multicultural competence, social justice, and counseling psychology: Expanding our roles. *The Counseling Psychologist, 31*, 253–272.

Vinson, T. S., & Neimeyer, G. J. (2003). The relationship between racial identity development and multicultural counseling competency: A second look. *Journal of Multicultural Counseling and Development, 31*, 262–277.

U.S. Surgeon General. (2001). *Mental Health: culture, race, and ethnicity*. Rockville, MD: Substance Abuse and Mental Health Services Administration.

Utsey, S. O., Ponterotto, J. G., Renolds, A. L., & Cancelli, A. A. (2000). Racial discrimination, coping, life satisfaction, and self-esteem among African Americans. *Journal of Counseling and Development, 78*, 72–80.

Walsh, R., Perrucci, A., & Severns, J. (1999). What's in a good moment: A hermeneutic study of psychotherapy values across levels of psychotherapy training. *Psychotherapy Research, 9*, 304–426.

Ward, T., & Mann, R. (2004). Good lives and the rehabilitation of offenders: A positive approach to sex offender treatment. In P. A. Linley and S. Joseph (Eds.), *Positive psychology in practice* (pp.598–616). Hoboken, NJ: John Wiley & Sons.

Webster, M. (2008). Review of promoting health through creativity: For professionals in health, arts and education. *Journal of Health Psychology, 13*, 299–300.

Weishaar, M. E. (1993). *Aaron T. Beck*. Thousand Oaks, CA: Sage.

Westen, D., & Gabbard, G. O. (2002). Developments in cognitive neuroscience: I. Conflict, compromise, and connectionism. *Journal of the American Psychoanalytic Association, 50*, 53–98.

White, J. L., & Parham, T. A. (1990). *The psychology of Blacks: An African American perspective*. New York: Prentice Hall.

Wilkson, K. (2008). *The happiness factor: How to be happy no matter what*. Austin, TX: Ovation.

Williams, D. R., Neighbors, H. W., & Jackson, J. S. (2003). Racial/ethnic discrimination and health: Findings from community studies. *American Journal of Public Health, 93*, 200–208.

Wilson, K. G. (1997). Science and treatment development: Lessons from the history of behavior therapy. *Behavior Therapy, 28*, 547–558.

Wilson, S. M., & Miles, M. S. (2001). Spirituality in African-American mothers coping with a seriously ill infant. *Journal of the Society of Pediatric Nurses, 6*, 116–122.

Wolpe, J. (1982). Missing the point: A reply to Wogan and Norcross. *American Psychologist, 37*, 1286–1287.

Wolpe, J., & Lazarus, A. A. (1966). *Behaviour therapy techniques: A guide to the treatment of neuroses.* Oxford, England: Pergamon Press.

Wong, J. (2006). The future of positive psychology. *Psychotherapy: Theory, Research, Practice, Training, 43*, 151–153.

Yalom, I. D. (1980). *Existential therapy.* New York: Basic Books.

# Index